Talking the Talk

Language makes us human, but how do we use it and how do children learn it? *Talking the Talk* is an introduction to the psychology of language. Written for the reader with no background in the area or knowledge of psychology, it explains how we actually "do" language: how we speak, listen, and read.

This book provides an accessible and comprehensive introduction to psycholinguistics, the study of the psychological processes involved in language. It shows how it's possible to study language experimentally, and how psychologists use these experiments to build models of language processing. The book focuses on controversy in modern psycholinguistics, and covers all the main topics, including how children acquire language, how language is related to the brain, and what can go wrong – and what can be done when something does go wrong.

Structured around questions that people often ask about language, the emphasis of *Talking the Talk* is how scientific knowledge can be applied to practical problems. This book also stresses how language is related to other aspects of psychology, particularly in whether animals can learn language, and the relation between language and thought.

Lively and amusing, the book will be essential reading for all undergraduate students and those new to the topic, as well as the interested lay reader.

Trevor A. Harley completed his undergraduate degree and PhD at the University of Cambridge. He moved to the University of Dundee in 1996 from the University of Warwick. He holds a Personal Chair in Cognitive Psychology and is currently Head of the School of Psychology. He is a Chartered Psychologist and his main research interest is in normal and pathological speech production.

Talking the Talk

Language, Psychology and Science

■ Trevor A. Harley

 Psychology Press
Taylor & Francis Group

HOVE AND NEW YORK

First published 2010
by Psychology Press
27 Church Road, Hove, East Sussex, BN3 2FA

Simultaneously published in the USA and
Canada
by Psychology Press
270 Madison Avenue, New York, NY 10016

*Psychology Press is an imprint of the Taylor &
Francis Group, an Informa business*

Typeset in Sabon by RefineCatch Limited,
Bungay, Suffolk
Printed and bound in Great Britain by
TJ International Ltd, Padstow, Cornwall
Cover design by Design Deluxe

The publisher makes no representation,
express or implied, with regard to the
accuracy of the information contained in this
book and cannot accept any legal
responsibility or liability for any errors or
omissions that may be made.

*British Library Cataloguing in Publication
Data*
A catalogue record for this book is available
from the British Library

*Library of Congress Cataloging-in-
Publication Data*
Harley, Trevor A.
   Talking the talk : languge, psychology and
science / Trevor Harley.
      p. cm.
   Includes bibliographical references and
index.
   ISBN 978-1-84169-339-2 (hb : alk. paper)
– ISBN 978-1-84169-340-8 (solf cover : alk.
paper) 1. Psycholinguistics. I. Title.
   BF455.H27133 2010
   401′.9–dc22
                    2009026996

ISBN: 978-1-84169-339-2 (hbk)
ISBN: 978-1-84169-340-8 (pbk)

Dedication

To Siobhan, Sheila, Hazel, and Bill too

Contents

List of figures

Preface

I am lucky enough to be the author of a successful text on the psychology of language. I know it must be successful because it's reached its third edition. Why then does the world need yet another book on the psychology of language, particularly another by Trevor Harley?

I hope this book will find a different readership from my text *The Psychology of Language* – although of course I hope eventually everyone will read both. I think there is room for a more introductory book; I also hope there is room for something a bit more personal. There are a number of popular and semi-popular books on language already available, but I think this is the most up-to-date one about the *processes* involved in producing and understanding language. I want it to be read by psychology and linguistics undergraduates, by people who want to learn about the subject before university, and, perhaps most importantly of all, by the lay reader. In short, I hope that it will be perfect reading for anyone who wants to know about how we think and how we communicate. With a bit of luck, the film rights will soon follow.

I hope therefore that it's also one of the most approachable books on the subject. I think that the psychology of language has become an increasingly complex and difficult subject over the past 10 years or so. The third edition (2008) of my text is considerably longer and harder than the first (1995). The subject is certainly one many undergraduates find difficult, I think for two main reasons.

First, there is now so much material available. My main text is already huge, but still some researchers and teachers wanted me to include more about this topic, while others wanted more of that topic. Clearly there are limits to how big a text can be! Indeed, I think the world needs a shorter overview, not a longer one. Brevity can only be achieved at the cost of selection, and my personal preferences and interests reveal themselves in this selection. Omitting something, however, is bound to upset someone.

The second reason people find the psychology of language difficult is that often it is difficult to come to any conclusion other than "we don't yet know". We are often left with two (or more!) alternative explanations of the same data, and it is rare that we can say with near certainty that this is how the mind always works. This lack of certainly is unsettling. In this book, although I've obviously tried to be balanced, I have tried to come to some definite conclusion more often, which means saying what I think is the more likely or compelling conclusion. I could of course be wrong, and again it will offend people. I've tried to avoid going into the details of the arguments and counter-arguments that pervade modern psycholinguistics, and I hope the consequences are clarity and simplicity – but not over-simplicity.

Because I've wanted to tell more of a story, I've avoided putting too many detours around the main theme, and I've tried to keep the number of references to a minimum. If I've missed something important out, I'm sorry. Not everything can be included. Although I've tried to show something of the controversies active in current research, for a book such as this I think the tried-and-tested results are more robust and their contribution to knowledge easier to assess, so there is a bias towards older references (say, compared with my text) – these older references, as well as standing the test of time, also often contain the first systematic description of the basic data that often remain to be fully explained. Because I'm trying to tell a story, I think the book is best read like a novel, from beginning to end; it's not meant to be dipped into. The section with further reading ("Next") also contains some sidelines and additional ideas that would have disrupted the flow of the main text if they'd been put there.

So in addition to being shorter, more selective, more approachable, and personal, this book might be more upsetting to more people; perhaps the more people it upsets, the more successful it has been. The last thing I want to do, though, is upset someone because of an inaccuracy, or misreporting or misunderstanding something. One of the most time-consuming aspects of writing a book such as this is checking things. Nevertheless, I will be amazed if some errors haven't crept in. If you spot any, or think I have presented something unfairly, I'd love to know about it, preferably by email (currently *t.a.harley@dundee.ac.uk*).

I have one other wish, and that is that this book goes some way to persuading people that cognitive psychology is a real science. Psychology sometimes gets a bad press: it's a very broad subject, tackled by many different sorts of approaches, but I think the experimental (in tandem with the computational–mathematical) approach has made huge strides in understanding human behaviour. Just because the subject of the subject is ourselves doesn't make the enterprise any less scientific. Psychology is a real science, up there with physics, chemistry, and biology. Indeed, in many ways if you want to see science working the processes are clearer in psychology. This preamble just explains the subtitle of the book – and is another reason why the psychology of language is hard.

I'd like to thank Matt Jarvis, Alan Kennedy, Annukka Lindell, Nick Lund, and Glen Whitehead for their comments on a draft of this book. I promise I considered every suggestion made very carefully, even if I didn't implement them all. It might of course be that the suggestions I ignored will turn out to have been correct. I am particularly and eternally grateful to them for helping me avoid making several potentially very embarrassing errors. I'd particularly like to thank Bill Thompson for reading a draft with the intelligent lay person's eye (and brain). I owe him a very great debt. I haven't always taken his advice, but seeing the book through his brain was an exceptionally helpful (if occasionally odd) experience. This book was planned and written in Scrivener on an Apple iMac. I can't imagine doing it any other way. All the photographs (bar one) are my own.

Professor Trevor Harley
University of Dundee
May 2009

Chapter 1

Language

I HAVE A FRIEND who says that studying the psychology of
language is a waste of time. He expounds this idea very
eloquently and at great length. He says it in nice, beautifully enunciated – if rather loud – sentences to anyone who
will listen (and often to people who won't). I think this
irony is wasted on him.

One of his reasons for thinking that investigating language is pointless is that, according to him, there's nothing
special about language. We learn language as we learn any
other skill: we learn to speak like we might learn to ride
a bike. It makes use of the same psychological resources
and processes as everything else we do. For him there's no
difference between speaking a sentence and navigating our
way home.

I think he wants things both ways, because when I put
the alternative to him – that there is something special
about language, that maybe we don't learn it like we learn
other things, and maybe it doesn't use the same psychological processes as everything else – he says that in that case
it's just a special case, and therefore not very interesting
either.

Using language is one of the most impressive things
we do. I find only vision comes close. We routinely produce
utterances of amazing complexity and originality. Think

1

back to the last few things you've said; have you ever said exactly those things before? Probably not, or if you have, you won't have to wait long before you say something no one else in the world has ever said in just that way ever before. Our use of language is creative. We combine words and sentence structures in novel ways all the time. And we do this combination incredibly quickly and with amazing accuracy. We can do this combination in speech or writing. We can also decode what other people say – we listen and read, and extract the meaning and intended message, again apparently effortlessly.

Language is also important. We spend a lot of time using it or even just thinking in it. Most of us have a running voice in the head telling us what to do and what we're thinking, and it's easy to think of that voice as being the core of us. The complexity of modern life is unthinkable without it: how could we have designed and built cars, computers, and atom smashers without it? Indeed, it's difficult to imagine being human without language.

Perhaps unwittingly, my conversations with my friend touch upon three of the most interesting issues in the modern study of language. First, how do we actually *do* language? What are the processes involved in speaking, writing, listening, and reading? Second, how do children acquire language? They're not born talking, but they soon are chattering away, if not at first quite like adults. Third, to what extent does acquiring and using language depend on knowledge and mechanisms specific to language?

This book is about the psychology of language. I find the "psychology of language" to be a bit of a mouthful, and what on earth do you call people who do it? Psychologists of language? In the sixties and seventies there was a perfectly good word, "psycholinguistics", with the people who did psycholinguistics called psycholinguists. For reasons I've never understood these words became unfashionable about the same time as flares stopped being widely available. I don't think these events were linked, but perhaps if "psycholinguistics" can be brought back into fashion, even flares stand a chance again.

"Psycholinguistics" and "psycholinguists": I'm going to use these words. Perhaps they will be deservedly revived.

What is language?

Type "language definition" in to your favourite search engine. Here's one I've adapted from www.thefreedictionary.com, according to which language is:

1   communication of thoughts and feelings through a system of arbitrary signs such as voice sounds or gestures
2   such a system including its rules for combining its components such as words
3   such a system as used by a nation or people.

This definition covers the most important aspects of what language is, but it's worth considering these points in more detail.

First, language is primarily a system for communication: its main purpose is to transfer information from one person to another. I think I'd add to this point that the communication is intended. Animals communicate to each other – for example, a blackbird singing communicates that a male is resident in a territory and available to females – but it's far from obvious that there is always a deliberate intention to convey information. In contrast, when we talk, we intend to convey specific information. This is not to say that everything we communicate is intentional: I might say something foolish and thereby communicate my ignorance, but this is a side-effect of what I say rather than its main effect, and certainly language didn't arise to convey side-effects. It is also not to say that the only function of language is strictly intentional communication: we often use language for social bonding, as a means of emotional expression ("darnation!", and sometimes perhaps a little stronger), and even for play (telling puns and jokes). And language seems to play a central role in guiding and perhaps even determining our thoughts.

Second, language is a system of words and rules for combining them. Words mean something; they are signs that stand for something. "Cat", "chase", "rat, "truth", "kick", and "big" all refer to objects in the world, events, ideas, actions, or properties of things. We know thousands of words: we know their meanings, and what they look and sound like. All this knowledge is stored in a huge mental dictionary we call the *lexicon*. But language is clearly much more than a list of words; we combine words together to form sentences, and sentences convey complex meanings about the relation between things: essentially, who did what to whom. But we don't just combine words in any old fashion; like computer languages, we can only combine words in particular ways. We can say "the cat chases the rat" or "the rat chases the cat", but not "the cat rat the chases" or "the the chases cat rat". That is, we know some rules that enable us to combine words together in particular ways. We call these rules the *syntactic rules* (sometimes just the *syntax*) of the language. What is more, word order is vitally important (in languages such as English at least): "the cat chases the rat" means something different from "the rat chases the cat". It is our ability to use rules to combine words that gives language its immense power, and that enables us to convey a huge (infinite, in fact) number of ideas.

The distinction between the lexicon and syntax is an important one in psycholinguistics. If syntax makes you think of grammar, you're right: we use the word *grammar* in a more general way to describe the complete set of rules that describe a language, primarily the syntax, how words can be made up, and even what sorts of sounds are permitted and how they are combined in a particular language. Be warned, though, that "grammar" is unfortunately one of those words that can mean what we want it to mean; sometimes it's used almost synonymously with "syntax", sometimes as the more general term to refer to the complete set of rules for a language. No wonder psycholinguistics is hard.

Third, the relation between the meaning and appearance or sound of words is arbitrary: you can't tell what a word means just by hearing it; you have to know it. Of course there are a few words that sound rather like what they depict (such words are called onomatopoeic) – but there are just a few, and even then the meaning isn't completely predictable. "Whisper" sounds a bit like the sound of whispering, but perhaps "sisper" would have done just as well. Knowing how "hermeneutical" is pronounced tells you nothing about what it means.

Fourth, although we have defined language in the abstract, there are many specific languages in the world. We say that English, French, Russian, and Igbo (a Nigerian language) are all different languages, but they are nevertheless all *types* of language: they all use words and syntactic rules to form messages.

How do languages differ?

A motif of this book is how bad I am at language and languages. I'm not proud of this fact; it's just the way it is. Indeed, I think I should have your sympathy for reasons that will become apparent later. It's perhaps odd that someone so bad at language should carry out research into language, but perhaps there's something in the adage about psychologists really just being interested in their own particular problems. Being hopeless at foreign (to me) languages, I had to ask members of my linguistically diverse psychology department how they would say the following in their own languages (I could manage the first):

> The cat on the mat chased the giant rat. (English)
> Le chat qui était sur le tapis a couru après le rat géant. (French)
> Die Katze auf der Matte jagte die gigantische Ratte. (German)
> Il gatto sullo stoino inseguiva il topo gigante. (Italian)
> De kat op de mat joeg op de gigantische rat. (Dutch)
> Pisica de pe pres a sarit la sobolanul gigantic. (Romanian)
> Kot ktòry był na macie, gonił ogromnego szczura. (Polish)
> A macska a szőnyegen kergette az óriás patkányt. (Hungarian)
> Matto-no ue-no neko-ga ookina nezumi-o oikaketa. (Japanese)

I think I know what's going on in the French, Dutch, and German translations. It is fairly obvious that there are similarities between them and English, and I remember enough school French to be able to work out the rest. Italian looks a bit more different to me but is still recognisable. Polish, Hungarian, and Japanese are very different and unrecognisable to me; for all I know, my colleagues could be pulling my leg and causing me to write unwitting obscenities. I apologise if they have.

There are differences other than just the vocabulary ("cat", "chat", and "Katze" all mean the same thing). In German what is called the *case* of the noun and the form of the verb are much more important than in English; the form of nouns and verbs changes by a process called *inflection* to reflect their grammatical role – for example, whether something is the subject or the object of the sentence – the thing doing the action or the thing having the action done to it. (There are other cases: I still remember nominative, accusative, vocative, genitive, and dative from my Latin lessons.) We do this a bit in English, when, for example, we use "she" as the subject of the sentence and "her" as the object, but nowhere near as much as in heavily inflected languages, of which German is one. If you know any Latin, you will realise that Latin is extremely heavily inflected, so much so that word order is relatively unimportant. To satisfy my nostalgia for being 12 again, here are the inflected cases of a Latin word, *stella* ("star"):

stella – the star	stellae – the stars (nominative case)
stella – o star	stellae – o stars (vocative)
stellam – the star	stellas – the stars (accusative, for direct objects)
stellae – of the star	stellarum – of the stars (genitive)
stellae – to the star	stellis – to the stars (dative)
stella – from the star	stellis – from the stars (ablative)

Japanese constructs its sentences very differently: I'm told the best translation is "mat on cat big rat chased"; notice how in Japanese also the verb comes at the end of the sentence. Turkish, like Finnish, Japanese, and Swahili, runs words modifying each other together, making it what is called an *agglutinative* language. Here is an example:

Ögretemediklerimizdenmisiniz? – Are you the one who we failed to teach?

(Where *Ögret* – to teach, *emedik* – failed, *lerimiz* – we, *den* – are you, *misiniz* – the one who). In agglutinative languages each unit in a word expresses a particular grammatical meaning in a very clear way.

The sounds different languages use can differ, too. To an English speaker, the properly pronounced "ch" sound in the Scottish "loch" and German "Bach" sounds slightly odd; that's because it's not a sound used in "normal" English. Technically, it's called a *voiceless velar fricative* because of the way it's made and the vocal tract being constricted as air is pushed out through it, and English doesn't use voiceless velar fricatives (see Figure 1.1 for a diagram of the articulatory apparatus). Arabic sounds different to English speakers because it makes use of *pharyngeal* sounds, where the root of the tongue is raised to the pharynx at the back of the mouth – and, of course, English sounds different to Arabic speakers because English doesn't make use of pharyngeal sounds. Some African languages, such as Bantu and Khoisan, make use of loud click sounds as consonants. Japanese doesn't make a distinction between the "l" and "r" sounds, which is

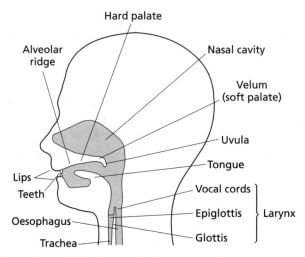

FIGURE 1.1 The structure of the human vocal tract

why Japanese people learning English have difficulty in producing these sounds correctly. "L" and "r" are called *liquid* sounds; Irish Gaelic has 10 liquids, and of course native English speakers would have difficulty learning all these distinctions. The list of differences in sounds between languages is clearly going to be enormous, and has obvious consequences for adult speakers trying to learn a new language.

I also asked a colleague in Iran for a translation; here are the results in Farsi and Arabic, along with Greek, Japanese, and Chinese (below). These don't even use the same *script*, or method of writing. Farsi, Arabic, and Hebrew are written from right to left.

Greek

Η γάτα στο χαλί κυνήγησε τον γιγάντιο αρουραίο.

Japanese

マットの上の猫が大きなネズミを追いかけた。

Chinese

那只大老鼠　　在毯子上　　　被　　　　猫　　追赶。
(The giant rat) (On the mat) (Passive expression) (The cat) (Chased)

Translation to Farsi

chased   the giant   rat mat on cat

گربه روی فرش موش صحرا یی بزرگ را تعقیب کرد.

V   O   Prep.   S

orbe(cat) rouye(on) farsh(mat) moush-e sahraie-ye(rat) bozorg(the giant)
ra taghib kard(chased) Farsi

Translation to Arabic

the giant rat chased mat on cat

القطه علي حصيرطاردت الجرن العملاق

O   V   S

Al-ghetta(cat) ala(on) hasir(mat) taradat(chased) Al-jerza al-amlagh(the giant
rat) Arabic

Translation to Hebrew

החותול אל השטיח רדף אחרי החולדה האנקות

H' chatul al h' shatiach radaf acharey h' chulda h' anakit

So languages clearly differ in many ways: the words they use (the vocabulary),
the preferred order of words, the syntactic rules they use, the extent to and way in
which they inflect words to mark grammatical role, the way grammatical units are
combined, the sounds they use, and the ways in which they write words down.

Although there are differences, there are also many similarities. Some languages (English, French, German, Dutch, and Italian) are obviously related to each
other, but all languages use separate words for separate concepts (they all have
different words for rat, mat, cat, giant, and chased), and they all have a means of
telling us what did what to whom – that is, of marking the *grammatical role*. We
know that it's the cat chasing the rat, not the other way round. All languages use
words, and all languages use rules to combine these words, and it turns out these
combination rules are often similar to each other in very systematic ways.

How many languages are there?

My wife is a Geordie (she comes from Newcastle). Fortunately, when I choose
to, most of the time I can understand what she says, but I have a great deal
of difficulty with some of her relatives. Geordie is a *dialect* (it has identifiable
vocabulary and grammatical features) with a strong *accent* (it sounds distinctive).
Although Geordie differs from RP English (received pronunciation, as spoken
by the Queen and BBC announcers in the good old days), and I have difficulty

understanding it, most people would still label it as a type of English. But when does a dialect become a different language? There are no hard and fast rules, and for this reason it is difficult to be precise about how many languages there currently are in the world.

Linguists estimate that there are 5000–6000 languages in the world, but some languages with small numbers of speakers are dying out, perhaps even as you read this. Some languages are as endangered as the black robin (apparently only five of which were left off the coast of New Zealand in the early 1980s). Over the past few centuries countless languages have been extinguished, sometimes deliberately, sometimes because the number of speakers has become too small for the language to be viable, sometimes because another language takes over.

Occasionally languages close to extinction make a resurgence. Welsh is an interesting case study of this (Price, 1984). It is the oldest language still spoken in mainland Britain. At the end of the sixth century or so the Brythonic language (an old Celtic language itself closely related to the Gaelic languages of Scotland and Ireland) became differentiated into Welsh, Cornish, Cumbric, and Breton. It had a long and rich literary tradition and was spoken extensively. English encroachment in the thirteenth century began to reduce the geographical area of Welsh. The Act of Union of England and Wales in 1536 did not actually proscribe Welsh, but stipulated that public officials had to use English. A rapid decline in the late eighteenth and early nineteenth centuries followed, and in the middle part of the nineteenth century English became the primary target language in state schools. The large number of English immigrants, particularly attracted by industrialisation in the south, further reduced the relative number of speakers and its perceived importance. You might have heard about the "Welsh knot", which was a piece of wood hung around the necks of school children who spoke Welsh at school in the nineteenth century. In one tradition the knot would be passed on if the wearer heard another child speaking Welsh, and at the end of the day the final wearer would be given a good thrashing. It is hardly surprising that such means discouraged the use of Welsh.

A resurgence in the Welsh language started in the 1930s, with the first state system Welsh medium school opened in Llanelli in 1947. The Welsh Language Act of 1967 allowed any legal proceeding to be in Welsh. Nevertheless the number of bilingual speakers declined from 929,824 (50% of the population) in 1901 to 508,207 (19%) in 1981; the decline in monolingual speakers is even more dramatic, correspondingly 280,905 to just 21,583. Broadcasting was mostly in English until the launch of S4C in 1982. The Welsh Language Act of 1993 and Government of Wales Act of 1998 now mean that Welsh and English should be treated equally. Signs and official papers, for example, must now all be produced bilingually. As a result the use of Welsh has now seen an upsurge, with currently 611,000 speakers (21.7% of the population in 2004). As ever, it is difficult to determine the causes of historical events, but it's reasonable to say that the determination of a few individuals has played a significant role in the resurgence of Welsh. For example, Clive Betts, in his 1976 book *Culture in Crisis*, argued for the establishment of a "Welsh heartland" where at least 70% of speakers would be Welsh and where Welsh would be the official language, and English would be a second-class language, to be used only when necessary, and to be taught only in Anglicised Heartland towns, such as Bangor, Aberystwyth, and Carmarthen (Price, 1984). Desperate situations need desperate plans.

So although Welsh was in decline, the situation is now not as bleak as it might have been. Contrast the history of Welsh with the history of Cornish, where the number of speakers was much smaller and speakers occupied a relatively small part of England. As English spread, Cornish became marginalised further and further to the west, particularly after 1500. The decline was rapid after that, with the last known monoglot speaker (someone speaking just one language) dying in 1676 and – although it's often debated – the last native speaker, Dolly Pontreath, dying in

I love Welsh scenery, and I love Welsh road signs nearly as much. This "Landscape with (very small) Welsh road sign (on the left)" is one of my classic photographs; it displays just about every mistake known to real photographers. How many can you spot? Translation between languages can sometimes go very wrong, such as in the road sign reported in the BBC News in October 2008 which read in English at the top: "No entry for heavy goods vehicles. Residential site only". The translation in Welsh beneath said: "I am not in the office at the moment. Send any work to be translated"

Mousehole, a fishing port near Penzance, in 1777. There are now some attempts to revive Cornish in everyday use, although it remains to be seen how successful these will be.

How has English changed?

Type "Shakespeare insult generator" into your favourite search engine. There are a number of sites that will generate an insult for you based on words found in Shakespeare; it didn't take me long to come up with "Methink you stinks thou beslubbering onion-eyed hugger-mugger". I quite like that, but it's unlikely to cut many people to the quick when they steal that parking space you've been nursing for two minutes.

It's obvious that language has changed considerably over time: we don't say "forsooth", "pribbling", or "coxcomb" too much these days. At least, though, Shakespeare is readily comprehensible (most of the time) to English speakers; go back a bit further and Chaucer is much more problematic for the unskilled reader.

> And somme seyen that we loven best
> To be free, and do right as us lest,
> And that no man repreve us of oure vice,
> But seye that we be wise, and no thyng nyce.
> For trewely ther is noon of us alle,
> If any wight wol clawe us on the galle,
> That we nel kike, for he seith us sooth.
>
> Chaucer, *The Wife of Bath's tale*, 935–941, written around 1390

It makes more sense if you speak it aloud, but it's still hard going, and the last two lines have me flummoxed.

The history of English is the history of England. English is a ragbag of languages, and England has often been described as a "mongrel nation". It doesn't sound very kind, but it conveys the idea. The history of England before the Norman Conquest was one of waves of invasions: Celts, Romans, Angles, Saxons, Jutes, and Danes, all leaving their linguistic mark. By the early eleventh century things had settled down, and the dominant language was Anglo-Saxon, a Germanic language, with Celtic languages (Cornish, Cumbrian, Manx, and Gaelic) spoken at the fringes. The Norman Conquest of 1066 was the last major invasion, and had a profound influence, producing for a while a two-tier system, with French the language of the ruling aristocracy, court, and law, and English the language of the vanquished majority. After a while the Germanic language reasserted itself, partly because more people spoke it, and partly because the Norman aristocracy became isolated from France, so that the language lost the source of its renewal, and marriages between

Normans and Anglo-Saxons became more common. Nevertheless, it was not until Henry IV was crowned king in 1399 that the country was ruled by a native speaker of English, although Edward III had made English the official language of Parliament in 1362. By then of course the English language had absorbed a huge number of French words and phrases. The class distinction of the French-speaking rulers and Anglo-Saxon-speaking peasants even became reflected in the names of trades: the more prestigious, skilled trades used names based on French, such as tailor, painter, and mason, while the less prestigious ones carried on with Anglo-Saxon names, such as miller, baker, shoemaker (Bryson, 1990). English still has several thousand words derived from French, mostly to do with court, law, and fashion.

Of course it isn't just vocabulary that changed; the rules of grammar changed as well. Mostly in its time in exile English became simplified. Grammatical inflections were lost, gender (whether a noun is male, female, or neuter, as they still are in languages such as French and German) vanished, and the number of word endings reduced. It's worth noting that early English was highly variable, much more so than today, not just from one region to another, or within regions, but even within speakers. Chaucer sometimes talks of "doughtren" and sometimes of "doughtres" (for the plural daughters). The invention of the printing press and the availability of printed material had a standardising effect.

Latin has also influenced the development of English. As the official language of the Church, its effect on religious matters, law, and education has been profound. Many important seventeenth-century scholastic works were first published in Latin (including Newton's *Principia* and Harvey's treatise on the circulation of blood, *Exercitatio Anatomica de Motu Cordis et Sanguinis in Animalibus*). A large number of Latin words survive, although their derivation is often obscured by Norman being a Romance language, like Latin. Latin was held in such high prestige that the early scholars of English grammar thought that the formal rules of English should be based on Latin.

Language has never stood still. Victorian language sounds distinctive to modern readers. All sorts of influences work on languages over time: they become simplified, they incorporate parts of other languages, they adapt or coin new words when needed, dialects spread while others become modified (look at the recent success of "Estuarine English"), and new phrases become fashionable. "Transistor", "television", "aeroplane", and "computer" are all relatively recent additions. A few years ago I liked to think of myself as one of the earliest ipodologists. And, of course, language is still changing. Not many people now tell me that it's heavy, man, or that I'm a groovy cat; and who knows how long it will be before people stare at you oddly when you say "chav"?

English has been exported too, particularly to America. Geographical spread also leads to linguistic isolation and change. I still can't get used to saying elevator, hood, sidewalk, and gotten when in the USA.

Some change offends some people. There are people out there (sometimes I'm one) who get upset about split infinitives ("to boldly go where no man has gone before", or, as the joke goes, "to boldly split infinitives no one has split before"), but even I can't raise much enthusiasm about dangling prepositions ("he was the man she gave the present to" rather than the so-called correct "he was the man to whom she gave the present"). Incidentally, this rule arose because Latin infinitives can't be split, so, said the early authorities, neither can English ones. The distinctions between "who" and "whom" and different uses of "shall" and "will" are now close to having become extinct. Some people get agitated about pronunciation: make sure you pronounce both those rs in "library", and don't say "libary" instead! And by the way, it's mispronunciation, not mispronounciation. I think what's important is that language losing its distinctions and language using its power are bad things; so every time we don't say "whom" instead of "who", it makes it a little bit harder for whoever has to understand the sentence. But it's difficult to believe that language will be degraded into a powerless mishmash of incomprehensible ambiguity. New distinctions and ways of making old ones will evolve. Things change. Get over it (but please get "its" and "it's" right).

How has language changed?

We've noted that some languages seem similar to each other. *Linguists* (people who

A house in Stratford-upon-Avon; my memory is that it's Shakespeare's

study language) have grouped together languages that appear to be related into language *families*. It's obvious that French, Italian, and Spanish are related, and these are grouped together into the *Romance* family; English, Dutch, and German also have much in common, and these are grouped to form the *Germanic* family of languages. Why should they be similar? The most obvious explanation is that members of the same family are historically derived from the same language root. If we went far enough back in time, we would find one language – for example, let's call it proto-Germanic – that over time, as speakers of the language became geographically dispersed and relatively isolated, split into the languages we speak today.

But the Romance and Germanic languages aren't really that different from each other, which means that if we go back a bit further in time, Romance and Germanic languages are derived from just one language. They also have features in common with other languages: the word "mother" is "mere" in French, "Mutter" in German, "moeder" in Dutch, "moder" in Swedish, "madre" in Italian and Spanish, "matka" in Polish, "maht" in Russian, "máthair" in Irish, and "mata" in Sanskrit. The number of similarities between other words (numbers provide a striking example) suggests that these similarities cannot be due to coincidence. So at one time all these languages must once have been related. Indeed, most of the languages of Europe and West Asia are all thought to have been derived from a language called proto-Indo-European, and members of the family are called *Indo-European* languages. In this way we can construct a family tree for related languages, as shown in Figure 1.2. But it's important to note that not all languages spoken in these areas are Indo-European. Basque, spoken by the Basque people

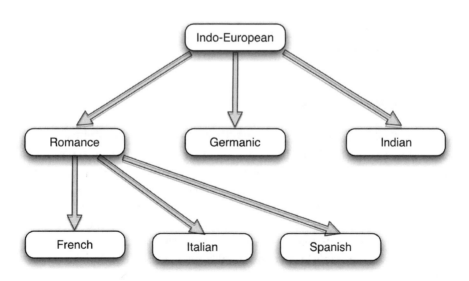

FIGURE 1.2 Part of a simplified family tree for some Indo-European languages

of northern Spain and south-western France, is thought to be an isolated remnant of a language spoken in Europe before the invasion of the peoples who spoke and spread Indo-European. Finnish and Estonian belong to the Finno-Ugric family; presumably the invasion of Indo-Europeans just didn't get that far. Hungarian Magyar is a more distant relative of the Ugric languages (and this observation suggests that we can learn about the movements of early peoples by looking at the distribution of related languages across the globe).

We can discover when languages split by looking at which words they share. All Indo-European languages have similar words for horses and sheep, but not for vines or palms, suggesting that the source language came from a place where horses were common but where there were no palms. Such observations suggest that the original speakers of Indo-European came from northern central Europe. Using such differences, and looking at the degree of similarity between words, we can construct a family tree of linguistic resemblance that shows how languages split from one another.

It's possible to construct similar family trees for other groups of languages. The Altaic language family includes Turkish and Mongolic languages of central Asia. The Sino-Tibetan family comprises 250 languages of East Asia, including the Chinese languages. The largest family, the Niger-Congo family, comprises over 1500 families. However, we've already noted that Basque doesn't have any obvious relation to Indo-European: there's a large number of other isolates that don't seem to fit into the predominant family of that area. The natural question then is if we go far enough back in time, will we find the ultimate great-great-grandmother language, the single language from which all other languages are descended, which means that language was "invented" just once (called the *monogenesis* theory)? Or were there several original languages? Those are questions about which it's easy to speculate, but difficult to say very much that's sensible. They do however touch on the ultimate origin of language.

Where did language come from?

In 1866 the Société de Linguistique de Paris (the Linguistic Society of Paris) banned all debate about the origin of language: there was too much conjecture and too little evidence. And there have been plenty of speculative theories: according to the "bow wow" theory, language began in imitation of natural sounds; the "heave ho" theory says that it originated in rhythmic chants of early men as they collaborated in heavy work; the "sing song" theory says that it came out of courtship, cooing, and laughing; and the "eureka!" theory (my personal favourite) says that some clever early man consciously invented it. But what can science tell us about the origin of language?

For a long time I wondered how on earth there could be any hard evidence about how language originated, let alone too little. But there are two main sources of evidence, none complete, and even in total leaving much to speculation. First, we can hypothesise about how language has evolved by looking at changes in the structure of the jaw and skull in the fossil evidence. Second, there's what we can learn from the analysis of remnants of DNA in these fossils.

When did language evolve? Obviously spoken language must have arisen some time after the genus *Homo* split away from other primates, with *Homo habilis* about 2.5 million years ago, and the modern behaviour by the first true human, *Homo sapiens*, about 50,000 years ago. The best we can do to be more specific is estimate this by looking at when humans possessed the articulatory apparatus to produce speech similar to the way we do now. There are indications from fossils that early hominids, as long as two million years ago, possessed a well-developed Broca's area – a region towards the front of the brain on the left-hand side that we know plays a significant role in producing speech. However, it's now known that great apes show signs of this same sort of asymmetry (Cantalupo & Hopkins, 2001). Perhaps in humans Broca's area took over some other function, such as making complex hand manoeuvres.

The Neanderthals were very close relatives of humans (some think a sub-species) that became extinct about 30,000 years ago. For some time it was believed that the shape of the skull of Neanderthal man strongly suggested that they were incapable of making complex speech sounds: their larynx, or voice box, was not in an appropriate position, being closer to the position in other primates than in humans, and they lacked fine control over the movements of their tongue (Lieberman & Crelin, 1971). More recent evidence suggests that Neanderthals might not have been as incapable as originally thought. In 1983 a Neanderthal hyoid bone – the bone in the neck that supports the base of the tongue – was discovered in Israel; the fact that this bone existed at all suggests Neanderthals were capable of some speech, but the structure of the bone was remarkably similar to that of humans (Arensburg et al., 1989). Recent extraction of DNA from bones suggested that Neanderthals possessed a version of the FOXP2 gene similar to that found in modern humans; as we will see, this gene is thought to play a significant role in language (Krause et al., 2007).

In 2008 Robert McCarthy, an anthropologist from Florida, used computer modelling to produce speech as it might have been spoken by Neanderthals. The speech is croaky and high-pitched, and they lacked the ability to produce the rich vowel sounds we do, but it could easily have formed a rich communication system. (Samples of the speech are widely available on the net.) Neanderthals used tools, buried their dead, controlled fire, lived in shelters, and possibly might even have practised rituals and religion and made music, and I find it hard to see how they could have reached this level of sophistication without language. If Neanderthals did share our FOXP2 gene, and did use language, these genetic changes must have taken place before modern humans and Neanderthals diverged 300,000 to 400,000 years ago. This line of reasoning is controversial, because the mutated FOXP2 gene might just have been present in the sample because of some interbreeding between *Homo sapiens* and Neanderthals.

Modern human behaviour can be traced to a flowering of human art, technology, and culture at least 40,000 years ago – and possibly much earlier in Africa – with the transition from the Palaeolithic to Neolithic phases of the Stone Age. Stone tools became more complex, art flourished, and personal jewellery appeared for the first time. Corballis (2004) argued that this cultural and techno-logical flowering was made possible by the development of language and the changes in the ways of thinking that language allows. With proper language, humans could move beyond the here-and-now, and could talk about things and ideas other than objects immediately in front of them. They could reason about possibilities. They could speculate, talk about the future, make plans, and talk hypothetically about "what if?" They could form complex conditional plans for the future ("if you do this I'll do that or else if . . ."). Fossil evidence shows that the articulatory apparatus – the tongue, teeth, larynx, and muscles that control them – hasn't changed significantly in the past 50,000 years – since about the same time as this cultural flowering. Here then is a more conservative estimate of the origin of true language: something happened about 50,000 years ago. Whatever it was fixed our vocal apparatus in its modern form, enabled modern language to develop, which in turn freed our hands for other uses, and these changes in turn led to the development of culture. What might have happened about then? The likely answer is a mutation in what is known as the FOXP2 gene within the past 100,000 years that led to its current form. In other primates this gene is responsible for controlling complex movements, and co-ordinating sensory input and output. The mutation led to an enlarged Broca's region of the brain and an enhanced ability to produce complex sequences – which is just what we need for language (Fisher & Marcus, 2006). We'll meet the FOXP2 gene again, but it's worth noting here that some researchers argue that damage to the gene in humans today leads to difficulty in acquiring language, particularly in the ability to order sounds. Consistent with this date for the emergence of language is that language must almost certainly have developed before humans spread out of Africa, around 60,000 years ago (Renfrew, 2007); it's inconceivable that language could have evolved in the same way in parallel in many different locations.

Primates use calls to communicate with each other, as we will see in the next chapter. The simplest suggestion for the origin of speech is that the enhanced devel-opment of the brain of early man meant that these calls could become increasingly complex and put into sequences. But higher primates make a great deal of use of gesture to communicate. A chimp, for example, extends an open hand when it sees another chimp with something it wants, such as food. We've already noted that great apes have broadly similar brains, and that in them Broca's area might control hand movements. Perhaps spoken language originated from hand and arm gestures? This idea is a popular one; the famous developmental psychologist Jean Piaget suggested in the 1930s that language arose from vocal gestures made to supplement manual gestures. Corballis (2004) argued that the mutation in the FOXP2 gene meant that we could make complex sequences of vocal gestures, and no longer needed to rely on the hands to communicate. This development meant that a more complex communication system could develop, and also that we could communicate while our hands did other things, such as simultaneously making tools. These developments in turn enabled culture to flourish. Although the differential reliance of evolution on calls and gestures is a current controversy in the literature, perhaps they shouldn't be seen as alternatives. The freeing of the brain from gestures meant that the vocal repertoire could be developed and extended.

It's also probably a mistake to see language as all or nothing: that we either have it or we don't. Bickerton (1990) postulated the existence of a proto-language that's intermediate between human language and primate communication systems. With proto-language early humans would have been able to label a large number of objects, but not to combine those labels with a rich syntax.

However and whenever language evolved, it conferred a significant evolutionary advantage, at some cost: the position of the structures in the throat that enable us to make so many rich sounds means that we are at perpetual risk of choking on our food, in a way that all other animals are not.

How do we do psycholinguistics?

We have some idea now what language is and where it came from. We're interested in how we produce, understand, and remember language, and how language interacts with other psychological processes. That is, we're interested in the psychology of language – a subject that we can give the name *psycholinguistics*.

It's nice to be able to date things exactly, isn't it? The origin of psycholinguistics is often traced to a conference held in the summer of 1951 at Cornell University in the USA, and the word is first used in print in Osgood and Sebeok's (1954) book describing that conference. But scientists were doing psycholinguistic-like things well before the term was coined. The early neurologists, such as Paul Broca (1824–1880) and Carl Wernicke (1848–1905), studied how the brain was linked to language by looking at the effects of brain damage (the structure of the brain, including Broca's area and Wernicke's area, is shown in Figure 1.3). The idea is a simple one. Brain trauma (perhaps by a stroke, which cuts off the blood supply to part of the brain, or a head injury) destroys part of the brain, which leads to a change in behaviour. After the person's death an autopsy will reveal exactly which part of the brain was affected. Wernicke in particular pieced together an account of how the brain processes language that isn't very different from that in favour today. We'll look at the relation between brain and language in depth

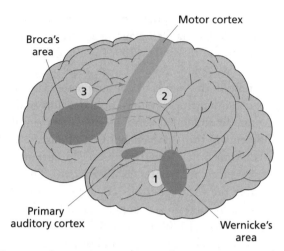

FIGURE 1.3 The location of Wernicke's area (1) and Broca's area (3). When someone speaks a word, activation proceeds from Wernicke's area through the arcuate fasciculus (2) to Broca's area

later. At the turn of the century, two German researchers, Meringer and Mayer, collected and analysed slips of the tongue in a way that is remarkably similar to more modern studies. (Their 1895 book was called *Versprechen und Verlesen: Eine Psychologisch-Linguistische Studie* [To mis-speak and to misread: A psychological–linguistic study], and I think Meringer and Mayer should get the credit for the first use of the word "psycholinguistic".) Freud picked up on their analysis of slips of the tongue in his 1901 book *The Psychopathology of Everyday Life*; although he tried to explain slips in terms of the repressed unconscious, he too was concerned with why we make slips of the tongue and the psychological processes involved in their occurrence. This emphasis on the psychological processes is the hallmark of psycholinguistics.

As a very crude generalisation, early psychologists were concerned with measurement or introspection. Then, throughout the 1930s, 1940s, and 1950s, *behaviourism* became the predominant paradigm in psychology. Behaviourism, popularised by J.B. Watson and B.F. Skinner, studied how an input, the stimulus, was related to an output, the response, without the necessity of hypothetical intervening constructs such as the mind. For behaviourists, thinking is just covert speech – speech we don't articulate aloud. Children learn language in the same way as rats learn to navigate a maze for the reward of a food pellet. The inadequacy of this approach was demonstrated by the American linguist Noam Chomsky in his influential 1959 book review of Skinner's *Verbal Behavior* – this is a rare example of a book review becoming more famous than the book on which it was based. Chomsky showed that the principles of learning derived from animal research were inadequate in accounting for how children learn language, and the creativity of both children and adults: we can produce an infinite variety of sentences, which of necessity we could not have heard before. Instead, a much richer account of language and how children learn it is necessary. Most psychologists believe that Chomsky's review spelt the end for behaviourism as an account of human psychology, and ushered in the information-processing account that still underlies cognitive psychology today: we're concerned with the mental processes and representations involved in behaviour.

Modern psychology is a science. That often comes as a surprise to students, many of whom think it's all going to be about Freud, or helping people, or helping them to understand themselves. Then they arrive at university and it's suddenly all statistics and computers and carrying out experiments. Psychology is harder than people think, and psycholinguistics is hardest of all: across the psychology degree curriculum it's usually the subject that most students find difficult to understand. It's difficult because the ideas are complex; there's a great deal of terminology, and few definitive answers. Psycholinguistics is not for the faint-hearted; it's not for wimps. But because language is at the heart of what it means to be human, and is so central to so much of what we do, the study of psycholinguistics can be exceptionally rewarding.

What does it mean to say it's a science? We form hypotheses, conjectures about how something works, and then carry out experiments to test those hypotheses. I'm using "experiment" pretty loosely here. For me, collecting slips of the tongue in the pub or systematically recording every utterance a young child makes in the attempt to test an idea about how the mind works is as much an experiment as using a computer to measure how quickly people respond in different conditions (although, admittedly, this particular technique has played a particularly important role in psycholinguistics). So we do psycholinguistics by carrying out experiments on how humans use language: how they speak, listen, understand, write, read, acquire, and remember language.

We psycholinguists are pretty methodologically promiscuous; across the past half century we've used many techniques and ideas borrowed from other fields. Given the importance of the brain to psychology, it is hardly surprising that we use data from neuropsychology (the study of the relation between the brain and the mind), and, given that psycholinguistics is about the processes involved in language, we would expect it to link with linguistics (the study of language itself). Psycholinguistics has also drawn from computing (in constructing models based on and using computers), anthropology, philosophy, and of course other fields of psychology. That's why psycholinguistics is often said to be an interdisciplinary subject.

Are there any answers in psycholinguistics? This might strike you as an odd question. Of course there must be answers, I hear you think. Of course psychologists must know a lot about how the mind works! You just said psychology's a science, didn't you? I did science subjects at school and university. (I mean "traditional" or "other" science subjects, before I did psychology.) I used text-books for physics and chemistry, and they were stuffed full of answers; they were full of what we know.

But psychology texts, particularly I think ones in psycholinguistics, aren't like that. Of course there must be answers to all our questions, but we often don't yet know what they are. Or rather, different people think they know the answers, but they often can't agree on what these answers are. So psycholinguistics texts are full of conflicting accounts, each account apparently being bolstered by experiments finding contradictory results. Another psycholinguist might argue about why you got that particular result; perhaps you didn't do that experiment quite properly, perhaps you forgot to take into account how common the words you used are, perhaps you didn't make the task quite difficult enough; or perhaps the findings of your experiment are just a special case, and my account is more general, subsuming your findings and explaining when we get them – and when we don't. The list of excuses can be pretty big when you put your mind to it. I have a memory of a television show where two puppets representing celebrities would stand in a ring and start fighting; one would get knocked down, get up, and then knock the other one down, and this process would be repeated several times. Psycholinguistics is like that. It's rare for a researcher to say "you're right! I'm wrong"; after being set an apparently insuperable hurdle, they'll be back.

So there are some answers in psycholinguistics, but not as many as there should be, and we will come across many occasions where researchers have exactly opposite views. And that's one reason why psycholinguistics is not for wimps.

What is an explanation?

What constitutes a good explanation in psycholinguistics? What would make a psycholinguist dance with joy? We carry out experiments and collect masses of numerical data, and then what?

We want a *model* of our experimental results. A model is an account that explains the data we've collected, but which goes beyond it. A *theory* is a more overarching account covering a wider range of phenomena and results. We might have a model of the time it takes to recognise a word, but a theory of word recognition in general. However, the terms are often used interchangeably, and it's not a distinction we should get too agitated about.

Here's a very simple example. Suppose we carry out an experiment to discover whether how long it takes us to be able to start to name a word aloud is related to the length of the word in letters. We carry out the appropriate experiment and find the following (rather made-up) results (and let's not worry about exactly how we should measure the time it takes us to start speaking):

3 letters   400 milliseconds (a millisecond is a thousandth of a second)
4 letters   500
5 letters   600

Let's draw a graph of the results. Plot the number of letters in the word on the x-axis and the naming time on the y-axis. What do we get in this experiment? A straight line. The most simple relationship between two variables we can find; we say there's a linear relationship.

So we've accounted for the results of our specific experiment, but can we go further? How long would it take to name a word containing six letters? You could probably work it out just by looking at these figures, but if you have any mathematical or statistical expertise you'll know that we can easily derive an equation that relates word length to naming time that takes the form:

$$y = ax + b$$

Here it would be:

Naming time in milliseconds = (number of letters in word × 100) + 100

This apparently simple mathematical model is pretty powerful. Not only have we got an account of how naming time and word length are related, but we can now go beyond the data we have already collected. How long will it take to start reading aloud a seven-letter word? Type the numbers into the equation above, and you have the answer: it should take 800 milliseconds. (That's nearly a whole second; I said I'd made the numbers up.) So now we're using our model to make predictions. We could carry out another experiment to test these predictions. Suppose we find that six-, seven-, eight-, and nine-letter words all take 600 milliseconds, just like five-letter ones; in that case, I'd think we'd all agree that the model hasn't done a very good job of generalising to novel data; it's been falsified. Back to the drawing board in search of another model that does a better job. And this is, supposedly, the way science works.

I think mathematical models are among the most satisfying accounts of behaviour in psychology. They have an elegance and a simplicity: all those data reduced to one line. But some of you might still be left a little dissatisfied. Is this equation really an explanation? Why should the relation be linear? It need not have been; a polynomial function (involving curves) is on the face of it just as plausible. So we shouldn't be overly impressed by the maths; we need to explain why the relationship is as it is. Really this model isn't much more than a rigorous description of the data that makes it easy for us to make some predictions. Why is the equation as it is?

We're almost back where we started. What would be a good explanation?

We could explain the results in terms of other psychological processes. Perhaps we can relate it to the speed with which we can retrieve information from memory. Perhaps it's the time it takes us to start assembling all the sounds of the words we're going to say. Perhaps it's both of these. But then we can push back our enquiry further: why should the time it takes to retrieve words from memory be related to their length in this way? Should we try to relate our findings to the way in which the neurons of the brain are connected together and the rate at which they fire? What would ultimately be a satisfactory account?

I think to be satisfactory a model has to have two characteristics. First, it has to make predictions that are in principle *falsifiable*. Falsifiable means that there is an obvious way of testing the prediction that could prove it wrong. So for our model above we predict that for a seven-letter word the reaction time to start speaking should be 800 milliseconds. That's a falsifiable prediction, because we could run an experiment to measure the reaction time. If the prediction's not verified, the model is wrong (or at least needs revision). If it is, good; the model lives to fight another day. The more novel and outrageous the prediction, the better: I predict that Torquay won't win the Premiership before 2020. No offence is meant to the players and supporters of Torquay; I suspect they'll agree with my prediction. But when (if) this prediction is proved right, you'll hardly be impressed by my football acumen, will you? But if I say I have a complete model of psychology and society and it predicts that Torquay *will* win the league in 2019, and they do, then that's impressive. My model must be good. Second, the explanation should not be circular. It should involve concepts that are from outside our original domain of thinking. Ideally we could derive our equation from a theory of memory, or how neurons in the brain are connected together. Good models should *transcend levels of description*. I think there's a limit, though, on how much looking at neurons and even whole brains can tell you. Ultimately all behaviour and psychological processes are grounded in the brain, but you can't do without psychology: not now, not ever. We still need to cross-reference what the brain is doing to what the person is thinking, feeling, and doing, and how a person is interacting with others. This book is about the psychology of language, not the neurology.

Quite often psychological models are based on metaphors. For example, we could have a model for how we search the mental dictionary based on a library, with words stored in particular places on mental shelves and a catalogue system for looking them up. Indeed, one of the best known models of word recognition, the serial search model, uses this analogy. One of the most commonly used metaphors in psycholinguistics is that of *activation*; you'll read about some words having a high activation level and others a low one, and words being in competition and the most highly activated one winning. Activation is a quantity rather like energy or temperature; some items have a lot, some not very much, but it's a continuous scale. So what would a good model of some psycholinguistic phenomenon look like? What about word recognition? A complete model of word recognition should explain what makes it hard, how long it takes to recognise words, the difference between recognition times for different sorts of words, what happens when we recognise a word, the difference between recognising and being able to name and access the meaning (if any), the difference between spoken and written word recognition, what happens during the recognition process in different parts of the brain, what makes recognition easier or harder, how it relates to other psychological processes, how it's affected by brain damage, and how it develops. That's quite a list of requirements.

What is a statistical model?

Let's step back a bit and look at two broad types of model. Psychology abounds in metaphors. Across the years we've had the mind as spirit, pump, rat, computer, gas, even tin cans; the mind has further been likened to cars, calculators, chocolate factories, radios, television sets, and smoke coming out of factories. Through much of the 1960s through to the 1980s the dominant metaphor was that the mind was like a digital computer: it had memory, a processor, it carried out operations that transformed one representation into another. Computers at that time were also pretty much serial: they just did one thing at a time. Now if you know anything about computer programming you might know something about the principles of good programming practice: try to make your code as modular as possible and as easy to debug as possible. Stick commonly used bits of codes in separate subroutines, and don't let your subroutines fiddle around with the insides of other subroutines. The East Coast model is typically serial – one thing happens at a time, modular, and bottom-up; it starts work on the input and grinds away without using any external information.

I remember in 1983 thinking that the computer was the ultimate metaphor for psychology; the mind was indeed a computer. The next year the importance of connectionist modelling became apparent, as was the fact that I was wrong in my conviction of just the year before.

Connectionist models typically use many very simple processing units that are simultaneously active and massively interconnected. The analogy is often made between connectionism and the brain: the brain is made up of a huge number (about 100 billion) of very simple nerve cells – neurons – and each neuron is connected to thousands of other neurons. All human behaviour, language, thoughts, feelings, actions, and consciousness emerge from this massively interconnected network of neurons. Each neuron is pretty dumb; it either fires in a certain situation or it doesn't, but out of this mass dumbness comes great cleverness.

An advantage of connectionist networks is that we don't just tell them how to behave; they learn. They use a variety of complex algorithms, which do things like ensuring that if two things occur together, the link between them is strengthened, or if we are trying to get the network to learn to recognise a pattern, we see what its current best guess is and then tell it how wrong it is. Because the networks learn, we can examine how they learn, and furthermore how that learning depends on the input we supply. One of the key points here is that the networks don't learn because they're told an explicit rule; they learn implicitly, by discovering statistical regularities in the input, and their subsequent behaviour is then guided by these regularities rather than rules (this sort of approach would be the West Coast thing again).

What is a statistical regularity? It's a pattern that occurs quite frequently. It's time for a literary diversion. Here is a little message written in a cipher.

Uif dbu dibtfe b mjuumf npvtf. Uif eph uifo dibtfe uif dbu, uif npvtf ftdbqfe.

Stop and think before reading on. Any ideas on how to go about breaking this cipher? If you've never come across this technique before, what do you think is going on? It seems that one letter has been substituted for another to render the original message meaningless. How do we work out what the correspondence is between the two sets of letters, the original and the cipher? Look at the message. There's one three-letter string that's used several times – more than any other, in fact. Now what's the most common three-letter word in English? (If you're still stuck, and need a hint, it was used in that sentence.) There's also a single-letter word: which is one of only two single-letter words in English? (Same hint as the last.) You might not even have needed that second clue, but should now have enough information to be able to decode this message. Congratulations: you have just made use of statistical regularities in English. Some words of certain lengths are more common than others. (This was a literary diversion because the technique of frequency analysis is explained much more elegantly – and entertainingly – in Arthur Conan Doyle's Sherlock Holmes short story *The Adventure of the Dancing Men*, and Edgar Allen Poe's short story *The Gold Bug*, both well worth reading.)

For a more psycholinguistic example consider the difficulties facing an infant trying to understand speech. If you listen carefully to someone speaking, there aren't many pauses in normal speech; words and sounds slur into each other. So one of the first difficulties facing a child trying to learn what words mean is trying to distinguish separate words in the first place. But the task isn't as impossible as it might at first sound. Imagine you know no language and hear:

Themanlovesthewomanandthewomanlovesthemanthemansdogchasedthe
womanscatthewomanlovedhercat

Hardly an inspiring sentence for a baby to hear, but some sounds seem to stick together quite a bit: "the". So it's likely that "the" is a distinct word. "C", "a", and "t" turn up together a few times too, so it wouldn't be a bad guess that "cat" is another word. And off the child goes. I'm not saying that the child reasons like this; the learning is done unconsciously. Connectionist models aren't conscious, yet they can easily detect these sorts of statistical regularities.

Statistical regularities are important in language. They simplify the task of children learning a language and people trying to understand what other people are saying.

What are the issues in psycholinguistics?

Psycholinguistics today is dominated by four controversies. Many studies cast light on one or more of these issues, even if at first sight that is not the primary concern of the researchers. It's worth spending some time outlining these controversies because they recur so often.

First, is our language behaviour governed by the use of rules or by multiple constraints and statistical regularities? When we hear a complex sentence, do we try to work out its structure according to the rules of grammar, or make use of our experience to tell us what the structure of that sort of sentence has usually been in the past?

Second is the issue of nature versus nurture: where does knowledge come from? Is it innate and in our genes, or is it learned? The question of how much knowledge a baby is born with has been a central one in the history of philosophy. According to the *nativism* view, we are born with particular information; we can say that the knowledge is hard-wired into the brain. According to the blank slate, or *empiricist*, view, we are born an empty canvas, and have to learn things from experience. No one would say that everything's innate or learned; for example, even if you think you learn everything, you have to ask where does the learning mechanism itself come from. You have to start with something. So the question is one of degree: how much specific knowledge about language are we born with? Is some knowledge about language encoded in our genes, or do we just pick it up using general-purpose cognitive mechanisms?

Third, is processing modular or interactive? A *module* is a self-contained unit. University courses are now often taught as modules – separate teaching units with their own assessment and structure. In a modular degree you might be able to pick and choose from a history module, a geography module, a biochemistry module, and of course a psychology module. Importantly, in a modular system you would only be examined in your psychology module exam on psychology; you wouldn't be expected to know any history or biochemistry. The courses are separate from each other. You can buy modular furniture, where you can choose from a range of furniture modules to customise the precise layout of your bedroom or living room to your taste. You can, I see from Google, even design modular concrete houses to your own specification. All of these systems have in common the fact that you can

25

pick and choose from a set of existing modules (courses, furniture, houses), but you can't change the contents of the module itself. So you can choose a psychology module but you can't choose whether you get social or cognitive psychology (unless they're modules in their own right, of course).

So a module is a self-contained unit that does something specific. The philosopher Jerry Fodor argued in 1983 in his landmark book *The Modularity of Mind* that the mind is made up of distinct modules responsible for carrying out specific tasks, such as parts of visual processing. Fodor describes several characteristics of modules, such as processing inside a module being fast, not accessible to consciousness, and mandatory (once it starts, it finishes; you can't not choose to read a word, and when you start you can't help but finish it), but the most important is that processes within a module are immune from outside interference – "you can't tinker around inside a module". It makes sense to argue further that the mind has evolved in this way: for example, suppose, as many psychologists believe, there is a face-processing module; that module has evolved under evolutionary pressure to enable us to recognise faces quickly and automatically because it confers an advantage to be able to do so. A final step in the argument is the unsurprising one that if these cognitive modules have evolved, they almost certainly correspond to distinct and identifiable regions of the brain.

This idea of modularity might seem to be getting away from language. But many psycholinguists argue that there are language-processing modules that carry out specific tasks, such as word recognition and syntactic processing. For example, when we try to understand language, do we process word order using just information about word order, or do we use other sorts of knowledge, such as meaning? When reading or listening we often come to a point of syntactic ambiguity, where there is more than one possible syntactic structure for what we have so far: so when we hear "The policeman arrested . . .", we could have either a structure as in "The policeman arrested the burglar" (most likely) or a different structure, as in "The policeman arrested by the fraud squad made a run for it". You're probably not aware of this ambiguity, but it's there. Do we then resolve that ambiguity using just syntactic (to do with word order) information or do we use semantic (to do with meaning) information to assist us? The former view is *modular*, the latter *interactive*. I discuss this issue in more detail in the chapter called "Understanding". We can take another example from the production of words; obviously we move from the general direction of meaning to sound, but perhaps sound-level information can influence our choice of words? The account where no such interaction is permitted is the modular one. The interactive account is not as implausible as it first might seem, and I discuss it in the chapter called "Speaking".

So we have two broad accounts of how we process language: a modular one, where lots of simple little modules carry out their individual tasks in splendid isolation, and an interactive one, where different sorts of process are talking to and interfering with each other all over the place.

An East Coast view: conservative and modular

In this sense language itself might be one big module (albeit in turn made up of smaller ones). This brings us to the fourth issue, one we touched upon when asking what is innate in language, that of whether the knowledge and processes we use to produce and understand language are specific to language, or whether they are general-purpose. Chomsky argued that language forms a separate mental organ – that we have a language faculty that occupies a distinct region of the brain and whose structure is innate (e.g. Chomsky, 1975). On this view, language processes run along nicely without any help or interference from other cognitive processes. The alternative view is that there's nothing special about language; instead of there being dedicated language processes, language makes use of the same cognitive processes that run the rest of our lives. There isn't a separate pool of linguistic knowledge, just a pool of

27

A West Coast view: liberal and hang loose

language. (This argument is of course the same as that of my friend at the start of this chapter.)

To give a concrete example, when we process the structure of sentences, we have to make use of some sort of memory. When you hear "the woman the man kissed laughed" you have to store "the woman" somewhere while you're processing the bit about her being kissed by a man until you get to the main verb of the sentence – "laughed". Where do you store it? Is there some special store that only syntactic processing can use (in which case sentence processing shouldn't impinge on other memory tasks) or does it use the same sort of memory we use when trying to remember a telephone number (in which case syntactic processing definitely should impinge on other memory tasks)? Or consider children learning language; do they learn language independently of everything else, or does its development depend on general cognitive development?

These could possibly be independent issues, but in practice they're related. People who argue that language is governed by rules tend to argue that we make use of language-specific knowledge that's in part innate and that processing is modular. People who think that language processing makes use of statistical regularities and constraints tend to believe that it's interactive and learned through general-purpose mechanisms.

It has also been observed that in the USA, people who believe in innate modular rules tend to live on the east coast (mostly in and around Boston), and those who believe in the laid-back general patterns acquired by experience tend to live on the west (mostly around Los Angeles). It's true. I like to think of them as conservative versus liberal, while making no claims about the political beliefs of anyone. The conservatives will argue that when formulating a model we should make the minimum number of assumptions about what's going on: we should go for the simplest account. Parsimony is often held up as a virtue in science: make as few assumptions as possible. Unfortunately, it isn't always obvious which is the simplest. And making few assumptions about one thing might entail having to make a lot about something else. Life is hard, and so is psycholinguistics.

Enough background. Let's look a bit more closely at what language is, and one of the most interesting ways of doing that is to look at how other animals communicate.

Chapter 2

Animals

WHEN I WAS YOUNG the *Chronicles of Narnia* left a profound impression on me. I remember though that I was more optimistic that something odd might lurk at the back of my mother's wardrobe than that animals would start speaking to me. The idea of animals talking like humans has obviously fascinated people across the centuries. We have talking animals in folklore, fairy tales (remember those three little pigs), talking rabbits in *Watership Down*, toads and rats in *Wind in the Willows*, and all sorts of creatures in *Narnia* and the *Dr Dolittle* books and films.

Why can't they talk? The simple answer is that only humans have a sufficiently complex articulatory apparatus. So why can't they use some other channel for language? Could we teach them human language? Just spend a few minutes watching a nature documentary; it's obvious that at least some animals communicate with each other. By *communicate* I mean that they transfer information; afterwards the second animal "knows" something (There's a snake out there! Great pollen over that way!) they didn't "know" before. I'm not saying that the animal is aware of this knowledge; just that their behaviour is likely to be different afterwards. There are also two types of communication: deliberate, where the first animal in some sense (again, certainly not necessarily consciously) intends to convey information; and unintentional. When a flock of birds is spooked, another bird will react to this by flying away too. Fear or danger has been communicated. It's the first sort of communication, involving the deliberate transfer of information from one animal to another, that we're interested in.

How do animals communicate, and what are the limits on animal communication? What separates us from them?

How do animals communicate?

I can't say I'm that keen on insects. They have too many legs and move around far too quickly for their size. But I do like watching ants. Try this experiment with some friendly local ants; they're pretty ubiquitous, even in towns. Find a place near where you know some ants pass, and put down something sweet; anything will do. Now sit back and watch. After a while, if you're lucky, your little drop will be swarming with ants. Then you can watch a little trail of them, carrying food back to their nest.

What's happened? Obviously an ant out on patrol has found the marmalade and has somehow communicated her (worker ants are female) exciting find to her colleagues. Ants communicate with pheromones, chemical signals; we can think of pheromone detection as "smelling", and ants smell pheromones with their antennae, which can detect both the direction and intensity of pheromones on the ground. When ants leave the colony they mark their way with drops of pheromone produced by special glands; if they find food they return along the same pathway, marking it with more pheromones and hence making the smell on that pathway stronger. Other ants pick up on it, and follow the pheromone highway, and if they too find food they reinforce the scent (Jackson & Ratnieks, 2006). In this way routes that lead to food quickly accumulate a strong pheromone trail. When the source of food is finished, ants wander away empty-mouthed in search of a new source, so the original trail is no longer strengthened and the pheromones gradually fade. Different sorts of pheromones indicate different things: in addition to the trail pheromone, there's also an alarm pheromone that stimulates ants to defend the colony, and a special pheromone that the queen produces while breeding that inhibits workers from raising new queens. Pheromones are used widely for communication among insects, to communicate about food, territory, danger, and sex. Pheromones enable butterflies to detect a potential mate up to six miles away.

Pheromones aren't restricted to insects, though. It's widely accepted that a group of women living together will eventually menstruate in synchrony, with the synchronisation effected by pheromones (Stern & McClintock, 1998). I'd call the insect pheromone system intentional communication, in that the purpose of the pheromone (not the individual ant) is to communicate a trail, or distress, or sexual availability, while I'd call the pheromone system involved in synchronising human menstrual systems unintentional, in that synchronisation isn't its primary purpose, but this isn't a distinction upon which we should get too hung up. You might have seen adverts for pheromone-based scents, guaranteed to make you more attractive to the opposite sex; as yet there's no hard evidence that these work.

Insect communication isn't just based on pheromones. Honey bees make honey for food as a means of storing energy, and to do that they need nectar from flowers. They also need pollen from plants as a source of protein to feed the young of the hive. How do they find the nectar and pollen? Do they just fly around randomly and optimistically until they spot a likely flower? Towards the end of the Second World War, the Austrian scientist Karl von Frisch discovered that the flight of the bee isn't random; they know where they're going, because other bees have told them where to go (von Frisch, 1974).

When a bee finds a source of food, she returns to the hive and performs a *bee dance*, where the pollen-laden bee "dances" on the honeycomb, moving in an ellipse or figure-of-eight shape, sometimes crossing the ellipse in a *waggle* or zigzag pattern (Figure 2.1). This dance had been known about since at least the time of Aristotle, who more or less got it right in thinking that the purpose of the dance was to attract the attention of other bees. Von Frisch showed that the dance conveyed information about the location of the source of the nectar and pollen relative to the hive: the direction of the axis of the figure-of-eight shape conveys information about the relative position of the sun to the food source, and the length of the waggle part of the dance conveys information about distance. Bees even adjust the direction of the axis to take into account the movement of the sun since they discovered the source of the nectar. Von Frisch received the Nobel Prize for Physiology for this work in 1973.

Von Frisch called his work "the language of bees", but here the term "language" is being used metaphorically. Bees can communicate detailed information, but all they can communicate is the direction and distance of the food source. All ants can communicate about with pheromones are things like the

FIGURE 2.1 The waggle dance

direction of food and whether they're being attacked. They can't talk about the weather on the way, or what colour the flowers are, or what they are looking forward to the next day, let alone whether that was a particularly good waggle dance or not. Insect communication systems are very impressive, but they aren't language.

What do monkeys talk about?

Of course, it isn't that surprising that insects, with their tiny brains, have very limited communication systems. What about something genetically much closer to us, such as other primates?

Primates include humans, along with apes, monkeys, lemurs, and related groups. Primates are highly social animals, living in groups, and as a consequence non-human primates have a rich communicative repertoire, communicating by sound, touch, and smell, using gestures, facial expressions, grooming, and calls. The communication system is used both to ensure the smooth running of the social group and to protect it from outside threats. For example, certain facial gestures indicate that the animal is angry, and are used to prevent or at least reduce the amount of fighting; these facial expressions are easily recognisable by us, as our own facial expressions are related. A dominant male baboon can scare off less dominant baboons just by blinking in the right way. Vervet monkeys have a particularly rich communicative repertoire. They groom and greet each other by touching noses to reinforce social bonds; they have a number of displays mostly to monitor and reinforce social dominance within the group. They have a large number of vocalisations, including some to reinforce social bonds, for infants to communicate distress to their mother, and even a purring sound when young are just playing with each other. Most notably, they have different alarm calls depending on whether the threat is a snake in the grass nearby, an eagle overhead, or if they've spotted a distant leopard, and each call elicits a different response from other members of the group (Struhsaker, 1967).

Non-human primates clearly have rich communication systems, but they fall a considerable way short of being like human language. They can "talk" about more than the direction of a source of food, but what they can "talk" about is still very limited: food, threats, I want a fight, I don't want a fight, and so on. It is true that each call or gesture has a meaning, but the range of meanings is limited to the here and now – things right in front of the primate's eyes. Furthermore, the calls aren't combined in the way we combine words using the rules of grammar to generate a large number of sentences, so the restricted number of calls and the lack of grammar mean that the communications of primates in the wild are very limited.

My visit to Monkey World. The one on the left is clearly winding up the clockwork one on the right

Do whales and dolphins use language?

Every year I teach the topic of language and animals, someone will say "but it's well known that whales [or dolphins] have a language . . .". This belief is close to having the status of an urban myth.

Cetaceans – including whales, dolphins, and porpoises – do indeed communicate with each other by a sound. They are often considered to be among the most intelligent species in the world, although this can be difficult to measure. Many species, particularly dolphins, are highly social animals, and tight social groups rely on communication for safety and coherence. Dolphins also use tools; they break pieces of sponge off the sea floor and wear them to protect their noses while foraging, and have been observed teaching this behaviour to their young (Krutzen et al., 2005). Dolphins play, and have been observed apparently choosing to interact with human swimmers. There's little evidence, however, that dolphins are particularly good at solving problems, or reasoning and planning a sequence of future actions.

The toothed whales, which include dolphins, make a variety of high-frequency clicks and whistles by passing air through a special structure in their head that rather resembles the human nose in its design, but containing a pair of phonic

Who has whom trained?

lips that, just like human lips, can be closed together to modify the sound. Single clicks are used to help the dolphin locate itself using echo-location, similar to bat sonar or radar. While some whistles may help other dolphins identify exactly where each individual of the group is located, generally the sounds serve some communicative purpose that is poorly understood (Frankell, 1998).

The large baleen whales produce the long, low-frequency sounds often called *whale song*. The sounds they make can be very loud and travel for many miles underwater. The exact way in which the sounds are produced is still unclear, but seems to involve recycling air through a larynx-like structure that enables sound to resonate (but differs from that of humans in not having vocal chords); structures like sinuses might further help the sound to resonate. The purpose of the sounds is also poorly understood. Some of the sounds may be used for echo-location to help the whale navigate, and some to help the whales co-ordinate group feeding. The complex song of the humpback whale is particularly famous, and as it has only been observed in the mating season it may be used for sexual selection – to attract a mate or to define a territory, or both. If this is correct, its restriction to the mating system seems to me to refute the popularly held belief that humpback whales can sing just for pleasure.

It's easy and tempting to anthropomorphise appealing animals, but as scientists we should stick to the evidence. And although there's clearly a great deal that just isn't known about cetacean communication, there's no evidence whatsoever that they're using language in the sense of being able to combine discrete sounds with arbitrary meanings (words) using grammatical rules in order to be able to generate an infinite number of sentences, or even that they can communicate about anything other than what's in front of their cute little snouts.

Can we teach language to animals?

Some animals, then, have sophisticated communication systems, but at least as far as we know they're limited to communicating about the here-and-now, have a very limited number of things they communicate about, and don't use a set of rules of grammar to combine symbols into sentences. Perhaps, though, at least some could do this if only they were taught? Perhaps it's just an accident of evolution that only humans have language?

You might teach your dog to "sit" and "fetch", and if you're lucky to stop rolling around in filth or chasing after another dog, but I doubt that you're under any illusion that you're teaching it language. Rover knows only a few specific commands. You could spend a lifetime teaching it the difference between "the big dog chases the cat" and "the cat is chased by the dog", and I doubt you'd get very far. You'll get even less far with your cat, although it seems to exude superiority. Of course most people don't try to teach their dog as much as possible, so we need to be a bit cautious about their limitations. One border collie called Rico was taught the names of over 200 objects, and could fetch the appropriate object from around the house even when he couldn't see the trainer. When faced with a new name, he inferred that the name belonged to an as yet unnamed object, rather than being just another name for an object with which he was already familiar (Kaminski et al., 2004). But Rico's abilities were nevertheless very limited. His knowledge was limited to the names of objects, there was no indication that he knew that words we know are related in meaning go together (we know – and very young children know – that the words "doll" and "ball", although they refer to physically very dissimilar objects, are the names of types of toy), and he couldn't produce the names, let alone combine them into sentences.

If we're going to try to teach human language to an animal, let's make our job as easy as possible by choosing a clever one. We could use dolphins, but all that water gets in the way, so most of the attempts to teach language to animals have used our closest relatives, non-human primates.

Can parrots talk?

Before we examine the research on teaching language to chimpanzees, it's worth having a detour with a parrot.

Parrots and myna birds are very vocal and excellent mimics that can be trained to produce particular human-like sounds. Occasionally one hears stories about people's secrets given away by their pet parrot saying the wrong thing at the wrong time. There's no evidence at all from these anecdotes that these parrots understand the sounds they're making or are able to combine them in novel ways.

But we need to move beyond anecdote and look more systematically at what parrots can and cannot do. Irene Pepperberg, an animal psychologist in the USA, did just that with a 30-year study of an African grey parrot called Alex (named after Avian Learning Experiment). Pepperberg bought Alex in a pet shop in 1977 when he was about one year old. When he was in his mid-twenties, he could name about 50 different objects and had a vocabulary of about 150 words (Pepperberg, 2002). In addition to the names he used adjectives and some verbs. He could classify objects together depending on characteristics such as their colour, their shape, and what they were made of, and make discriminations such as one thing being larger than another. He could count up to six and use those numbers appropriately, and, Pepperbeg claimed, had a concept of zero (for when things were absent or missing). There are some charming anecdotes that suggest something about the inner life of the parrot; once when he said "I want a banana", he was offered a nut. He stared at the nut in silence, asked for a banana again, and eventually threw the nut at the researcher. Alex died suddenly in 2007, but the work is being continued by Pepperberg with another parrot, called Griffin.

As with whales and dolphins, we must be careful about anthropomorphising these stories too much, and thinking that because an animal seems to behave like us, it must be having the same thoughts and feelings. Pepperberg is aware of this danger, and the research on Alex is thorough and carefully documented. Pepperberg has also been careful to avoid making too strong a claim about what Alex can do, and has avoided words such as "language" and "conscious". Nevertheless, Alex's linguistic abilities are clearly very limited. He never learned many verbs, and there's no clear evidence that he could relate nouns using verbs. Verbs are essential for language; by definition, you can't construct a sentence without one. Alex was stuck at the one-word stage, with very little or no ability to combine them – the hallmark of language. And some researchers think that Alex did nothing more than rote learning, and had no understanding of the meanings of his vocalisations.

Let's not be too hasty, though, in dismissing Alex as being totally without language. It's worth putting a final decision on hold until we've discussed some further examples.

Although Rico and Alex might not be using human language, their stories do show that we should be very careful about thinking animals to be dumb. I find both stories very impressive, and some animals are clearly cleverer than once thought. At the very least Alex showed some rudimentary reasoning ability. I now look at Rover in a new light, even if I know he's never going to start talking to me about the nature and limitations of animal communication systems. And if dogs and even parrots can be taught so much, how much more could we teach a chimpanzee?

What about chimps?

I've just ordered *Me Cheeta: The Autobiography* from Amazon. It's the story of Cheeta, the real star of the 1930s Tarzan films, also starring Johnny Weismuller and Maureen O'Sullivan. I was surprised to discover that Cheeta is still alive and well and living a happy retirement in Palm Springs. In his autobiography, which looks to be both well written and very funny, he dishes the dirt on the stars.

Of course it's ghost written, but then whose autobiography isn't these days? And who's to say this isn't what Cheeta would have said, if only he could have talked?

Higher primates, particularly chimpanzees, are our nearest genetic neighbours. Although there's a bit of controversy about the exact figure, we share at least 95% of our genetic material with chimpanzees, and perhaps as much as 98.5%. Chimpanzees are highly social animals, and highly intelligent; very broadly speaking their intelligence is on a par with that of a toddler aged about three (Hayes & Nissen, 1971). Some of their hunting strategies require a great deal of co-operation, and they have recently been shown to make tools such as spears (Pruetz & Bertolani, 2007). They play, they seem to mourn their dead, display curiosity, and may even show empathy and respect towards other species. As we've already noted, primates have sophisticated communication systems, using displays, gestures, and vocalisations. If we can teach any animal to use language, surely it would be a chimp? Not surprisingly, therefore, most of the research on teaching language to animals has been with chimps.

The basic idea of the early research was to raise a chimpanzee like a human child in a family setting, a process known as *cross-fostering*. The first attempt at this was reported by Kellogg and Kellogg (1933), who raised a female chimpanzee called Gua along with their own son Donald for nine months. At the start of the experiment Gua was seven and a half months old and Donald was 10 months. The Kelloggs' emphasis was to examine the differential effects of heredity and environment on development, rather than on just language; they wanted to discover how human a chimpanzee could become when raised in a completely human environment. Nevertheless, it was obvious that Donald had superior language abilities from an early age, particularly in production, where Gua produced just her native barks, screams, and cries; she couldn't produce any recognisably word-like sounds. At first her comprehension of language was better than that of the child; from an early age she could understand "no no" and "kiss kiss". Within a few months, however, Donald overtook Gua's comprehension skills. At the end of the study Gua's language remained extremely limited.

A similar enterprise was undertaken a couple of decades later with a female chimp named Viki (Hayes, 1951). Hayes reared Viki like a human child, and tried to teach her to speak. After six years the only recognisable words she could produce were "mama", "papa", "up", and "cup", and even these four words were poorly articulated. Hayes reported that Viki demonstrated a high level of language comprehension, although the stories are largely anecdotal and it's therefore difficult to be certain how much Viki actually understood.

It's a reasonable conclusion from these early studies that chimpanzees are cognitively and linguistically similar to human children of the same age until the time children start to speak in earnest – at around the age of 18 months. But there's one very good reason why we shouldn't have any great expectations of the ability of chimpanzees to speak. We saw in the previous chapter that one of the great evolutionary steps forward in human language was a redesign of the vocal apparatus that enables us to produce complex sounds so fluently. Chimps never took this great leap forward, so we should hardly be surprised that they struggle to produce sounds. What they are good at, however, is using their hands. Subsequent attempts to teach language to chimpanzees made use of this skill.

The most famous study of cross-fostering and teaching language to a chimp is that of Washoe by Beatrix and Allen Gardner in Nevada (as described, for example, in Gardner & Gardner, 1969, 1975). From when she was about one year old, Washoe was raised as a child by the Gardners, whose innovation was to try to teach Washoe ASL, the form of sign language used by the hearing impaired in North America. Sign language uses combinations of hand movements to convey meaning; it has words and grammatical rules, and is equal in power and complexity to spoken language.

By the age of four, Washoe could produce about 85 signs, and understand many more; a few years later she had acquired a vocabulary of around 200 words. These words came from all syntactic categories: in addition to nouns, names of things, she had a rich vocabulary of verbs and grammatical words such as negatives and pronouns. Washoe also learnt words in the same way as human children, making the same sort of errors that human children do. When children start producing language, they sometimes use words incorrectly, extending ones they know inappropriately. They might, for example, start using the word "moon" to refer to all round things, or "dog" to all four-legged animals. These sorts of mistakes are called over-generalisations, because the child has clearly learned some aspect of the meaning of the word, but not that it can only be used in restricted contexts – that "dog" can only be used to refer to four-legged animals of a certain sort. Washoe seemed to make over-generalisation errors. Early on, she used the sign for "flower" to refer not just to flowers, but to all things with a flower-like scent. She used the word "hurt" to refer to a tattoo. Even more remarkably, she was able to make up words for things for which she hadn't yet been taught the sign; most famously, when she first saw a duck, she signed "water bird".

We've seen that human language gets its power from our ability to combine words using rules. Washoe learned to combine signs and produce them in strings several words long. In the earliest stage she produced two-word utterances, just like human children, saying things like "Washoe sorry", "go in", and "hug hurry"; later she would produce utterances such as "out open please hurry". She could answer questions correctly. She was sensitive to the importance of word order, knowing the difference between "You tickle me" and "I tickle you".

Perhaps most extraordinary of all, researchers noticed that Washoe's adopted son, Loulis, started using sign language without any training from them. Loulis acquired signs both by just observing Washoe and by actively being taught by her (Fouts et al., 1989).

What did Washoe know?

At first sight Washoe's accomplishments are impressive, but this work sparked a fierce debate in the language community. There are two types of criticism of this work with chimps. The first criticism is methodological: the rigour of the experimental work wasn't sufficient to enable strong conclusions such as "Washoe acquired language" to be drawn. Pioneers of new techniques always have my sympathy: it's virtually impossible to anticipate every problem in advance, and it's very easy to be wise and criticise with hindsight. Nevertheless, critics noted that the Gardners and their colleagues drew attention to Washoe's successes. In order to evaluate Washoe's language, you would need a complete, systematic corpus of all the utterances Washoe produced in a particular period of time, along with the errors she made. There isn't such a corpus. The reports of Washoe's utterances were also cleaned up to some degree, such as by deleting repeated signs, in order to make the meaning more obvious – but this also made it harder to evaluate (Seidenberg & Petitto, 1979). Washoe's creative use of the sign for "flower" would be much less impressive if she went round that day calling everything a flower, or her creativity in calling a duck a "water bird" would be less meaningful if she'd been in a period when she prefixed everything with water: water dog, water banana, and water hug aren't quite as significant. It's also important that the utterances are recorded accurately and neutrally; hearing-impaired signers often thought Washoe had said something else (or nothing at all) compared with what her trainers thought (Pinker, 1994). While it seems most unlikely that she was just signing randomly, it's difficult to evaluate the details of what she was doing.

Comparisons have been made between Washoe and the case of Clever Hans. Clever Hans was a horse owned by a Mr Von Osten in Germany at the start of the twentieth century who appeared be able to solve arithmetic problems and tell the time, indicating the answer by tapping his hoof. The horse would get the right answer even if Mr Von Osten wasn't present. It turned out that the horse was very sensitive to the demeanour of the person asking the question; as Hans got near the right answer, the facial expression and posture of the person would change. The horse used this information to choose the right answer – or get close to it. Clever, but not that clever. Washoe built up a strong social bond with her trainers, and in everyday settings they doubtless would have conveyed some information about what would have been an appropriate response. However, it seems most unlikely that this could have been the sole cause of all Washoe's success.

The second criticism of Washoe's language is that she in fact learned much less than she seemed to have done. She tended to make more relative use of signs that are related in meaning to what they denote. The sign for "drive" looks like the act of turning a steering wheel, while the sign for "give" resembles the motion of passing something to someone by hand. Her utterances were also largely tied to the here and now: what was happening then in front of her. More significantly, the utterances lacked the syntactic structure of those made by a human child with a vocabulary of a similar size. There was also little evidence that Washoe had learned grammatical rules: she didn't order her words in a consistent way. Similar work with other chimps showed that apparently learning the rules to be able to produce utterances such as "insert apple pail" and "red dish" didn't lead to the ability to combine them to be able to generate utterances such as "insert apple red pail" (Fodor et al., 1974).

Other attempts about the same time to teach language to chimps drew attention to the limits of what an ape could acquire. These studies tried to pre-empt the above sorts of methodological criticism by testing the chimps in the laboratory.

A slightly different approach from teaching ASL was taken by David Premack with the chimp Sarah. Sarah was raised and taught in a laboratory environment to manipulate small plastic symbols, called lexigrams. These symbols corresponded to words, and they could be combined according to rules to form sentences in a language that became known as *Premackese* (Figure 2.2). Although less

FIGURE 2.2 Here we see another of Premack's chimpanzees, Elizabeth. The message on the board says "Elizabeth give apple Amy". Adapted from Premack (1976)

spontaneous than sign language, this system has the advantage that when conversing the array is always to the animal, so the memory load on her is less, and also that the relation between the symbols and the thing represented can be completely arbitrary. Sarah learned a sizeable vocabulary and was able to combine the lexigrams according to rules to form quite complex utterances (Premack, 1971; Premack & Premack, 1983). However, her ability to produce novel utterances was limited to substituting one word for another: for example, having learned "Randy give apple Sarah", she could produce "Randy give banana Sarah". There was none of the creativity and originality we observe with children. And it's also worth noting that Premack worked with five chimpanzees, two of which failed to learn any words. People focus on successes. But I don't think it's fair to compare these particular chimps with children. Training and testing in the laboratory gives you control over what's going on, but you lose the spontaneity, interaction with the environment and social interaction with other people, and the sheer amount of time exposed to and using language that you can get with cross-fostering. How much language would a child learn if just trained for a few hours a week in a laboratory by men in white coats? And Sarah was already five years old by the time training began – this could be significant, as we'll see in the next chapter.

Nim Chimpksy was named after Noam Chomsky. Nim learned 125 signs, and his trainers systematically recorded all his utterances over two years (Terrace et al., 1979). His trainers were pessimistic about how much Nim had learned. Although his two-word utterances showed signs of regularity (for example, the place something was was always the second thing mentioned), this regularity broke down with longer utterances. His longer utterances showed much more repetition, in a way reminiscent of Washoe ("banana me eat banana"); his longest sentence was 16 words long: "Give orange me give eat orange me eat orange give me eat orange give me you". This is very different from the types of 16-word-long sentences that humans routinely produce. Nim rarely signed spontaneously – unlike Washoe – and many of his utterances were about the here and now; as many as 40% were just repetitions of what the trainers had just signed. His utterances were almost invariably geared towards getting specific outcomes, such as getting another banana: very different to the wide range of utterances produced by children. Although Nim was raised with a family, he was trained on ASL and tested in a laboratory, opening up this case to the same sorts of criticism as with Sarah: this just isn't the way children learn language, so why should a chimpanzee be able to do it?

Both Sarah and Nim's utterances were much more limited than those of children, and there was no clear evidence that they learned a grammar in the sense of acquiring a system of rules that enables us to combine words in novel ways. At best they seemed to learn a few sentence frames into which they could insert words. But we have to bear in mind the limitations in the way in which they were taught: methodological stringency comes at a heavy cost.

I'm left with a vague sense of unease by all these criticisms. Perhaps I've read too many books about the importance of positive thinking, but they do dwell on the negatives so. These chimps are showing much more competence with communication than might have been expected before the research programme began in the middle of the last century. Ultimately the debate comes down to questions of exactly what is language, and what has been learnt, and what are the possible limits of learning, which are at the heart of the nature of language, and indeed of what it means to be human. I'll return to these questions after looking at another world-famous chimp, Kanzi.

Why is Kanzi important?

The earlier studies of teaching language to primates generated a great deal of interest. But, like a great deal of pioneering work, they provoked nearly as many questions as they answered. At the same time, the techniques available, and the knowledge of what had to be done to carry out the research in a way that would convince sceptics, evolved.

The earlier work studied the common chimpanzee, *Pan troglodytes*. The bonobo (formerly known as the pygmy chimpanzee), *Pan paniscus*, is even more intelligent, more social, and has a richer native communicative repertoire than the common chimpanzee, making it a prime candidate for carrying out language research. Kanzi (b. 1980) is a male bonobo who many believe has acquired significant language abilities.

The first extraordinary thing about Kanzi is that he wasn't originally taught language at all. When he was young he accompanied his adoptive mother Matata to her training sessions; in Savage-Rumbaugh's research programme, bonobos were being taught to communicate through a language based on symbols (lexigrams) displayed on a keyboard (Savage-Rumbaugh et al., 1986; Savage-Rumbaugh & Lewin, 1994). Matata struggled to make progress in training. Although it was reported that Kanzi appeared to show no interest in what was happening in these sessions, one day in Matata's absence he spontaneously started using lexigrams. Hardly surprisingly, the emphasis of the research programme then switched to Kanzi. Kanzi interacted with humans in an enriched environment. He acquired language by interaction, rather than by explicit training.

By the age of 30 months, Kanzi had learned at least seven symbols (for orange, apple, banana, peanut, bedroom, chase, and Austin), by the age of 46 months he had learned nearly 50 symbols and had produced 800 combinations of them, and at the age of six years he had acquired around 200 symbols. He was sensitive to word order and verb meaning; he could respond appropriately to "put the hat on your ball" and "put the ball on your hat", and "get the rock" and "take the rock". Spontaneous utterances – which he initiates, rather than just responding to someone's command or request – formed the majority of his utterances.

In addition to being able to express himself with the lexigram keyboard, Kanzi also understands a great deal of spoken English. Generally Kanzi appears to perform at the same level of language as a two-and-a-half-year-old human child (Savage-Rumbaugh et al., 1993). In addition to his linguistic achievements, Kanzi is an accomplished user and maker of tools (he is particularly good at making knives), and the dominant male of his group. His favourite food happens to be onions.

The researchers were of course sensitive to the criticisms of the earlier work, and this research programme is methodologically very strong, building upon what was learned in the earlier studies. Therefore if the level of Kanzi's language skills is truly equivalent to that of a young child, and if he learned largely by observation rather than by intense training, it is a remarkable achievement with important consequences, not just for how we think of other primates but for how humans learn language. Not surprisingly, this claim has been disputed. First, some have questioned whether Kanzi learned as much by observation as is claimed, rather than by direct training using explicit rewards. Although Savage-Rumbaugh and colleagues were careful not to give Kanzi food just after a correct response or utterance, there are other ways of reinforcing people and animals trying to learn things. Smiles, verbal prompts, praise, even things of which we are usually unconscious, such as the posture we adopt, might have made a difference (Sundberg, 1996). Although, as we shall see in the next chapter, human children aren't explicitly taught language in a rigorous training regime, there is occasional reinforcement of utterances (although these don't always have an effect!), and parents do praise and prompt their children. The difference between Kanzi's upbringing and that of a human child isn't that great.

The second issue with Kanzi is whether he uses language in the same way as we do. What exactly has he learned? He might have learned language like a child, and might know as many words as a child, but does he use language like a child? A number of researchers have pointed out some differences. Most of Kanzi's utterances are requests for things he wants, rather than comments on the world. The grammatical structures Kanzi produces are relatively simple, and he learned grammar more slowly than children. A controversy has raged over whether Kanzi uses word meanings in the same way as children: he used the word "strawberry", for example, as a name, as a request to eat strawberries, and as a request to travel. Does he know that it's the name of an object? Are his words representing the world in our way? There's plenty of argument (Seidenberg & Petitto, 1987) and counter-argument (Nelson, 1987; Savage-Rumbaugh, 1987) but little agreement.

Why are animals relatively poor at language?

Whether animals can't use language at all, or just have very limited abilities, they're clearly greatly inferior to humans. Even Kanzi, the superstar of the animal language world, is still only equivalent in ability to a toddler. Some chimps never seem to get the rudiments of language at all, however much effort is put into teaching them. And they all need considerable exposure to language before they acquire anything, with arguable amounts of explicit training; in contrast, human children will develop a language in the absence of any linguistic input, as we'll see in the next chapter.

Why are animals so poor? Chimpanzees have much smaller brains than humans. A chimpanzee's brain weighs well under 500 grams; the average human brain weighs about 1300 grams. Now of course there's some variation in brain size, and there is a far from perfect correlation between brain weight and intelligence, but this difference is a huge one. So one possible explanation for their poor linguistic ability is that chimpanzees just aren't clever enough to be able to learn language well because their brains aren't big enough. Remember that some chimps just don't seem to be able to get language at all. Well, that's not surprising. Chimps, like humans, vary in their intelligence and cognitive skills, and in these tasks they could be performing right at the edge of their cognitive abilities. Only the smartest apes, like Kanzi, seem to get it.

So one explanation is that possessing language depends on having a high level of relevant cognitive skills – put simply, having a big brain and being clever. According to this viewpoint, some apes can acquire some language. But others argue that only humans can acquire language because language depends on specific, innate processes that only humans have: it's in the human genetic make-up, and human alone. For these researchers chimps even like Kanzi haven't really acquired language.

Of course, you might argue, it all depends how we define language. Let's say it's the ability to combine a finite number of words using a finite number of rules to be able to communicate an infinite number of messages. Does Kanzi meet this definition?

Let's think about words first. Clearly Kanzi is using words in the right contexts, but is this the same as what humans do? What has Kanzi really learned? We can train a pigeon to discriminate between pictures by Picasso and pictures by Monet; they get rewarded with food for pecking when they see pictures of one sort but not the other (Watanabe et al., 1995). After a while they only peck to pictures by one artist. This sort of learning is called *operant conditioning*. So it shouldn't be too difficult to be able to train pigeons to peck differently when they see the lexigrams for "banana" and "train". But would you say that pigeons have really learned the words in the way that we have? We know so much more than just being able to distinguish a type of sign; we know that a banana is yellow and tastes good and is a fruit and that it grows on trees in the Tropics; we know that it's related to mangoes and blueberries but not so closely to sweet potatoes; we know that a banana is a banana whether it's growing on a tree, being transported in a plane, or nicely packaged in a supermarket. We know similar things about trains. We know that bananas are living things and that trains aren't, even when a banana is being flown around the world and a train is stationary in the goods yard. Would a pigeon know all this? Of course not. So are linguistic chimps more like pigeons or more like us? There is no agreement between researchers. You might say "in between", but what does that mean? Is there even an in between?

A similar issue arises with grammar. We order words according to syntax, the rules of grammar. Do chimps produce their multi-word utterances using grammar, or do they just learn a few simple word orders, or frames, with no insight into what they are doing? So they might know "Give me banana" and "Give me peanut", and that saying one results in them being given a banana and the other a peanut, but little more. In this case they've just learned by operant conditioning again. But we know so much more. We know that we can put any noun into this syntactic structure, and that "give" is related to "take". We know that "I give you a banana" is similar in syntactic structure to "You give me a banana", but very different in meaning (or at least outcome); we know that "I gave you a banana" means the same as "A banana was given to you by me", even though here the syntax is different. We know that "I give you a banana" is grammatically acceptable, but "Me give you a banana" is not. Critics argue that Kanzi doesn't know any of this; again, all he's doing is that he's learned to press the right keys in the right order to get a banana. And Kanzi's comprehension is still markedly better than his production, and, as we know, human adults and young children are skilful and voluble producers of language.

Well, maybe, you say, that's all true, and chimps don't do all of that, but perhaps it's just a matter of degree. Maybe humans have just learnt a lot more by operant conditioning? There are several reasons why we're smarter than that, and why what we know is more sophisticated than something that can be acquired just by making associations between things. One of Chomsky's great achievements was to show that language was so powerful – remember that it can communicate a potentially infinite number of messages – that it could never be learnt just by conditioning. Although the argument is long and complex, you can gain an insight into what is involved if we look at *recursion* in language. Recursion is a process that involves itself. A simple example is the old joke of the dictionary definition of "recursion" as "see recursion". Recursive rules in language enable us to generate an infinite number of sentences that are in principle grammatically acceptable (although perhaps not readily comprehensible). The most commonly given example is that of embedding one sentence in another; we can repeat this as often as we like. Let's start off with the sentence "The rat escaped" and embed within it the other sentence "The rat was chased by the cat". Embedding and combining the two gives us:

The rat the cat chased escaped.

But we needn't stop there:

The rat the cat the man loved chased escaped.

I must admit that this is stretching my limits of comprehension and memory, but in principle we could go on:

The rat the cat the man the woman kissed loved chased escaped.

Recursion gives language enormous power, and there is no unambiguous evidence that chimps learning language can use it.

Perhaps you're not too impressed by the absence of recursion in animal language; perhaps you'll shrug your shoulders and say it seems a bit specialist, that you're happy to call what Kanzi does language. Perhaps we should move away from the idea of having or not having language, or being able or not able to learn language, as the only options; perhaps we should view language abilities as falling on a continuum. If you recall Bickerton's argument from the previous chapter that early men developed proto-language on the way to developing language, perhaps we could settle on chimps like Kanzi getting at least to the proto-language stage.

At the moment there's something of an impasse in the research literature, with the pro-animal-language people (the minority) and the anti-animal-language people (the majority) firmly entrenched in their positions. This type of research is very expensive and time-consuming to carry out. We're very unlikely to have all the answers to everyone's questions any time soon.

I must admit, though, that in writing this chapter I've become increasingly impressed by how smart some animals are. Anyone who talks about dumb animals is just a bit dumb themselves.

Chapter 3

Children

A NEWBORN BABY is very good at screaming, but can't talk or understand a word. Few things look more pathetic, hopeless, and vulnerable than a newborn infant. But in a few years they're running around, often of course still screaming, but producing and understanding sentences with a facility far beyond that of the best-trained chimpanzee or most expensive computer. What brings about this remarkable transformation?

The contrast between children and chimps is remarkable. We struggle to teach chimps just a few signs; only a very small number of chimps seem able to learn anything just by observation. Kanzi's productions are limited, and he is frozen at the linguistic level of a two-year-old. Yet children seem to learn language effortlessly, with little conscious tuition from their parents. Indeed, attempts to tell children what to do are often spectacularly unsuccessful, and children can be as woefully disobedient when instructed in language as they can be in everything else. Yet it doesn't seem to matter. They grow up talking (often too much for my liking) regardless. What makes all this happen?

When do children learn language?

Children make plenty of noise before they start speaking. They cry, burp, and scream; over the next few months they start cooing, and from four months or so they start laughing. After six months or so they start making the speech-like sounds known as babbling, marked by syllables (consonants and vowels, such as "ba" and "da"), often repeated several times. Around nine months infants show extensive signs of comprehension – they start noticing that certain sounds occur regularly in certain situations – although they might well comprehend a few words a bit earlier. A little later, they start producing their first recognisable words. At about 18 months there is a dramatic increase in the number of words the child knows – this phase has been given the name "the vocabulary explosion". About the same time children start combining words in their productions. At first they produce two-word utterances, but they soon start producing longer ones. These early longer utterances are appreciably grammatically different from the corresponding adult version, often lacking the grammatical detail, and are usually called *telegraphic speech*, to emphasise their clipped, abbreviated nature (e.g. "more car", "bye-bye car"). As the child grows, they acquire the finer syntactic detail, while all the time their vocabulary is increasing quite dramatically. By two and a half they are starting to speak like little adults. Obviously development continues after this; it takes some time to acquire the finer points of the syntax of the language, with the finer points depending on which language the child is acquiring. Vocabulary acquisition continues throughout life, although the rate of acquisition slows down as we get older. It's been estimated that the average young teenager is still acquiring 10 new words a day.

So, putting aside babbling for now, the typical child starts to show signs of knowing some words around six to nine months, becomes linguistically very active around 18 months to two years, and although acquisition does slow down the process never really stops. There is of course a great deal of variation in these timings, and a great deal of variation in the order of exactly what is acquired. No two children are exactly the same. The following is a *typical* scheme of language acquisition: if Junior isn't saying your name on her 366th day, don't worry!

1 month	Burp
4 months	Laugh
6 months	Ba da ba da ba da – babbles consonants
9 months	Some comprehension of words and simple instructions
12 months	Ma – first words
18 months	Bad dog! Vocabulary explosion and two-word utterances
24 months	Three-word utterances and longer
36 months	Increasingly large vocabulary of thousands of words, full sentences, use of grammatical rules

Can a foetus learn language?

It's been fashionable for some time now for mothers to talk to their children in the womb. Naturally the mother's voice is going to reflect her mood, and this in turn will affect the levels of hormones in circulation in her body, which could affect her child's development. But can the sounds and content of what she says influence the child? The foetus develops behind a protective wall of skin, fat and muscle, and is bathed in amniotic fluid. If you think this means that the sounds a foetus will hear will be limited, you're quite right: it's a bit like listening to someone speaking with your head under water. The important components of speech include sounds with frequencies up to 4000 Hz (cycles per second); the telephone restricts that to under 3000 Hz; the foetus will only hear up to 1000 Hz, so what they hear will sound very muffled (Altmann, 1997).

What's the evidence that a foetus in the womb can make use of anything they hear? DeCasper et al. (1994) got mothers to read aloud a short children's rhyme every day between the 34th and 38th weeks of pregnancy. They then played either the same rhyme or a new, different one through speakers connected to the mother's abdomen, so the foetus would be able to hear this new story but the mother wouldn't. They monitored the heart rate of the foetus and that it decreased when the foetus "heard" the familiar rhyme (presumably because it was old and comforting), but not when the new one was played (presumably because the foetus had detected novelty). So the foetus can hear sufficiently well to be able to influence their behaviour.

But if the foetus is unlikely to be able to make out individual words, what use is the ability to hear in the womb? They will be able to hear the *rhythm* of speech: the way in which our voices rise and fall as we speak, and where we place emphasis. Different languages have different rhythms. Mehler et al. (1988) played tapes of French speech to four-day-old babies from monolingual French families; babies are extremely unlikely to have been able to learn much about language in four days. They got the babies to suck on teats so that the rate of sucking controlled the presentation of the speech samples; as long as the baby carried on sucking, they heard the speech. Babies love novelty, and will suck to hear something different, but will stop as soon as they get bored. Hence this technique is very good for detecting change: if you change what the baby is exposed to and if they detect the change their sucking rate will go up, because they want to hear more of the novel stimulus, but if they can't see or hear anything different, the sucking rate won't change. When the babies had become used to – or to give it its technical name, *habituated* to – the French tapes, the researchers changed to tapes of the same person speaking Russian. The babies detected the change in language, as measured by their sucking rates.

Mehler et al. played the tapes with the high frequencies filtered so that all the baby could hear were the low-frequency sounds, so the babies would not have been able to distinguish the languages on the basis of their different sounds. The speech samples were also read by the same person, so there was no clue to the difference there. The only reasonable explanation is that young babies can distinguish the rhythms of different languages.

This study shows that babies are sensitive to the rhythm of language from a very early age. But Mehler et al. also found that the French babies preferred to listen to the French samples; the babies that heard the French sample sucked significantly more than those who heard the Russian sample first. Given the very young age of the babies, this preference could only have arisen because they'd already become familiar with the rhythm of the language in the womb. Further evidence for this idea is that although the babies could distinguish their own language from others, they couldn't distinguish two foreign languages.

Although foetal exposure helps with the rhythm, it doesn't provide the child with detailed information about the ambient language, the specific language to which they're primarily exposed. Infants at the age of six months can distinguish between sounds that are not used in their own language, so the children could not have learnt this in the womb. For example, English makes a distinction between the "l" and "r" sounds ("rate" and "late" are different words), but Japanese does not. Early on, a Japanese child would be able to recognise the "l" and "r" sounds as being distinct. However, by the age of about a year, they have lost this ability. They have become focused on their own language (Werker & Tees, 1984),

So exposure to sounds in the womb gives the child a flying start by making them sensitive to the rhythm of the language to which they're going to be exposed after birth, but not enough to help them narrow down the sounds of their ambient language. Babies might not be talking, but they're born knowing something about what their language sounds like. They're born prepared to pay attention to speech, and particularly to the speech they've already heard the most – their mother's.

Why do babies babble?

It's said that the ancient Greeks had a name for foreigners; foreigners babbled an unintelligible language that sounded just like "ba ba ba", so that's what the Greeks called them. The Romans picked this usage up, and we got the word "barbarian".

Before they start speaking, from the age of about six months, babies babble, but not like the Ostrogoths and Visgoths. Babbling is the repetitive production of speech-like sounds, and there are two basic types: reduplicative babbling, which is the production of repeated syllables (a syllable is a consonant followed by a vowel), such as "babababababa"; and variegated babbling, which is the production of chains of largely non-repeated syllables ("badokabodabo"). The babbling phase lasts up to nine months, on and off of course, gradually being replaced by true speech.

If I ever thought about why babies babble before I became a psycholinguist, I suppose I thought the baby could hear people speaking and, not wanting to be left out, had a go themselves, so that babbling is a baby talking before they can talk. We know my naive hypothesis can't be right: babies who have been deaf from birth start to produce sounds, although they don't then go on to produce the repeated syllables that hearing children make (Oller & Eilers, 1988; Sykes, 1940), and infant non-human primates, such as pygmy marmosets, babble in the sense of making early repeated sequences of call-like sounds (Elowson et al., 1998).

The finding that deaf babies' babbling is different to that of hearing children suggests that babbling is influenced by the language the baby hears. Babbling isn't the random production of sounds: regardless of to which language the baby has been exposed, 95% of babbled consonants are the following 12: p, b, t, d, m, n, k, g, s, w, j, and h, which happen to be the most commonly used consonants, on average, across all languages. However, there are some small differences in babbling between languages (De Boysson-Bardies et al., 1984): French adults could distinguish the babbling of French babies from the babbling of Chinese and Arabic babies. The influence of the environment is shown most strongly by deaf babies developing in an environment of signing adults: the infants then babble with their hands (Petitto & Marentette, 1991). Results such as these show that later babbling isn't tied to the speech mode, but is instead related to the abstract structure of the language to which the child is exposed.

Why then do babies babble? One early idea was that there is a continuum between babbling and early speech so that the former merges into the latter (Mowrer, 1960). The child starts off producing all the sounds in all the languages of the world, but this gradually gets narrowed down by exposure so that sounds the child never hears drop out, leaving just the sounds of the appropriate language. We know this idea can't be quite right. First, babies don't produce all the possible sounds of possible languages when they babble. They mostly produce just the 12 consonants mentioned above, and never produce consonant clusters (two or more consonants strung together – as at the start of "strung") in babbling. Second, parents don't particularly reinforce some sounds at the expense of others; they just encourage their child to make any sounds, so it can't be that the parents are actively reinforcing the sounds of just their language. Third, there isn't much evidence of a gradual shift towards the appropriate sounds (Locke, 1983). But although there was once thought to be a discontinuity between babbling and true speech, with the sudden dropping of sounds that aren't present in the target language (Jakobson, 1968), it's now known that babbling and early speech just merge into each other, with a phase where the child is both sometimes babbling and sometimes producing words.

There's clearly a biological drive for the infant to babble, and its form is influenced by the world around them – babies exposed to signing babble in the manual mode. But the sounds of babbling don't gradually change into the sounds of language. It's most likely that babbling is the baby playing with sound, practising and gaining control over their motor apparatus, and learning how sounds differ from one another and how they're made (Clark & Clark, 1977). They might be practising getting the rhythm, or the overall sound, of their particular language right as well (Crystal, 1986). Babbling is like warming up before a football game: you practise some of the moves, but it's nothing like the real game.

How do young children segment speech?

It's obvious that comprehension precedes production. To be able to use a word, the child has to know (more or less) what it means. So one of the first tasks facing the developing child is working out what words mean. But before they can do that they have to identify the words, and that means they have to be able to *segment* the speech they hear into words. Put yourself in the place of a baby: all you can hear is a rapid stream of meaningless sounds. If you have difficulty doing this, you should try listening to a language with which you are completely unfamiliar. You don't know where one word ends and another begins.

The task of segmenting the speech stream isn't as difficult as it might first appear. First, there are pauses between some words, and, it turns out, adults help young children by making their speech very clear and often by inserting clear gaps between words. But there are other ways of solving the problem without too much help.

Let's consider a visual analogue of part of the first paragraph above as it might be heard by a child.

oneofthefirsttasksfacingayoungchildlearningalanguageissegmentingthespeech
theyhearintowordsputyourselfintheplaceofababyallyoucanhearisarapidstream
ofmeaninglesssoundsifyouhavedifficultydoingthisyoushouldtrylisteningtoa
languagewithwhichyouarecompletelyunfamiliar

Looking at this, the stream isn't completely random. There are regularities; for example, the string of letters "you" turns up repeatedly, as does "the" and "a". We say that certain letters (and sounds in speech) tend to cluster together. These clusters are likely candidates for being distinct, whole words. Just a few lines and we can work out what at least three words are. We mentioned the idea of statistical regularities in language earlier: this is the idea that the language we hear contains a great deal of order and regularity, and humans use this order to make processing language easier. There are other types of regularity you might employ to work out what words are. For example, you might notice that "ing" tends to occur together, particularly at the end of words, so something following "ing" is likely to be the start of a new word. A sequence like "mp" never starts a word, so if it turns up its likely to be within a word or straddle a word boundary. An isolated consonant cannot be a whole word. And so on. There's a great deal of regularity in language.

The task still sounds daunting, but computer models show that it is in fact quite straightforward to segment speech and identify words in this way, given a sufficient amount of input – which babies certainly get (Batchelder, 2002). And there's experimental evidence that babies do segment fluent speech using this kind of statistical regularity in the input: eight-month-old infants quickly learn which sounds go together to form words. Once they've identified a word, they spend longer listening to novel stimuli that they don't recognise as words, rather than to the words they've already identified. (Babies love novelty, remember.) What's more, they learn extremely quickly, needing only a few minutes' exposure to speech to be able to isolate any words in it (Saffran et al., 1996).

The child is likely to hear the sounds making up "mother" (or "mama", or "mom", or "ma", or "mammy", or "mum", or "mater", or whatever) occurring together very often; they're likely to form a word. Not only that but the sounds occur when a certain person is present – when they work this out, the child is off the linguistic mark. By the age of eight months, children start responding appropriately to what they hear. When they hear "Where's daddy?", they might turn round and start looking for him. They probably haven't learnt the meaning of each word in the phrase, or even necessarily yet even identified what all the words are, but are using a number of cues to work out what was intended (Fernald & Marchman, 2006).

It's estimated that the average 10-month-old understands approximately 40 words. Once you've started learning a few words, it becomes easier and easier to work out what the other ones must be – this idea of using a bit of information to learn more is called *bootstrapping*, after the idea of pulling yourself up with your own boot laces, and is an important and recurrent idea in how children learn language. So it's not surprising that the word-learning process quickly accelerates, so that by 18 months a child understands an average of more than 250 words.

What are the early words?

I remember my little brother's first words very clearly: "pretty light". Except I don't think it could really have worked like that, because it seems too complicated for a very first utterance. We've already noted that children start to produce identifiable words that clearly relate to things in the world from the age of about one year, but things don't really get going until the vocabulary explosion at around 18 months. What do babies talk about?

It's perhaps hardly surprising that there's some uniformity in children's first words. The worlds of young babies are quite similar to each other, with parents and food and cots and bright lights and things that feel nice and things that feel nasty. Babies talk about what they can see. The earliest words tend to be the names of people, toys, food, and animals (Nelson, 1973). Although there is of course a great deal of variability in the first words, Nelson noticed that children fall into two very broad types: a *referential group*, that tends to name objects first, and an *expressive group*, that tends to name more people and feelings first. These differences in language might arise because of differences in what the children think language is for: those who think it is for labelling objects are going to develop the referential style, while those who think it's mainly for social interaction are going to develop the expressive style. Parents also vary in the degree to which they spend time with their children labelling objects; the more they do so, the more likely the child is to develop in the referential style (Pine, 1994). The consequences – if any – of these differences for later linguistic and psychological development are unclear; both types of children reach the milestone of 50 words at about the same time (Bates et al., 1994).

Although there's some uniformity in what the early words are, there's also great variability in when children start speaking. Some children show signs of understanding individual words (other than their name, which can come very early) as young as eight months, while others might not do this until several months later. Some children speak their first words before their first birthday, whereas others might not do so until they're 15 months old (Fernald & Marchman, 2006). This variability means that if your child is in this sort of range and hasn't yet started speaking, there probably isn't anything to worry about; variation is normal. Relatively late acquisition doesn't appear to have any consequences for late development, either, although obviously the longer the delay, the greater the risk of a language disorder.

I've already remarked that the child's vocabulary grows considerably around the age of 18 months when the child can already speak about 50 words. This apparent sudden growth has been called the vocabulary spurt. One suggestion is that around this age the child suddenly "gets" language because of other significant changes in cognitive development. One significant development is that around this time, according to the noted developmental psychologist Jean Piaget, the child acquires the concept of object permanence – the idea that objects continue to exist even when they are out of sight – so the child acquires the notion that there are discrete, permanent, objects in the world – that is, that there are things to name, an idea called the *naming insight*.

It should be said that there is something of a controversy, though, about whether the vocabulary spurt is real or apparent and, if it is real, what causes it. Is there a discontinuity in the rate of growth of the child's vocabulary? Some researchers argue that there is no spurt, but instead the rate of vocabulary acquisition in early childhood is relatively constant (Bloom, 2000). Part of the difficulty is in defining "spurt"; how big a change in rate does there have to be for it to be necessary to say there's something significant to explain? Also, the rate is going to vary over time; sometimes the child will be learning more words, sometimes fewer, but again does this need explaining in terms of fundamental changes in what the child is doing?

The child often simplifies the sound of the first words, tending to make them shorter. They might omit the final consonant, turn consonant clusters into single consonants, and omit syllables that aren't stressed (Smith, 1973). Sounds that weren't in the child's babbling repertoire tend to be substituted by ones that were. So, for example, "ball" becomes "ba", "stop" becomes "top", and "tomato" "mado". There are probably several reasons why words are simplified. The likely explanation is that the child prefers to use sounds that they can produce comfortably.

Finally, no one knows why the child has to be a year old or so before they start producing words. A number of abilities need to coalesce before the child can start producing words in any quantity: they must have a certain level of perceptual skills to be able to see the world in sufficient detail and process and segment the sounds they hear; they must have the ability to distinguish and produce speech sounds; they need to know that objects exist and can be named; they need to be able to categorise objects in the world; they need to have attained the memory milestone of being able to store the object–name link for a sufficiently long time; and perhaps they need to have some idea about what language is for (Bloom, 2000).

How do children learn words?

Imagine you're standing in the centre of Tokyo. A Japanese person comes up to you and just says "kumo". What do they mean? (I'm assuming for the purpose of this experiment that you're a native English speaker and know no Japanese, which is certainly true of me.) You'd have no idea, and, assuming they say it once and then walk away, you'd probably never be able to work it out. You might try to fumble your way through your Japanese–English dictionary, or maybe try to remember it and write it down for explanation later. But almost certainly, you wouldn't have a clue what they were talking about. (In fact they've just said "cloud" to you, and now you think about it, there is a particularly nice fluffy one high above your head.)

Being an infant is a bit like this, but in some ways it must be worse. If you're a year old you don't hear isolated words; you hear whole sentences, coming at you rapidly. How on earth do you work out what the words mean?

Things aren't quite that bad. Imagine yourself in another scene in Japan. You're in a wood and a group of people come running to you, covered in ash and soot. They turn around as they run past and shout "kaji da!", pointing backwards. You look where they're pointing and you see orange flames leaping through the wood. Now what do you think they said? You'd probably guess "fire!", and you'd be right.

Adults do provide this sort of help to children, if not normally as dramatically, but the task facing a child is still daunting. Put yourself in the small shoes of a toddler in front of whom your mother has placed a playful puppy. Your mother is now pointing at the puppy, saying, slowly and carefully, "dog . . . dog . . . dog". What is your guess as to what she's talking about? Even if you work out that she's trying to name something for you, what is it? Is it the leg that's got the name "dog", or the paw, or the fur? Or the little barking sound it's making? Or its colour? Or is it the whole thing? You might think that would be a reasonable guess, but suppose she instead says "puppy . . . puppy" or "Rover"? And how do you know it's still a dog when it's out for a walk or in the bath?

This difficulty is called the *mapping problem*: how do children learn to map language onto the world? Although it's a problem, children solve it remarkably well: children as young as three learned how to use a new word with just a few exposures to it ("bring me the chromium tray, not the blue one, the chromium one"). This rapid learning of some or all of a word's meaning after just one or two exposures is called *fast mapping* (coined in Carey & Bartlett, 1978).

It's difficult to see how the child could solve the mapping problem without some kind of help. The first piece of help is that adults don't carry on speaking around the child as they do with adults; they speak distinctly, slowly, and repetitively. They talk about things to which they are jointly attending with their child. It's more like the "fire!" situation than the "cloud" one.

The second piece of help is that the child must be constrained in some way about the sorts of guesses they're allowed to make. Psycholinguists have identified several types of constraint that children might use (Golinkoff et al., 1994; Markman, 1990; Waxman, 1999). Perhaps the most obvious is the assumption that unless there's evidence to the contrary, a new word refers to the whole object, rather than a part. There's some supporting evidence for this idea in the observation that when adults point to an object and give a novel name, it usually does refer to the name of the whole object. Mommy doesn't point at a dog and say "paw". If the adult is deviating from this principle they will try to make it very clear, often naming the whole object as well. They might point very specifically to the paw and say "this is the PAW of the dog". Children also make mistakes that suggest they sometimes use this principle a little too enthusiastically, assuming that a new word incorrectly refers to the name of a whole object (for example, using the attribute "pretty" as the name for a flower). Another likely constraint is that children assume, at least at first, that things can only have one name, and yet another is the related idea that if there's only one thing in front of them for which they don't have a name, a novel word is likely to be that missing name. They also seem biased towards assuming that names label categories of similar things: "dog" labels the category of things that look like dogs, rather than everything that might go with a particular dog – its lead, food, and dog bowl, for instance.

Third, after the child has made a start, language itself provides clues. "I see Rover" suggests that Rover is a proper name, while "I see a dog" suggests that "dog" is a common noun. With more advanced children you can explain things in terms of other words ("Rover is your dog"; "a dog is a sort of animal that barks") – another example of bootstrapping, and clearly one reason why vocabulary acquisition accelerates. It's also worth commenting that the sorts of categories humans have are those that seem easiest for the child to acquire; we don't have words like "stog", meaning "sandy-coloured dogs on a Tuesday". This list of possible constraints is by no means exhaustive.

You might think the idea of constraints is all very well, but it just pushes the problem back a stage, because we then need to explain where these constraints come from. And here we have to say we don't really know. The environment is structured in a certain way: objects are physically coherent and distinct, uniquely occupying part of space, and parts of an object move together, distinct from other objects. Perhaps then it's not surprising that children give some preference to objects. The child can't really be a completely blank slate: we must come with basic cognitive apparatus, if only certain means of learning things. There is something of the last resort in saying that it is innate: perhaps the whole-object assumption, as it's called, is innate, but perhaps it emerges in some way from other aspects of cognition. We just don't know.

I mentioned the mistakes children make when naming, and it's worth looking at these in a little more detail. Young children make two main sorts of error when first using names: they either use them too specifically or too generally. They do occasionally use words in a way that has no overlap whatsoever with the adult usage, but these are rare and fleeting, quickly disappearing from the child's speech. The most common sort of error is *over-extension*, using a word too generally, so that it refers to a wider range of things than is appropriate (Clark, 1973). For example, Eve Clark's child used the word "moon" to name cakes, round postcards, the letter "O", and round marks on a window, as well as the moon, and "horse" to name cows, calves, pigs, and, at first, all four-legged animals. What's happened here is that the child has picked up on a particular attribute (roundness, having four legs) and used this attribute to define a category; they haven't yet worked out that the word defines a more specific category. Over-extensions are very common, with children over-extending perhaps as much as a third of the earliest words, and occur across cultures. They also sometimes occur in comprehension. Over-extensions are mostly based on the appearance of things, rather than their function.

Clark and Clark (1977) proposed that over-extensions develop in two stages. In the first stage, the child fixates on an attribute of an object, usually perceptual, and uses that to define the category, not realising that the object is in fact defined by several attributes. They hence use the word too generally, to name anything with that attribute. After a while they work out that something isn't quite right, and that the word has in fact got a more specific meaning than the one they're using, but they don't yet know the names of those other objects. At this stage they're using the word as a shorthand for "things shaped like the moon that I don't know the name of yet".

The usual caveat applies: there is controversy here, particularly about the proportion of over-extensions that occur because of incomplete semantic development, rather than being just mistakes, or the child's attempt to communicate as best they can when they don't know very many words. Nevertheless, these sorts of early errors show how children's semantic representations, their meanings, develop and gradually converge with those of adults. Language acquisition is a process of the semantic representations of adult and child converging, with words attached to just the right meanings. Also, the idea that you should look at what children, and people in general, get wrong, as well as what they get right, is an important idea in psycholinguistics to which I will return. And the "mistakes" children make while learning language shouldn't obscure the central fact that they do an amazing job of going from very little language to being fluent and competent in just a few months.

How do adults talk to children?

> Ooh, he's a clever little boy – he's a clever little boy. Do you like your rattle? Do you like your rattle? Look at his little eyes following it . . . look at his iggy piggy piggy little eyeballs eh . . . oo . . . he's got a tubby tum-tum. Oh, he's got a tubby tum-tum.
>
> *Monty Python's Flying Circus*

It's easy to focus on the difficulty of the task facing the child trying to understand language. Chomsky (1965) commented on the *degenerate* nature of the input he thought children must hear: it's full of mistakes, hesitations, grammatical errors, false starts, slurred speech, and ums and ahs that have nothing obvious to do with the message being conveyed. He argued that the degenerate input, together with the circumscribed nature of the language they hear – in particular, they don't get given examples of non-grammatical sentences (such as "now listen carefully Ziggy, 'the cat the rat the man loved' is NOT a grammatically acceptable complete sentence, have you got that?") – must make the child's job impossible.

Although our everyday speech might normally be degenerate (in more ways than one), children do get a lot of help from adults. Adults have a special way of talking to children, called *child-directed speech*, or CDS for short (Snow, 1994). CDS is colloquially called baby talk or motherese, which is a misleading term because although mothers do use it most, most adults talk to young children in this way, and even older children talk to younger ones in a form of CDS. CDS is very clear and simplified. The vocabulary is restricted and the sentences short and grammatically simplified; speech is slower, with more pauses between words, and repetitive; and the stress and intonation, the way in which our voice rises and falls as we speak, is often exaggerated. Adults tend to talk about what is in front of the child, often establishing joint attention with it, so as to ensure that they are both talking about the same thing. CDS contains relatively more nouns but fewer word endings. Phonologically difficult words (words that are relatively complicated in terms of the sounds that make them up) might be simplified – although this cannot be the only explanation for some of the changes in vocabulary, as it isn't obvious to me that "bow wow" is easier to say than "dog", or "moo moo" easier than "cow". Speech is often marked by a high pitch. The younger the child to whom the person is speaking, the more exaggerated is the form of the CDS.

Given a choice, infants prefer to listen to CDS than normal speech (Fernald, 1991), and you can see why. Slow, simplified, clearly segmented speech is going to be easier to understand.

However, although it makes life easier, it can't be essential, because the amount it's used varies considerably, and children still manage to acquire language without too much difficulty. On the one hand, the drive to use CDS means that it turns up in other forms of language in addition to spoken: mothers using sign language use a simplified form, with clear, exaggerated signs presented at a slower rate when signing to their infants (Masataka, 1996). On the other hand, although CDS is widespread across different cultures, it is far from ubiquitous, and when it is present there is considerable variability in the amount and style (Lieven, 1994). What seems to be important is a culture's view of children; if the dominant cultural belief is that a child is helpless and understands nothing, adults are less likely to engage actively with their children than if the dominant belief is that very young children are capable of understanding a great deal. It is of course possible that cultures that appear to lack CDS compensate for it in other ways; one suggestion is that mothers might involve the child in everyday communal life more.

There does seem to be a contradiction here, but the contradiction is more apparent than real. One possible explanation is that it's not the simplification that's important in CDS so much as engaging and maintaining the child's attention, and ensuring that the adult and child are attending to the same thing. Most of the features of CDS mentioned above have this effect, and cultures that don't use CDS as ours does ensure this in other ways. Joint attention – speaker and child paying attention to the same thing – is of central importance in language development (Tomasello, 1992).

This statement is a long way from saying that the content of what the mother says is of no importance. It's generally accepted that the development of vocabulary and language skills of children in lower-status socioeconomic groups lags behind that of children in higher-status families (Rowe, 2008). One important contributing factor seems to be the way in which the mother interacts with her child. Mothers from higher-status groups tend to say more to their children (perhaps if only because they have more time), use more variety, and speak in longer utterances (Hoff, 2003). The children who learn fastest are those who receive most encouragement and acknowledgement of what they say, who have the opportunity to share attention with their mothers while talking, who are questioned most, and whose comments get amplified by their parents (Cross, 1978). Put simply, quality time makes a difference. As with cross-cultural differences, what seems to be important is what adults believe about child development; the more adults know about the current theory of what young children know and how much they really understand, the more likely the adults are to talk and interact with their children in rich ways (Rowe, 2008).

What are the early sentences?

Typically about the age of 18 months, soon after the start of the rapid increase in vocabulary acquisition, children start combining words. Before this the child uses single words to convey a quite complex meaning: saying "ma" might stand for "give me a hug", rather than just naming a person. This stage is called *holophrastic speech*, because a single word stands for a whole sentence. Then many children go through a short transitional phrase when they juxtapose two words that are related in meaning. For example, a child who woke one morning with a sore eye said "Ow. Eye" (Hoff-Ginsberg, 1997). Following this children start producing two-word utterances, of which the following are examples (from Braine, 1976):

Daddy coffee
Mommy book
Big balloon
Little banana
More glass
Two raisins
Mommy sit
Daddy sleep

It's obvious that these aren't random combinations of words. The first two examples are of the form "the possessor of something followed by the thing possessed", the next two "attribute of something and the thing", the next two "indicator of quantity and a thing", and the final two "person and action". Most of the child's utterances in the month studied followed either these or other patterns. In fact the range of meanings conveyed by these early sentences is quite limited: across cultures just eight combinations like these account for the great majority of early utterances (Brown, 1973). Sometimes the same two-word utterance can be used to mean different things: a young girl named Kathyrn used "mommy sock" on one occasion to refer to the act of the mother putting the sock on, and on another to the mother's sock (Bloom, 1970); nevertheless, both utterances use one of the primary combinations.

It's also notable that children don't violate these patterns by saying things like "banana little" or "coffee daddy". So even at this stage we can discern that the child appears to be using rules. From early on they're using a grammar, with a syntax, or a system for ordering words. The rules aren't exactly the same as the adult grammar, and it's obviously much simpler, but it's a grammar nonetheless. We can see syntactic development as the process whereby the child's grammar converges with that of the adult.

Some children stay in the two-word stage for some months, while others pass through it very quickly, but the average length of the child's utterance increases with time. It's the upper limit that changes: Hoff-Ginsberg (1997) noted all the utterances of one two-year-old child over breakfast, and while just one was longer than three words, some were three words, and most were still just one or two words long. The early three-word utterances can often be described in terms of combining and simplifying the two-word structures available to the child. So "I watch it" is a combination of "I watch" (person and action) and "watch it" (action and object). These early sentences talk about what's in front of the child, and generally make positive statements. They're made mainly of nouns, adjectives, and verbs, omitting many of the short grammatical words that are very common in adult speech, so much so that this type of speech is called *telegraphic*, after the old practice of omitting less important words in telegrams when they were charged by the word. In addition to grammatical words, word endings that grammatically modify nouns and verbs are scarce. This telegraphic simplification seems common across many languages and cultures, although there are differences: in Turkish, word endings are particularly prominent and important, and these are produced very early by Turkish children (Aksu-Koc & Slobin, 1985).

Learning syntax is difficult, and it's happening at a time when their memory capacity and skills haven't yet fully developed. Children probably simplify because at a time when their resources are stretched they omit what is less important at conveying meaning. In Turkish, where the grammatical elements are important for conveying meaning, they're acquired much earlier. It's also probable that at this stage children don't really understand exactly what these grammatical elements do and how they work. Later development involves learning more complex grammatical structures so that longer and more complex ideas can be expressed, and learning how to use grammatical elements.

In this early stage children are learning rules, or at least patterns – let's not worry too much about the difference. They learn that a valid sentence can take the form "noun phrase verb noun phrase", where a noun phrase contains a noun, such as "the cat chases the rat", but not "verb noun phrase noun phrase" (we don't, and children don't, say "chases the cat the rat"). To be able to make use of these sorts of patterns, however, children have to know what's a noun and what's a verb. Of course they don't need to know this explicitly, but they do implicitly – they need to know which words are acceptable in which slots, and which are not.

This task is quite a difficult one, and a number of explanations have been proposed for how children acquire this information. One possibility is that know-ledge of these syntactic categories (noun, verb, adjective, and so on) is innate (Pinker, 1984). According to this account, children are also born with a set of what are called *linking rules* that enable them to relate syntactic categories to semantic ones – so that, for example, objects and people, the things doing actions or having actions done to them, are linked to nouns, and actions to verbs. So once they've worked out whether a word is referring to a thing or action, they can use their innate knowledge to work out the sort of syntactic roles that word can have. Because this approach depends on working out the meaning first, and using this to discover syntactic knowledge, it is called *semantic bootstrapping* – that bootstrapping again, pulling yourself up high with a little bit of initial knowledge.

Other researchers have pointed to several problems with this approach in addition to my earlier and more general contention that there's something defeatist about saying something is difficult, and therefore it must be innate. The first prob-lem is that the success of the enterprise depends on the child hearing plenty of sentences early on in which it is straightforward to identify what's doing what to what, but although we've noted that CDS tends to be about the here and now, it's far from true of all utterances. In fact it can be quite difficult to work out from the context what are the objects and what are the actions, particularly if the utterance isn't about the immediate here and now, and sometimes even if it is. What is a child to make of the meaning of verbs such as "see", "want", or "know", even if the context is right in front of them (Gleitman, 1990)? In what sense are they actions, like "kiss" and "kick"? Second, the detailed predictions of the model haven't always been supported by the data. If children do learn semantic bootstrapping through linking rules, then verbs that are easier to link to the associated actions (such as "fall" and "chase", where the things doing the falling and chasing are immediately apparent) should be acquired earlier than those that are more difficult (such as "have" and "lose"). This order of acquisition is not always found, how-ever, and sometimes children have more difficulty learning verbs that should be easier to link to the semantic roles associated with them (Bowerman, 1990).

The idea that's emerged as the main alternative to innate knowledge is that children learn to spot statistical regularities in the linguistic input, and the notion of grammatical categories emerges from these regularities (e.g. Levy & Schlesinger, 1988; Valian, 1986). According to this *distributional* account, children are spotting patterns of what can go where in a sentence, and use these patterns to form rules. As a very simple example, in most simple – what are called declarative – English sentences, words referring to living things come first, followed by actions, followed by other living things or objects. So a category emerges of "types of things that can come first in a sentence", which happens to be a noun. Or consider what are called "count" and "mass" nouns. Count nouns refer to single objects (e.g. cup, horse) and mass nouns (e.g. furniture, sand) stand for substances or a collection of many things. This distinction can be quite hard to grasp, particularly for a child, and it's difficult to give a straightforward semantic account of the difference. There are however striking and reliable syntactic differences between count and mass nouns: we can say "a cup", "a horse", but not "a furniture" or "a water"; on the other hand we say "some sand" or "some water", but we can't say "some horse". We can easily form a plural of count nouns ("horses"), but it's more complicated for mass nouns ("sands" is a word, but not the straightforward plural of "sand", and "furnitures" isn't acceptable at all). Children acquire this distinction using these syntactic cues rather than grasping the intricacies of the semantics (Gathercole, 1985; Gordon, 1985). Computer modelling shows that this distributional account works: it's possible to learn syntactic categories just on a statistical basis by repeated exposure to many sentences (Mintz, 2003).

The advantage of the distributional account is that it's more parsimonious than a model that postulates innate knowledge: all children have to do is listen to language and spot patterns. Of course parsimony in itself is not sufficient, but the distributional account does a good job of explaining a range of data across several languages.

When does language acquisition stop?

I remember my fifth birthday very clearly. I had a record that you could sing along to saying "five today", and I remember the scene as though it were a photograph. In my mind, aged five, I was essentially the same person, with the same skills and abilities, as I am now. Clearly this cannot be right. The language skills of a five-year-old are very different from those of an adult. My vocabulary would have been much smaller than what I have now, and the range of syntactic constructions considerably more restricted. Not to mention that I could barely read and probably couldn't write. But in spite of these obvious differences, the average five-year-old is strikingly linguistically advanced.

Obviously many skills have to be acquired after the telegraphic stage before a child can be considered a fully competent user of language, but I can't help but think that by that stage the battle is largely won. The child's vocabulary is still relatively small between the ages of two and three, their syntactic constructions very limited, and grammatical words are virtually absent, as are word endings, such as those that mark the number of nouns or the tense of verbs. Any complete account of language acquisition has to be able to explain the development of these phenomena. At some point children start being able to talk about language itself: we call this ability to talk about our own language metalinguistic, so that *metalinguistic skills* allow us to talk about our language, and metalinguistic knowledge is knowledge about our language. Obviously it's a great advantage if we can communicate about words and sentences themselves. From this point on children can talk about language and we can talk to them about what they can't do.

Language skills continue to develop throughout life. We learn new words occasionally, hone our writing skills, and learn the correct pronunciation of words we thought we knew. But although we continue to develop, it's apparent that the bulk of linguistic development happens in early childhood after the age of 18 months.

Language acquisition never stops – only the day before I wrote that phrase I learnt that a duduk is a traditional Armenian reed instrument. Even children as old as 12 have difficulty spotting inconsistencies in stories that arise as a consequence of the meaning of the individual words, and therefore fail to realise that they haven't properly understood what they've been reading (Markman, 1979). I've used the following example before, but I like it . . .

> There is absolutely no light at the bottom of the ocean. Some fish that live at the bottom of the ocean know their food by its colour. They will only eat red fungus.

. . . If only because it took me some time to spot why it doesn't really make sense. I'm sure I'm not alone in still finding the same problem, usually with something I wrote a couple of days ago.

Are we driven to produce language?

The French Pyrenean village of Aas looks a very pretty little place; Google it and you'll probably find a picture of a church with attractive houses nestling on the side of a valley, with the distant mountains disappearing into the clouds. Pretty, yet unremarkable but for one remarkable fact about the inhabitants. Shepherds spent long summers tending their flocks, based in cabins that, because of the wide areas involved, were sparsely distributed and some distance from the village. They created a whistling language to communicate with other shepherds – a 100 dB language that could be heard and understood two miles away, with variations in the pitch of the whistle conveying the meaning. The "language" was still in use until the early part of the twentieth century, when it died out as easier means of communication over distance became widely available. Whistling languages still occur in parts of the world, particularly in association with what are called tonal languages, where the pitch of vowels is important. There is some debate as to whether these languages are fully expressive in the sense of being able to convey an infinite number of meanings, but they served their purpose for thousands of years, enabling the whistling shepherds, or *siffleurs*, to keep in touch.

The whistling language illustrates the extent to which people will go to communicate. Children in particular seem to have a drive to learn language. One now famous example is that of ISN, Idioma de Señas de Nicaragua (Nicaraguan Sign

The Pyrenees: Mountains are home to whistlers, yodellers, and echo-makers

Language). Before the 1970s deaf people were isolated in the community, with little formal provision of teaching sign language. In 1977 a school specifically for deaf children opened in west Nicaragua; however, the teaching was based on lip-reading Spanish and using a few elementary signs. Unsurprisingly, the programme failed to teach Spanish effectively. However, when the children were brought into proximity for the first time, something interesting happened: they collaborated to create their own sign language to communicate. At first children communicated with each other with a mixture of gestures and the few signs that they had been using at home, but gradually a full sign language, with rich vocabulary and a sophisticated system of grammatical rules, emerged (Kegl et al., 1999; Senghas et al., 2004). It's worth repeating the import of ISN: children without language found a means of inventing one.

The two-stage creation of ISN reflects the distinction between pidgins and creoles. *Pidgins* are simplified languages that enable two (or more) groups of people who don't have a language in common to communicate. Typically they emerge when the two groups are in prolonged contact and there is a need to communicate; often they were the result of slavery or trade, and so notable pidgins developed in the Caribbean, China, the South Pacific, and Hawaii. There aren't any native speakers of pidgin – for everyone it's their second (or third) language. Pidgins combine words and grammars, but are usually based on one language rather than another. Sounds, words, and grammatical rules become simplified and restricted. So we hear utterances such as "Da book stay on top da table" (The book is on top of the table) in Hawaiian Pidgin, and "Hab gat lening kum daun" (There's rain coming down) in Chinese Pidgin English.

Some pidgins stay pidgins, many have died out, but some evolve into *creoles*. Whereas pidgins have no native speakers, creoles do; children born in an environment where they're heavily exposed to a pidgin turn the pidgin into a proper language, the creole form. It's as though children who grow up hearing the cobbled-together, impoverished language turn it into a real one. Creole languages are found around the world, but naturally in the areas where pidgins developed. Whereas pidgins are simplified, creoles are not; whereas the sounds, vocabulary, and grammars of pidgins are restricted, again those of creoles are not. Often it is possible to discern the primary influence of one underlying language. An example is Jamaican patois; in a sentence such as "mi a di tiicha" ("I am the teacher"), the underlying influence of English is apparent. There is no agreement about exactly how creoles develop and how the language becomes standardised. For our purposes the important fact is merely that they exist: where there was no suitable language before, people invent one.

All these examples suggest we are *driven* not just to communicate, but to use a fully expressive language with a grammar. This idea that there is a biological drive to develop syntax is called the language bioprogramme hypothesis (Bickerton, 1984).

How do we learn language?

It's obvious then *why* children learn language: to communicate. There's this thing everyone else around them is doing, and when you start doing it, the world becomes a simpler place. You start getting that ice cream just when you want it, and you get the right flavour too, and you get ice cream and not jelly. We've seen what happens *when* children learn. The next obvious question is *how* they learn.

The simplest explanation is that infants imitate what they hear around them. Imitation undoubtedly does play a role in language development, and we shouldn't underestimate its importance. Just a little time with a child will show how often – and how well – they imitate. There is also now a body of research literature showing how important imitation is across several domains, and how difficulty in imitating can lead to developmental disorders. There has recently been a great deal of interest in *mirror neurons*, which are located in parts of the frontal cortex of the brain, and which become active whenever we carry out an action and see others carrying out the same action. Mirror neurons are thought to be very important for imitation, and it's been argued that they played an essential role in the evolution of higher cognitive abilities in humans, including gesture and language. The mirror neuron system might play a role in imitating the gestures of adults from a very early age. Newborn babies not only imitate their carers; they also initiate previously imitated gestures, and engage in gestural "conversations" with their carers. So children are born with a ready-made imitation machinery that plays an important role in learning to communicate (Nagy, 2006).

However, imitation is not sufficient to account for much of language acquisition. Children make mistakes and do things they never hear adults do. Often they are unable to imitate adult speech correctly, even when they try. Most importantly, though, our grammar enables us to generate a potentially infinite number of utterances. How can a child produce an utterance or construction they've never heard before?

Earlier we saw how one of the defining moments in the history of psycholinguistics was Chomsky's review and rebuttal of the behaviourist account of language learning. According to early behaviourists, children learn language as they do anything else – by a process of conditioning, so that correct utterances are reinforced while incorrect ones are not, so incorrect usage drops out of the child's production to be replaced by just correct ones. A baby might be babbling away and randomly produces a string of sounds that resemble "mama"; the mother comes over, gives the child a kiss and attention, says "that's right, mama", and the child is then more likely to say "mama" next time. Gradually the sounds the child makes approximate to those of the right word. If the baby says "dada", mother looks upset and says "no, mama", and the child is less likely to say something like "dada" next time. In this way the child learns which sounds go with objects; the rest of language was thought to be learned in a similar way.

Of course that phrase "in a similar way" disguises a huge and complex task, and Chomsky provided a mathematical argument as to why it wouldn't work. The details needn't detain us, but essentially he showed that it was impossible to learn a grammar that could generate an infinite number of sentences and no non-sentences just by exposure to examples of sentences.

Observation of children's language is sufficient, though, to show that imitation and reinforcement can't be the whole story. Adults generally aren't too bothered about the details of what the child says as long as it's true and reasonably comprehensible; they don't go round correcting children a great deal. And even if adults try, their corrections often have little or no effect (Brown & Hanlon, 1970; De Villiers & De Villers, 1979). The following are some famous, indeed notorious, examples of what happens when adults to try to correct children:

Adult: Say "Tur".
Child: "Tur".
Adult: Say "Tle".
Child: "Tle".
Adult: Say "turtle".
Child: "Kurka".

> *Child:* My teacher holded the rabbits and we patted them.
> *Adult:* Did you say teacher held the baby rabbits?
> *Child:* Yes.
> *Adult:* What did you say she did?
> *Child:* She holded the baby rabbits and we patted them.
> *Adult:* Did you say she held them tightly?
> *Child:* No, she holded them loosely.

On the other hand we have:

> *Child:* Mama isn't boy, he a girl.
> *Adult:* That's right.

Another problem for any account of language acquisition based primarily on simple observation of adult speech is that children sometimes regress from getting things right to getting them wrong. The most famous example of regressive production is the pattern of acquisition of the past tense. It's well known that while English forms the past tense of most verbs by adding "ed" to the end of the verb (or a "d" if the verb already ends in a vowel), there are many exceptions, called irregular verbs. So while we can happily form "loved" from "loves" and "kissed" from "kiss", verbs such as "give", "has", "seek", "blow", "go", and many, many more are much more problematic. It's been known for some time that children start off using the irregular form correctly (gave), but then they start making errors. They still correctly produce the past tenses of regular verbs, but they make errors known as over-regularisations with irregular verbs – they start producing the past tense of the irregular verbs as though they were regular; so, for example, they might produce "gived", "haved", and "goed". Then later still they go back to correctly produce the regular forms and the exceptions. If we plot a graph of the number of errors children make against time, the number starts off low, increases, and then declines, in the shape of an inverted U (Kuczaj, 1977).

It's difficult to see how classical learning theory based on conditioning of correct responses could account for this pattern. Once children get it systematically right, they shouldn't then start getting it systematically wrong. There has however been considerable controversy over exactly what the child has learned. I think most people would agree that the child has learned some kind of pattern, but there the agreement ends.

There are two hotly debated theories of how children learn the past tense. The classic explanation is that first of all children just learn the past tenses on a case-by-case basis, so that everything is individually memorised. They then spot a rule: you form a past tense by adding "-ed" to the end of the verb. The trouble is, they apply it too generally, not realising that the rule has exceptions. They later observe that the rule has exceptions, and learn these exceptions. This account says that children are basically *learning rules*, and have a separate mechanism to deal with exceptions (Pinker & Prince, 1988). According to this view, adults process regular and irregular forms by two different routes – one that uses a rule if an exception can't be quickly retrieved directly from memory. This view gains some support from imaging studies of brain activation, which find different patterns of activation depending on whether regular or irregular verbs are being processed (Pinker & Ullman, 2002).

The alternative view is that we don't need two different processing routes. In a classic computational study, Rumelhart and McClelland (1986) simulated how children learn the past tense. They trained a computer to produce the correct inflected form of the past tense (e.g. "gave") given the root form of the verb ("give") using a technique known as back-propagation, which gradually reduces the discrepancy between what the computer actually produces and what it should be producing, over many thousands of iterations. They found that the way in which the model is trained is crucially important. It so happens that many irregular forms are very frequent in speech, and if the computer is trained selectively on these common irregular forms first, it gets them right very quickly. As the child gets a little older, they learn many of the less common verbs too, so after the initial phase the computer was exposed to many medium-frequency verbs. This increasing exposure to a range of verbs seems to confuse the model, and the result is that the computer programme demonstrates the inverted-U-shaped learning curve: it starts off well, then performs badly, but then learns to get all the items right. So on this account the errors children make depend on the way in which they are exposed to language. The data on brain imaging in adults are explained by the processing of regular and irregular verbs relying differentially on different types of knowledge, with the processing of regular forms making much use of the processing of sound regularities.

Few topics in psycholinguistics have generated as much controversy as this one, which is a good example of the east coast–west coast EW schism in psycholinguistics, with deeply entrenched views on both sides (see "Next" for some more references).

No, children aren't simply observing; they're trying to detect regularities in the input. We also need to bear in mind the impact of that input – to what are children actually exposed?

Do we need innate knowledge?

We've seen that Chomsky argued that the quality of the input that children hear is insufficient for them to be able to acquire language. It is, he argued, degenerate in that it is replete with hesitations, mistakes, and grammatical errors. It's also the case that it can be shown mathematically that to acquire a complex language with characteristics that are found in all human languages (such as recursive rules – rules that call themselves, such as is necessary to produce centre-embedded constructions such as "The cat the rat chased died"), exposure to sentences is not enough; children also need to hear negative evidence – they need to be provided with some examples of sentences that are not grammatical. And this doesn't happen. Taken together, these two ideas merge to form what is called the idea of the poverty of the stimulus – there isn't sufficient information in what children hear for them to be able to learn the rules of syntax just by hearing language alone. But they clearly do, so, Chomsky argued, children must receive some additional assistance. What might this assistance be? Chomsky (1965, 1980) proposed that children are born with an innate *language acquisition device*, or LAD.

Chomsky's terminology changed over the years. He also argued that although human languages are superficially very different, deep down they're all similar. As Pinker says, "a visiting Martian scientist would surely conclude that aside from their mutually unintelligible vocabularies, Earthlings speak a single language" (Pinker, 1994: 232). Many people's first reaction to this quote is that it is a preposterous one: putting aside the very different vocabularies, surely our grammars are also very different? Even something as basic as where the verb usually goes in the sentence can vary: in English, it goes between the thing doing the action and the thing having the action done to it, and hence English is called a subject-verb-object or SVO language; but in Japanese the verb usually goes after the subject and object, making it a SOV language; and in Gaelic the verb comes first (it's VSO). Surely then languages are very different?

Not according to nativists, who make two points. The first is that these differences between languages are superficial. Languages share a great deal, particularly at a fundamental level. They all have different grammatical categories corresponding to objects and actions – nouns and verbs. All languages have pronouns (words like "he", "she", "it"). They all have similar sorts of grammatical rules. In a classic study of similarities between languages, Joseph Greenberg (1963) surveyed 30 languages from all over the world, and found several syntactic features that were common to all of them. The features shared by languages are called *linguistic universals*. And, nativists argue, although grammars differ, they do so only in circumscribed ways. So although word order differs between languages, it isn't a total free-for-all. Languages that put the object before the subject are extremely rare, accounting for less than 1% of all languages, if that (given that linguists don't agree on how these particular languages should be classified).

The second point is that although there are variations, these variations are highly systematic and correlated, in that once you know one property of a language, you can deduce others. The correlations are so large that linguists consider them to be another type of universal, called *implicational universals*. These can be specified as rules. One of the best known examples of an implicational universal concerns how we form questions. English forms questions by putting the question word at the start of the sentence ("What did you have for dinner?", "Who did you kiss?", "Where did the cat catch the rat?"). The position of the question word is very systematic; indeed, we can phrase it as a rule: all SVO languages put the question word at the start of the sentence, whereas all SOV languages put the question word at the end. Another example concerns prepositions – words that indicate relations between things, such as "on", "in", "at", and "to". In English, prepositions come before the phrase they're related to – we say "on the mat", "in the box", "at the fair", and so on, but many languages, such as Japanese and Hungarian, have postpositions, where these little grammatical words follow their associated phrase. Here is the rule: if a language is SVO, it uses mostly prepositions, but if it is SOV, it has postpositions.

So once we know one thing about a language, such as where the verb typically goes, we suddenly know a lot more. Chomsky called those aspects of language that are free to vary (like whether it has prepositions or postpositions, and whether the question word goes at the beginning or end) *parameters*. You can think of them as switches, which can only be in a limited number of positions; and once you know which way one of them goes, you can be pretty certain how many of the others go too.

These universals are so common that they couldn't arise by chance. Chomsky said that they're a consequence of the language acquisition device. We're born with the switches. Indeed, we're born with a basis that's common to all languages, what he called *universal grammar*. Children – and only human children, which is why animals are so bad at learning languages – come with a framework of parameters that get fixed by exposure to a particular language.

Over the past 20 years or so the nativist framework of Chomsky has come under attack from several directions, all of which share the idea that children don't need to be born with language-specific knowledge. Where do universals come from? All humans share basic cognitive processes and live in the same world; it's not surprising that we all distinguish between things as basic as objects and actions given the biological constraints. Having said this, it's unclear how specifying what goes with what could be constructed in this way. On the other hand, just to say "it's innate" doesn't add much either. The point is that these matters are up for debate.

The premises of Chomsky's arguments have all been questioned. First, it's debatable whether human language is quite as powerful as Chomsky first proposed. Although in practice we might be capable of infinite recursion, of carrying on embedding one sentence in another, a bit like this, for ever and ever, in principle we don't – we can't. Even the simplest centre-embedded sentences are quite difficult, and many people find them ungrammatical. And in any case children do get some negative evidence – they do get corrected some of the time when they produce ungrammatical utterances, even if they then appear to take no notice (Pullum & Scholz, 2002), and they do get provided with implicit negative evidence, in that parents tend to repeat ill-formed utterances more than well-formed ones, and tend to follow ill-formed utterance with questions rather than continuing with the topic of conversation (Sokolov & Snow, 1994).

The second and related strand in the criticism of nativism comes from the impact of connectionist modelling of language acquisition. These computer models of learning emphasise exactly what and how children learn, and pay particular attention to the language to which children are exposed. Computer models show that children can in fact learn very human-like grammars from exposure to positive evidence alone (Elman, 2005). What seems to be critical here is that the models aren't just thrown in at the deep end. The models can learn to analyse embedded sentences, but only if they are first trained to analyse non-embedded sentences, and only if the programmes were given reduced memory storage that was gradually increased. This idea – solving simpler problems before solving bigger ones – is known as "the importance of starting small", or "less is more". Children of course do something similar. They don't start with the most complicated problems, they start with the simpler ones; they don't try to do everything at once; and as we've seen with CDS, adults simplify what they say to children, and hence what children are initially exposed to. Children have shorter memory spans than adults, and this might be advantageous when learning complex patterns – essentially, a smaller memory span means they have to focus on the essentials, and so are less likely to get distracted by less central aspects of the task (Newport, 1990). And in further support of this idea, adults learning a new language find it easier if at first they're only exposed to full segments of the novel language, rather than to the full complexity (Kersten & Earles, 2001).

A third difficulty is that in the absence of a detailed theory that spans psychology, neurology, and genetics, it's difficult to see exactly how genes encode language knowledge and processing. I'll talk about the alleged "gene for language", the FOXP2 gene, in the next section, but it would be naive to think that genes directly encode linguistic processes. We know that genes express themselves in producing an RNA copy that directs protein synthesis. We need to map out this chain from protein synthesis to behaviour in such a way that it explains why this information is restricted to language. In recent years Chomsky has greatly reduced the quantity of what he thinks has to be supplied by the language acquisition device, so much so that he now argues that the distinguishing feature of language, and the skill that distinguishes humans from other animals, and the only skill that has to be somehow genetically encoded, is recursion: the operation that allows a rule to use itself and thereby gives language its complexity and open-endedness by allowing us to embed structures within other structures (Fitch et al., 2005).

What are we to conclude from all this East–West thrust and counter-thrust? There's certainly no consensus among researchers as to how necessary is innate language-specific knowledge – we find the usual East–West split. Although the nativist position is for many still compelling, the core assumptions about the poverty of the stimulus have been disputed, computational modelling has shown that it is possible to learn a great deal of language by exposure alone, and new empirical evidence contradicts some of the original arguments in favour of nativism. We can see that it's important to take a child's-eye view of the task, and look at what they actually do. We should remember children are not little adults. And it's certainly worth taking the empiricist position and running with it: how far can we get without recourse to innate knowledge about language?

Are there language-specific impairments?

At this point, even though I'm at heart a West Coast ageing hippy, and am generally happy to go along with the conclusion of the previous section, I get troubled by remembering the FOXP2 gene. Remember that the FOXP2 gene mutated in humans within the past 100,000 years, leading to an enlarged Broca's region of the brain and an enhanced ability to produce complex sequences. FOXP2 has been talked about as a (note, not "the", as presumably many are involved) "gene for language", particularly a "gene for grammar" (Lai et al., 2001; Pinker, 2001). What does this gene do?

The KE family of London has been much studied in recent years. About half the members of the large family, spanning three generations, have some difficulty with language (Vargha-Khadem et al., 1995). Those affected have difficulty making clear speech sounds because they have difficulty in controlling their articulatory apparatus, particularly their tongues. The distribution of the problem throughout the family clearly suggests that the problem is inherited and caused by a dominant gene, and the disorder has been associated with a mutation in part of the FOXP2 gene (Lai et al., 2001).

The KE family don't just have problems with articulation, though. Members of the family with the problem also show what is called *developmental verbal dyspraxia*. Dyspraxia is difficulty in planning and carrying out movements and tasks, and it's developmental because people are born with it, in contrast with acquiring it as a result of some later brain trauma. The affected people have trouble identifying sounds, understanding speech, understanding and producing grammatical inflections, and making judgements about whether sentences are grammatical or not. So in addition to their articulation difficulties, they appear to have higher-level language problems too. Lai et al. (2001) propose that the mutation in FOXP2 has the consequence that the brain circuitry for language fails to develop properly.

Of course language and speech production and perception must have some genetic underpinning; the question is, are there genes that control aspects of language and nothing else? Does the human FOXP2 gene control only language? If the difficulties shown by the KE family are restricted to language, then the answer would appear to be "yes". Hence the debate has centred around the question of whether or not the deficit shown by the KEs is a *specific language impairment* (SLI). Affected members do have other problems, and critics of the grammar gene position argued that any grammatical or language problem arises from factors such as lower general intelligence, difficulties with motor planning and co-ordination, and difficulties in perceiving the sounds of speech, all of which could give rise to a pattern of impairments that looked like it was a problem with grammar. The FOXP2 mutation is associated with lower scores on intelligence tests, but this could be a consequence of impaired verbal abilities, not the cause, and in any case there is some overlap with the normal range, suggesting that lower IQ does not automatically lead to a language impairment. Nativists argue that the higher-level problems to do with grammar could not arise from lower-level ones such as difficulties in producing and planning speech, while critics of the nativist position argue that they could.

Moving beyond the KE family, people with SLI have difficulty with grammar, failing to develop language normally for their age, while otherwise appearing to develop normally. Is there any unambiguous evidence that SLI exists more generally, and that people can be born with problems with grammar and grammar alone? The existence of such a disorder would clearly support the nativist position (Gopnik, 1997). Others argue that SLI results not from a specific language impairment but from more general subtle difficulties in perceptual and cognitive processing. One proposal is that grammatical difficulties could arise from a perceptual deficit, particularly one that leads to difficulty in keeping sound-based representations in working memory (Joanisse & Seidenberg, 2003). To be able to learn how to give verbs the right endings – to learn how to inflect them – for example, you have to be able to hear the sounds properly. You need to know that the past tense of "bake" is "baked", sounded with a "t" sound at the end, but the past tense of "try" is "tried" (with a "d" sound), and that of "wait" is "waited" (with a whole new sound added). We can express these different endings as a rule: if the final consonant doesn't involve the vocal chords vibrating (we say sounds like "k" are voiceless), add a "t"; if the final consonant or vowel is voiced (the vocal chords do vibrate, as with "try"), add a "d"; and if the word ends with "t" or "d", add a vowel as well as a "d". Obviously if a person has difficulty hearing these sounds, they're going to have difficulty learning this rule. Put another way, the expression of the grammatical rule to do with forming the past tense has a phonological (or sound) component (Joanisse & Seidenberg, 1998). Other problems with syntax could arise because affected people find it more difficult to remember sentences – we know that an important component of short-term memory involves maintaining material in a phonological form. If present from early on, this difficulty could have clear knock-on consequences for language development.

Critics of the critics reply that not all children with SLI have perceptual impairments, so that cannot be the underlying cause (Gopnik & Goad, 1997), although this has in turn been debated, and in any case it is not clear how all the observed grammatical impairments can be related to perceptual deficits. Once again the positions are deeply entrenched, and although the front is edging towards the nativist camp, there's a long way to go yet.

Is there a critical period for language acquisition?

It's certainly a widespread belief that the younger you are, the easier it is to learn something. It doesn't just apply to language; I always think I'd have been a better swimmer, footballer, pianist (insert just about any skill of your choice) if I could have started earlier. And it seems strikingly, almost self-evidently, true of language acquisition: unless you start to learn a second language early, you've had it (and I didn't start French until 11, which I'm always telling people is one reason for my abominable ability with it). The advantages of early learning aren't restricted to humans. Young songbirds have to be exposed to song in their first two weeks in order to be able to produce it properly later. The limited window in which something has to happen if subsequent development is to proceed normally is called the *critical period*. According to the critical period hypothesis, you need to start learning language early on. What exactly is meant by "early" varies, some thinking that the critical period ends as early as five, others arguing that it goes on until puberty, although the ability to learn might decrease the older you get. And to learn a language, you obviously have to be exposed to it. The idea of a critical period for language acquisition fits in well with our intuitions about learning a second language; unless we start to learn it early, in the critical period, we're always going to struggle, and can never be as fluent as a native speaker. But our intuitions aren't always right.

Given the importance of helping people to learn a second language, it's not surprising that there's been a considerable amount of research on whether timing matters. Is it really hopeless unless you start learning another language very early? The results have been rather inconclusive. One thing to bear in mind is that for all their apparent linguistic supremacy, children spend a lot of time doing it. One might say that a child has little else to do than learn language; it's their full-time job. Contrast that with an adult, who might struggle to find a couple of free hours a week. Is it any surprise they're relatively bad? If we're going to make any claim stronger than that children spend more time on it, we have to control for this factor somehow. When we do this, it's far less obvious that children are better than adults; indeed, adults, who have a wider range of study skills and learning techniques, might do better. In a comparison of English adults and English children in their first year in the Netherlands learning Dutch, Snow and Hoefnagel-Hohle (1978) found that the children aged three to four years did worst. The one clear way in which children do better is that they are less likely to be left with a significant accent.

Other researchers have found some evidence for a critical period for learning a new language. In a classic study, Johnson and Newport (1989) carried out a detailed analysis of Chinese and Korean immigrants of different ages trying to learn English after arriving in the USA. They focused on the acquisition of syntax, asking the immigrants to make judgements about whether or not a sentence was grammatical. They did find that the earlier in life the person started learning the new language, the better they performed. After the age of 15, though, the variability in the level of attainment was much higher, and the correlation between ability and age of arrival was low. But this wasn't a dramatic cut-off; performance started declining gradually from around the age of seven. Johnson and Newport explained their results as the consequence of the maturation of the developing brain: after the age of seven it starts to become less responsive and adaptable, and reaches an adult-like steady state around the age of 16.

Two things are clear from this research. First, there isn't a dramatic cut-off point after which it suddenly becomes impossible, or at best very difficult, to learn a new language. There is a decline in ability, but it's a gradual one. Second, when considering how well people can learn new skills, the total time a person, adult or child, can spend doing it is important.

If there is a critical period for language in which you must be exposed to language to learn it properly, what happens if linguistic input is absent during this period? There are a few charming legends about historical rulers carrying out devious and damningly unethical experiments. James IV of Scotland wanted to know which language was spoken in Eden, so around 1500 he allegedly had two children abandoned on the isolated Inchkeith Island in the Firth of Forth with only a deaf and dumb woman to look after them; it was later claimed that many years later they were found speaking very good Hebrew, hence providing support for the then widespread idea that Hebrew was the parent language from which all others are descended. An earlier story involving the Pharaoh Psammetichus I has the first word of children in a similar predicament being "bekos" – which is Phrygian for bread, making Phyrgian the original language. And yet another story involves the Holy Roman Emperor Frederick II, but this time the children died without saying a word.

There are several accounts of *feral children* through the ages. Feral children have been either lost or abandoned by their parents in the wilderness, and have managed to grow up fending for themselves. Romulus and Remus, the legendary founders of Rome, were abandoned on the banks of the River Tiber and raised by a wolf – hence the alternative name for these children, wolf children. Many subsequent accounts have not been much better documented. One of the most famous is the "wolf child of Aveyron", the basis for Francois Truffaut's 1970 film *L'Enfant Sauvage*. A male child, later named Victor, was found wandering in wild woods near the village of Saint-Sernin in the south of France in January 1800 (Shattuck, 1994). He stood upright, wore only a tattered shirt, and could not speak. The efforts of a medical student, Dr Itard, to educate and tutor him in social skills and language were largely unsuccessful. He only ever managed to speak two words: "lait" (milk) and the phrase "Oh Dieu" (Oh God). Victor died in 1828. Although of course it's impossible to be certain about his age when he emerged from the wilderness, he appeared to be about 11 or 12 years old. There are a few dozen other similar stories, more recently including the girls Amala and Kamala, apparently rescued from a wolves' den in India in 1920, and Ramu, the wolf boy of Lucknow, India, found in 1954.

None of these feral children acquired language. But even if we were to accept the veracity of these accounts, before we accept their stories as evidence for a critical period, we need to be aware that there is an intractable problem with this type of anecdotal evidence: we know nothing about the linguistic abilities of such children before they were abandoned. It's very likely that their parents abandoned these children because they were different in some way – perhaps they were autistic, or had brain damage, or were showing early signs of having difficulty with language. That is, we can't be sure with these cases that their linguistic impairments were a consequence of their linguistic deprivation in the critical period: they might well have ended up that way regardless.

Neither can we carry out experiments on linguistic deprivation, for obvious ethical reasons, so we are reliant on investigating occasional cases when and if they should unfortunately occur. One such famous case is that of the girl known as "Genie". Genie was over 13 when she was discovered by the Los Angeles authorities in November 1970 (Curtiss, 1977; Fromkin et al., 1974). From the age of about 20 months until she was discovered, she had been locked in a small bedroom, with aluminium foil over the windows to keep out the light, most of the time strapped to a potty during the day, and in a small enclosed crib at night. Her father was very intolerant of noise, so there was no speech in the house, not even a television or radio. Genie was punished if she made any noise. Her father forbade her mother and brother to talk to her, and instead they were only allowed to communicate to her by barking and growling at her like dogs. The only contact she had with other people was a few minutes when she was fed in silence by her mother.

Given that by the time therapists could begin working with Genie she was almost 14, she should make an excellent test of the critical period hypothesis. By all accounts the critical period is over by that age, so if the hypothesis is correct, it should have been impossible for Genie to learn language; if it is wrong, it should have been possible to teach her to become fully linguistically competent. As is usually the case with psychology, the results lay between these two possible extremes. Genie learned some language, but her language differed in several significant ways from the language of young children. First, her syntactic development lagged considerably behind her vocabulary development, so that compared with children using the same number of words, her sentences were simpler and more idiosyncratic. She used few grammatical words; she tended to form negatives by putting negatives at the start of the sentence rather than with the verb; she used fewer question words; she didn't use auxiliary words; she didn't properly acquire the passive construction (which enables us to transform a sentence such as "The cat chases the rat" into "The rat is chased by the cat"); and she didn't really learn how to inflect verbs and nouns to form past tenses and plurals. Unlike most right-handed children, she didn't show the usual right-ear advantage for processing speech sounds, hinting that her brain might have become wired up differently in some way.

Disputes about the proper care of Genie and difficulties in obtaining funding meant that further scientific research ground to a halt. Genie now lives in sheltered accommodation in a secret accommodation in California. Little is known about her current condition, other than she can only speak a few words, but knows a little sign language.

Unfortunately there is some dispute about how normal Genie was at birth. Her father (who subsequently committed suicide) said that when Genie was between one and two years old a doctor said that she was developmentally delayed and perhaps retarded. The father interpreted this as "very retarded", and bizarrely thought he was acting in Genie's best interests. This claim muddies the water somewhat, but even children with quite a severe reduction in intellectual ability can acquire language. Nevertheless, the possibility of a developmental disorder, plus extreme social, emotional, and physical neglect make it difficult to assert with any confidence that Genie could not acquire language only because she wasn't exposed to it in a critical period. The case though is suggestive of the need for exposure to language early on in order to be able to acquire language normally.

Other cases of extreme abuse and social and linguistic deprivation do occur. One of the most recent is the case of Danielle Crockett, found in Florida in 2005, aged six. Danielle had been kept in their house by her mother in what was described by the local police as "unimaginable squalor". Danielle could not and still cannot talk. One of the other most famous cases is that of Isabelle, who suffered extreme social deprivation until the age of six, and who required a year of help and training before she could speak normally (Davis, 1947). A case like Isabelle is important because it shows that it's possible to overcome the effects of extreme linguistic deprivation if the child is young enough.

There's a contrast here between the older feral children, who learn little or no language, and the Nicaraguan deaf children, who formed their own sign language. The obvious difference is that the Nicaraguan children began communicating when they were rather younger, which would appear to provide some support for the critical period hypothesis. There are however other explanations for this contrast. The first explanation, as I've mentioned already, is that it's difficult to rule out the possibility that these feral children were born with severe cognitive or linguistic deficits. The second possible explanation is that the feral children were isolated, whereas the Nicaraguan children were in a thriving social group including many children of the same age. The third, related point is that feral children have all had severe emotional and social deprivation. We know that social interaction is essential for proper language development – that's why all societies use CDS or some special form of interaction with children.

The importance of children learning language in context is brought home by the case of "Jim". Jim was the hearing child of deaf parents. Jim had normal hearing, and his parents wanted him to learn speech rather than the sign language they used, so they avoided signing around him and hoped he would learn language just from listening to the television and radio (Sachs et al., 1981). When Jim entered nursery school about the age of three, he had acquired some language, but from what we have seen above it's not surprising that his language was impoverished and unusual. His articulation was so poor that some of his utterances were unintelligible; his intonation was very flat – his voice didn't rise and fall as he spoke; and his grammar was very idiosyncratic. He couldn't turn a singular noun plural by adding "s" to the end, and so he would say things such as "House. Two house. Not one house". His comprehension was also very poor. Fortunately Jim was still very young when therapy could begin, and within a few months his language was almost normal. Jim's case shows that mere exposure to language is not sufficient for normal development; it has to be within a social context, and directed towards the here and now.

I'm struck by the resemblance of Genie's language, the performance of linguistic apes, and Bickerton's idea, mentioned earlier, of a *proto-language*. Bickerton (1990) argued that language couldn't have evolved in one step; instead there was an intermediate step, the proto-language, out of which arose our syntactically rich, fully expressive language. A proto-language is a system of words but with only very basic or no syntax. A theme that does emerge from all this work is that it's our syntactic ability, our ability to produce and understand ordered sentences with correctly placed grammatical units, that is most sensitive to linguistic deprivation during the critical period.

The pioneering work on the biological basis of the critical period for language was carried out by the linguist and neurologist Eric Lenneberg (1967). Lenneberg was interested in how brain damage affects language development. He noted that the younger the child, the greater the likelihood that the child would recover from brain damage that would devastate an adult. Lenneberg promoted the idea of *neural plasticity* – the idea that intact parts of the brain could take over the functions of a damaged part, but only if the damage occurs when the child is still very young. He argued that at birth the brain is very plastic, but this plasticity is quickly lost, and is much reduced after the age of five or so.

Lenneberg was most interested in the development of lateralisation. It's widely known that the brain is divided into two hemispheres that specialise in different sorts of tasks. Very broadly, for most right-handed people, the left hemisphere specialises in serial and analytic processing, whereas the right hemisphere is more concerned with holistic processing. The popular conception of "left brain versus right brain" greatly simplifies and exaggerates the differences, but the germ of the idea is correct. Most importantly, two key areas of the brain concerned with language, Broca's and Wernicke's regions, are located in the left hemisphere. So language processing is highly asymmetrically distributed in the brain, with most processes concerned with word retrieval, comprehension, planning, and articulating speech localised in the left hemisphere. Given this, it's hardly surprising that damage to the left hemisphere – particularly if it involves Broca's or Wernicke's areas – results in impaired language ability, a condition called *aphasia*. Although adults recover some functions with time, progress is slow, and if a large amount of the language centre is destroyed, there is nearly always some permanent impairment. Language functions seem tied to particular regions of the adult brain. Lenneberg noted that, in contrast, children with damage to the left hemisphere language areas recovered much more quickly, and often recovered completely. The younger the child when the damage occurred, the better the prognosis.

The ability of young children to recover is shown most strikingly by what happens following the operation known as *hemi-decortication*. Hemi-decortication is a last-resort treatment for exceptionally severe epilepsy, and involves the surgical removal of all of the cortex of one side of the brain with the aim of destroying the sources of the seizures and preventing the seizures spreading to undamaged brain tissue. If carried out on an adult, left-hemisphere hemi-decortication would almost completely obliterate a person's language abilities. The language abilities of children who have had hemispherectomies (the name of the operation) in infancy and very early childhood are in very striking contrast: these children do go on to acquire language, although not completely normally. There is some debate about how different the language of these children is, partly because this operation generally lowers IQ (Bishop, 1983). Vocabulary is less affected, but there is some impairment in understanding complex syntax and in producing fluent speech.

With young children, then, the right hemisphere can take on the functions of the left hemisphere – but only if the child is young enough. What's striking here isn't so much that the right hemisphere doesn't acquire language anywhere near perfectly (and that's hardly surprising, given the loss of so much brain matter, and that now the right hemisphere has to do the job of two), but that it acquires so much. Lenneberg argued that the brain isn't born lateralised, but becomes lateralised in the first five years. If part of the brain, even a whole hemisphere, is damaged, other parts can take over those functions. Another way of putting it is that there's a great deal of neural plasticity in early childhood, which declines as the child gets older. This period of maximum neural plasticity corresponds to the critical period. Whether or not the two hemispheres of the brain begin by being indistinguishable (an idea known as *equipotenitality*), or whether we are born with the left hemisphere structures predisposed towards becoming associated with language, is a matter of some debate (Thomas, 2003). We know that the brain is lateralised to some degree from a very early age. Entus (1977) used the sucking technique to examine the listening preferences of three-week-old infants, and found that they preferred speech when it was presented to the right ear. Adults show the same advantage: because of the way in which the ear is wired to the brain, speech in the right ear gets delivered more quickly to the speech centres of the left hemisphere than speech in the left ear. The electrical activity of the left and right hemispheres differs to speech and non-speech stimuli in babies as young as one week (Molfese, 1977). Nevertheless, evidence of some early lateralisation doesn't detract from the key point that neural plasticity is greater when you are younger.

Changes in neural plasticity might tell us why children can recover relatively well from brain injury, but why should they mean that it's difficult to acquire language as you get older? One idea is that exposure to language produces dedicated pathways in the brain that help us learn and use language. This idea is called *native language neural commitment*, or NLNC for short (Kuhl, 2000, 2004). The young brain develops special networks that enable it to become attuned to the particular characteristics of the ambient language. There's some evidence that dedicated networks speed up acquisition: there were differences in seven-month-old infants tested on perceiving the sounds of their own and foreign languages, and these differences predicted later language skills – but negatively, so that the children who became linguistically more advanced later had become focused on their language early on. Narrowness is an advantage. In summary, we can acquire language best if we can develop networks in the brain dedicated to language process, and this development depends on neural plasticity.

I think we can reject the notion of a sharply defined critical period that ends at five. And neither is it the case that without exposure to a language we are incapable of learning anything. The brain continues to develop throughout childhood, and this development places constraints on what can be learned. There is a gradual decline in what can be learned in childhood, so that if a child receives virtually no exposure to language, their syntactic ability will be greatly impaired. So yes, there is a critical period for language, particularly syntactic development, and this critical period is a consequence of declining neural plasticity.

What is bilingualism?

When I'm abroad, foreign words fly by me. I can't distinguish many of the sounds I hear, even in supposedly "familiar" languages such as French and Spanish. I once wrote a note to the maid apologising for having broken a glass; unfortunately I actually said that she had broken it, and I was very sorry about it. No wonder she looked bemused, perhaps even a little angry, the next day. I'm always therefore extremely impressed when I meet people fluent in a second language. I'm amazed at how they can do it.

If I'd been born into a linguistic community where more than one language is commonly spoken, things would have been different. There are many regions of the world where two languages are spoken: English and Welsh in Wales, particularly north Wales; English and French in parts of Canada; the Netherlands has two official languages, Dutch and Frisian; and Belgium has three official languages, Dutch, French, and German. In fact regions with multiple languages are very common across the world. In other cases workers might move to a new country, and a child might grow up exposed to one language at home and another language outside the home.

We call the ability to use more than one language with a good degree of competency *bilingualism*; some people are multilingual, being fluent in three or more languages. This definition is a little vague because there's a lack of precision in words like competent and fluent, but it's better to think of degrees of bilingualism, with proficiency in different languages lying on a continuum.

Even in a multilingual environment, it's very unlikely that children will be equally exposed to all the surrounding languages. Even if each parent is speaking in a different language to the infant, the child is almost certain to be exposed to one more than the other (usually the mother's). We label the language the child is exposed to most often as L1, and the second L2 (and we could add L3 and so on if we wished). We call it simultaneous bilingualism if the child is exposed to both languages from very early on (with definitions of "very early" ranging from birth to three); if exposed to one first, and then another later, we refer to sequential bilingualism. The longer the delay before the person is exposed to L2, the more bilingualism merges into second language acquisition.

Early studies reported diaries of the linguistic development of their own bilingual children. The most famous of these was by Leopold (1939–1949), who detailed the linguistic development of his daughter Hildegard in five volumes. Leopold was a German linguist who moved to the USA with his American wife. He brought up his daughter with a "one parent, one language" rule, although of course English was the ambient language. Leopold noted that Hildegard at first jumbled up both languages. This observation gave rise to the model that the bilingual child goes through an initial stage when L1 and L2 are undifferentiated, such that they are essentially monolingual, but with words from languages mixed up. The vocabularies of the two languages then become differentiated, and after that two languages become fully differentiated, with separate syntax (Genesee & Nicoladis, 2006).

Recent work shows that accomplished bilinguals are not just two monolinguals in the same brain (Hernandez et al., 2007). Many studies show that the strategies that people use to process sentences in L1 and L2 get mixed up, so that a strategy that is optimal for understanding L1 is applied to L2, where it might be sub-optimal, and vice versa. For example, languages differ in how subjects and verbs agree. In English what matters most is word order, and not so much the word endings: "I love you", "You love them", "They love you", "We love him", "He loves you", "He loves them" – the verb ending does change a little (for the third person), but it's generally not very predictive. In other languages, such as Spanish, the verbs are more widely and systematically inflected, and therefore looking at the verb ending tells you much more – to the extent that the pronoun can be dropped in languages such as Spanish, but not in English. When processing sentences like these, monolingual English speakers rely almost exclusively on word order, monolingual

Spanish speakers rely almost exclusively on verb endings, and bilingual speakers use both strategies in both languages. Bilingual speakers also show *code-switching* – switching between L1 and L2, sometimes even within a sentence. Code-switching can happen by mistake, but is often used in conversations between two bilinguals, and happens for a number of reasons – one of which is that sometimes an idea is easier to express or more accessible in one language than another. So there aren't just two separate language systems; the processing of one language influences the other.

Most of the time, doing two things at once has a cost. Is learning two languages simultaneously more difficult than just one? If there is a cost it isn't a great one: bilingual children reach the developmental milestones at about the same time as monolingual children (Genesee & Nicoladis, 2006). Some researchers have found some cost as indicated by interference between languages, while others have noted that sequential bilinguals learning L2 start to show reduced facility in accessing L1. However, any differences are minor. It's also debatable whether it's truly possible for learners to achieve true monolingual-like attainment in both languages, but performance on L2 can be very good (Harley & Wang, 1997). Indeed, there's evidence that bilingualism can lead to other benefits; some researchers have found that bilingual speakers tend to be more verbally fluent and have greater awareness of how language works, others have found that bilingual children score higher on tests of creativity than monolingual children (Bialystock, 2001b; Lambert et al., 1973), and bilingual speakers perform better on non-verbal measures of attention than monolinguals, suggesting that having to cope with two languages leads to a general increase in controlling attention (Bialystock et al., 2004). Learning a second language seems to produce long-lasting changes in the brain, with bilinguals having denser grey matter (effectively, more connections among brain cells) in the left parietal cortex, a region of the brain known to be important for performance on tasks of verbal fluency (Mechelli et al., 2004). A cognitive advantage is apparent from a very early age: eye-measurement studies have found that infants as young as seven months who have been exposed to two languages perform better at a task involving searching a visual display than infants of the same age who have been exposed to just one language (Kovacs & Mehler, 2009). So bilingualism both rewires the brain and generates cognitive benefits from an early age.

Attention does play an important role in ensuring that the two languages don't interfere too much when the speakers don't want them to. Bilingual speakers turn out to be remarkably efficient at suppressing the non-desired language when they have to. In one study, researchers told bilingual speakers to press a button when they saw a word in one of their languages, and to ignore words in their other language. The monitoring of the brain's electrical activity showed that the non-target words weren't processed very much at all – the participants in the experiment weren't even sensitive to how common the words were, ignoring highly frequent words just as well as less frequent words (Rodriguez-Fornells et al., 2002). In fact the non-target words seemed to be treated in just the same way as non-words (such as NATE).

What's the best way to learn a second language?

In a distant place, a long, long time ago, I learned Latin and French at school. It seems odd now that we didn't learn them in very different ways. Sure, there was a bit more emphasis on listening, talking, and conversation in French, but both were taught from books. Both sets of lessons were centred around teaching formal grammar. We learned verb conjugations. We learned grammatical rules. There was a lot of emphasis on learning tables of things by rote. There was much more emphasis on reading than there was on making ourselves understood.

Things are very different now. If it's some time since you learned a language at school, take a look at one of the many books available on teaching yourself a language. Rules are rare; instead the emphasis – at least at first – is on conversation and effective communication. Most of the books will have an accompanying CD so that you can hear the language. Many courses just involve listening, with sophisticated audio-visual materials. Nevertheless, learning a new language is difficult, and to do it well is very time-consuming. One of the major obstacles to learning is just finding the time to get sufficient practise. You also need to practise with a competent speaker; there's a limit to how far you can get by yourself with multimedia aids. Adults in particular face additional problems, because they expect to be successful very quickly. One of my difficulties with trying to learn a new language is just lack of patience.

It perhaps isn't surprising, given the facility with which children learn language, that the best way to learn a second language is to be as child-like as possible, which in practice means a lot of listening to the language, a lot of time, and plenty of opportunities to make mistakes without worrying too much about the consequences. The *immersion method* throws learners right in at the deep end; all of the tuition takes place in the new language. The most famous examples of immersion teaching are some schools in Canada where, as part of a drive to increase English–French bilingualism, all education of the native-English-speaking children is carried out in French, usually from the age of five. The emphasis in these schools is not on rushing or forcing the children into speaking French, or on emphasising grammatical accuracy, but on waiting until they are ready to speak, and encouraging fluency and communicative accuracy. Immersion is the best way of teaching a new language. There is some initial cost, because the children lag behind their non-immersed peers in terms of educational attainment for the first few years; however, they soon catch up and perform at the same level, they eventually attain a very high level of competence in the second language, and there is no discernible cost apparent in their first language (Baker, 2006).

The point that second language learning takes time is emphasised in the influential work of Krashen (1982, 2003). Krashen points to the differences between traditional approaches to teaching a second language and the way in which a child learns their first language. Children spend a great deal of time just listening – they say nothing at all for many months, even when they are fully immersed in their ambient language. Even though an adult might have a longer memory span and be a more proficient learner, they are rushed, and feel rushed, into speaking. The learner has to have a comprehensible input; we've seen that children don't learn language by listening to a fast-talking television star, so why should older children or adults? Indeed, we've seen that parents simplify and exaggerate their speech with CDS; why shouldn't the same be necessary with adults? Language needs to be learned in context. Krashen distinguishes between the natural acquisition process, which is largely unconscious, and a more conscious, deliberate monitoring process involving checking what we're about to say to ensure that it's correct. For Krashen, learning the rules so that we can monitor effectively is the only appropriate role for learning: eventually students need to know the rules of the new language in order to be able to ensure their final output is correct; and Krashen acknowledges it often might not be appropriate to use our monitor – we might want to ensure that we get our writing right, but in conversation communication and speed are more important than accuracy. Formal learning is less effective than informal acquisition.

Of course, much depends on what your goal on learning a new language might be. Becoming fluent in a language takes vastly more time and effort than getting by on holiday; and having to pass an exam is another matter altogether. Children don't have to sit exams in language acquisition (yet), which is just one reason why they do so well at it.

Chapter 4

Thought

I HAVE A FRIEND (not the same one who thinks that language is a waste of time) who says he thinks in pictures. I find this incredible; in fact I find it incomprehensible; and the more I think about it, I don't really believe him. I think in words. Or at least, sort of words. My head is continually full of an inner dialogue, or a stream of words telling me what to do next or what I should be doing now. At least, that's my experience. But my head is certainly full of words. And I bet my friend thinks in words (or sorts of words) more than he realises. In fact I find it inconceivable to think of thinking without words. How are language and thought related?

What is thought?

What is thought? I started to write an answer to this question thinking it would be easy, but then had to take an aspirin and a very long break. It's one of those slippery notions that we all think is straightforward and that we can explain very easily, until we have to define it in a sentence. So I cheated and looked up some online definitions. One definition of "thought" was "the act or process of thinking"; not very helpful. "The faculty of thinking or reasoning" – reasoning at least adds something different. "Think" gives us "to reason about, reflect on, or ponder", "to visualise", and "to concentrate one's thoughts", "to exercise the power or reason", "to solve problems". We're slowly building up a picture.

I turned to textbooks of cognitive psychology for help. The most useful (some others don't define "thinking", or barely mention it) was Eysenck and Keane's (2005) *Cognitive Psychology: A Student's Handbook*, which says that the "our ability to reflect in a complex way on our lives, to plan and solve problems that arise on a daily basis, is the bedrock of thinking behaviour" (p. 429). While stopping short of a formal definition, it is a very good outline of when we think. They go on to say that "clearly thinking must involve conscious awareness; however, we tend to be conscious of the products of thinking rather than the processes themselves".

I'll be bold and say that thought is the manipulation of ideas with an outcome that can enter consciousness – and be vague for now about what I mean by "consciousness" and "idea". But as we'll see, some of the research on language and thought really ranges further than this, and in practice this chapter is about the question: how is consciousness related to the rest of cognition and perception?

The behaviourists, who tried to dispense with internal constructs such as the mind, were faced with a bit of a problem with thought, because it would take even a very bold psychologist to deny that they think. So the behaviourists said that language and thought are the same thing. Now not even behaviourists went around speaking their thoughts aloud, so they said that thinking is nothing other than subvocal speech – and Jacobsen (1932) provided some evidence for this hypothesis when he detected electrical activity in people's throat muscles when they were asked to think. So thinking is speaking, but with the sounds being stopped just in time. As J.B. Watson famously said, "according to my view, thought processes are really motor habits in the larynx" (1913, p. 174).

But this doesn't seem intuitively right: although intuitions are often unreliable, I think most of us believe we can talk aloud and think about something different at the same time. One of my favourite experiments of all time showed that thinking isn't just small motor movements in the articulatory apparatus. Smith et al. (1947) used tubocurarine to paralyse the muscles of a volunteer – the fearless Smith. Tubocurarine is the toxin in tubocurare, one of the poisons used on arrow heads in South America. Curare, for short, is an extremely effective muscle relaxant, causing paralysis, and was used for some time alongside anaesthetic in surgery for that reason. In itself therefore it's not fatal, as long as the person is given artificial ventilation until the paralysing effects of the curare wear off in about 20 minutes. Curare doesn't affect the central nervous system, so here is a perfect test: if thinking is just small movements in the articulatory tract, you shouldn't be able to think while under its effects. Smith could, reporting afterwards that he could think in words and solve mathematical problems.

So thinking is more than mere subvocal speech. Certainly some of the time at least we have the impression of an inner voice, watching, chiding, and guiding us. Surprisingly, there hasn't been a great deal of research on inner speech – surprising I think because in some respects this inner speech is as close as we get to the real "I" – but there has been some. There's been a recent flurry of research on how the inner voice might be involved in some pathologies, such as schizophrenia and autism, where the problems might arise in part from difficulties in self-monitoring (e.g. Jones & Fernyhough, 2007; Whitehouse et al., 2006). Much of the work stems from the idea that inner speech is a form of self-monitoring and self-regulation, mediating intellectual and social interaction, promoted by the Russian psychologist Lev Vygotsky. We'll return to the work of Vygotsky later.

Articulatory suppression – interfering with the inner voice by speaking aloud – impairs our performance on a number of cognitive tasks, particularly planning and retrieving things from memory (Miyake et al., 2004). There have even been studies on the sorts of slips of the tongue people make in inner speech. A comparison of these errors with those commonly made in overt speech shows some differences – in particular, in overt speech there's a tendency for the sounds involved in some slips to be similar to each other (an "r" is more likely to swap with an "l" than with a "b", for example), whereas there's no such tendency in internal speech (Oppenheim & Dell, 2008). On the other hand, like overt speech, slips in inner speech tend to result in outcomes that are words more often than you'd expect by chance (for example, if you say an "r" sound instead of the "l" at the start of the word "leaf", you still end up with a word). So inner speech is a form of mental imagery we use to monitor our thoughts and behaviour, which assists us in several ways in cognition, and which, true to our intuition, is speech-like, but is also different, being impoverished at the level of the final details of sounds. But thinking isn't just inner speech; the very fact that we can make slips of the (inner) tongue in inner speech, leading to a mismatch between our intention and inner speech, shows that. What then is an intention? And we occasionally (often in my case) find ourselves saying or thinking "I didn't mean that". Clearly there's a level of thought that isn't just linguistic, and that involves things like intentions. Of course, thought can involve visual mental imagery too. And although the product of thinking might enter consciousness, all the processes leading to that product need not. I've no idea what my non-linguistic intentions are really like other than that they're a product of my brain.

The other point to make about thought is that it involves categorisation. Indeed, I think it's self-evident that an undifferentiated world is inconceivable – which is why the mental life of a newborn is impossible to imagine, even if they are born with some mental categories. Cognition involves dealing with categories of things picked out in some way that differentiates them from other categories. We give some categories names – we have the labels "cat" and "dog" for different categories of animal (itself a category) – but we don't have a separate word for the category of "black dogs", or even "black dogs and cats but not other black animals", although at least at first sight we might. So language, thought, and categorisation are all manifestly intertwined.

But perhaps we're being unnecessarily pernickety in thinking too much about exactly what thinking is. We don't have to go along with Einstein all the time ("if you can't explain it simply, you don't understand it well enough"). We're interested in how language is related to the rest of cognition, both in terms of how cognitive and language development are related and in adults. I'll begin at the beginning, with children.

Is language development dependent on cognitive development?

Jean Piaget (1896–1980) was one of the most important developmental psychologists of all time, famous for his theories of cognitive development. Piaget was interested in the structure and origin of human knowledge. His contributions were massive and wide-ranging, and it's easy to over-simplify them. He mapped out how children's intellectual structures develop through a series of stages, and what drives the changes from one stage to another.

Piaget called the stage between birth and about two the *sensorimotor period*, in which infants understand the world only through acting upon it. The motor actions of the infant become sensorimotor schemas – general patterns for action involving action and perception. By the end of this stage the child is capable of forming a mental representation of the outside world. One of the key attainments of this stage, as we've already seen, is that of object permanence – the idea that there are individuated objects in the world that continue to exist when they're out of sight. In the *pre-operational stage* (from the ages of about two to seven) the child uses mental representations of the world, but their ability to reason is limited by their reliance on perception and by their egocentrism: the way in which they think of themselves as at the centre of the universe, and in which they are unable to adopt alternative points of view. In the *concrete-operational* stage (ages seven to eleven) children start to think logically and overcome the limitations of egocentric thought. They are less constrained by perception and can adopt alternative points of view. Finally, in the *formal-operational stage*, from 11, children reason logically and scientifically (at least some of the time). As Flavell et al. (2002) put it, the child moves from knowing about the world through actions on it, to static representations of it, to mental operations on representations, to mental operations on operations. External actions turn into internal ones. Piaget saw cognitive development as driven by the complementary processes of assimilation and accommodation, where assimilation means applying what you already know to the world, while accommodation means adjusting your knowledge to something new and surprising in the world. So knowledge grows as the child interacts with the world, and knowledge structures change when they are unable to explain everything about the world. So this account is both constructivist – the child constructs knowledge of the world from their experience of it – and environmentally driven. In this sense Piaget was an empiricist, because he stressed the way in which knowledge comes from experience, but this is not to say that there aren't nativist aspects to his theorisation as well – the drives to assimilate and accommodate have to come from somewhere.

Where does this leave us in thinking about the development of language? For this sort of approach, there's just nothing different or special about language development. It's a cognitive process like any other, dependent on other cognitive processes, and on possessing certain cognitive abilities. We've already seen how the putative vocabulary explosion around 18 months might be linked to the child's attainment of the concept of object permanence towards the end of the sensorimotor stage; more generally, as we've just seen above, Piaget argued that children aren't born representing the world, but that representation develops in the sensorimotor period and emerges in the pre-operational stage. Representation involves symbols – something in the mind standing for something outside it – and a word is something that stands for something else, and thus language and representation are inextricably intertwined. So language is unthinkable until the child develops mental representations. It's possible to take Piaget's idea further with the idea that children can only talk about what they know about, and what they know about is dependent on the current state of their cognitive system (Flavell et al., 2002). Researchers have investigated a number of links between cognition and language, of which the naming and object permanence link is one. Another is the finding that words relating to the ideas of the relative quantities of an object, such as "more", or of disappearance, such as "gone", only emerge in the later stages of the acquisition of object permanence (Gopnik & Meltzoff, 1986).

The idea that cognitive development drives language development is sometimes called the *cognition hypothesis* (Sinclair-deZwart, 1973). What are we to make of it? The hypothesis is strongest when talking about how the systematic use of words is dependent on particular cognitive precursors being in place; it is weaker when it talks about how particular concepts and labels emerge from cognitive development; and it is at its weakest when talking about grammatical development, about which it is almost silent. Indeed, at the very time in which the child is making huge leaps in vocabulary and syntax, between the ages of two and four, Piagetian theory emphasises the limitations of cognition, the egocentrism (the idea that the child can only see things from their point of view and can't adopt the perspective of others), and the dependence on perception (Flavell et al., 2002). Even the apparent dependence of naming on object permanence is shakier than it first seems. We've seen that most children are producing some words before 18 months, and are clearly understanding them much earlier, so it can't be that object permanence is a prerequisite of word use. What is it a prerequisite for, then? Tying the vocabulary explosion to object permanence is meaningless if, as we've seen some theorists argue, the vocabulary explosion doesn't really represent a discontinuity in development. It's even possible that the causal relation is the other way round – having unique names for objects helps children to understand that objects are distinct. Hearing two distinct labels for two different objects (e.g. a toy duck and a ball) helped nine-month-old infants to discriminate them in a way that associating them with different facial expressions did not (Xu, 2002).

Another problem is that the relation between cognitive abilities and linguistic abilities is not clear-cut. If the cognition hypothesis is correct, then if cognitive development is delayed or impaired, aspects of linguistic development should also be delayed or impaired. Yamada (1990) described the case of Laura, a young woman with severe cognitive impairments and an estimated IQ of about 40 (that's four standard deviations beneath the mean). Laura was nevertheless able to produce and understand syntactically complex sentences. The content of her speech was very different from that of people of similar age, but the form was similar. Yamada interpreted these results as showing that cognitive and syntactic processes are distinct. Laura isn't an isolated case: other case studies show that the correlation between verbal abilities and non-verbal IQ is low. Another notable case is that of Christopher, who is so intellectually impaired that he is unable to look after himself, but is able to translate between 15 different languages (Smith & Tsimpli, 1995).

Williams syndrome (WS) is a rare developmental disorder caused by the absence of genes on chromosome seven. Physically it's characterised by an "elfin-faced" appearance, but the cognitive and behavioural changes are more marked. Children with WS are often very cheerful and out-going, but with occasional negative outbursts. WS affects IQ, leading to severe mental disability, with very low IQ, typically about 60; children with WS perform very poorly on classical Piagetian tasks such as conservation (where children have to understand that water poured from a tall narrow glass to a wide one doesn't change in volume). Nevertheless the speech of people with WS is very fluent and grammatically accurate, often with a rich and unusual vocabulary, the children seeming to delight in rare words. One child, when asked to name all the animals they could, began: "brontosaurus, tyrandon, dinosaurs, ibex, brontosaurus rex [sic], elephant, dog, cat, lion, baby hippopotamus, whale, bull, yak, zebra, puppy, kitten, tiger, koala, dragon"; in contrast, a matched Down syndrome child produced: "dogs, cats, fish, bird, fish". In WS, then, the linguistic skills are better than you would expect given their general level of cognitive ability (Bellugi et al., 1999).

The final testing ground for the relation between cognitive and language development is that of blind children. Not surprisingly, severe visual impairment changes and delays cognitive development: the child is less mobile, has less feedback from the environment, and has restricted experiences; there is just less information available to drive important early cognitive constructs such as object permanence, causality, and conservation. If language development were dependent on cognitive development we would expect clear differences in language development; however, any differences are subtle and controversial, with perform-ance being highly variable (Hindley, 2005; Lewis, 1987). The first words are pro-duced about the same time as by sighted children, and are broadly similar, although there might be fewer object names. Unsurprisingly, blind children don't name objects that are visually salient, going instead by tactile and auditory salience. There's been some argument that blind children have some early difficulty general-ising words to contexts beyond that in which they were originally acquired (Dun-lea, 1989), and early syntax differs in small ways. For example, there might be a delay in the acquisition of the auxiliary verbs "will" and "can" (Landau & Gleit-man, 1985). However, these minor differences should be considered in the light of the fact that although there are differences in cognitive development between blind and seeing children, there are also necessarily differences in social interaction and development, and also in the way that adults talk to the children. For example, adults tend to make direct statements to blind children ("take the doll") rather than ask questions involving auxiliary verbs ("can you take the doll?") – and so it's not surprising that their children's acquisition of these verbs is rather later. Indeed, some have suggested that some aspects of the speech of blind children that were once thought to reflect impairment and delay in fact are advantageous; the more repetitive speech of some children, for example, might serve a communicative func-tion in prolonging social contact (Pérez-Perieira & Conti-Ramsden, 1999).

In summary, there's little evidence that cognitive development drives linguistic development. There's no obvious link between milestones of cognitive develop-ment and notable features of language acquisition, and the study of linguistic savants, children with Williams syndrome, and blind children shows that at the very least cognitive impairments do not lead to clear-cut linguistic impairments, while many would go further and conclude that the advanced linguistic abilities of some members of these groups show that language and cognition are completely independent. If there is any link between the two, it's a subtle and complex one. So in this respect my friend is wrong: language isn't just a cognitive process like any other.

Is language development dependent on social development?

It's sometimes unfortunate, to say the least, when you mistakenly speak your thoughts aloud. Inner speech is meant to remain private. Children, though, don't seem quite so adept at self-censorship. Piaget (1926) observed that the conversa-tions of preschool children weren't like the conversations of adults; although children took it in turn to speak, just like adults, what they said often wasn't at all related to what the previous speaker had said. Each child was producing a monologue, and when a group of children get together, you don't, said Piaget, get a conversation, you get a *collective monologue*. (In my experience the same is in fact true of many adults as well.) Piaget thought the nature of monologues followed in part from his idea that young children were egocentric, because their egocentrism prevented them taking the point of view of other participants in the conversation. But also, he thought, as well as lacking the skill to engage in conversation, they lacked the will: they're just not bothered about communicating and engaging in dialogue.

In addition to these monologues, children talk to themselves a great deal – they don't need listeners, as a famous study by Weir (1962) shows. Weir recorded the speech of her two-and-a-half-year-old son as he fell asleep by himself in his bedroom. The child produced charming sequences such as "Mommy's too weak. Alice strong. Alice too weak. Alice too weak. Daddy's too weak". What function could this self-talk serve? Weir argued that the child was practising and exploring language. The speech of children to themselves can be longer and more complex than what they produce in conversation (see Hoff-Ginsberg, 1997, for more detail).

For Piaget then, monologues arise because the child lacks the skill and the will to converse with others, and when the child is alone, they are a form of practice. As they get older, they fade away, particularly when they acquire the cognitive skills that enable them to overcome their egocentrism and take the points of view of their listeners. A different viewpoint was proposed by Vygotsky (1934/1962). I've already mentioned Vygotsky, noting his idea that inner speech is a form of self-regulation and self-monitoring. Vygotsky had the insight that inner speech and the monologues of children are related. In fact, he said, they're the same thing, except young children haven't yet learned to internalise their monologues. On this account monologues don't just fade away, but become internalised to become our inner speech. In both the overt and covert case it plays the same role, but young children can only speak their thoughts aloud.

It's important not to over-simplify these positions. Not all soliloquies need be directive; sometimes the child might just be playing with language. And the speech of young children clearly isn't always a monologue. Nevertheless, there is a difference between Piaget and Vygotsky's views on the function and future of much of the child's monologues. There is some experimental support for Vygotsky's contention that self-talk has some guiding role in that the kind of private talk a child produces while they're trying to solve a problem predicts how likely they are to be able to solve that problem, and the harder the problem gets, the more private speech the child produces (Behrend et al., 1992). The internalisation of thought occurs around the age of three, although there are variations, with children exposed to more language and more cognitive stimulation at home tending to internalise earlier (Quay & Blaney, 1992).

Vygotsky then saw a more complex relation between language and cognition. He also stressed the importance of the social and cultural contexts in which interaction and development take place. Vygotsky thought that language was the most sophisticated and complex system available for higher thought; hence in older children and adults, cognition depended on language. He also recognised that infants have developed cognitively before they begin to use language. For Vygotsky, the moment when speech and cognition begin to interact was the most important moment in a child's intellectual development, and was marked by the emergence of private speech, which would later be internalised. Before this moment speech served a purely social, communicative function, but after it also guided and assisted reasoning, while early thought was prelinguistic. Language enables children to separate themselves from the immediate context, and thereby talk and reason about things that aren't immediately in front of them. So after initially separate beginnings, language and thought become interdependent.

Vygotsky's ideas have always struck me as sensible and unobjectionable, and therein perhaps lies the problem: it's all a bit vague – certainly compared with some of the empirical work I've discussed elsewhere in this book. The idea on the internalisation of egocentric speech into inner speech is a plausible and intriguing one, but I know of no research testing this idea, and I find it difficult to think about how it could be tested. The idea that language and thought are interdependent and develop in a complex way is plausible, and more consistent with the data than the cognition hypothesis, but again, it's short on detail, and there's been little work on translating the idea into specific, testable predictions, so it lacks detail. Indeed, given that we can reject any strong statement of the cognition hypothesis, logically it's either got to be this sort of complex relationship, or one of the two alternatives I've yet to discuss. So it's case not proved, but sounds plausible enough.

Vygotsky's argument that we need to consider the context in which development occurs is also a sensible reminder that neither language nor cognitive development happens in isolation. Jerome Bruner (1983) stressed the importance of the social context in particular in which language development occurs, particularly the mother–child pair (or as it's often called, *dyad*) that helps the child learn so much about the meaning of what is being communicated. In rejoinder to Chomsky's innate LAD (language acquisition device), he talked about language acquisition taking place in the context of a LASS (language acquisition socialisation system). We've already seen how adults moderate their language when talking to children, and how joint attention, where mothers talk about what they and the child are jointly attending to, is important in helping children discover the meanings of words. Social interaction is also essential for helping children learn the skills necessary to maintain conversations. When we talk, we don't (usually) all talk at once; we take turns. This turn-taking is managed by a number of cues, such as gaze (you tend to look away when you want to keep talking, but look at the other person when you're ready to yield the floor), the way in which our voice rises and falls as we speak, and the content of what we say. We can trace back this pattern of I talk, you talk, I talk, very early. Schaeffer (1975) proposed that conversational turn-taking goes right back to the start–stop pattern of feeding, while a little later in the course of development, mothers respond to the infant's burps and yawns as though they're utterances (Snow, 1977). One has only to observe the pattern of vocal interaction between a mother and her baby to see that the beginnings of turn-taking are present from a very early age. The mother tends to look at where the infant is gazing, so co-operation and joint attention are also present from very early on.

Of course language acquisition depends on social interaction and an appropriate social context; we only have to remind ourselves of Jim, who struggled to learn language from watching television, to see that. Of course social interaction is an enormous benefit to the child; after all, the primary purpose of language is to communicate with others. But it can't be the whole story.

Is language a special, separate module?

Delve around inside your abdomen and you'll find a number of distinct organs with specific functions: lungs, liver, stomach, pancreas, and so on. For Chomsky, the relation between language and thought is simple: there isn't one. The mind is divided up into organs – or faculties, or modules – and language is an independent module. The development of language doesn't depend on cognitive development. Instead, as we've seen, it has a genetic basis in the language acquisition device, or LAD, which means that the child is born with the foundation of universal grammar. All that has to happen now is that the switches, or parameters, have to be set to the appropriate value by exposure to the ambient language.

There are several intertwined themes in this East Coast view of language. We've seen that the original motivation was the poverty of the stimulus – the idea that the child doesn't receive sufficient information from just listening to language to be able to learn it. (Incidentally, this is why many people don't like to talk of children *learning* language, like they might learn how to ride a bicycle, because this phraseology implies it's all out there, that the child is a blank slate; instead, children *acquire* language, hinting that they come with more to the party.) We've seen that there are several problems with the poverty of the stimulus, which is why evidence such as the role of the FOXP2 gene, specific language impairments, savants with high-functioning language ability but very poor other cognitive skills, and all experimental results that show that language processing is modular and rule-based are picked up with glee by the East Coasters – and questioned or rejected by the West Coasters.

For the outsider, it's difficult to know what to conclude. It's also difficult to imagine what sort of evidence could prove or disprove this approach. It's particularly difficult to envisage what would confirm a modular model stressing the importance of innate language-specific knowledge other than a sophisticated and complex model of psychological processing relating behaviour to genes through brain structures. As we begin to chip away at the complexity of the problem, particularly with connectionist modelling, we see how we don't need rules of innate knowledge, but can explain language in terms of general cognitive processing.

What is the Sapir-Whorf hypothesis?

Clear your mind and then read aloud the following sentence. "The chairman brought the meeting to order." What came to mind? In your mind's eye, what did the chairman look like? I'm ashamed to say that in mine there was a vague image of a slightly corpulent gentleman in a pin-stripe suit; ashamed because it was a man. Do you think if you'd read "The chair brought the meeting to order" it would have been any different (putting aside for now disturbing images of animate chairs)? We try and avoid sexist language because, at least some of us think, it leads us to make assumptions. We're more likely to think that a chairman is a man than a chair is a man – or at least, we now modify our language to act as though it's that way. (I draw the line at objecting to "masterly", though.) We avoid sexist language in case the words affect our thoughts.

The idea that language can constrain our thoughts and beliefs is of course not a new one. In the novel *Nineteen Eighty-Four*, George Orwell invented "Newspeak", described as "The official language of Oceania and had been devised to meet the ideological needs . . . of English Socialism" (1949: p. 241). The purpose of Newspeak was to make thoughts alien to the ideology impossible – in other words, people would come to think only what their leaders wanted them to think because you could only think what Newspeak allowed you to think. For example, the meaning of the word "free" had been changed so that it could only be used in the sense of "this dog is free of lice" – it could no longer be used to mean politically free, or free speech, or free thought. Words became short and sentences simple, with the idea that thinking would become short and simple; indeed, there was no word for "thought". Newspeak isn't as incredible as it might sound: the American military invented the term "collateral damage" because it didn't have the implications of "civilians unfortunately killed or injured as a consequence of military action". Some of my other favourite euphemisms include "adult movie", "economical with the truth", "tired and emotional", and "I need to wash my hands" (see "Next" for translations). All of them make unpalatable thoughts less unpleasant and therefore acceptable.

The idea then that language can influence thought is well known in popular culture, and has been for some time. In psychology the idea came to prominence with the work of the American linguist Edward Sapir and his student Benjamin Lee Whorf. Whorf died young, and is remembered for his collected writings, published posthumously in 1956. Together the two gave their name to the Sapir-Whorf hypothesis, the idea that the form of our language influences the way in which we think. Whorf wrote that the idea of language influencing thought came to him in his time as a fire prevention inspector in Connecticut. On one occasion a worker threw a cigarette end into an "empty" drum of petrol that was of course full of petrol fumes – with predictable results. He came to the conclusion that accidents were happening because people misperceive the situation because of the way in which they have labelled it with words (see Pinker, 1994, for further examples and detail). The idea that language determines thought is called *linguistic determinism*. Another way of putting this idea is that thoughts are constrained by the form of the language in which they're expressed, and therefore differences between languages will lead to differences in ways of thinking, an idea properly called *linguistic relativism*. However, the terms "linguistic relativism" and "determinism" are often used inter-changeably. We could in principle have determinism without relativism, but let's not let details of terminology muddy our thoughts. To add to the confusion, the whole idea is sometimes called the Whorfian hypothesis, a phrase to which Whorf himself reputedly objected because the word "the" implied he'd only ever had one hypothesis, when in fact he'd had many.

Just as it would take a very brave person to say that cognition has no influence on language, it would take an equally brave person to deny that language has any effect whatsoever on cognition. However, the extreme version, that language completely determines the form of our thoughts, is also incorrect. The question then is how much does language influence thought?

Whorf's work was mostly anthropological. He studied Native American languages, and concluded that these languages were very different from English – not just in the very obvious differences of their vocabulary and syntax, but also in the way in which they appeared to structure the world. Whorf's most famous example is his discussion of how Apache speakers talk about springs (1956, p. 214):

> We might isolate something in nature by saying "It is a dripping spring". Apache erects the statement on the verb *ga* "be white" (including clear, uncoloured, and so on). With a prefix *no-* the meaning of downward motion enters: "whiteness moves downward". Then *to*, meaning both "water" and "spring", is prefixed. The result corresponds to our "dripping spring", but synthetically it is "as water, or springs, whiteness moves downward". How utterly unlike our way of thinking!

For Whorf, this translation showed that speakers of Apache don't divide the world clearly into things and actions that happen to or because of actions in the way that English does. Whorf provides plenty of other examples: the Apache equivalent of "he invites people to a feast" becomes translated as "he, or somebody, goes for eaters of cooked food", and "he cleans a gun with a ramrod" becomes "he directs a hollow moving dry spot by movement of tool" (see Pinker, 1994, for further discussion of these examples).

The phrase "how utterly unlike our way of thinking" has become legendary. Several researchers have pointed to the absurdity of the arbitrariness and literalness of this translation (e.g. Clark & Clark, 1977; Pinker, 1994). It's like the way I used to translate French at school, word for word, trying to find exact correspondences between the elements of the two languages. Both English and Apache identify the elements of clearness, water, and moving downwards as being key concepts in both languages – "how utterly like our way of thinking!" (Clark & Clark). Turning the tables, Pinker points out that "he walks" could be translated as "as solitary masculinity, leggedness proceeds".

In addition to the arbitrariness of the translations, there is an element of circularity here (Pinker, 1994). Apaches speak differently from us, so they must think differently. How do we know they think differently? Because they speak differently! We need an independent measure of "thinking" before we can begin to talk about such things.

We can't conclude much from comparing languages. The point is reiterated if we look at the way in which different languages map the world on to words. One of the few things many people know about languages is that the Inuit have many different words for snow. The observation dates back to the work of the anthropologist Franz Boas (1911). Boas noted that the Inuit used different kinds of construction for talking about different types of snow: *aput* for "snow on the ground", *gana* for "falling snow", *piqsirpoq* for "drifting snow", and *qimuqsuq* for "a snow drift". Boas was interested in how different languages use different root words for constructing words; whereas we have one root word (snow), Inuit has four. Whorf (1940, reprinted in his 1956 collection) went further to add that to the Inuit these types of snow are "sensuously and operationally different". He also inflated the number of types of snow to seven – meaning falling, on the ground, packed hard, slushy, flying, and other kinds (Pullum, 1989). In the same way that Bartlett's famous (1932) study of memory shows how stories get distorted and simplified by time and retelling, the number of Inuit words for snow has become distorted and detached from the original data. I remember being told at school there were 13 words for snow, but I think this number might have arisen from a similar confusion about the number of Filipino words for rice. An editorial in the *New York Times* of 9 February 1984 gave the number as 100; I've seen "400" a few times; and the highest I can reach in an online search is now "thousands". It does seem that in cyberspace at least it's widely accepted that most people think the total is over 100 (although "40" is another common total, which shows how all over the place these numbers are). The exact number doesn't matter; in Geoffrey Pullum's charming phrase, everyone knows there's a bucketful. But never believe anything you read. How did the number get so inflated? In part by misreporting and distortion, in a manner Bartlett would have recognised; in part by deliberate hoax; in part by satire getting confused with reality; in part by mistranslation; and in part by confusion over what constitutes a word. And once a pseudo-fact has caught the public imagination, it's very difficult to slay; I shudder to wonder how many pseudo-facts I believe I know.

But let's take Boas's original four as the correct number (although there is some debate about the right number; it could be as low as two – *qanik* for "snow in the air", and *aput* for "snow on the ground" – and if anyone tries to insist that there are more than four, ask them what they are). Whorf's point was that because people have different words, they categorise the world in different ways: in his famous phrase "we dissect nature along lines laid down by our native language". If our words differ, we see the world differently. This conclusion is of course total conjecture. It would not be surprising if Inuit did have more words for snow, or Filipino more words for rice, but that hardly means that we see these objects differently – that because someone has two words for snow, they see the two sorts as differently as we do chalk and cheese. Once again this argument is circular – they have different words and therefore perceive the world differently; how do we know they perceive the world differently? Because they have different words! And we do in fact have different words for different sorts of snow: snow, slush, and sleet, and you might want to include blizzard and avalanche too. Skiers, who have a higher level of expertise with snow, have more: powder, corn, crust, and piste, perhaps – see what I mean by the difficulty in deciding on a word for snow? And even if we don't have a single word, we could easily make more: dry snow, wet snow, snow on wires, snow that's just fallen off a branch on to my head, and so on. Inuit is an agglutinative language – it makes up words from root words by combining words together, so these sorts of concepts could be represented as a single word – would you say that these compound words are all different words for snow? The number is just a consequence of the way different languages combine words to form complex concepts.

I'm sure by now you're as fed up with snow as I am. Let me give you another example about words and how we see the world. When I was young, and had much more free time, I was quite a keen birdwatcher. Where you might see a "seagull" (or perhaps even just a "bird"), I would see a black-headed gull, or herring gull, or common gull, or lesser black-backed gull . . . you get the idea. And other bird-watchers more expert than I was were able to tell races apart, so they would talk about seeing a *Larus fuscus fuscus* or a *Larus fuscus graellsii*, or even a second-winter or third-winter juvenile. But are we seeing different things? Of course not. We might be differentially sensitive to detail, but when I've pointed out to you that you've got to pay attention to whether the legs are yellow or pink, or whether there are white tips on the ends of the wing, you can tell the difference too. But that information was present in the visual scene before you had to attend to those features – you might not have noticed them because you weren't paying that much attention, or might not have realised how important they were. Our perceptions might not differ, but our ability to dissect the world, in Whorf's phrase, does. I can tell the difference between different types of seagulls, but because I have the expertise, not because I have the names for them.

One domain that has seen a recent flurry of research activity as a testing ground for the Sapir-Whorf hypothesis is that of numerical cognition – how we understand numbers and mathematics. The Piraha tribe are hunter-gatherers in Brazil who have only three words for numbers, corresponding to one, two, and many. Gordon (2004) examined the mathematical abilities of members of the tribe on a range of tasks. They performed much worse when they had to deal with more than three things. For example, they found it difficult to remember whether a picture had four fish in it or five, and they found it difficult to match the number of sticks or nuts to those laid out in a row if there were more than three. One explanation for their poor performance is that they found reasoning and counting with larger numbers difficult because they didn't have the words available to facilitate making the appropriate distinctions. Of course, we might ask why the tribe didn't distinguish numbers above two; the standard reply is "because they don't need them", which I find difficult to believe. But it could be that they have less need for differentiating three or more things, which would lead to lack of practice and expertise with dealing with larger quantities. In addition to their vocabularies differing from ours, their lifestyles also differ.

Other studies have not found the same results: Warlpiri is an indigenous Australian language that also has words for one, two, and many, and Anindilyakwa a language that has words for one, two, three or four, and many. Monolingual children speaking these languages possessed just the same numerical concepts and abilities as monolingual English-speaking indigenous Australian children (Butterworth et al., 2008). What is perhaps most striking is that the Munduruku, another Amazonian tribe very similar in most respects to the Piraha, do have numbers for three, four, and five as well as one, two, and many, but the Munduruku were also poor on some arithmetical tasks involving numbers smaller than five (Pica et al., 2004; Pinker, 2007). These results suggest that lifestyle and culture play a large role in mathematical ability. Pica et al. found that the Munduruku were capable of sophisticated numerical competence in the absence of number words, but the lack of these words nevertheless hampered them on some more precise tasks.

The way languages use numbers does make some difference, though. Although Welsh numbers have the same number of syllables as the corresponding English numbers, the vowel sounds are longer so many of them take longer to say. Given that we know that our working memory represents things by the way words sound, this vowel difference should be reflected in differences of memory for numbers. Essentially you can squeeze more short things into working memory than long things. English–Welsh bilingual speakers (and the bilingualism is key here, as it enables us to compare the same person's performance in the two different languages) performed slightly worse in memory tests for Welsh numbers compared with English. They also tended to make slightly more errors when doing mental arithmetic in Welsh compared with English – presumably because they could remember the numbers slightly less well (Ellis & Hennelly, 1980). Although numbers take longer to say in Welsh than English, it's even faster to say them in Chinese, which has very short names for numbers, and accordingly Chinese speakers can remember more digits than English speakers (typically 10 instead of 7; Dehaene, 2000). The English number system is relatively complex: we have 13 primitive number names (zero through to 12), and then a special rule for naming 13 through to 19; then up to 100 we have a fairly simple rule-based system, but we still have to learn special names for 20, 30, 40, and so on; and then a new rule applies. Contrast this with the much simpler naming system of Chinese, where a child just has to learn 11 basic terms for zero to 10, and then the three special names for 100, 1000, and 10,000. In Chinese, "eleven" is simply "ten plus one", "twelve" is just "ten plus two", and so on, in a simple, predictable fashion. It should come as no surprise that Chinese children are faster to learn to count, particularly in the "teens" (Hunt & Agnoli, 1991; Miller & Stigler, 1987). Some languages have single words that express quite complex concepts in other languages, and the existence of these words must make it easier to access those concepts: examples include *Weltanschauung*, meaning "a comprehensive view of the world" and *Schadenfreude* (I get this a lot: joy in other people's misfortune) in German, and *mokita*, a word in the Kivila language of New Guinea that beautifully means "the truth everybody knows but nobody speaks".

Having words readily available might well assist reasoning and classification, but it's another thing to say that if you don't have the word, you can't do the task. I'm reminded of the story of the Hawaiian islanders not being able to see Captain Cook's ships when they first arrived because they didn't have the concept of such things. This story is so completely unbelievable that it makes the point.

What can we learn from how people name colours?

Let's continue with this idea about what having words readily available can do for us. First though, think about a rainbow. How many colours do you see? Seven, of course, you'll say. There are even several mnemonics for the colours and the order they're in. I learned "Richard of York gave battle in vain" at school, but I think I now prefer "run over your gerbil because it's vicious". In fact, when I look at a rainbow, although there are supposed to be seven colours, I can never see seven; I can only ever see six. My colour incompetence aside, the way in which we name colours turns out to have been a battlefield in the understanding of the relation between language and thought.

Some colours are easier to describe than others. You can look at a colour and think "that's a good red", or "that's a strong yellow", or perhaps "that's a pale

A very arty picture of "as snow, whiteness turning a bit dirty and slushy"

orange-pink". Other colours are much more difficult to describe. A number of early studies showed that the people have better memory for colours that are easier to name. The researchers showed colour patches that varied in colour saturation, brightness, and hue (you can get an idea of what the materials looked like by looking at some leaflets of paint samples) to participants, and examined how well they remembered the patch. What's more, these effects seemed robust across languages (Brown & Lenneberg, 1954; Lantz & Stefflre, 1964).

Doesn't this support the Sapir-Whorf hypothesis? At first sight, yes: having a word or words readily available for a colour affects how easily we can remember that colour. But in drawing this conclusion we're assuming that the correspondence between the colour name and the colour is an arbitrary one: that we're free to divide up the colour spectrum with language, and however we divide it up, we'll

There's a pot of gold just outside my back door

always be better with those colours we happen to have named. We might have come up with a "grue" between green and blue, instead of green and blue, and then we would have had better memory for that colour. It turns out that biology plays a big role in colour naming. There's a great deal of order in the colour names used by different languages and cultures (Figure 4.1); they're not all over the colour spectrum, but are highly constrained (Berlin & Kay, 1969).

In the same way that not all cultures have numbers corresponding to the same

English	purple blue green yellow red orange
Shona	cipswuka citema cicena cipswuka
Bassa	hui ziza
Dani	mili mola

FIGURE 4.1 Comparison of colour hue division in English, Shona, Bassa, and Dani. Based on Gleason (1961).

ones as in English, cultures differ in the colour terms they use. Berlin and Kay (1969) examined the distribution of what are called basic colour terms. These are, as the name implies, the core colour terms available to a language. A colour name has to meet several criteria before being acceptable as such: it has to contain just one unit of meaning (so "red" is acceptable, but not "dark red"), it must be applicable to anything ("blond" can only be used to talk about hair colour or skin type), it must be generally known or derived from another object ("saffron" is out), and it can't be a subtype of another colour (in the way that "scarlet" is a type of red). The number of basic colour terms in use is rather small. What's more, across cultures, they form a hierarchy. If a culture has just two basic colour terms, they always correspond to black and white. Languages that have three colour terms have names corresponding to black, white, and red. If they have four, five, or six colours, they will be black, white, and red plus some or all of yellow, green, and blue. And if they have seven, the seventh will correspond to our brown. And if they have more, the colours will correspond to one or more of our purple, pink, grey, and orange (Figure 4.2).

However, it's not the name that matters most, but the corresponding colour. Four-month-old infants prefer to attend to colours that lie centrally in the categories spanned by the colour names rather than those at the border; put another way, they prefer a good clear blue or red to a murky one in between (Bornstein, 1985). In a classic cross-cultural study, Rosch Heider (1972) showed that people in different cultures treat a colour in just the same way, regardless of whether or not they have a name for it. She looked at people's memory for *focal colours*; these are the best examples of colours corresponding to a colour term. If you showed 100 people samples of different types of blue and asked them to pick out the best blue, they would mostly agree about which sample it should be, and the one they would agree on would be the focal blue. If I ask you to shut your eyes and imagine a blue square, that is likely to be in focal blue, too.

Rosch Heider looked at how members of the Dani tribe of New Guinea used colours. The Dani are one of those cultures with just two basic colour terms: *mola*, corresponding to our white and used to talk about light colours, and *mili*,

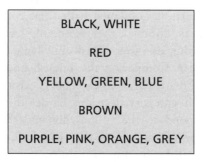

BLACK, WHITE

RED

YELLOW, GREEN, BLUE

BROWN

PURPLE, PINK, ORANGE, GREY

FIGURE 4.2 Hierarchy of colour names. Based on Berlin and Kay (1969)

corresponding to our black and used to talk about dark colours. Rosch Heider taught the Dani names for other colours. She found that it was easier to teach them names for the other focal colours than for non-focal colours. They could also remember focal colours more easily, even though they didn't have names for them. So people behave in just the same way as Brown and Lenneberg originally found, even though they don't have names available! Having a word available doesn't seem to have anything to do with it after all. Heider also investigated colour preference among Dani children, and found what by now you will expect: the children preferred focal colours to non-focal ones, and found them easier to remember, even though they didn't have words for them.

What could explain this systematicity among colour names? The obvious candidate is the biology of the colour perception system. The rods and cones in the retina, and cells sensitive to colour in the part of the brain known as the lateral geniculate nucleus, respond differentially to different light frequencies, although the response distributions overlap, and the visual system records differences, meaning that we process colours in terms of opposing pairs, such as blue–yellow and red–green – which is why if you look at a patch of intense yellow for 30 seconds and then look at a white sheet of paper you will have the illusion of seeing a blue patch (see Lennie, 1984). The details need not detain us, but we therefore know that the visual system is more sensitive to some colours than others, and the focal colours are those to which the system is most sensitive. So the colour naming studies are telling us about the biology of the visual system, not how our perception and cognition are influenced by which words we have available. By 1976 Roger Brown had changed his mind, concluding that colour naming doesn't tell us anything much about how language influences cognition.

So it's the biology that's determining the language, not our language influencing our cognition. Or at least that's what I was taught when I was young, and in turn have taught for years. More recent work has shown that there are limits on how much our biology constrains our colour naming, and that there is some influence of the availability of colour terms on thought. The Berinmo, a hunter-gatherer tribe from New Guinea, have five colour terms. In particular, they do not divide blue and green as we do; most of the whole blue–green range is called "nol" by them, with a small portion, combined with what corresponds to our yellow, called "wor". Nevertheless, although they essentially have just one word for the whole blue–green range, they do not find tasks involving the focal colours that we call blue and green easier. Comparing the English and Berinmo colour name schemes, the Berinmo find their cross-category decisions easier than English speakers, and their within-category decisions harder than English, regardless of how the colours correspond to the supposedly underlying focal colours. The Berinmo don't show any of the effects that Rosch found with the Dani and focal colours: they show no facilitation of learning and no recognition advantage (Davidoff, 2001; Davidoff et al., 1999; Roberson et al., 2000). Indeed, there is now even debate over whether the Dani really just have two colour names. So the evidence that biology determines cognition doesn't stand up. Indeed, Davidoff (2001) concludes that perceptual categorisation is determined by linguistic relativity. At the very least we can conclude that the domain of colours might not be the best one to use to be able to draw strong conclusions in any direction.

Given that we know that the language processing is predominantly localised in the left-hand side of the brain, we might expect that any effects of language on perception will be more pronounced in the left hemisphere. Gilbert et al. (2006) showed that we are faster to distinguish target colours from distractors when the two colours have different names only when the colours are presented to the left hemisphere; reaction times to colours presented to the right hemisphere were not affected by colour names. We can easily control which side of the brain gets what because the left side of our visual field (that is, the left half of what both the left and right eye see) is wired to the right hemisphere, and the right side of our visual field to the left side of the brain. Hence by presenting colours to just the right visual field we can preferentially direct them to the left hemisphere of the brain, where the colour names will be more strongly represented. Gilbert et al. conclude that we view the right, but not the left, half of our visual world through the lens of our native language.

Does language influence memory and reasoning?

There are a few psychology experiments whose results are so surprising that they're difficult to believe: my favourite is that if young people read a list of words describing elderly people, they walk away from the lab more slowly than if they'd read something else (Bargh et al., 1996).

Language, then, can affect action and behaviour. This isn't quite the same as the Sapir-Whorf hypothesis, but it does show the complexity and interconnectedness of human behaviour. Given there are such subtle effects as these, it would be surprising if there were no effects of language on thought. As you now realise with psycholinguistics, the effects range from the subtle and less controversial to the more controversial. Generally it's the cross-cultural differences that generate more controversy.

Let's start with the less controversial stuff first. There's a wealth of evidence that shows that language facilitates and distorts reasoning and memory. We only have to think of the famous research on eye-witness testimony by Elizabeth Loftus. In one of the best-known experiments, people were shown a short film clip of a minor car crash. They then had to fill out a questionnaire. For half the participants, one of the questions was "how fast were the cars going when they hit each other?" while the other half were asked "how fast were the cars going when they smashed into each other?" The participants in the "hit" condition estimated 34 mph, while those in the "smash" condition estimated 41 mph (Loftus & Palmer, 1974). As they were asked the question after they saw the film, the wording couldn't have influenced their perception of the incident; it must have affected their memory or judgement of it. But the same participants were asked some more questions about the film a week later. One of the questions was "did you see any broken glass?" Participants who had been in the "smash" condition were significantly more likely to answer "yes" than those in the "hit" condition (32% compared with 14%). There had been no broken glass in the film. The wording of the question had distorted people's memory – leading questions can lead. The importance of this in law can't be overstated; the study of language and thought isn't just of academic interest, but can be the difference between justice and injustice.

The idea that language influences memory was first shown in a simple but effective way by Carmichael et al. in 1932. They showed people simple line drawings – for example, two circles connected by a little straight line. Half the participants were given one label with each picture and the other half different labels. So some of the people were given the label "dumbbell" to go with the circles, the other half "eyeglass"; half the people shown a thin crescent saw it labelled "crescent moon", the other half "the letter C", and so on. Later the people were asked to draw what they'd seen from memory. I'm sure you can guess the results. The pictures people drew were influenced by the label they'd been given such that the pictures tended to migrate towards the label. Just having a label available can make something easier to remember; people shown nonsense shapes found them easier to remember if they'd also been supplied with an arbitrary label (Santa & Ranken, 1972).

Words can help or hinder our ability to solve problems, too. When solving problems, people are often reluctant to "think outside the box". That's one of those management phrases I detest, but is particularly apt for a description of the phenomenon known as *functional fixedness* (Duncker, 1945). People get fixated on the traditional functions of objects and are reluctant to think of novel ways of using them even when the alternative use would help them solve a problem. In the classic demonstration, people are shown a table with various materials on it such as a candle, a box of nails, pieces of string, drawing pins, and rubber bands. They're asked to build a construction such that the candle can be attached to the wall and burn all the way down to the bottom. People go to great trouble to make the most magnificent constructions – I remember my first attempt at doing this; Isambard Kingdom Brunel would have been proud. (Unfortunately my construction collapsed after a minute or two, and the burning candle fell to the ground; health and safety were less dominant then.) The easiest solution is just to pin the box to the wall and stand the candle on it. People seem very reluctant to think of the box in this way; presumably they're fixated on the box's function as a container because, well, that's what boxes do. It's possible to make the problem easier or harder to solve by manipulating the prominence of the box's function; if the materials are all in the box, that emphasises the container function more than if they are placed alongside it; and labelling the box with "nails" emphasises the containing function even more, making it less likely that people will think of it in any other way (Glucksberg & Weisberg, 1966).

The language we use can influence what sort of information we access. In one study, Chinese–English bilingual speakers read descriptions of people, and later were asked to provide descriptions of the people they'd read about (Hoffman et al., 1986). Some of the descriptions were written in Chinese, and some in English. After reading the description the participant had to fill in a questionnaire rating statements about the person who had been described. The ratings differed depending on which language had been used; bilingual people thinking in English applied an English stereotype, while those thinking in Chinese applied a Chinese stereotype. For example, Chinese has one word available to describe a socially skilled person devoted to his family but who is a little reserved, whereas English needs all those words. It's easier to think about that stereotype in Chinese than in English, and this ease skews the ratings.

The conclusion from this work is that language and words can influence our memories, judgements, and reasoning, but this claim is perhaps unsurprising and is certainly much weaker than the original linguistic relativity hypothesis. Languages differ in the ease with which they can express different concepts. A stronger finding would be if these differences between languages led to differences in people's ability to reason. The first study of this idea was by Carroll and Casagrande (1958), who examined some of the consequences of the grammatical differences between English and Navajo. Navajo differs from English in changing the form of the verb depending on the shape and rigidity of the object being discussed, so that, for example, the endings for the verb meaning "carry" depend on whether you're carrying a rope or a stick. Carroll and Casagrande argued that therefore Navajo-speaking children should pay more attention to the shape and rigidity of objects than English speakers. As all the children were bilingual, they compared the way more English-dominant children grouped objects with the way the more Navajo-dominant children grouped them. The Navajo-speaking children were more likely to group things together based on their shape than colour compared with the English-speaking group.

The way in which we think about time also seems to be influenced by the form of our language. We use spatial terms to describe time: in English we use a side-to-side metaphor, talking about going forwards and back in time, but Mandarin Chinese uses an up-and-down metaphor, with earlier events being described as "up" and later ones as "down". English speakers are faster to make judgements about time (does March come before April?) when they've just seen a horizontal array of objects, and Mandarin speakers when they've just seen a vertical array (Boroditsky, 2001). So the way in which we think about abstract domains such as time can be influenced by our language.

If I'd worked harder at school I would have been a millionaire by now. If Gavrilo Princip hadn't gone for a sandwich, then the first World War would never have begun. This type of construction is known as a counter-factual – if something in the past had been different, things would later be different. As we can see, English has a simple construction for making counter-factual statements; technically it's known as the *subjunctive mood*, a term that brings back very happy memories of school Latin. It's not so easy to make this type of counter-factual statement in Chinese; there aren't any grammatical markers for the subjunctive in the way there are in English. Look at the differences between the simple statement and the subjunctive counter-factual in English:

I did not work hard at school, so I did not become a millionaire.
If I had worked harder at school, then I would have been a millionaire.

These verb changes are big clues to us about what's going on – so much so that we can leave out some of the relational words (like "then") without making much difference. Verb changes are much less used in Chinese, which instead relies much more on these relational words and context. Bloom (1981) hypothesised that the lack of these clues would make it more difficult for native Chinese speakers to reason counter-factually. He compared their performance on how readily they could understand counter-factual statements with a group of native English speakers, and found that the Chinese speakers did indeed find them more difficult.

Earlier I noted that different languages use different word orders – some, such as English, put the verb, the action, before the object ("the pig chased the rat"); others put the verb after the object. Does this word order influence our behaviour when we're not speaking? It doesn't seem so. The word order people use in everyday speech doesn't influence non-verbal behaviour, as measured by performance on a communicative task (describing an event using gestures) and on a non-communicative task (reconstructing an event using a series of pictures). Speakers of English, Chinese, and Spanish (object-final languages) produced the same sorts of descriptions as speakers of Turkish (a verb-final language): agent–patient–act (Goldin-Meadow et al., 2008). This description order corresponds to the word order subject–object–verb. Goldin-Meadow et al. argue that this order is the natural sequence for representing events, with the agent and object, or patient, being more closely linked cognitively than the rather more abstract action. This order corresponds to that seen in emerging sign languages, too. This work argues against a strong version of the Sapir-Whorf hypothesis, suggesting that rather than language constraining the way we think, there are deep similarities in the way we think, and these similarities are reflected in our language.

In conclusion, there isn't a straightforward answer to whether the Sapir-Whorf hypothesis is right or wrong (no surprise there, then). It's useful to distinguish between a strong version of the hypothesis (language determines the form of our thought) and a weaker version (language can influence our memory and reasoning on some tasks), and while there isn't much support for the strong version, there's clearly a considerable amount of evidence for the weaker form. But language in turn reflects the world and the way in which our brains are structured to deal with the world.

Are there practical consequences of the way we use language?

When I was much younger, I remember my PhD supervisor asking me this question: "A man is involved in a car accident and is rushed to the local accident and emergency. The surgeon says, "I can't operate on this person, because he's my son". The surgeon is not the man's father. How can this be?" I don't know whether it was because of my ignorant and callow youth, or because even I harboured the same sexual stereotyping preferences as most other people in the early eighties, but it took me ages to work out the answer (or perhaps I just gave up and asked).

We have preconceptions about what words mean, and these preconceptions can affect the way we think. Certain words seem to imply certain things, and again, these implications might make us draw unwarranted inferences. I mentioned earlier the famous example of the word "chairman" of a committee; many believe that hearing "chairman" biases us towards assuming that the person talked about is a man, in a way that a more neutral phrase such as "chairperson" or "chair" does not. There has been surprisingly little research on this important topic; there's plenty on who is likely to use sexist language and when, but very little on its cognitive effects. But given that there are some clear influences of language on thought, at least at the margins of cognition – and we'll see in the chapter on understanding that people draw (often unwarranted) inferences from what they hear and read – it wouldn't be surprising if using particular words biased us towards drawing some inferences. And it only needs a small bias in a big population to make a large difference. Given that the remedy is as straightforward as avoiding sexist language, it seems self-evident to me that we should do so. (Although there are limits to the plausibility of this argument; I refuse to give up talking about "mastering a subject").

There are other differences in linguistic style that could have important implications, particularly for education. The British sociologist Basil Bernstein (1961) attempted to explain some of the differences in educational attainment of working- and middle-class children in terms of differences in their language. He argued that working-class people use a *restricted code*, while middle-class people use an *elaborated code*. The term "restricted" was an unfortunate choice; he did not mean that working-class people had a more restricted vocabulary, or middle-class people a more elaborate language; he meant that working-class people tend to draw more on a shared culture and use a type of language that reinforces a sense of belonging to their community. An elaborated code is more neutral with respect to assumptions and presumptions, and therefore more readily understood outside the immediate social group – and in that sense more effective for dealing with middle-class institutions. And, in particular, the education system is geared towards communication and education in elaborated code. It's important to note that we're talking about dialect differences here, not restrictions imposed by dialect. In another famous example, Labov (1972) studied African American Vernacular English (AAVE) – a dialect spoken by African Americans in the northern cities of the USA. Contrary to the beliefs prevalent at the time that AAVE was an impoverished linguistic system that the educational system should strive to eliminate, Labov showed that AAVE is as linguistically rich and powerful as any other dialect.

Of course people speak different dialects, but there's no evidence that any dialect is impoverished, or restricts thought, or that some form of language is better than others. It is true, however, that the dialect spoken by those in power and in charge of the education system has an advantage.

Are we forced to think in categories?

Language forces us to talk if not think categorically. When I produce a fascinating sentence such as "the cat chased the rat", I'm publicly committed to a belief that the thing doing the chasing is a cat, the thing being chased is a rat, and the action that unfolded was one of chasing. If we think this to ourselves, the effect is the same. Now I know a pedant might come along and say I might be lying, or harbouring unspoken doubts that perhaps it's a giant rat that looks like a cat chasing a small cat that looks like a rat, but for most people life's too short for this sort of worry. We say the things we do because our brains have dissected the world – both external, in the sense of our perceptions, and internal, in the sense of our beliefs and thoughts – in a particular way. Even if we hedge our bets overtly ("the cat-rat thing chased the rat-cat thing"), we're categorising things in the world in a particular way. That's the way round it is, mainly: world–brain–talk. The research on linguistic determinism shows that sometimes our language can influence our thoughts, so a more accurate model includes a little feedback (Figure 4.3).

Figure 4.3 conveys the idea. We categorise the world, and the categories we form aren't arbitrary; totally unsurprisingly, the categories we form reflect the interaction of our biology with the environment. (We could add a biology box in Figure 4.3 too, if we wished.) We have to survive and live in the world, our biology is geared towards doing so, we use language in part to communicate – so the sorts of categories we form are largely determined by this interaction between biology and the world. A child learning language maps words onto the categories they're forming – but that's not to say that the words can't refine and define categories too. It's one thing for an adult to point to a dog and say "dog", and

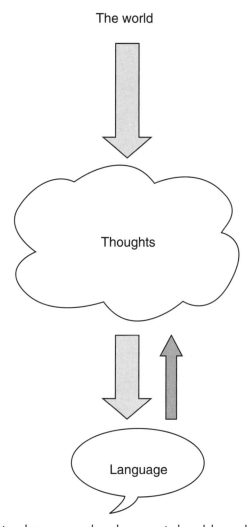

The world

Thoughts

Language

FIGURE 4.3 Interactions between our thoughts, our mind, and the world

hope the child will learn that that label goes with that category by a combination of a predisposition to dissect the world into concrete objects, the whole object principle, and the novel name principle; it's another to point to a dog and a cat and say "they're mammals" and hope that biology and cognition can do the rest without assistance.

Chapter 5

Meaning

A T SCHOOL THERE WAS a new teacher who made the dreadful mistake of starting off nice. You can't give schoolboys an inch. (I assume he's learnt his lesson and is now nasty and very successful somewhere.) Very soon his classes degenerated into mayhem. One day the headmaster walked into the riot and demanded "What is the meaning of this?" We didn't know how to answer him then, and I still don't really know what he meant. There – without noticing it, I referred to "meaning" again.

"Meaning" is one of those many words in language that we think we know the meaning of, but the more we think about them the more slippery they become. Meaning underlies language – it's the starting point of language production and the end point of language comprehension. It underpins all activities: linguistic, cognitive, and social. Without it our lives are unthinkable – dare I say it, meaningless?

What has meaning? Words do. Sentences do. The meaning of sentences is derived from the meaning of the constituent words interplaying with the syntax. But do objects have a meaning? Does a conversation? Some even talk about the meaning of life. At least if psycholinguists aren't sure what meaning is, they have happily given its study a name: semantics.

What's the meaning of meaning?

I had a friend at University who mocked philosophy and philosophers mercilessly. Whenever either was mentioned he would screw his face up and say in a high-pitched whine, "Yes, but what's the meaning of meaning?"

As ever, when stuck for meaning, let's look it up in a dictionary. And, as ever, let's be prepared to be disappointed. The online Freedictionary says meaning is:

1   something that is conveyed or signified; sense or significance
2   something that one wishes to convey
3   an interpreted goal, intent, or end
4   inner significance.

Here the act of looking "meaning" up in the dictionary is perhaps more interesting than what we found. Many people find out the meaning of something by looking it up in the dictionary; therefore, meaning is the dictionary definition. Perhaps we each have a mental dictionary, and a word's meaning is what's stored in its entry? And when we learn a new word, we create a new entry? And the meaning of a sentence somehow combines all these entries, indicating how they are related?

The problem with the dictionary account is that in the end we just go round in circles. By definition, words have to be defined in terms of other words. Pick a word at random in a dictionary. "Meaning" will do. Part of its definition is the word "sense". Look that up, and, among other things, we get:

A meaning that's conveyed.

That was a pretty small circle! Nearly as short as Steven Pinker's (2007) example:

Endless loop: n. See loop, endless
Loop, endless: n. See endless loop.

If we had an English-speaking man who knew no Chinese, and who sat in a little room with a big Chinese dictionary, and we gave him Chinese words written on scraps of paper that we fed him under the door, would we wish to say that this man knew the meanings of these words? Of course not. What this account clearly lacks is any reference to the outside world. Bringing the outside world into psycholinguistics and the brain is one of the big challenges facing modern psychology, and has been surprisingly largely ignored by psycholinguistics until recent times. No wonder we've gone round in circles.

What's a dog?

My friend was wrong about philosophers (and linguists). One very useful distinction they've given us is between the denotation and connotation of the meaning. The *denotation* is the primary meaning – its core, essential meaning that everyone agrees on (or would agree on if they expressed it). There should be no room for doubt about the denotation of a word (although one sometimes wonders, as when Bill Clinton said "it depends upon what the meaning of the word 'is' is"). When I talk about "semantics" I mean denotation. The *connotation* is the secondary meaning – all the associations we have to a word.

We can see that meaning somehow has to refer to the world; the real problem is what is the nature of this relation. For some things it seems very easy. There's just one moon (pedants, please, I'm just talking about our moon, the one everyone talks about) and just one sun, so the meaning of "moon" and "sun" relate in quite a straightforward way to the world. With "dog" things get a little trickier, because there's a very large number of them, of many different sorts, but at least they're very obvious things that form a pretty straightforward category (we call them a *natural kind*). "Mammal" gets trickier still, but we can still use the very useful following trick: we can point to something and say "yes, that's a mammal", or "no, it's not". Perhaps the meaning is in some way related to the rule that enables us to decide whether or not something is a member of a category? But then we get on to yet more abstract words, such as "truth" and "justice"; it's obvious that these words don't refer to objects, so our pointing rule won't work any more. We can apply the same sort of analysis to adjectives: we can point to things that are yellow or dead, admitting that we might be troubled by relativity (some things might be big relative to others, but relative to other things they might be small) or subjectivity (beauty is in the eye of the beholder, they say). We could do something similar for verbs, but with more difficulty. Grammatical words – let's not even go there yet.

Referring to things or properties in the world, then, is an important aspect of meaning. Our knowledge of meaning enables us to say whether a thing is a dog or not a dog, but this is most definitely not the same thing as saying that we represent the meaning of a word like "dog" as some kind of decision rule. The psychological representation of meaning is sufficiently powerful to enable us to do this sort of thing, but that doesn't mean it is that thing.

And here's another problem with pointing: we don't always know what things are in the world. The classic example is that of Hesperus and Phosphorus. The early Greeks called the bright star that sometimes lights up the evening western sky "Hesperus"; they called the bright star that could be seen some mornings in the east "Phosphorus". We now know that they both refer to the same thing – the planet Venus. Both words refer to the same thing, but it doesn't seem at all right to say therefore that for the ancient Greeks they had the same meaning. We need to distinguish two aspects of meaning: the thing referred to in the world, and the sense that captures the world as we understand it. The *intension*, or sense, is our internal, abstract specification that enables us to pick things out in the world; the *extension*, or reference, is the thing, or set of things, referred to. So for the Greeks Hesperus and Phosphorus had different intensions but the same extension.

This debate isn't as philosophical as it might at first seem because our knowledge of the world changes. A little while ago Pluto was demoted from being a planet to a dwarf planet. It's still the same thing (it still has the same extension), but its intension has changed.

What is a dog, then? I phoned up my mother and asked her that question. Being apprehensive about what psychologists get up to, I think she suspected it was a trick question, and needed some reassurance before she said "An animal with four legs. It's kept as a pet. I could go on". I then asked the mother-in-law too, and got: "A small domesticated wolf, often referred to as 'man's best friend' because of its loyalty to its owner". Neither is terribly good in my opinion! (I hope they don't read this.) Yet I'm sure they know a dog when they see one. In this case at least our implicit knowledge of meaning is demonstrably better than our explicit knowledge. But I then started getting carried away with people's definitions of "dog", so I asked a friendly professional psycholinguist, and got: "I'd look in a dictionary". Undeterred, I asked another and got: "Animal who walks on four legs, has a tail that wags in response to happiness or interest in surroundings, can be domesticated; prefers to live in packs (but not necessarily with other dogs, but could be with people, for example), lives in the moment, loves to play, fiercely loyal to the pack and will defend said pack courageously". I should have known better than to ask psycholinguists. And I thought it was just a four-legged animal that barks and is kept as a pet.

Let's look at it the other way round, and when we do, we see that we have a preferred way of talking about things. Let's try another experiment. If you show people the picture on p. 122, and ask them what it is, what are they most likely to say?

Most of them will say "dog". They're unlikely to say "animal", very unlikely I think to say "mammal", and probably unlikely to give the breed of dog. "Dog" seems to be just the right level of specificity for talking about things most of the time; it's got the right balance between being just informative and discriminative enough (in a way that "animal" and "mammal" aren't), on one hand, and general and economical on the other. This sort of level ("dog", "cat", "chair", "car") is called the *basic level* (Rosch, 1973, 1978). Above the basic level we have one or more superordinate categories ("mammal", "animal", "furniture", "vehicle"), and beneath we have category members or subordinates ("poodle", "Siamese", "office", "easy", Volkswagen, Chrysler), which in turn might be subdivided. We tend to categorise, and perhaps think, at the basic level; there's a large loss in distinctiveness as we go from the basic level to the superordinate category, but not much to be gained most of the time by making unnecessarily fine distinctions between subordinates below. Objects at the basic level tend to look alike, at least in profile. Basic-level objects have several psychological advantages: children usually learn basic-level names first, it's the highest level at which we can form a mental image (try forming a mental picture of "animal" without thinking of something more specific), people can find most things to say about basic-level things, and we process basic-level names more quickly than those at other levels (Jolicoeur et al., 1984; Rosch et al., 1976). When people misremember stories, they move from the direction of subordinate terms to using the basic-level name (Pansky & Koriat, 2004). Of course the basic level might change depending on one's level of expertise; my knowledge of seagulls used to be such that the basic level for me was the species, rather than seagull, or bird.

None of this is to deny that some categories are fuzzy (in the way that the distinction between this chapter and the next is now getting fuzzy). Category membership is determined by the underlying concept, but that's straying more deeply into the realm of meaning.

Are meanings captured by networks?

A dog's an animal. A setter and a poodle are sorts of dogs. Everything that's true of an animal is also true of a dog, and everything that's true of a dog is also true of

Another artistic composition, this one of Hesperus. It's there, honest

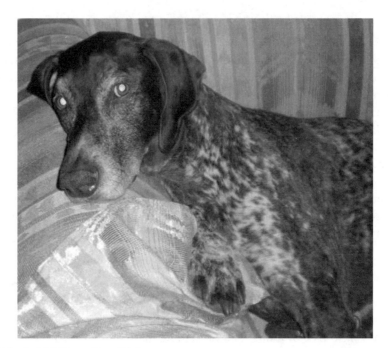

Mum. What's this? It's my friend Felix

setters, poodles, Alsations, and rottweilers. Collins and Quillian (1969) realised that once you've specified information at one level, you don't need to do it again at a lower one. They presented a model of semantic memory known as a semantic network. In their model, knowledge is stored in a hierarchy. Concepts are represented as nodes connected by links; these nodes are connected by links, and these links can have values. In their model, the most common one is called an ISA link; no prizes for guessing what ISA means ("is a" or if you want to pad it out a bit, "is an example of"). Attributes are stored at the highest possible node; so "has wings" is stored at the "bird" node, because it's true of all birds, but not all animals. It's easy to understand when seen in a diagram.

Models are fine, but are much more impressive when supported by experimental evidence. How can we test this sort of hierarchical model? Think about how we might verify a statement such as "a canary is a bird". We'd start off at the CANARY node, and travel up to the BIRD node. The two nodes are connected by an ISA link, so the statement is true. What about "a canary is an animal"? Just the same, only this time we have longer to travel to establish a connection. So the crucial prediction is that it should take longer to verify "a canary is an animal" than "a canary is a bird". What about "a canary is yellow"? Easy, we retrieve the IS YELLOW information directly from the CANARY node, so we should be relatively fast. What about "a canary has wings"? We have to travel up to the BIRD node to be able to retrieve that information, so that should take longer. And for "a canary has a liver",we have to go all the way up to the ANIMAL node, which should take longer still.

Collins and Quillian tested these predictions using a *sentence verification task*. This task is very simple: you present people with a sentence on a computer screen, such as "a canary has wings", and ask them to press one key if the statement is true and another if it's false, and you measure how long it takes them to make the decision. Obviously it's going to take people some time to read the sentences and some time to press the key, but these should be constant across sentences. Any *differences* in response time should therefore reflect differences in decision time.

The results from the sentence verification task supported the model. Essentially the further you have to travel along the hierarchy, the longer it takes you to retrieve that information and make a judgement about the veracity of a sentence containing it. We have to make the additional assumption about how people decide on the falsity of statements ("a fish has wings") somehow, perhaps by going up until we find a superordinate that can then lead us down to the appropriate node again (we can go up from fish to animal and then down another branch to find bird, which has wings), or perhaps just by rejecting statements as false if we don't find a match quickly enough.

It's been worth spending some time with this early model because although no one now thinks this is how we store all information about word meaning, the basic idea that meaning is represented by the interconnection of concepts is still very much alive. Some of the problems with the model are obvious: it's all very well for natural kind terms like birds and canaries, but what about our old friends truth and justice? Where do they live on a network? And think about "canary" and "wings" compared with "canary" and "liver"; the first two are always turning up together in sentences – we can say they're highly *associated* – but "canary" and "liver" do so much less frequently (I've never seen them together on the same page before now, I think) – they have a very weak associative strength. When we control for the strength of association of the words in the sentence, the linear distance effect is weaker, but not eliminated (Conrad, 1972; Wilkins, 1971). Other experimental results followed, showing that verification time isn't related to cognitive distance. We're faster to verify "a cow is an animal" than "a cow is a mammal", even though mammal is closer to cow than animal (Rips et al., 1973). If two things are related in some way, we find a false sentence more difficult to reject than one in which the two things are unrelated:

A pine is a church.
A pine is a flower.

Both are false, but the relatedness of the two words leads us to find the second sentence harder to reject, and therefore we're slower (Wilkins, 1971). And we're faster at dealing with items that are more typical of their category than ones that are not, a result called the typicality effect:

A penguin is a bird.

A robin is a bird.

Both are true, but robins are in some way "better" birds than penguins – they're more typical birds – so we're faster at verifying the first sentence than the second (Figure 5.1) (Rosch, 1973).

There are of course some pretty obvious modifications we could make to the model. Perhaps the most obvious is that although we called the model a network, it isn't really. We could introduce more links between things and vary the lengths of the connections, so that, for example, the ROBIN node is closer to the BIRD node than is the PENGUIN node. We haven't really talked about the mechanism whereby verification occurs – *what* travels along the links? If we think back to the first chapter, an obvious candidate is activation, that mental energy that inhabits our mental networks. The longer the link, the longer the activation takes to get there. Activation spreads out from an activated node to all those connected to it. These modifications constitute the Collins and Loftus (1975) *spreading activation network* model of semantic processing.

The details of these models needn't detain us. We've established a very

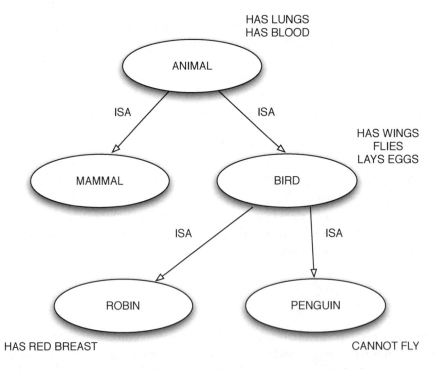

FIGURE 5.1 A small part of a Collins and Quillian type semantic network, showing property inheritance

important principle: knowledge can be represented in an interconnected network of information through which activation spreads (Figure 5.2).

What's a semantic feature?

Whatever their numerous and manifest deficiencies, the definitions I've discussed so far do have one subtle but important feature in common: they try to explain the meaning of something in terms of combinations of simpler units of meaning. The Collins and Quillian model does this to some extent as well: information such as

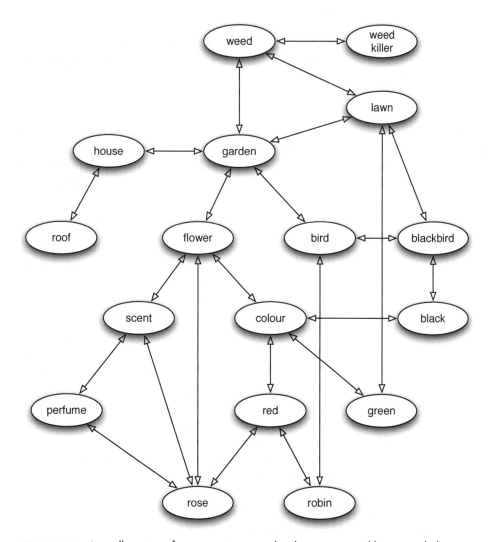

FIGURE 5.2 A small portion of my semantic network – things very quickly get tangled up

"has wings", "flies", "has liver" is stored at each node. Meaning is broken down into smaller units of meaning.

We can take this idea that meaning is best represented by combinations of smaller units of meaning much further so that it acts as the basis for a theory of semantic memory. We call such approaches decompositional theories. It works very well in some domains. The classic linguistic example is that of *kinship terms*. Think about how we might define your relatives relative to yourself. There's some redundancy in the meanings: if you know the gender of your ancestor, the generation, and whether it's maternal or paternal, you can work out who we're talking about. So female, maternal, second – that would be my grandmother Lillian on my mother's side. Male, paternal, second – that would be my grandfather Walter on my father's side. We can represent me, my two parents, and four grandparents – seven people – in terms of combinations of three things. That's parsimonious. We could extend the scheme to include siblings and take the ancestry further back just by extending the things, or *features*, as they're called, that we combine.

The idea of a semantic feature is a useful and powerful one: we represent the meanings of words by different combinations of a much smaller number of semantic features. The scheme has two big advantages. First, for most words, we no longer have to worry about meaning; all we have to worry about now is the meaning of a much smaller set of semantic features. The second advantage is that it's economical. Although economy might not, especially in the light of any conflicting evidence, be essential, it is elegant. It also reduces the circularity problem with our mental dictionary, if not obliterating it. Because of these advantages, feature-based approaches have been popular in artificial intelligence approaches to language and translation. Yorick Wilks (1976) described a computer simulation where the meanings of 600 words were captured by combinations of 80 features. An example, simplified and translated from the computer program LISP into English: the meaning of the verb "drink" is decomposed into "an action done by animate things to liquids causing the liquid to be in the animate thing via an opening in the animate thing". Let's not get too hung up on whether this is plausible; and remember this is a translation from features into a computer language and back to English. The important point is that we can capture the meaning of complex notions in terms of combinations of a small number of simple ones – and it works.

Some linguists argue that the meanings of words in all languages can be described in terms of combinations of a small – perhaps as small as 60 – number of features universal to all languages. The leading exponent of this approach is Anna Wierzbicka (e.g. 1996, 2004), whose major insight is that the complexity of meaning in different languages can be reduced to primitives that are common to all languages. The features include translated items corresponding to I, YOU, SOMEONE, SAY, TRUE, HAPPEN, MOVE, LIVE, DIE, and NOW. Now this is not to say that this way of describing language is how humans actually compute meaning in everyday life, but it does demonstrate the viability of the approach, and shows how it is possible to extend meaning from beyond the confines of an individual language. Their universality does give an inkling that these sorts of features might be the atoms of thought.

The other great advantage of semantic features is that they give us a way to build up the meaning of sentences. The meaning of a sentence is no longer the meaning of the individual words, but of a combination of semantic features. The combinatorial approach gives us a method of coping with ambiguity and explains why certain combinations of words strike us as anomalous (Katz & Fodor, 1963). The word "ball" is ambiguous. Here it is in three utterances.

Felix picked up the ball in his mouth and ran towards goal.
The pet owners' annual ball was held in the field this year.
The house kicked the ball.

The sense of "ball" meaning "small round object" is the only one that fits with an animate thing picking it up; the "dance" sense only fits with being at a location; and inanimate things can't carry out actions in either sense, so we find the final sentence anomalous.

How do semantic features fare at predicting performance in the sentence verification task? Very well, with some modifications. Rips et al. (1973) divided semantic features into two sorts, *defining* and *characteristic*. Defining features are those that are an essential part of the word's definition. A bird lays eggs and has wings. Characteristic features are usually true but aren't always: a bird usually flies, but it's not an essential, defining feature of birds. What happens when we have to verify a sentence such as "A penguin is a bird"? In Rips et al.'s account, when doing the sentence verification task, we first compare the overall featural similarity of the two key words in the sentence ("penguin" and "bird"). If there's a very high overlap (as there would be with "robin" and "bird"), we should respond TRUE, and if there's a very low overlap (as between "aardvark" and "bird), we should respond FALSE (assuming of course the person knows what an aardvark is). There are, however, pairs of words with a moderate amount of overlap, such as "penguin" and "bird", and "pine" and "flower"; in these cases we are forced to go to a second stage of comparison, where we carefully check the defining features alone.

Feature theories bear much similarity to network models, and the connectionist models we're just about to come to combine the two concepts. It's difficult and perhaps impossible to distinguish between the two, and now certainly not worth the effort. Feature-based accounts of meaning do face a number of problems, however, the foremost of which is that it's straightforward enough to list features for dogs and aardvarks, but what about our old acquaintances truth and justice? Furthermore, some words don't seem to have any defining features; the most famous example is "game" (Wittgenstein, 1953). What do all games have in common? For everything we can think of, there's a counter-example. Involves opponents? Solitaire. It's enjoyable? Tell that to a footballer or chess grandmaster on a bad day. One response to this difficulty is to ditch the whole idea of defining features, and say that category membership is defined by family resemblance, so that members of categories such as "game" merely resemble each other. But this apparent problem isn't really a problem at all for a feature-based theory; we merely dispense with the notion of necessary defining features, and look at the total amount of overlap.

We're still faced with the problem that we don't really know what the set of our semantic features is, and how we combine them to form the meanings of truth and justice. But I don't think we should worry about this too much; we know from the linguistic work of Wierzbicka that it can be done in principle. We need to move away from the idea that human semantic features have nice, straightforward linguistic correspondences like "has wings", "big", "has liver"; there's no reason at all why they should, and many good reasons why many of them won't. There's also no reason to suppose that a semantic feature is simply either "on" or "of"; it might have a value between one and zero, say. These are all characteristics of the connectionist models I describe in the coming sections, but it is worth reiterating the point that we don't know what our features are, and they might not be easy to express in words. We don't know what's in our heads. A related point is that features such as the sort we're thinking of here provide us with a means out of the terrible self-referential loop that confronts dictionaries because some of our semantic features can be linked to our perceptual systems. We can envisage the mind as a huge network. Words will link to other words and features, back perhaps through many levels of connections, to the sorts of representation with which vision, sound, touch, smell, and taste connect. Not all connections will need to go this far; some might even just connect to other words.

I don't want to give the impression that a theory of meaning is now in the bag. It should be made very clear that not everyone even agrees that decompositional semantics, where we break the meaning of a word down into smaller units of meaning, provides the best account of meaning: the leading alternative view is non-decompositional semantics, which maintains that for every word we know there's a concept that stands in a one-to-one relationship with the word. It's extremely difficult to distinguish the decompositional and non-decompositional approaches experimentally, and the impetus in current research is definitely with the decompositional approach. It's also difficult to see how the non-decompositional approach can be related to perception so readily.

This description sounds vague and speculative, but connectionist models show how it can all work in practice.

There's a rare (for Britain) bird somewhere in this photograph. Or perhaps it's an aardvark

What does neuropsychology tell us about meaning?

The brain is a delicate organ protected by a thick casing, the skull. Nevertheless there are numerous horrible ways in which it can be damaged, of which the most common are head injuries, particularly including missile wounds and brain damage from some car crashes, and strokes, when the blood supply is cut off to part of the brain – brain cells are very sensitive to oxygen starvation and die very quickly without a supply of oxygenated blood. I'll talk more about the range of disasters that can befall the brain in a later chapter, but here I want to focus on a disorder known as *deep dyslexia*. Deep dyslexia is a profound problem with reading that previously competent adult readers acquire as a result of severe damage to parts of the left hemisphere of the brain (Marshall & Newcombe, 1966, 1973). It's characterised by a number of symptoms, including great difficulty in reading aloud pronounceable non-words (often called pseudowords), such as DAT, NITE, SMOUTH, and GRAT. Normally, as I'll show in a later chapter, people have no difficulty in pronouncing strings of letters such as these, and what's more people agree on how they should be pronounced. People with deep dyslexia also find nouns easier to read than adjectives, and adjectives easier to read than verbs. They have particular difficulty in reading grammatical words, such as "of", "in", "their", "where", and "some", even though these words are very common and usually short. They also make errors that seem to be based on the visual appearance of the word, mispronouncing it for another that looks quite similar, such as saying "perfume" for "perform" and "signal" when asked to read "single", and derivational errors, where they misread the word as another one grammatically derived from it, such as saying "performance" instead of "performing" and "entertain" instead of "entertainment". Perhaps unsurprisingly, they also make what are called mixed errors, where the word said is related to the target in both meaning and sound (e.g. saying "late" for "last").

In these respects deep dyslexia is very similar to another acquired disorder known as phonological dyslexia, but deep dyslexia is characterised by the presence of a very curious sort of error known as *semantic paralexia*. When a person makes a semantic paralexia, they pronounce a word as though it's related in meaning to the one they're trying to read. A few examples should make this clear.

> Daughter is read as "sister".
> Kill is read as "hate".
> Rose is read as "flower".
> Sergeant is read as "soldier".

They find words referring to more imageable concepts easier to read than words referring to less imageable ones. Imageability is simply how easy it is to form a mental image of the thing the word refers to. Close your eyes, sit back, and try to form images of these words: "poppy", "cloud", "dog"; now try the same with "justice", "truth", "knowledge". The difference in the ease with which you can form an image should be striking.

Semantic paralexias seem mysterious enough by themselves, but the really interesting thing about these symptoms is that they always occur together in deep dyslexia. If a patient has the defining characteristic of making semantic paralexias, they will also always have difficulty with non-words, grammatical words, and also make visual errors, and so on (although the proportion of types of error might vary from patient to patient). Why should this be? At first sight semantic paralexias look like a completely different sort of thing altogether from visual errors and the type of part of speech. There's no apparent reason why they should all occur together. For some time researchers struggled to find an explanation for this pattern. Deep dyslexia is one of the most severe of the acquired reading disorders, and some researchers argued that it's the outcome of a highly damaged system trying to read normally (Morton & Patterson, 1980). Although this approach sounds very plausible, it lacks detail, and doesn't explain why things go together as they do. Other researchers adopted a completely different approach, noting that as deep dyslexia is found when a patient has extensive damage to the left hemisphere with the loss of much of the brain that normally deals with reading, perhaps it doesn't reflect the normal reading system struggling bravely on at all, but reflects the performance of a much inferior system. One suggestion was that it reflects the performance of a right-hemisphere reading system that's normally suppressed by the much more effective reading system, but can come to the fore when the usual left-hemisphere system is virtually obliterated (Coltheart, 1980; Zaidel & Peters, 1981). This hypothesis does have some appealing aspects, because we know from various sources that the right hemisphere of the brain can read in a very limited way but makes many semantic errors; however, it can't account for the precise range of symptoms found in deep dyslexia, and in particular cannot explain why all the other symptoms occur in addition to semantic paralexias.

We're not much further forward in explaining the pattern of reading difficulties in deep dyslexia. It took a sophisticated computer simulation of meaning and how we access meaning in reading to illuminate the problem, and also to show how powerful a system based on decompositional semantics can be at explaining normal performance but also how brain damage can disrupt the system. Warning! The next section is hard going, and might need to be read a few times. It's worth it though.

Hinton and Shallice (1991) produced a computer simulation of aspects of reading, focusing on how we get to the meaning of a word from print. In their connectionist model, they used many simple processing units arranged in layers, with each unit in one layer connected to every unit in the level above. In the lowest level there were 28 units representing *graphemes*, the smallest unit of printed language that can make a difference to the meaning of a word. This is more or less a fancy way of saying a letter – such as "c", "o", "a", and "t". Hinton and Shallice used 28 graphemes rather than 26 because they also wanted to represent information about the place of the letter in the word. So the input level is a way of representing the visual appearance of the printed word.

The output level was 68 units, each corresponding to a semantic feature. These features were things like "mammal", "has-legs", "brown", "main-shape-2D", "soft", and "fierce". Now no one would pretend that human semantic features are anything like these, but the underlying principle is the same. These features were sufficient to encode the meanings of 40 short words such as "cat", "cot", "cow", "rat", and "bed". So, for example, the meaning of "cat" would correspond to the positive activation of the semantic features "max-size-foot-to-two-yards", "main-shape-3D", "has-legs", "moves", "mammal", "fierce", "carnivore", among others. The idea is that when we read, we activate the appropriate letters, or graphemic input units, and out comes the right meaning, or pattern of activation on the semantic units.

The model was trained to produce approximately the right output to any given input. In this sort of model the outputs don't have to be exactly right, they just have to be good enough – as long as the output is closer to the target output than the semantic representation of another word, that's the meaning that will be "accessed". The model was trained using a learning algorithm known as back-propagation. We've met this technique before. Each connection in the network has a weight or connection strength associated with it. We apply activation to the input unit and activation flows along the connections to the output units. Suppose we had a very simple network where we wired whole words directly to semantic features. So when we pressed the switch for CAT the connection strength to "has-legs", "moves", "mammal", and so on, would be +1, ensuring that those semantic features then light up at the other end, and the connection strengths to "sweet", "tastes-strong", and "made-of-wood" would be zero, because we don't want those features to light up. The Hinton and Shallice network is much more complicated than that, because it has to learn to produce the right semantic outputs for 40 words based on the input of their letters. So the input pattern CAT has to activate a very different output pattern from COT even though there's a lot of overlap in the letters. In addition, to learn material like this it's been shown that we must have an intermediate level of units (called the hidden units) that just mediate between the input and output. Hinton and Shallice used 40 of these (the exact number isn't critical). That means that the complete network had nearly 4000 connections in it – which is one reason why this sort of approach wasn't really feasible until powerful computers were readily available. The network starts off with random connection strengths (between plus and minus 0.3), and would there-fore at first produce utter rubbish. It's trained to produce the right patterns, more or less, by repetitively presenting all the inputs to the network, seeing what the network outputs for that particular input, comparing it to what it should output, and grad-ually changing the connection strengths so that the next time the output it produces is a bit more like what it should be. It then moves on to the next input. This whole process is then repeated perhaps many thousands of times until a criterion of good performance is reached: the network produces the appropriate semantic output for each word it's presented with. The network has been taught to read.

No one is claiming that humans learn anything by back-propagation, although the process of learning by gradually reducing the errors we make has some plausi-bility to it. The important thing is that back-propagation provides modellers with a means of constructing networks without having to craft every aspect by hand. Indeed, with a network of this complexity, it would be near impossible to do so.

In fact the model was even more complicated. There's something unsatisfac-tory about being so dictatorial about exactly what the semantic units should be doing. It would be nice if the system could learn something about how the semantic units are related to each other – for example, that mammals can move but can't be made of glass. We want the semantic units to have some interdependencies. Also, at first the network didn't work terribly well with the structure I've just described. It tended to confuse similar inputs – it tended to create semantic outputs for words like "cat" and "cot" that are visually similar, unless the network was given a huge amount of learning. Hinton and Shallice therefore introduced another layer of units, connected just to the semantic features, called "clean-up units". In fact there's a feedback loop between the semantic units and the clean-up units (Figure 5.3). This type of network is called a *recurrent network*, and the result is a system that can

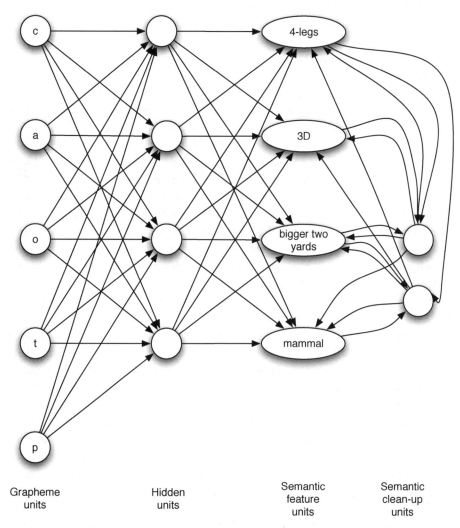

FIGURE 5.3 Simplified portion of the Hinton and Shallice connectionist network model of deep dyslexia. The figure gives some idea of the complexity of the model. There's an input level of graphemes representing the visual appearance of the word, a level of hidden units essential for the model to be able to learn, and an output level of semantic features representing a word's meaning. The semantic features are connected to clean-up units in both directions, enabling the semantic system to develop structure with experience

learn more efficiently and develop its own semantic structure, learning regularities in the semantic representation of words.

Now we have a system that has both learned to read and developed its own semantic representations. It's a functioning adult reader, albeit in a very limited way. How can we simulate the effects of brain damage? There are several ways, which we can call *lesioning* the network – in just the same way as brains are lesioned. We can randomly reset some of the connection weights to zero, or a random value, and of course there are types of connection (input to hidden, hidden to output, and semantic to clean-up) we could disrupt. The details of how we lesion turn out not to be too important, although damage to the connections involving the clean-up units is the most interesting.

The advantage of connectionist models such as Hinton and Shallice's is that they display what we call *graceful degradation*. If you remove one transistor from your computer, it will stop working altogether. That's not graceful. But if you take a trained connectionist network and damage it just a little, tiny bit, you probably won't notice any difference. As you increase the amount of damage, the network starts to make errors. What's more, these errors aren't random, as we shall see. The more you damage it, the more errors it makes. Of course, there comes a point when it behaves terribly, and another when it behaves randomly; if you zero every connection then it won't work at all. But this degradation of performance is a gradual one.

When you inflict a moderate amount of damage to the Hinton and Shallice network, it makes errors like the semantic paralexias of a deep dyslexic. For example, given the visual input corresponding to the word "cot", it produces the semantic output corresponding to (or at least closest to) the word "bed"; it might say "dog" for "cat" and "hip" for "rib".

Perhaps this outcome isn't too surprising; after all, the network was trained to associate meaning with visual appearance, so damage to it is going to disrupt that matching. It's the fact that the lesioned network systematically produces semantic errors, rather than some random output, that's intriguing. But that is by no means all: it also produces visual errors, such as saying "cot" for "cat" and "log" for "dog". Now that is surprising – why should the visual appearance of words matter?

The explanation illuminates the way in which humans represent meaning. Remember that the clean-up units allow the semantic features to discover structure among themselves. It's this structure that's important. We've moved away from the simple presence or absence of semantic features to something much more complex and interesting. The structure of our semantic space is best thought of using a visual analogy or two. Imagine you have a bowl and drop a marble into it. It lands on the side. Where will it end up? It will of course roll to the bottom of the bowl. It's obvious that wherever you drop the marble into the bowl, wherever it hits the side, it will roll to the bottom. The bottom of the bowl is called an *attractor*. Semantic space in Hinton and Shallice's simulations ends up being structured in the same way; you can think of semantic space as a landscape, seen from a plane, a rolling countryside with many valleys separated by mountains. If from your plane you drop a football, it will land and then roll to the lowest point in the valley nearby – the nearest attractor. The lowest point in the valley is the semantic attractor, and the football the input from visual processing. What brain damage does is to change the landscape, at first by eroding the hills and mountains between the semantic valleys. The erosion could lead to the ball ending up in a different place. When you see "cat", the ball should end up in the semantic attractor corresponding to the meaning of "cat", but damage to the scenery means that it might land in the basin of another meaning; remember it's not where the ball lands that's important, but the attractor. It's obvious that valleys nearby in the landscape will be of closely related meanings, so although the ball for "cat" lands in the same place, it might end up in a damaged landscape at the bottom of the valley for "dog" or "rat".

I think this account of why we get semantic errors is straightforward and intuitively clear, but it's far less obvious why we should get visual errors as well. The key point to understanding the explanation is to appreciate the importance of it not being where the ball lands that's important, but where it ends up, and that balls landing in places that are very close together could end up a long way apart. The key insight is that the system learns in a way such that the visually similar representations (like cat and cot) initially point to quite close points in semantic space; the clean-up units then ensure that the ball falls to the proper valley. It's as though the scenery has some wide valleys separated by peaks, and the ball is directed on to the peaks. These are some way away from the valley bottoms, but gravity will do its work and guide the ball to the appropriate valley bottom. But damage to the system erodes the area where the balls first land, so once again, although they land in the same place, they will fall into the wrong valley, but because of the initial mappings this valley might be one of a word related in appearance or one related in meaning. Of course, a word related in both meaning and appearance will have even more potent attractors, explaining why we get so many mixed errors.

The "landscape" is much more complex than this analogy of a landscape suggests, and we would find it impossible to visualise. Because each semantic feature can have an activation level that varies continuously, our semantic landscape has as many dimensions as we have features. It sounds like one of those fantastic theories of modern physics. It does though help to explain what might be the puzzling feature, that landing at an initial point in semantic space can take you to both visually and semantically related attractors. This puzzle is only a problem in two- or three-dimensional space; this behaviour arises as a consequence of the geometry of multidimensional space. (I did say psycholinguistics was hard.)

The model can explain another striking aspect of deep dyslexia: the imageability effect, where words are more likely to read correctly the easier it is to form a mental image of the related concept (so "rose" is more imageable than "abstraction"). In this approach, the high-imageability word has more active semantic features underlying its meaning than a low-imageability one. The more concrete and imageable a word, the richer is its semantic representation. So in the model the word "post" needs 16 features to specify its meaning, but the word "past" has just two (has-duration and refers-to-time). Semantic representations underlain by many features are going to be more robust to damage, and will be able to pass on more activation to the next processing stage, that of producing the sounds of the words; semantic representations underlain by few active features are less robust and can pass on less activation.

I've spent some time with this model because although it is a model of a specific neuropsychological disorder, it shows how we can develop the semantic feature approach to construct a coherent and plausible account of how the mind deals with meaning. If we scale up the model to human cognition, the semantic representation becomes even more complex, but the same principles apply. The underlying semantic features will be much more numerous and, as I said earlier, likely to be abstract and not necessarily with any straightforward linguistic correspondence. They also provide contact with the perceptual system, which "earths" the semantic system in the real world. Word meanings still correspond to semantic attractors. What happens in language acquisition is that the child abstracts semantic features, and the attractors gradually come to resemble those of adult speakers. Note that in this approach not everyone's semantic space will look exactly the same; all that needs to happen is that our attractors correspond enough for us to be able to communicate. In the terminology introduced earlier, the attractors are the denotations of meaning. Differences in the shape of semantic space give us differences in connotations. This variability is in fact desirable; we all have slightly different associations to particular words, and this approach captures those differences. You might be very fond of tarantulas, although the thought makes me shiver, but we can still talk about them (just) and be confident that we're talking about the same thing.

How can we explain what goes wrong in dementia?

The semantic feature approach explains another neuropsychological disorder in a very straightforward way. The neurodegenerative diseases that fall under the umbrella term "dementia", of which Alzheimer's disease is the best known, display a number of psychological problems. Although the exact cause of dementia isn't known (and there are several types, and there are probably several different causes), the basic pattern is the same: a progressive loss of cognitive and motor functions. The brain of a person with Alzheimer's disease shows a loss in the number of neurons and the presence of tangles and plaques (where the nerve cells become bunched up and knotted together, and surrounded by dead cells and deposits of protein). The earliest symptoms of Alzheimer's disease include subtle difficulties in planning and loss of memory, particularly for recently learned things. Language is noticeably affected by dementia from quite early on, with difficulty in remembering names and a diminishing vocabulary; the grammatical rules seem relatively well preserved. It's this loss of vocabulary and the increasing inability to remember the names of things that's of interest here. (Don't worry, some difficulty in remembering names is an aspect of normal ageing, too.) Given pictures of common objects to name, people with moderate dementia will struggle. What could explain the difficulty in naming and the shrinking vocabulary? Given that dementia involves progressive loss of neurons, I think the most obvious explanation is that the loss of brain matter means that the person is losing their semantic features.

Researchers have modelled the effects of the progressive loss of semantic features with a connectionist model that shares many feature of the Hinton and Shallice model. Tippett and Farah (1994) constructed a model centred around 32 semantic feature units. These were connected on one side to 16 units that represented the spoken names, and on the other to 16 units that represented the visual appearance of a small set of objects. The model was trained so that activation of an input pattern corresponding to a particular object gave rise to the right pattern of semantic activation, in turn producing the correct name for that object in the name units. Similarly, the model was trained so that the activation of the name units gave rise to the appropriate semantic representation. After training, the model was damaged or *lesioned* by removing semantic units at random.

As you would by now expect, destroying semantic units impaired naming, and the degradation in performance was graceful in that a small amount of damage impaired naming ability, but didn't destroy it completely. As the amount of damage increased, naming performance deteriorated. But the beauty of connectionist models is that they show us how things we might not think are related can in fact be so. The lesioned network had more difficulty with less common names than more frequent ones (frequency had been implemented by giving more training to high-frequency names than to low-frequency ones). The damaged network became very sensitive to the clarity of the visual input pattern; if a weak pattern was presented, corresponding to a degraded image, naming was even worse – and it's been known for some time that the naming ability of people with dementia is sensitive to the quality of the picture; they do better with colour photographs than black-and-white photographs, which in turn lead to better performance than line drawings. Finally, naming could be improved by providing a bit of help with the sound of the name; naming by people with dementia is improved by giving them the hint of the initial sound of the word ("l" for "lion", a technique known as *phonological priming*). So a simple model can give rise to sophisticated and realistic behaviour. The central idea, though, is that the vocabulary and naming problems in dementia are caused by the progressive loss of semantic features.

How is semantic memory organised?

One of the most peculiar neuropsychological deficits of meaning was first studied in detail by Warrington and Shallice in 1984. They noticed that their patient JBR performed much better at naming inanimate objects than animate ones. So he was much better at naming pictures of vehicles than of animals. His difficulties went beyond naming, though, because he also found it more difficult to understand words denoting living things than non-living things, matching the right picture to the name, and even producing a gesture appropriate to the word. This pattern of results, where a patient shows good performance with members of one semantic category and poor performance with another, is called a *semantic category-specific disorder*. It later emerged that other patients show the reverse pattern, performing better with animate things compared to inanimate (Warrington & McCarthy, 1987). The most obvious explanation for these findings is that knowledge of living things is stored in a different part of the brain from knowledge about non-living things.

Although category specificity involving the living–non-living distinction turns out to be a relatively common one (although these disorders are in absolute terms rare), several more specific disorders have been found. One patient had particular difficulty just with fruit and vegetables (Hart et al., 1985); others show problems with proper names (Semenza & Zettin, 1988).

At face value, these deficits suggest that special parts of the brain store different types of information: knowledge about living things in one part and about non-living things in another. It was immediately apparent that this simple explanation was unlikely to be right. JBR's naming was more complex than this initial picture suggests. For a start, he was good at naming parts of the body, even though these are parts of living things. He was also poor at naming several types of non-living things: musical instruments, precious stones, types of material, and foods. The reliable co-occurrence of these categories with living things is difficult to explain: why should damage to the part of the brain storing knowledge of living things also lead to problems with musical instruments and gem stones?

One explanation is that these categories have something in common, and what the brain damage has disrupted is the processing of this shared characteristic, rather than knowledge of the categories themselves. What might this common characteristic be? What do living things, gemstones, foods, musical instruments, and materials have in common that other artefacts don't? One possibility is that we distinguish and describe the first group primarily in terms of their appearance, while we describe artefacts in terms of what we do with them. To give a very simple example, think about how you'd define a "giraffe": it might be something like "an African mammal with a very long neck and long legs and a tan skin with spots and little horns and a happy face that chews the leaves from the top of the woodland canopy", and then contrast that with a definition for a "chair", which might be something like "a piece of furniture with a seat and back used for sitting in". Contrast "diamond" ("extremely hard, highly reflective form of carbon") with "hammer" ("a hand tool with a head that's used for striking things hard"). I'm not saying that the animate and related things are defined just in terms of their sensory attributes and the artefacts their function, but that animate things depend relatively more on sensory information (Warrington & McCarthy, 1987; Warrington & Shallice, 1984). This observation is supported by an analysis of a large number of dictionary definitions: for living things, the ratio of perceptual to functional attributes is just under 8 to 1, but for non-living things it's much lower, about 1.5 to 1 (Farah & McClelland, 1991).

The idea that different categories depend differentially on sensory and functional information is called the *sensory-functional theory*. So what gets damaged in these patients isn't the categories themselves, but the ability to access the sensory or functional information that underlies them. Imaging studies of blood flow in the brain show that the temporal lobes of the brain don't respond differentially to living and non-living things, but different parts of the brain do respond to perceptual and non-perceptual information (Lee et al., 2002).

It wouldn't be psycholinguistics without a good argument. The American neuroscientist Alfonso Caramazza has produced robust criticisms of the sensory-functional theory. If the theory is correct, he's argued, a patient who performs badly on living things does so because of a problem in processing sensory features, and therefore will perform badly on all tasks involving living things, and on all other categories (the musical instruments, gemstones, materials, and so on) that also depend heavily on sensory information. But this isn't always the case (Caramazza & Shelton, 1998). There are patients impaired at tasks involving animals but not foodstuffs, whereas others are impaired at foodstuffs but not animals; some patients are impaired at animals but not musical instruments; and knowledge of animals can be spared or damaged independently of plants. It is of course conceivable that some categories rely more on particular sorts of sensory information than others, so what is damaged isn't a wholesale ability to deal with sensory information but just particular types of sensory information, but such an approach would need much more spelling out to be convincing. Caramazza and Shelton also point out that while the idea of sensory information has some coherence (it's just what things look, taste, smell, feel, or sound like), the category of functional information is much less coherent. The concept of "what something is used for" is very restricted; is all non-sensory information functional? What about "a long neck to reach the canopy"? "Lives in the desert"? They also point to imaging studies that suggest that different parts of the brain are in fact differentially activated when processing animals and other categories. Put very broadly, knowledge about animals is stored more towards the back of the lower left temporal lobe of the brain, while knowledge of tools is stored more towards the side, where the temporal, occipital, and parietal lobes of the brain meet (Caramazza & Shelton, 1998;

Vigliocco et al., 2004). An alternative account, the *domain-specific knowledge hypothesis* (thankfully often abbreviated to DSKH), says that because of the obvious evolutionary importance of distinguishing between living and non-living things, the brain has evolved separate mechanisms for dealing with them. So on this account knowledge about different categories is processed in different parts of the brain. Further evidence for some genetic basis to the distinction between living and non-living things comes from the study of a 16-year-old boy known as "Adam", who suffered a stroke the day after he was born. Adam has great difficulty recognising and retrieving information about living things; the fact that the damage occurred so early rules out the possibility that any learned information could have been affected. We are born with different neural systems to store knowledge about living and non-living things.

Clearly we have much to learn about how the brain represents knowledge. I don't find *where* something is stored that useful or interesting or interesting in itself. But neuroscience can tell us a great deal about the principles upon which human knowledge is constructed and stored.

What are statistical models of meaning?

The idea that everything is linked to everything else is deservedly enjoying vogue in the popular science press. Psycholinguists, with their semantic network model of

A bundle of mainly perceptual features

A bundle of mainly functional features

meaning, got there first – or at least early on. I've shown how connectionist modelling provides an account of meaning at two levels. At the the lower level we have semantic features, which capture aspects of meaning, and which are the atoms or "primitive" of thought. These are interconnected in an enormous mental network, with connections to words in one direction and sensory representations in the other. The features are also connected to each other in a way that enables the mind to discover structure and regularity among them. This ability enables us to view semantic representations at a higher level as multidimensional landscapes, with peaks and valleys, and the meaning of words corresponding to semantic attractors.

An approach that's very similar in spirit is called *latent semantic analysis* (Landauer & Dumais, 1997). The motivation of this approach is that meaning arises from co-occurrence. As we're exposed to language, from infancy on, some words tend to occur frequently with other words, some occasionally with other words, and some combinations occur rarely or never. For example, "doctor" and "nurse", "bread" and "butter", and "dog" and "cat" are highly associated; "proton" and "xylophone" might never have occurred in proximity before I wrote this (although rather to my amazement a Google search with both terms present in pages generated over 5,300 hits). For any word, we can identify the frequency of occurrence of all others within a certain distance.

Landauer and Dumais worked out (using a computer; this approach is another that would be unthinkable without a good fast computer) how often every word in an encyclopaedia co-occurred with every other word in the same encyclopaedia entry. The encyclopaedia contained over 4.5 million words, made up of 60,768 different words, arranged in 30,473 entries. You could represent this co-occurrence in a huge, 60,768 by 60,768 grid. Each cell would signify how many times that word pair co-occurred in the same encyclopaedia entry (the score for xylophone and proton probably being zero). They then simplified this down to 300 dimensions. Words with similar patterns on these 300 dimensions should have very similar meanings, and highly similar patterns should mean that the words have very similar meanings indeed – that is, they're synonyms. Unfortunately "xylophone" doesn't have synonyms, but you can play with online synonym generators to discover that synonyms of "happy" include "blessed" and "blissful", and those of "miserable" include "abject" and "wretched". The synonyms generated by their model corresponded very well with published lists of synonyms. We know that we're faster to recognise a word if it's preceded by one similar in meaning – so we're faster to identify "butter" if we see "bread" immediately beforehand. The degree to which recognition is speeded up depends on how closely related the two words are, and this distance, and therefore the magnitude of the recognition benefit, is predicted quite well by this sort of multidimensional analysis of 300 million words taken from online messages (Lund et al., 1995).

This approach captures aspects of meaning, but it's a much bigger step to say that this is how meaning originates in humans. Something seems to be missing from the account: the real world. You can't learn language just by listening to a stream of words; children pay a great deal of attention to the environment – as indeed we all do. Meaning is more than association to other words; it's grounding in perception and action too. This claim does not deny that the shape of semantic space isn't modified by co-occurrence information – it's probably one of the sources of information that influences the way clean-up units structure semantic space. This type of statistical analysis is interesting and useful, and says a lot about how words connect to words, but not how words connect to the world.

What's grounding?

Even the best dictionaries have an element of circularity about them. However careful the lexicographers are, eventually they have to end up defining words in terms of other words. The same limitation is present in computer databases. And it would be very difficult to take a robot seriously unless it had some way of taking in information from the environment in real time, such as robo-eyes and robo-ears, no matter how wonderfully structured and enormous its database. Humans are special in that meanings ultimately connect with the world. I've said several times before that our internal representations are *grounded* in our perceptions, actions, and feelings. Concepts have very direct links to the world (Barsalou, 2003, 2008; Glenberg, 2007). Our minds don't work in isolation – they are *situated* within the world. According to this view, concepts and meaning aren't just abstract, amodal things: thinking about real-world objects, for example, involves the visual perceptual system. Furthermore, according to the situated cognition idea, concepts are less stable than has usually been thought, varying depending on the context and situation. Barsalou (2003) had people perform two tasks simultaneously: using their hands to imagine performing some manual operations, and identifying the properties of concepts. Sometimes the actions being performed were relevant to the concepts being described, in which case the participants were more likely to mention related aspects of the concepts. For example, if they were performing the action of opening a drawer, they were more likely to mention clothes likely to be found inside a clothes dresser than otherwise.

There is some evidence that our mental situation in the world takes a very concrete form, in that there are direct links between representations of perceptions and actions. What happens in the brain when we hear the word "kick"? We see Wernicke's region, the part of the left temporal lobe of the brain that we know plays a vital role in accessing word meanings, light up like a Christmas tree when seen using brain imaging. It would be worrying if it didn't. We also see some activation in Broca's area, a region towards the front of the left hemisphere that we know to be involved in producing speech. Perhaps there are echoes here of the behaviourist idea that thought is language, but this result isn't too surprising. What is very surprising is that the functional magnetic resonance imaging (fMRI) scans show that there is activation in the parts of the brain that deal with motor control – and the motor control of the leg at that (Glenberg, 2007; Hauk et al., 2004). It's as though when we hear "kick", we give a little mental kick. Similarly, if we hear a word like "catch", we see some activation in the parts of the brain that control the movements of the hand, and if you hear "I eat an apple", you get activation of the parts that control the mouth (Tettamanti et al., 2005). This motor activity peaks very quickly – within 20 milliseconds of the peak activation in the parts of the brain traditionally thought to be involved in recognising words and processing meaning (Pulvermüller et al., 2003), which is so fast that it would appear to rule out the explanation that people are just consciously reflecting on or rehearsing what they've just heard. This idea that thinking or understanding language causes activation in the parts of the brain to do with how the body deals with these concepts is called *embodiment*. Language is grounded to the world, and that grounding happens in the parts of the brain that deal with perception and action. Just like you'd think.

Chapter 6

Words

THE FIRST STEP IN understanding both spoken and written language is doing something with words. Words are the building blocks of language.

I don't want to claim that we necessarily understand language on a strictly word-by-word basis. Sometimes we might use information from other words to identify some words. If you hear "The cat chased the [slurred speech sound] -ouse", you'll probably decide the final word is "mouse" rather than "house" or "louse". The extent to which surrounding information influences the identification of words is one of the most important controversies in the field. But to get to the point of wondering whether it's a mouse or a louse, you have to have identified most of the other words in the utterance. We say that word recognition is primarily a bottom-up or *data-driven* process. We're trying to understand what's in front of us, visually or aurally, primarily on the basis of what's in front of us. The alternative to data-driven processing is top-down processing, where we use general knowledge or hunches about what we're processing to identify it. Although there might be some role for it, clearly top-down processing by itself would be a terribly inefficient way to understand language. We're not going to get far by ignoring what the other person says and claim we know what they mean because we think we do (although in my experience many people act this way). So recognising words and understanding language has got to be mainly data-driven. The question is what is the role of top-down processing – if any.

For once we don't need a dictionary to tell us what a word is, but the rest of the process isn't as clear. Note that I began by saying "doing something with words". I've also been a bit sneaky using words such as "recognise", and "understand" and "identify", without really explaining them. It's time to unpack these ideas a little. Let's think about our goal when listening or reading: it's getting enough meaning from the words to be able to construct a representation of the meaning of the sentence, which we can then use to do something with. *Recognising* a word means you've made a decision in some way that the word is familiar; you know that NIGHT is a word and you've seen it before, and you know that NITE isn't. Strictly speaking, recognition doesn't necessarily entail anything more: you could in principle decide something's a word you know and not do anything more with it. *Identifying* a word means that you've made some commitment to what the word is – sufficiently so to be able to initiate some response. *Understanding* a word means that you access the word's meaning. *Naming* a word is accessing the sound of a word, which in turn could mean saying it aloud, or saying it to yourself. When we're reading, do we automatically and necessarily access the sounds of the word? And then there's a term much liked by psycholinguists, *lexical access*: that means accessing our mental dictionary, the lexicon, and obtaining potentially all knowledge about the word – its meaning, sound, appearance, and syntactic information about it.

Psycholinguists have used several tasks to investigate word processing, and these tasks relate to these distinctions I've just made. One of the most popular tasks is the *lexical decision task*; imagine you're sitting in front of a computer screen, and a string of letters is flashed up in front of you. You have to press one key if you think the string of letters forms a word, and another if you think it's a non-word. So you might see NIGHT or NITE. Researchers measure how long it takes the person to make their decision, and also how many errors they make. In a lexical decision, you don't have to access the meaning or the sound of the word, you just have to say whether it's familiar or not – whether it's in that set of things you know to be words; you *might* access the sound or meaning, but you don't have to. Contrast lexical decision with the *naming task*, where you see a word on the screen and have to say it aloud, and researchers measure how long it takes you to start speaking. In naming all you have to do is pronounce it, which means that you don't *have* to access the meaning or even decide whether it's familiar or not; and even if you do access the meaning, we don't know that it happens before you start naming. There are other tasks, but these two illustrate the difficulties involved in talking about word processing: access to meaning, the sound of a word, and its familiarity could happen at different times, and we have to be clear about what we think we're measuring.

Many researchers believe that there's a "magic moment" in word processing, where a person has recognised a word but hasn't yet accessed the meaning. Put slightly more formally, this is the point at which a word becomes sufficiently activated for a person to carry out some sort of response to it, but this point is before we start to access the meaning. As Balota (1990) points out, this assumption sounds like a reasonable one, and at first sight how could it be otherwise? Surely we have to identify the word before we can access its meaning? No, we don't have to, because we could start accessing something about meaning as soon as there's some information about the word coming through, and this meaning might be used to influence the identification process. If this idea is correct, then we have to be very careful about what we conclude from lexical decision and naming, because these judgements might be influenced by meaning.

You can tell by now that word processing isn't going to be straightforward. We have to be very careful about what tasks we use to study it and what assumptions we make. We can't assume that when we start naming a word we've accessed its meaning, or that we can decide whether something is familiar or not before we access the meaning. Even "accessing the meaning" is a phrase full of pitfalls. When we hear or read a word, like TIGER, how much of its meaning do we access? Must we access everything we know about it? Do we automatically and necessarily retrieve how many legs it's got and that it's got stripes and whiskers? I think two features of word processing make our life easier: most of the time it's just "good enough", so we only do as much with the incoming words as needed to get by on, and it's got a statistical or probabilistic element to it so that, some of the time at least, we're almost just guessing. One problem with the area of research into word processing is that it's been dominated by metaphors that we have come to believe to be true. We talk about searching the lexicon as though we're looking through a dictionary, and then we have models of lexical access based on a dictionary search.

We know that many factors can influence the ease with which we can recognise a word (Harley, 2008). Obviously the clarity of the perceptual stimulus matters; it's going to be more difficult to recognise a very quiet, mumbled word spoken against a lot of background noise than a nicely enunciated loud one spoken against a background of silence. As I've mentioned before, the frequency of a word is an extremely important variable in word processing – the more common a word is, the easier it is to recognise. It's thought that the age at which we are first exposed to a word – a variable called age-of-acquisition – is independently important, such that we're faster to process words we learn earlier. Having seen a word in the recent past makes it easier to identify. Finally, I must mention semantic priming – we find it easier to identify a word if it is preceded by one related in meaning (such as DOCTOR and NURSE).

How do we recognise spoken words?

Have you ever tried listening to someone speaking a language you don't know? You can't even make the words out. I find it difficult even with a language I know a tiny bit about, like Spanish or French; listening to a native speaker talking at their normal speed is a chastening experience. I can occasionally make out the odd word, but mostly it's just a string of sounds. It's the same problem babies face when learning language: segmentation. The sounds of speech are usually slurred together. Of course there are some pauses, and small gaps after some sounds (those called stop consonants, that necessitate closing the airstream very briefly, such as p, b, t, d), but although speech is rapid, we're very effective at processing it. If we're given a mixed-up sequence of buzzes, hisses, tones, and vowels, we can only distinguish the order of the sounds if they come at a rate slower than 1.5 sounds a second; but we can understand speech at the rate of 20 sounds a second, and sometimes faster (Warren & Warren, 1970). We're good at processing speech.

The basic unit of speech is called the *phoneme*. A phoneme is the smallest unit of a language that makes a difference to the meaning. So the sounds "p", "b", "r", and "c" are all phonemes, because if we swap them around we get different words with "pat", "bat", "rat", and "cat". By convention, we put phonemes in sloping lines, like this: /p/. Phonemes vary from language to language; /l/ and /r/ are different phonemes in English (as testified by the difference between "lot" and "rot"), but not in Japanese. Other languages make distinctions that English doesn't. You might want to try the following in private. Put a hand in front of your mouth and say the word "pin"; you should be able to feel a puff of air accompanying the "p" sound. Now say "spin"; there isn't any such puff. Physically they're different sounds – we say the "p" in "pin" is aspirated and that in "spin" is unaspirated – but the difference isn't a critical one in English. In some languages, such as Thai and Korean, it is; whether or not the "p" is aspirated can change the meaning of the word.

This point illustrates the fact that a phoneme can vary considerably, which is another factor that makes speech processing difficult. To make matters even more complex, the precise sound changes depending on what other sounds it's surrounded by: the /b/ phonemes in "bill", "ball", "able", and "rub" are all acoustically slightly different. This phenomenon is called *co-articulation*. It happens because as we say any sound, the articulatory apparatus is moving, getting ready to produce the next sound (and indeed has moved into position having just produced the previous one). Co-articulation could be of some assistance, because it means that a sound gives information not just about itself but also about surrounding sounds, but it is another source of variability in sound. And of course, no two people speak in exactly the same way – in addition to systematic differences such as age, gender, and regional accent, there are individual differences. All these ways in which sounds vary depending on the context also make speech recognition very difficult. They rule out models of sound recognition based on templates, where we compare each sound to an internal idealised phoneme, because the incoming sounds are just too variable.

Even though speech is highly variable, we're not that sensitive to the differences. Of course we can identify the gross characteristics of the speech, enough to be able to identify them, their age, and gender, but we don't hear all these variations in sound as different phonemes. To the English ear an aspirated and unaspirated "p" are just /p/s. And what happens if we hear a sound that's intermediate between two sounds? We categorise it as one thing or another. We simplify what we hear.

It's worth dwelling on this point about intermediate sounds a little more. Let's take as an example pairs of sounds like /p/ and /b/, and /t/ and /d/. The words in these pairs lie on the ends of a continuum. The difference between the ends of the continuum, between a /p/ and a /b/, is called their *voice onset time*. With *voiced* consonants (/b/, /d/), the vocal chords start vibrating (you can feel them vibrate if you put your fingertips to your throat) as soon as the lips close (/b/) or the tongue goes to that little ridge above the teeth (/d/); the voice onset time for voiced consonants is close to 0 milliseconds. With voiceless consonants (/p/, /t/) there's a bit of a delay (60 milliseconds or so) before the vocal chords start vibrating. This small difference in voice onset time is all that separates a /p/ from a /b/ and a /t/ from a /d/. But what happens if you hear a sound halfway between, with a voice onset time of 30 milliseconds? Do we hear a sound halfway between a /p/ and a /b/?

No, we don't, we hear either a /p/ or a /b/; there's no halfway house, in that all variants of the same phoneme sound the same to us, a phenomenon known as *categorical perception* (Liberman et al., 1957). Which we hear varies from person to person and depending on the circumstances. The closer the voice onset time to the 0 milliseconds end of the continuum, the more likely we are to categorise it as /b/, and the nearer to the 60 milliseconds end the more likely we are to categorise it as /p/, but there's no in-between stage where we hear something halfway. If we go up the onset time continuum we switch suddenly from hearing /b/ to /p/. And the same is true of /d/ and /t/. Although there is a distinct boundary between the categories, it isn't fixed. We can move the boundary up or down by fatiguing the feature detectors that identify the sound by repeated exposure to a sound from one end of the continuum; so if you hear /p/ repeated several times, you become a bit more likely to identify a sound halfway along the continuum as a /b/ (Eimas & Corbit, 1973). The categorical perception of sounds is probably a result of the way in which the brain is wired rather than being a skill we learn; babies as young as one month show it (Eimas et al., 1987). It isn't even unique to humans: chinchillas, a cute sort of little South American rodent, categorise syllables such as "ta" and "da" in just the way humans do (Kuhl & Miller, 1975). The phenomenon of categorical perception is not even restricted to speech, as musicians appear to perceive musical intervals categorically (Siegel & Siegel, 1977).

Another possible source of assistance when listening to speech is the knowledge we have about what the speaker might mean – what we call the context. The importance of context is demonstrated powerfully by a famous psycholinguistic phenomenon known as the *phoneme restoration effect* (Warren, 1970; Warren & Warren, 1970). You hear the following sentences:

> It was found that the *eel was on the orange.
> It was found that the *eel was on the shoe.
> It was found that the *eel was on the axle.
> It was found that the *eel was on the table.

They're constructed by splicing tapes together (so easily done digitally these days; I wonder at the perseverance of researchers having to do these experiments without the full panoply of modern computing tools) so that the only word that differs is the final one. The asterisk represents a 0.12 second portion of speech that's excised from the tape and replaced with a cough. People then say they hear "peel" in the first instance, "heel" in the second, "wheel" in the third, and "meal" in the fourth. They don't hear there's anything missing, and can't even reliably locate the cough in the right place. People say they actually hear the sound that isn't there. The only explanation for this is that the "top down" knowledge of the word is affecting the perception of the speech stream. The precise sound doesn't matter – buzzes and tones elicit the effect just as well, and you can excise larger amounts of the word and still get the effect. There are limits on how much and when people will restore, though: you can't get away with just replacing the phoneme with a short period of silence; people notice that.

The influence of context on speech perception isn't restricted to speech; what we see can influence what we hear, as demonstrated by the McGurk effect (McGurk & MacDonald, 1976). Suppose the sound "ba" is played to you through head-phones while you simultaneously see a video of someone saying the sound "ga". What you hear isn't the sound "ba" at all, but a sound in between the one you should hear and the one you hear": "da". The McGurk effect demonstrates an interaction between visual and auditory perception; we are using information about the shape of a speaker's lips to deduce (of course, not consciously) what sound they are producing, and this information in turn influences what we hear.

So although there's a great deal of variability in speech, we have ways of simplifying that variability. We just deal with categories of sound, rather than every subtle shade of variation, and use the context to narrow down the search.

I want to examine briefly a couple of models of speech recognition. They share the underlying idea that when we hear speech, the sounds of words activate words that could possibly correspond to the perceptual input. I said earlier that the concept of activation is a powerful one, and it pays its way here.

The *cohort model* of William Marslen-Wilson emphasises the way speech unfolds across time (Gaskell & Marslen-Wilson, 2002; Marslen-Wilson, 1990; Marslen-Wilson & Welsh, 1978). You're listening to a word, and of course you

don't hear it all at once, you hear it sound by sound. So suppose you're sitting in a lovely drawing room watching an old lady sewing, and she says the following:

Be a dear and pass me some thread for my –

Now what could come next? The syntax provides some constraints – only an adjective or noun makes sense. Context provides others; it's most unlikely that the word coming up is going to be "elephant". So already the *cohort* of candidate words that could be next has been greatly reduced. Next you hear the first phoneme, /t/. This small amount of perceptual information makes an enormous difference and can eliminate tens of thousands of words from the cohort of candidates. What could the word be? I can only think of a few plausible candidates that could now be left in the cohort, "tablecloth", "tapestry", "togs", "tea cosy" perhaps, although some of these are less likely than others. If the next sound is "a" (as in "tapestry"), I think we're really only left with "tapestry" remaining in the cohort – the context precludes the possibility that she might be asking for some thread for her tapeworm. In this way the elimination of candidates from the cohort can be rapid, and therefore spoken word identification is very fast and effective.

All spoken words have a point at which they become unique – that is, based on perceptual information alone, we can say with absolute certainty "this word I'm hearing is tapestry, not tapeworm or tabulation". That point is called the *uniqueness point*. We can find out what each word's uniqueness point is using what's known as the *gating task*, in which participants are played increasingly large segments of a word, perhaps in 20 millisecond slices, and asked to say what word they're hearing. They start getting it right after the uniqueness point. The gating task shows the importance of context; people need on average 333 milliseconds to identify a word in isolation, but only 199 milliseconds to hear a word in an appropriate context. So we're slow identifying "camel" in isolation, but much faster when we hear it in "At the zoo, the kids rode on the camel" (Grosjean, 1980).

What's in the cohort matters. If what you're hearing has a very unusual phonological form ("xy-"), the cohort of words is going to be very small, but if you hear something that has a common phonological form ("sp-"), the cohort of candidates is going to be very large. It's hardly surprising therefore that cohort size affects word recognition time; if the cohort is large, recognition is slower, and what's more, the relative frequency of all these neighbours matters. If the target word is "specious", it's as though the common words like "special" and "speech" are getting in the way. So you're faster to recognise a high-frequency word that has only low-frequency neighbours than vice versa (Goldinger et al., 1989; Marslen-Wilson, 1990).

This broad approach of activation-based models of word recognition has been implemented in a computer simulation known as TRACE (McClelland & Elman, 1986). In the TRACE model there are three levels of processing units. Each unit is very simple, simply accumulating activation from all the other units to which its connected and passing some of it on to other units. At the lowest level is a pool of phonetic features, in the middle level is a pool of phonemes, and at the highest level is a pool of words. Phonetic features are components of phonemes; for example, as we've seen, /b/ has a voiced feature, /p/ a voiceless feature; consonants are produced by constricting the vocal tract at some point; some sounds are strident, containing a burst of white noise, such as /s/ and /sh/. The details of these phonetic features needn't detain us; the important point is that it's possible to decompose phonemes into lower-level units, and specify how two phonemes differ in terms of their featural make-up. /b/ and /p/ differ, for example, by the presence and absence of voice.

In line with the principle that connectionist networks display massive inter-connection, every unit in one level is connected to every unit in the level above. However, there are three important points about these connections. First, they're bidirectional, which means that activation can flow down the network from the word level to phonemes and phonetic features as well as bottom up. Second, they're either excitatory or inhibitory. An excitatory connection is one that increases the activation level of the unit at the other end, and an inhibitory connection is one that decreases the activation level at the other end. So the phoneme /t/ has excitatory connections to TAKE and TASK, but inhibitory connections to CAKE and CASK (Figure 6.1). Third, each unit within a level is connected to all other units in that level by an inhibitory connection. All we have to do to get the model rolling is to apply activation to the input phonetic features corresponding to a word, and sit

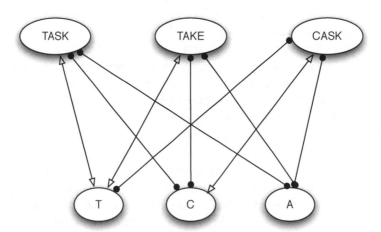

FIGURE 6.1 Portion of a TRACE-style network. This fragment simply shows some of the connections for the initial-letter position. T is in the first position of both TASK and TAKE, so the T-initial unit is connected to these units with bidirectional facilitatory connections. It isn't in CASK, so T is connected to that unit by an inhibitory connection. The reverse applies for the C-initial unit. A isn't in the initial position in any of these words (although it is of course in the second position), so the A-initial unit is connected with inhibitory connections

back and watch the activation flow up and down the network until only one word unit is left active – and that's the word the system has "recognised". Suppose we apply activation corresponding to the phonetic features unvoiced, consonant, tongue touches above the teeth; these are enough to get the /t/ phoneme going. This activation then spreads to TAKE and TASK, and these will inhibit incompatible patterns, such as CAKE and CASK. When an /s/ sound comes along a bit later, TASK will start inhibiting its competitor TAKE. Eventually only one word is left standing. Models like TRACE are called IAC models, short for interactive activation and competition. Competition is an important aspect of this network; as soon as a unit starts to pile up evidence for itself, it starts to inhibit its competitors. Truly do the rich get richer; the winner takes all.

Because activation is top-down as well as bottom-up, the model can deal with incomplete or corrupted evidence. Suppose the model is presented with a phoneme intermediate between /p/ and /b/ – the voicing feature is given 50% activation – but that is followed by -LUG. Only PLUG is a word, so that gets activated, and sends activation down to the /p/ unit, which then sends activation back down to the featural level. BLUG is not a word so /b/ doesn't get much of a look in, even though /p/ and /b/ sound very similar (differing in just the voice feature). So context exerts its influence by top-down activation spreading to lower levels. And because there's always got to be a winner, the model abhors intermediate values. It's got to be either a /p/ or a /b/ we're hearing, and one of them has got to win, so the model displays categorical perception of phonemes as well.

These models demonstrate the power of activation-based models and the usefulness of implementing your model in a computer program to show that the model really works. Often things drop out of the simulations you don't expect. Phenomena such as phoneme restoration and categorical perception of phonemes arise from the principles of top-down activation and competition; the explanations make sense, but there's nothing like demonstrating it in a computer program for reassurance. Needless to say, in psycholinguistics no model goes unchallenged. The main bone of contention here is exactly when context has its effect. Does it directly affect the very earliest, perceptual stage of processing, or much later, when we're trying to integrate what we've perceived with everything else? Is phoneme restoration a true perceptual effect, or does it reflect guessing? Can we trust what people report? The East Coast view is that perception is bottom-up, with context affecting only the later stages of processing, while the West Coast view is that context can affect early processing. The jury's still out.

The TRACE model as implemented is just a fragment of presumably what actually happens. The word units will in turn be connected in a similar way to the semantic feature units; meaning will seep back down to the word influence to supply activation to contextually appropriate words, which in turn will flow back down to the letter level, and so on. In this kind of model where activation is continually "cascading" through the system – where as soon as one unit sees evidence for itself it immediately sends out activation to all the other units to which it's connected – there can be no magic moment where we recognise a word but don't access any of its properties.

I've also been a bit vague about what "context" is. Potentially it's all the knowledge we have that could influence perception top-down. So if we're trying to identify a phoneme, it's the context of what word it could be, how the possible words fit in with the syntax of what we're hearing, our knowledge about the conversation, the situation, the weather – anything at all that could help narrow what's being said or read. And that's the problem with context: it's huge. And do we really want to override our perceptions too easily? If a lion bursts through my office door, should I act on the basis of my perception and run, or should I stop and reason with myself about the unlikeliness of this event and therefore how my perception could be wrong, while I get eaten?

How do we read?

I probably spend more time reading than talking, but I realise I'm almost certainly unusual in this respect. Writing has had a huge influence on culture and thought; by

Not the best time for a lot of top-down processing

154

Don't try this at home: cascading activation. Water is already pouring into the bowl even while it's still flowing out of the top glass

its enabling us to create and store external records of our thoughts and memories, we have increased our cognitive capacity enormously. It's impossible to imagine that civilisation could have progressed far, and that we could have developed any sophisticated technology, without written language. Indeed, the invention of writing is what separates history from prehistory.

Nevertheless, students often have the impression that a disproportionate amount of psycholinguistics is taken up with two apparently very specific topics: how we understand the sort of sentence known as the "garden path", which I'll come to in the next chapter, and how adults read single words. I used to worry about this restriction too, before, with respect to Dr Strangelove, I learned to stop worrying and love single-word recognition. If we understand how we read one word we know something about how we read them all. There is also the advantage that it's relatively easy research to carry out; these days all you need is a computer and you can carry out sophisticated priming and lexical decision experiments. And because it's easy to carry out, there's been a lot of research, so we know what's

A more conservative solution: discrete processing. The tall glass is empty; the short one is just about full and ready to pour in one go into the empty bowl

happening, and if we don't know the answer, we know the shape of the battleground, so word recognition exemplifies some of the key topics in psycholinguistics. Of course reading does involve much more than reading isolated words, so it's right not to get too carried away. In real life, we have an array of text in front of us, which means that we can jump around the text, looking back to earlier material if need be. It also means that the eye can take in information about more than one word at a time, which could be of considerable assistance in understanding them. There's now a considerable amount of evidence that when reading we can take in information about words that fall on the retina outside its most sensitive spot, the *fovea* (e.g. Kennedy & Pynte, 2005).

Recognising printed words presents a different set of problems from understanding spoken words. The words are usually (except in devious psycholinguistic experiments) fixed and unchanging in front of us for as long as we need. But we have to decide where to put our eyes to extract information from the printed page in a fairly efficient way. One thing we do know for certain is that in normal adults (those without brain damage), reading is like listening; you can't help yourself – you have to do it. You can't choose to stop the reading process halfway through once you've seen a word, in the same way that when you hear a word you can't help but understand it. That reading is mandatory is shown very clearly by the Stroop task (Stroop, 1935), in which you have to name the colour of ink a word is printed in. That sounds easy enough, but if the word is a colour name, and is different from the ink colour, you're much slower than when the name and ink colour are congruent. So naming the colour in RED (in red ink) is easy, but GREEN (in red) is hard. You can't stop yourself reading the word, and you can't stop the meaning interfering with what you're supposed to be doing.

Unlike speech, which could reasonably only have evolved once, writing seems to have been invented several times in man's history, almost certainly arising in the near and middle east, China, and the Mayan culture of ancient Mesoamerica. As speech might have evolved from gesture, writing almost certainly evolved from some simpler system, probably a means of keeping tallies of numbers.

I II III IIII IIIII

Those languages in the near and middle east originally used pictures to represent concepts, with the first probably being the cuneiform script of ancient Sumer around or before 3000BC. The well-known hieroglyphic system of ancient Egypt probably developed soon after, with the hieroglyphic system of Crete developing after that. These early systems used pictures to convey meaning, although the relation between the picture and the meaning gradually became looser, with some symbols coming to stand for sounds.

The big invention that changed western writing was the widespread adoption of the alphabetic principle, where the written symbols stand for individual sounds. The alphabet probably originally derived from the Egyptian system of hieroglyphs, but it became a central part of the Phoenician system of writing. As Phoenicia, located approximately in the modern coastal territories of Syria and Lebanon, was an important maritime trading state, the alphabet spread throughout the eastern Mediterranean. The Phoenician alphabet represented just the consonants of the language; the Greeks adopted it and added vowels. The Roman alphabet subsequently took over the Greek system, and the Roman Empire spread the alphabetic system throughout the western world. Today languages in the west are based on the Graeco-Roman alphabet, with those of China, Korea, and Japan based on the ancient Chinese system of pictures.

A legacy of this complex and multi-centred evolution is that today different languages use different means to map written words on to language. In a language such as Chinese, every word has a different symbol or combination of symbols associated with it, and you (more or less) have to learn each word separately. Such languages are called *logographic* languages. There are over 45,000 symbols in the full Chinese dictionary, although most of these are rarely used and so full literacy is possible with knowledge of under 4000. Contrast this complexity with the languages that use the *alphabetic* system, where each letter corresponds to a sound:

English of course uses just 26 letters. Even then there are different ways of mapping letters onto sound; the consonantal scripts of Hebrew and Arabic continue to represent just the consonants, with the vowels being filled in when reading. Most alphabetic languages – including English – represent both consonants and vowels. But even within these alphabetic languages, the details of the ways in which letters correspond to sounds differ. In some languages, such as Serbo-Croat, each letter corresponds to just one sound, and vice versa. We call these *regular* languages – or sometimes ones with shallow orthographies. In languages such as French, correspondences between letters and sounds are regular, but some sounds can be represented by different combinations of letters ("o", "eau", "au", "eaux", for example). In English the relation between sound and letters is complex, with some sounds being represented by different combinations of letters (consider for example "to", "too", "two", and "threw"), and some letters corresponding to different sounds (consider the "a" in "hat", "hate", and "father"). This lack of regularity makes English spelling particularly difficult to learn.

What's the dual-route model of reading?

"Xhjhhgz" is a non-word, but it's not a very interesting one. You can't pronounce it. Instead, let's take the examples of "gat", "smeat", and "nouse". You can pronounce – say aloud – these; they could be English words, but they happen not to be. We call pronounceable non-words like "gat", "smeat", and "nouse" *pseudowords* – they're like words, but aren't quite. The comedian Stanley Unwin made a decent living speaking in these, using his language Unwinese to comic effect (Elvis Presley was rather beautifully described as "wasp waist and swivel hippy"). What's more, if you ask a number of people to pronounce these pseudowords, they usually all give the same pronunciation. The most obvious explanation of how people can read things they've never seen before is that they build up the pronunciations, letter by letter, converting each letter into a sound, and assembling those sounds together.

Now consider a word like BEEF. Imagine you've never seen it before. How would you pronounce it? You could do just the same as with these pseudowords: you could convert letters into sounds and say B EE F – and your pronunciation would be quite right. Words like BEEF, where all the letters are given their most common pronunciations, are called *regular*.

Let's turn BEEF into STEAK. How would you pronounce that if you'd never seen it before? The common pronunciation of EA is "ee", as in "speak", "leak", and "bleat". So starting from scratch you'd get STEAK wrong, and you'd pronounce it "steek". Words like STEAK, where the letters or letter pairs don't have their most common pronunciations, are called *irregular* (or exception) words. English is full of irregular words. "Steak" is by no means the worst. What about "aisle", "ghost", "psychology"? You might have heard the following old joke:

How do you pronounce the word "ghoti"?

Pause for a moment if you haven't seen it before. The answer is "fish" (with "gh" as in "enough", "o" as in "women", "ti" as in "rational".

Here then are two critical observations about reading English. We can pronounce irregular words and we can pronounce novel pseudowords. The obvious explanation for these abilities is that reading involves two processes: we read pseudowords (and, in principle, regular words) by a process taking the word letter by letter, and turning each letter into a sound, a process we call *grapheme–phoneme conversion* (GPC). Grapheme–phoneme conversion won't work for irregular words. We just have to know them all by heart.

So without too much difficulty we've created a model of reading aloud, the dual-route model, championed across the years particularly by Max Coltheart (Coltheart, 1985; Coltheart et al., 2001). The dual-route model posits two routes from print to sound. First, there is a fast, direct route, where print activates an entry in our mental dictionary, the lexicon. When the entry is activated, we gain access to all information associated with the dictionary entry, including the word's meaning and sound. The direct route, called the *lexical route*, is fast and effective for skilled readers and well-learned words. Second, there's an indirect route, making use of letter–sound correspondences, called the *non-lexical route*. For skilled readers this route is much slower, but novice readers depend on it, using GPC to spell out the sound of a word and then using that sound to access the lexicon. We can think of the two routes in a perpetual race, with the lexical route becoming faster the more skilled a reader we become. We're very fast at reading regular words because there's no conflict between the direct and indirect routes, but with irregular words the two routes give conflicting answers, and that conflict slows us down, explaining why we're faster at reading regular words than frequency-matched irregular words (Baron & Strawson, 1976).

What does brain damage tell us about reading?

If there are two reading routes, it seems very plausible that these might be located in different parts of the brain. It follows that, by chance, some people will have damage to the part of the brain housing one route but not the other, and with other individuals the opposite should be the case. Put more concretely, we should find some adults who as a consequence of brain damage should have damage to the lexical route but not the non-lexical route, and other adults who have damage to the non-lexical route but not the lexical. Such a pattern, where two skills can be differentially impaired, is called a *double dissociation*. Note that I'm just talking about adult *acquired* dyslexia here – adults who could previously read well but suffer brain damage, often as a consequence of a stroke, that affects their reading

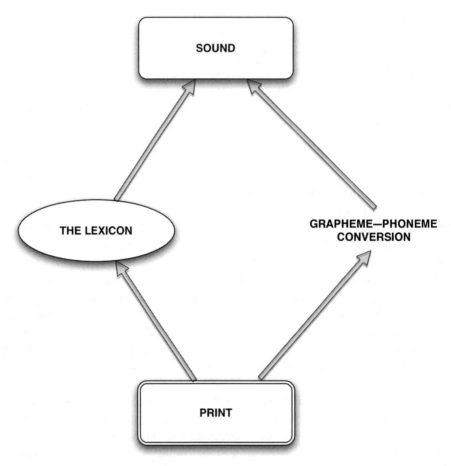

FIGURE 6.2 The dual-route model of reading

ability – in contrast to people, particularly children, who have difficulty in learning to read, a difficulty called *developmental dyslexia*.

What would such patterns look like? Remember that the lexical route is a direct route, where we access the pronunciation of a word directly, and is essential for the correct pronunciation of irregular words. People with damage to the lexical route will therefore have difficulty reading irregular words, but should be able to manage with regular words and pseudowords, because they can be read by the sublexical route. This pattern of impairment exists and is called *surface dyslexia* (Marshall & Newcombe, 1973). Patient MP (Bub et al., 1985) was almost perfect at reading non-words, showing that her sublexical route was completely preserved, but she was poor at reading irregular words, managing to read correctly 85% of high-frequency irregular words and just 40% of low-frequency irregular words, suggesting that the sublexical route was severely damaged. Surface dyslexics make just the type of errors you would expect if you try to read an irregular word through the sublexical route using grapheme–phoneme conversion; they try to regularise the irregular words, trying to pronounce them as though they were regular, hence producing errors such as "steek" for "steak", "eyesland" for "island", and "brode" for "broad". These are called *regularisation errors*. Put at its most dramatic, a person with surface dyslexia could read the regular word "speak", but not the very similar but irregular word "steak".

What about damage to the non-lexical route when the lexical route is left intact? People with this sort of impairment should be able to read words (e.g. SLEEP) but would be unable to read pseudowords (e.g. SLEEB). This pattern of reading is known as *phonological dyslexia* (Shallice & Warrington, 1975). A patient known as WB is a very striking case of someone with phonological dyslexia (Funnell, 1983); WB could not read any non-words at all, suggesting that the GPC sublexical route was completely obliterated, but could read 85% of words, indicating that his brain damage had almost totally spared his lexical route.

There are a few puzzling observations about phonological dyslexia, however, that make its interpretation a little more complex. First, for that vast majority of patients who have some sparing of the sublexical route, their reading performance is generally much better if the non-word when pronounced sounds like a word. Such pseudowords, called pseudohomophones, include as examples NITE, BRANE, and FOCKS. The most obvious explanation for this finding is that there is some sort of leakage between the lexical and non-lexical routes. Another finding is that phonological dyslexics tend to have particular trouble reading low-imageability low-frequency words, so it should come as no surprise that they find grammatical words particularly hard to read. They also have difficulty with word endings, finding inflected words difficult to read. Phonological dyslexia resembles deep dyslexia, but without the semantic paralexias; indeed, deep dyslexia sometimes resolves into phonological dyslexia as the patient recovers some ability after the brain trauma. Put at its most dramatic, a person with phonological dyslexia could read the word "sleep", but not the very similar non-word "sleeb".

Given the existence of these two types of dyslexia resulting from brain damage, it follows that different regions of the brain must be involved in different aspects of reading. Further evidence for specialisation of brain regions for different aspects of reading comes from a brain imaging study by Fiebach et. al (2002). They examined the way the brain becomes activated when it has to make lexical decisions as to words and pseudowords. Different parts of the brain lit up more depending on which type of stimulus was presented: words elicited more activation than pseudowords in the part of the brain around the bump known as the temporal gyrus, whereas pseudowords elicited more activation in more frontal and subcortical regions. Do the imaging data necessarily support the dual-route model? While the data are consistent with it, it would be too strong to say that they confirm the dual-route model. They're consistent with any model of reading that has at least two processing components. As we'll see, the triangle model says that there's a division of labour between the orthographic–phonological and semantic pathways. So as it stands, the imaging and neuropsychological evidence can't distinguish between the models.

What are the problems with the dual-route model?

So far, so good; the data support the dual-route model, although some of the observations concerning phonological dyslexia are a little unsettling. But it soon became apparent that we can't get away with a model of reading that's that simple. The three main obstacles to a simple life are that there are lexical effects on non-word reading, not all sorts of word are equivalent, and there are other types of acquired dyslexia that don't fit so well into the basic model.

That not all non-words are created equal was demonstrated in an ingenious experiment by Glushko (1979). Glushko examined the effects of word neighbours on pronouncing non-words. A neighbour is a word that's very similar to a word or non-word; for practical purposes we can say that two words are neighbours if you turn one into the other by changing one letter, so by this definition "gaze", "maze", and "laze" are all neighbours. Now consider the non-word TAZE, which has all those words as neighbours. What's important about these neighbours is that they're all regular words. Contrast that with the non-word TAVE; that has lots of neighbours, including the regular "gave", "save", and "rave", but it also has an exception neighbour, the frequent and potent "have". People are faster to name non-words with consistent lexical neighbours (like TAZE) than non-words with inconsistent, squabbling neighbours (like TAVE), although in every other respect they look very similar. So somehow words are influencing the pronunciation of non-words, a finding that can't be explained by the simple dual-route model. Glushko also showed that regularity among neighbours affects the pronunciation of words, which is difficult to explain if skilled readers pronounce words just by directly accessing their lexical entries. GANG is a word with nice friendly regular neighbours ("rang", "sang", "bang" "hang"), but BASE is a word with a nasty inconsistent neighbour ("vase", at least in English English) along with a regular neighbour ("case"). These squabbles among neighbours seem to impede the naming of regular words. Somehow the pronunciation of related words is influencing the pronunciation of regular words, and its difficult to see how this can be explained by the simple dual-route model.

There are several other experiments that show that non-words are not all equal. One of the most revealing was that of Kay and Marcel (1981), who showed that prior exposure to a word could influence the way in which a non-word is pronounced. Suppose you have to read aloud "yead"; in one condition it's preceded by the word "head", and in another by the word "bead". The way in which "yead" is pronounced is influenced by the pronunciation of the preceding word. It's as though people pronounce the non-word by *analogy* with what comes before. In fact this idea of analogy might have struck you a few pages back when I asked you to pronounce the non-words "smeat" and "nouse"; the latter in particular is very like the word "house", and although introspection is of course highly unreliable, I think that when I pronounce it I distinctly think of the word "house", and model the pronunciation on that. The analogy model of reading came to the fore in the late 1970s when the extent to which there are lexical effects on non-word reading became apparent. The idea is that we read non-words not by grapheme–phoneme conversion, but by finding similar words that we can use as the basis of an analogy (Glushko, 1979; Henderson. 1982; Kay & Marcel, 1981). As we're just reading using words, there's really only one route in this sort of model, and this idea became particularly important later on, as I will very soon show.

The other problem with a simple dual-route model is that it's not obvious how it can handle deep dyslexia. Worse is to come, though, because there are other types of dyslexia that don't fit in either. Patient WLP could pronounce words she didn't understand, a deficit known as *non-semantic reading* (Schwartz et al., 1979). She had great difficulty in retrieving the meaning of written words; she was completely unable to match written animal names to the appropriate picture. She could, however, read aloud their names, and crucially, she was just as good at reading irregular words. So she must be going through the lexicon somehow to retrieve the irregular names, but without accessing the word's meaning.

It's possible to explain lexical effects on non-word reading, neighbourhood effects in word pronunciation, and deep dyslexia and non-semantic reading by making additional assumptions about the model. The dual-route model has to be modified in at least two ways to accommodate all these findings. First, we could explain lexical effects in non-word reading if the non-lexical route had knowledge of spelling–sound correspondences for units larger in size than a phoneme. In particular, we could explain Glushko's results if in addition to GPC rules the route had knowledge of word endings – what psycholinguists call *rimes*. Rimes are the part of the word ending that give rise to rhyme: -ave, -eak, -ouse, -ead, and so on. If the system had ready access to this knowledge it could read easily by analogy. Second, we could explain the dissociations shown between deep dyslexia, where readers can access the appropriate meaning and not the correct sounds, and non-semantic reading, where readers can access the correct sound but not the meaning, if we split the direct, lexical route into two routes. What we would need would be a route that goes directly from print to the lexicon and then to sound without accessing semantics, and another route that gains access to sound through semantics (Patterson & Morton, 1985).

The model is starting to get unwieldy, and has lost the charming simplicity that made it so appealing initially. It's also unclear how the model explains all the symptoms of deep dyslexia, unless we incorporate a Hinton and Shallice type network into it. A computational model based on the revised dual-route model, called the *dual-route cascaded* (DRC) model, gives some indication of how such a system might work in practice (Coltheart et al., 2001). The model has two core assumptions. The first is that activation is cascaded throughout the network, just as it is in standard connectionist networks; as soon as a unit, such as a letter, is activated, it starts activating those units to which it's connected. The second core assumption is that there's a division of labour between a non-lexical reading system and a lexical reading system, which in turn is split into two routes, one where a representation of spelling is connected directly to a representation of sound, and another that is mediated through semantics. The model can simulate a range of results from experiments on reading, and damaging different parts of the model gives rise to different types of dyslexia.

What's the triangle model of reading?

It looks as though the complexity of the data necessitates a complex model, and compels a division of labour between lexical and non-lexical routes. Connectionist modellers have argued that this division isn't necessary. The most influential connectionist model has become known as the triangle model because of the shape of its overall architecture (Harm & Seidenberg, 2004; Plaut et al., 1996; Seidenberg &

Neighbours, every word needs good neighbours

McClelland, 1989). The triangle model describes a framework for understanding the relation between print, meaning, and sound, comprising orthographic, semantic, and phonological units connected to each other. However, all the work has been on the orthography-to-phonology pathway – print to sound.

The modellers make two strong claims that taken together make the triangle model a radical alternative to traditional models of reading and word recognition. The first bold claim, as you might have deduced from this description of the architecture, is that there is no lexicon in this account. There's no central repository where each word has its own entry and where you access that entry to get at a word's meaning and pronunciation. The sounds of words are patterns of activation across the phonological units; the meanings are patterns of activation across the semantic units; and the print forms are just patterns of activation across the orthographic units. We therefore can't decide if something is a word or non-word by looking it up in our lexicon, because there is no lexicon; all we can go by is what pattern of activation an input string produces across the network. The second bold claim is that we don't have separate lexical and non-lexical reading routes for pronouncing irregular words and pseudowords respectively; instead, the system's statistical knowledge of all spelling–sound correspondences is brought to bear when presented with an input string of letters, and in connectionist models all knowledge is encoded by the weights of the connections between units.

The simulations of orthographic to phonological processing used the sort of architecture you'll now recognise as being very familiar. An input pool of 105 units each representing graphemes (letters) in a particular position in a word (so the /k/ in "cat" was represented by a different unit from the one in "tack") was connected to an output pool of 61 units each representing phonemes (sounds), through an intermediate "hidden layer" containing 100 units. This hidden layer, you will remember, is just necessary computationally for these sorts of models to learn efficiently. Every unit is connected to every unit in the layer above. The model was trained using the back-propagation algorithm on a corpus of almost 3000 monosyllabic words until the model correctly pronounced all of them (a process that takes about 300 iterations – which means the whole process was carried out 300 times – across the whole corpus, or complete sample of words, with more frequent words being presented for training more often). It's important to realise that this corpus contains both regular and irregular words.

What happens when the trained model is then given non-words to pronounce? Plaut et al. presented the fully trained network with over 100 non-words. The network gave the "correct" (by which we mean the same pronunciation as a human would have given the non-word) pronunciation at about the same rate as humans. The important conclusion here is that a single route can produce human-like pronunciations of regular words, irregular words, and pseudowords. How can it do this? Because the connections encode the complete sum of knowledge about spelling–sound correspondences; it's a super-duper analogy model. The network

165

also gave a good account of other reading phenomena, such as the interaction between regularity and frequency, such that people are markedly slower at reading low-frequency irregular words.

Other simulations explored how surface dyslexia might arise in this architecture, although a full understanding involves broadening the scope of the model. Damage to the orthography–phonology pathway does give rise to reading errors that resemble those of surface dyslexics, but the fit isn't that good. In particular, damage to that pathway led to reading that wasn't bad enough for low-frequency irregular words, and too impaired for regular words, and didn't produce a sufficient number of regularisation errors. These problems led Plaut et al. to explore the possibility that damage to another part of the system leads to surface dyslexia, in particular the idea that surface dyslexic reading reflects the behaviour of an undamaged but isolated orthographic–phonological pathway that has developed with semantic support. After all, children don't learn spelling–sound mappings in isolation; they learn them associated with words that have meaning. So they trained another network where patterns of activation over the phonological units corresponding to words provided some additional support from semantics. After the network was trained, they cut the support from the semantics, and then found that the damaged network performed much more like a surface dyslexic. In terms of the mechanics of the model, what seems to be happening is that as the model learns, there's a division of labour between the semantic pathway, which becomes more responsible for irregular words, and the orthographic–phonological pathway, which becomes specialised in – but not dedicated to – regular spelling–sound correspondences. It's as though meaning glues together phonological patterns that correspond to irregular words. This idea is supported by the observation that with progressive dementia, people usually also become surface dyslexic, presumably because the semantic glue that normally helps us to read irregular words becomes gradually unstuck as the system loses semantic features (Patterson, Graham, & Hodges, 1994).

The triangle model does a good job of explaining normal reading, and explains surface dyslexia in terms of disruption to the semantic–phonology pathway. It would be straightforward to incorporate the Hinton and Shallice (1991) model as part of the orthography–semantic–phonology route. Where does phonological dyslexia fit in? Phonological dyslexia is thought to arise from damage to the representation of phonological information itself, an idea known as the general phonological deficit impairment (Farah et al., 1996; Harm & Seidenberg, 1999, 2001). Clearly words will have much more stable phonological representations than non-words: word sound patterns are much, much more familiar, and they receive support from semantics. So phonological dyslexia occurs when the phonological representations are themselves weakened; phonological representations corresponding to words can always rely on semantic support, but by definition there is no such support available for non-words. The general phonological deficit hypothesis is supported by the finding that people with phonological dyslexia aren't just bad at non-word reading, but are nearly always also bad at a variety of other tasks involving phonology. For example, they're bad at repeating non-words aloud, and at tasks involving manipulating the sound of words.

So here we have two different explicit accounts of reading: DRC and the triangle. Which, you want to know, is right? Scientists have known for many years that good theories must be falsifiable – that is, capable of being proved wrong. That means they must make predictions. So to distinguish between the dual-route and triangle models we need to be able to identify differential predictions. That is, the triangle model must predict something that could be proved wrong, and the dual-route model something different. There must be something that's right in one model and wrong in another. Unfortunately, life isn't that simple. With models such as these there is always a question about how good is the fit between the real-life data and the predictions of the model; no model purports to capture every aspect of the reading process, so there must be some tolerance in allowing a mismatch between prediction and data, but how much is reasonable? The DRC model is more complex, but its authors claim it accounts for a wider range of phenomena than the triangle model, but while it is good for accounting for the accuracy with which words are read, it isn't so good at accounting for the time it takes us to name words. And both models are limited to the reading of monosyllabic words. Yet again opinions are deeply entrenched and the neutral jury must remain out, but there is an elegance and simplicity to the triangle model that certainly makes it the one to beat (Figure 6.3).

Do we have to sound a word to understand it?

Read the following sentences to yourself, silently and normally:

> Ben planted his seeds in nice tidy little rows. He then got a watering can and watered the rose.

What do you find happens? Do you "hear" an internal voice sound out the words as you speak? What role does this internal voice play? We've spent some time with reading aloud, but most of the reading we do is silent reading. The goal of silent reading is to access the meaning of the words, but must we also access the sound of what we read? There are two ways in which sound might be involved in supposedly silent reading. It would hardly be surprising, given the architecture of the triangle model for example, if semantics activated by orthography then went on to activate phonology incidentally; more interesting is the case that we might have to access phonology to get at meaning, an idea called *phonological mediation*.

There is some experimental evidence for phonological mediation. In the category-decision task, you see a word on a computer screen and have to decide

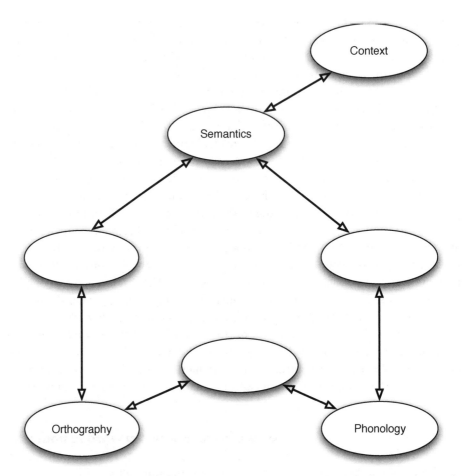

FIGURE 6.3 The triangle model of reading

whether or not the word belongs to a particular category. For example, you might be given the category "fruit", and see the word "pear", in which case you would have to press the YES button. Suppose you see "pair", which is a homophone of a word to which you should respond YES, but to which itself you should respond NO? People make many errors with homophones such as "pair"; it's as though the sound of the word is somehow interfering with the decision-making process (Frost, 1998; Van Orden et al., 1988, 1990). Note that to get this sort of interference the activation of phonology must be relatively early to be able to interfere with the semantic decision-making process.

The idea that we *must* access sound in order to be able to access meaning doesn't really fit in with either of the models we've discussed. The effect does seem to be sensitive to the details of the experiments that demonstrate it; for example, we find more interference if participants have to respond quickly. The effect also seems to be limited to low-frequency homophones (Jared & Seidenberg, 1991). Furthermore, we only find interference in certain sorts of tasks, such as category-decision. Some dyslexic patients can understand words without being able to read them; they can give perfect definitions of printed words, and match names to pictures, even though they can't pronounce them (Coltheart, 2004). We can explain the results apparently supporting phonological mediation with the idea that although orthography–semantics in the skilled reader is normally the fastest route, in some experimental conditions it might not be. There are two ways to activate the semantic units: the direct orthographic–semantic pathway, and the normally very slow orthography–phonology–semantics (there must be links from phonology to semantics because we can understand words we hear!). So in certain experimental conditions, such as in the category-decision task with low-frequency homophones, there's conflict at the semantic level, as both "pair" and "pear" become activated. It's this conflict that causes the interference and that slows us down and causes us to make errors.

Does speed reading work?

Along with "I used to have the memory of a sieve", advertisements promising faster, more effective reading are common in the Sunday supplements. These advertisements assure you that (for a suitable fee of course) a speed reading course will teach you to read faster. I've seen claims that you can learn to read at the rate of a second a page; if true, this would indeed be a considerable boost, as the normal reading rate is in the range of 200–350 words a minute. If the average page contains about 500 words, that means you can do in a second what it would normally take you well over a minute to do. If these claims are true, I think these courses would be a bargain.

It's true that many people could learn to read a little faster without any cost; sometimes our concentration wanders, sometimes our eyes linger too long on the page. Like all skills, reading skills lie along a continuum, and as with most things most people can probably improve a bit. Sometimes of course we want to read slowly; what's the point of skipping through good poetry as quickly as possible without savouring each word and hearing it in your inner ear?

Unfortunately the psycholinguistic evidence says that you can't increase your reading speed much without cost, and that cost is how much you understand and how much you remember. Just and Carpenter (1987) gave speed readers and normal readers two pieces of text to read – one that was considered "easy" to understand (it was an article from *Reader's Digest*), and another that was "difficult" (an article from *Scientific American*). They then asked both groups some questions to test their comprehension, and found that the normal readers scored 15% higher on both passages than the speed readers. In fact the speed readers did only slightly better than another group who were asked just to skim through the texts. To be fair, the speed readers still got the general gist of the text, but they were worse at the details. The eyes have it for reading; for a word to be processed properly – which means to access its meaning and to begin the process of integrating that meaning with the rest of the text, it has to "land" close to the fovea, the most sensitive part of the retina, and stay there for enough time for its semantics to become available (Rayner & Pollatsek, 1989). This explanation is supported by Just and Carpenter's additional finding that speed readers couldn't answer questions when the answers were located in parts of the text where the eyes hadn't fixated.

Which isn't to say that you can't learn to improve your memory for and understanding of text. But to do so takes more effort, not less. The most famous method is known as the PQ4R technique (Thomas & Robinson, 1972), and it must work because I've seen it recommended by several famous cognitive psychologists in their textbooks as being the ideal way to read their book. Suppose you need to read a textbook or article and understand it and remember as much of it as possible. First, you *preview* it: you survey the material, look through the contents, find out what's in it, look at the chapter introductions and conclusions, glance at the figures and tables. Speed reading, in the sense of skimming quickly through just to find out what the contents are is useful here. Then you make up some *questions* for each section, trying to make your questions related to your goals for reading the work, turning headers into questions (just as I have already helpfully done for you in this book). Then you should *read* the material carefully, section by section, trying to answer your questions. Next you should reflect on what you've just read; try to relate what you've read to things you already knew; do you really understand what you've just read? If not, why not? Reread the material you don't understand, without worrying too much, because difficult material might take several readings to understand. You might have to look things up elsewhere for clarification. Then after finishing each section you should try to *recall* what you've read; try and phrase it to yourself in your own words. What are the answers to your questions? When you've finished, you should *review* the material, trying to list the main points, arguments, and conclusions. When you've finished, skim through the material again. Repeat an hour later, and tomorrow if possible. And then come back to it several times more. This technique is hardly speed reading! Do I follow this recommended technique? Of course not.

As with everything in life, no sweat, no gain. Having said that, every so often I read about people who read a phenomenal amount. I remember reading that Bill Gates, the founder of Microsoft, often reads two books a day. While I envy him the time he must have available to do all this reading, not to mention the money he has to be able to afford all those books, I do wonder how much he remembers of what he reads.

What is the alphabetic principle?

Learning to talk comes naturally to children; learning to read most certainly does not. Many more children struggle to master reading than have spoken language difficulties. All I remember of my own experience of learning to read is an image of the letters of the alphabet posted around the classroom, with a picture of an apple above the letter "a", and presumably other pictures above the other letters. I have no idea what was above the "Z". Also for some reason great store was placed on being able to repeat the letters of the alphabet in sequence backwards. Somehow I went from reciting the alphabet backwards to being able to read scientific papers and write books such as this one.

I do dimly remember learning to read – in addition to my fun with letters. I remember seeing a picture of a black cat, with CAT printed beneath it, and being taught to spell out "c . . . a . . . t . . ." – "cat"! Easy! But it's not easy. To learn in this way, the child has to know several important things:

1   The spoken word "cat" is made out of three distinct sounds.
2   These sounds correspond to printed letters.
3   The printed word CAT is made up of three distinct elements.
4   And then of course the child has to know that c is the same as C, that a C with serif is the same thing as sanserif, and that my untidy scrawl that looks like a blotch of ink is also a c, and so on.

By "know", I don't mean that the child has to be able to explain this knowledge, just that in some way they have the skill to be able to make use of this information.

The central idea here is that sounds correspond to letters, and this is known as the *alphabetic principle*. Once you know it, you can get a long way. You might never have seen the word COT before, but once you know how the constituent sounds are pronounced, you can spell it out and recognise it. (Let's not worry for now about whether you have to spell it out first in order to recognise it.) Learning and mastering the alphabetic principle is the key achievement of learning to read.

However, children don't just learn the alphabetic principle and go from illiterate to literate; reading development seems to go through a number of phases (Ehri, 1992, 1997). Young children often go through a pre-alphabetic phase, where they haven't yet acquired the alphabetic principle, but can nevertheless still recognise a few words whose shapes they must have learned by rote. So they might recognise the word "yellow" because it's got two tall bits in the middle and a repetitive wiggle at the end. Children at this stage are associating the pattern of a word with the concept, not a particular word. In one famous example a child could recognise the name of the toothpaste, "Crest", but "read" it variously as "toothpaste" on one occasion and "brush teeth" on another. This phase is brief and by no means universal, and is clearly nothing like the direct access of skilled readers, where print is associated with a word rather than a concept. In the partial alphabetic reading phase, young children have some knowledge of letter names and their correspondences with sounds, particularly the initial and final letters of words. The child is still unable to segment the word's pronunciation into all of its component sounds. In the full alphabetic phase children have full knowledge of letters and sounds and how they correspond, so can read words they've never seen before. Gradually, with more practice, in the consolidated alphabetic phase, children read like adults: words are read directly without the need for grapheme–phoneme conversion, and children are aware that many spelling units, particularly rhymes (often also called *rimes*), are common to many words. Very poor readers will have difficulty getting beyond the third or even second stage.

What is phonological awareness?

To make use of the alphabetic principle you have to know that the spoken word "cat" comprises three sounds – and of course know what those sounds are. This knowledge of sounds and the ability to manipulate them is called *phonological awareness*. There are really two related sorts. You could tell that two words rhymed (horse and course, knight and fight), without being able to decompose and manipulate the sounds. We call this implicit awareness, while the more sophisticated sort of awareness you need to be able to do things with the sounds is called explicit awareness (Gombert, 1992).

Many tasks require phonological awareness; here are a few.

1   What's the first sound of "fun", "doll", and "cat"?
2   What sound do "bat" and "ball", and "cat" and "ham", have in common?
3   How many sounds are there in "cat", "most", and "shelves"?
4   What word would be left if you took the first sound away from "stand"?
5   What would be left if you took the second sound out of "stick"?
6   If you added the sound "t" to the start of "track", what word would you get?

Literacy and phonological awareness are very closely related. Illiterate adults perform poorly on phonological awareness tasks; a group of illiterate adults from an agricultural area of southern Portugal had particular difficulty with tasks manipulating sounds, such as adding and deleting phonemes to and from the start of words; adults who received some literacy training in adulthood performed much better (Morais et al., 1986). What's more, as you might expect, it's literacy in an alphabetic language that matters; adult Chinese speakers literate in both an alphabetic reading system and the logographic Chinese system find these tasks easy, but people who are only literate in the non-alphabetic logographic system find them much more difficult (Read et al., 1986).

Young, preliterate children perform very badly at phonological awareness tasks, and the obvious question is what's the direction of causality here? Does phonological awareness precede literacy, or does literacy in alphabetic languages lead to phonological awareness? Researchers disagree on the answer, although several pieces of evidence suggest that phonological awareness comes first. Training children on phonological awareness tasks leads to an improvement in reading ability (Bradley & Bryant, 1983; Hatcher et al., 1994). Children also seem to be able to be aware of units of speech, such as the beginnings and ends of words, before they learn to read (Goswami & Bryant, 1990). But although all this evidence is suggestive, other researchers urge caution, arguing that these studies failed to take account of the existing level of literacy skills among the children who were tested. Virtually all the studies arguing for a causal role for phonological awareness used children who already had some level of literacy, and by necessity all tasks involving explicit phonological awareness require some instruction or training in the nature of the task, letter names, and the nature of sounds (Castles & Coltheart, 2004).

A related controversy is whether children first learn correspondences between individual letters and the corresponding sounds, or whether they first learn correspondences between larger units and sounds. Young children are certainly aware of syllables from well before they start reading: children as young as four can tap out the number of syllables in words they hear, if instructed clearly (Liberman et al., 1974). One possibility is that children first learn to spot onsets and rimes (Goswami, 1986, 1993). *Onsets* are the beginnings of words: T in "tank" and CH in "church"; *rimes* are the final parts of words, the part that gives them their rhyme, so they'd be -ank and -urch in these two words. The controversy centres on whether the early ability to spot rimes or to segment words into phonemes is the better predictor of early reading ability; as yet there is little agreement (Bryant, 1998; Goswami, 1993; Muter et al., 1998). Although Goswami argues that young children begin reading by analogy, making particular use of the rime, many other studies find that young children need grapheme–phoneme decoding skills before they can learn to read. One telling piece of evidence is that young children find it easier to split words into phonemes than onsets and rimes (Seymour & Evans, 1994). The differences between the results are probably explicable in terms of differences in the materials researchers have used and in the particular instructions given to the children.

What is the best way of learning to read?

My early memory of being taught to read by learning the alphabet backwards can't be right, but learning which sounds go with which letters makes much more sense: "A is for Apple", with a big "A" underneath a picture of an apple; "B is for Bear", with a big "B" underneath a picture of a bear; "C is for cat", and so on; that method makes much more sense.

The age at which children start to learn to read doesn't seem to make much difference; even if the teaching of reading is delayed until the age of seven, the child soon catches up. The other side of the coin is that very early tuition doesn't seem to provide any particular long-lasting advantage either. There are two different approaches to teaching reading. At one extreme, we could teach the child what individual whole words sound like, an approach called the *whole-word* or *look-and-say method*; at the other extreme, we teach them how to turn letters into sounds, and then how to split words into sounds, an approach called the *phonics method*.

Of course neither method in isolation would work. It would be terribly inefficient to teach every word separately, not pointing out that cat, bat, rat, cats, and rats share something. And learning to spell ghost, aisle, and island by turning the words into their component sounds would lead to disaster. The question is which mechanism do we emphasise most, first. There are several studies that show that the phonics method is greatly superior, and a meta-analysis, which combines the results of several different studies into one, of all the studies carried out on how reading should be taught came to the same conclusion: phonics is better (Adams, 1990; Ehri et al., 2001). Indeed, the key to a child learning to read effectively is their discovery of the alphabetic principle, the idea that letters correspond to particular sounds, and anything that speeds up the discovery of this principle speeds up reading development. Other methods don't work anywhere near as well. Philip Seymour and Leona Elder (1986), then also of Dundee, examined the reading performance of a class of five-year-olds who had been taught without any explanation of the alphabetic principle, and found that these children were limited to being able to read only the words that they'd been taught, and even so they made many errors, resembling dyslexic readers.

Recent work by Rhona Johnston in Clackmannanshire in Scotland caused a flurry of activity in the press when a seven-year longitudinal comparison of children learning to read showed that synthetic phonics is the most effective means of teaching reading. What's more, it confers long-lasting advantages, with children taught by this method still having a reading advantage over children taught by other means several years later (Johnston & Watson, 2007). Synthetic phonics is an accelerated form of phonics instruction that emphasises letter sounds before they are exposed to print. The children are taught a few letters and what these sound like, and they are then taught how these can be blended together in different ways to make up different words. So they might be taught the letters P, T, S, and A, and the sounds /p/, /t/, /s/, and /a/, and then that by combining these they can make the words "tap", "pat", "taps", "pats", and so on. The children are then taught the correspondence between sounds and letters of the alphabet. Children aren't first taught the pronunciation of new words, but have to spell them out from the individual letters.

Teachers emphasise fluency over accuracy. This method enables the basics of reading to be taught in the first few months of the first school year. From 2007, synthetic phonics became the preferred method of teaching reading in the UK.

As Snow and Juel (2005, p. 518) put it, "attention to small units in early reading instruction is helpful for all children, harmful for none, and crucial to some". It's rare in psycholinguistics that we all agree, but this topic is one of those exceptions: reading should be taught in a way that allows the child to discover the alphabetic principle as soon as possible.

I showed in the previous chapter that languages differ in the way in which sounds are translated into print. We saw that even within alphabetic languages there are differences in the regularity with which sounds are mapped on to letters. In Finnish or Serbo-Croat a letter is always sounded in one way, and a sound always corresponds to one particular letter. Put another way, words are always regular in these sorts of language. But in English irregular words abound and the mapping is much more complicated. So we can arrange languages along a continuum of what is called orthographic depth, with Finnish at the shallow end, Greek and German in the middle, and English at the deep end (Goswami, 2008; Seymour, 2005). Languages also differ in the complexity of their syllable structure. In French and other Romance languages the syllable structure is simple and consistent, being mainly consonant–vowel, but in English and other Germanic languages it's more complicated, with a mixture of consonant–vowel (e.g. "ta" in "table") and consonant–vowel–consonant (e.g. "Pat"), and with some syllables involving consonant clusters ("strap" has a cluster of three consonants at the beginning). Given this difference in complexity, it comes as no surprise that French-speaking children acquire the notion of a syllable before English-speaking children (Seymour, 2005). So we can map languages into a two-dimensional grid:

Shallow		Deep
Simple	Finnish, Greek, Italian, Spanish, Portuguese, French	
Complex	German, Norwegian, Icelandic, Dutch, Swedish, Danish, English	

The ease with which children acquire phonological ability and literacy should be greatest at the top left of this grid and most difficult at the bottom right, which seems to be the case. English is *very* difficult, because everything conspires against it. In addition to the complex syllables and deep orthography, there's a very large number of syllables, and the way in which we stress words and sentences is complex and irregular. The English child has eventually to learn whole-word strategies for words like 'yacht" and "cough", rime-analogy strategies for words like "light', "right", and "fight", as well as grapheme–phoneme strategies for regular words (Ziegler & Goswami, 2005). I'm surprised I learned to read at all, let alone write and spell, which causes similar sorts of difficulty.

B is for very, very old banana

What is developmental dyslexia?

In 1896, William Pringle Morgan, a British doctor living in Sussex, described the case of Percy, a 14-year-old boy who, although achieving normally in other academic areas, experienced significant difficulty in learning to read and spell. Pringle Morgan could find no evidence of any brain damage or other obvious explanation, and concluded that Percy was unable to "store visual impressions" of words, what Pringle Morgan called "congenital word blindness".

Learning to read isn't like learning to talk. It isn't that easy, but some children have more difficulty than others. Like most skills, there's a continuum of ability; we'd expect to find good readers and bad readers. Children who find reading very difficult suffer from *developmental dyslexia*. Percy bore all the hallmarks of developmental dyslexia: difficulty in learning to read, difficulty spelling, average performance in other academic areas, and no obvious signs of brain damage or any other obvious impairment that could explain the difficulty.

There's some debate about the nature of developmental dyslexia: is it just very bad reading ability (in which case it's a quantitative difference), or is it something else (in which case there would be a qualitative difference)? Julian Elliott of the

University of Durham received particular attention in the press in 2005 when he questioned the validity of the term "dyslexia" (Elliot & Place, 2004). Although his original claim was that there were so many misunderstandings and misconceptions about "dyslexia" that the term had become virtually useless, this claim became translated, in a way that only journalists can, into "dyslexia doesn't exist". Elliott and others have a point: the term "dyslexia" has become stretched by some people to mean virtually any difficulty in reading, writing, or understanding, including grammatical and memory problems, or indeed, in the extreme, any discrepancy between the child's actual educational attainment and how the parents think the child should perform! It's for reasons such as these that in the past dyslexia was dismissed as "the middle class disease", with the implication that some parents don't like to accept that their child might not be excelling academically for other reasons.

If we wished to be pedantic, there's another possible confusion, in that developmental dyslexia is a difficulty with reading. Difficulty in learning to spell and write properly is called developmental dysgraphia. Unfortunately, developmental dysgraphia and dyslexia always go together, so we can use "dyslexia" to refer to both. All of this controversy and confusion is a great pity because of course developmental dyslexia exists, but the definition I'm going to work with is quite strict: it's a marked discrepancy in reading ability skills and non-verbal measures of IQ. The different ways in which the term "dyslexia" is used, and how it's measured, make its prevalence in the population difficult to estimate, but it's likely to lie between 10% and 4%. Note that developmental dyslexia affects someone all their lives, so although more attention has recently been paid to diagnosing it in childhood, there must be hundreds of thousands of adults in the UK who have undiagnosed developmental dyslexia.

There are different types of acquired reading disorder, so the question naturally arises as to whether or not there are different types of developmental disorder. Castles and Coltheart (1993) identified two subtypes of developmental dyslexia. People with surface developmental dyslexia have particular difficulty with irregular words. Their reading of non-words and their ability to convert graphemes into phonemes is relatively good, but they have difficulty in constructing the direct-access reading route. (I'll put aside the question of whether or not there are direct and indirect routes for now and put it this way for clarity, but we'll come back to an alternative interpretation shortly.) People with phonological developmental dyslexia have difficulty with grapheme–phoneme conversion; they have difficulty with non-words and spelling out new words, but can read both regular and irregular words they know by the whole-word, direct-access route. This division into good and bad grapheme–phoneme conversion, phonological skills versus good and whole-word, orthographic skills, is not limited to dyslexia. Adults in the population within the normal range of reading skills also vary in the degree to which they rely on these skills. Baron and Strawson (1976) distinguished between what they called

"Chinese readers", who are relatively good at orthographic skills but relatively poor at phonological, and "Phoenicians", who are relatively good at phonological skills and bad at orthographic (and of course some individuals will be good at both). Hence within the normal population we can identify individuals with a very mild form of phonological dyslexia and others with a very mild form of surface dyslexia.

What causes developmental dyslexia?

Researchers have proposed several causes of developmental dyslexia. From the outset I should make clear that there might be more than one type and more than one cause of developmental dyslexia, particularly given that there's more than one type of deficit. We should also bear in mind that there are also different levels of explanation, so that a genetic impairment might lead to a child having difficulty in representing sounds, for example.

Although I've been at pains to point out that dyslexia is a selective deficit in reading and spelling relative to other non-verbal skills, the reading problem does seem to be associated with a cluster of other problems. Sufferers tend to suffer more than we would expect from a depressingly lengthy list of additional problems, including dyspraxia (difficulty in planning movements), clumsiness, difficulty in processing sounds, difficulty in producing neat handwriting, and difficulty in producing sounds. None of these will make the dyslexic child's life any easier, but the extent to which they are necessarily related to pure dyslexia is uncertain. There is strong evidence that developmental dyslexia runs in families, and some researchers have tentatively identified a number of regions on chromosomes that might be implicated in dyslexia (Fisher et al., 1999; Pennington & Lefly, 2001; Schumacher et al., 2007). A genetic cause of, or at least predisposition to, dyslexia makes perfect sense, and it is also very plausible that it might be associated with this cluster of additional symptoms, although the precise way in which all these things hang together remains to be worked out.

In the popular mind at least, one of the most well-known theories of the origin of dyslexia is that it arises because the person has difficulty in visual perception. They tend to confuse similar looking letters, such as p and b, and m and n, and often report that the letters appear to dance across the page. These observations could be explained if the dyslexics have difficulty keeping the eyes stable when fixating on print, or difficulty in resolving fine detail in print, or both (Lovegrove et al., 1986). Brain imaging studies show increased activity in the occipital region of dyslexics, that part of the brain where much low-level visual processing is carried out, presumably reflecting the extra work necessary to try to make sense of print (Casey et al., 2001). Another low-level account says that dyslexia arises from a deficit in auditory processing. Dyslexics have difficulty processing rapidly changing sounds, of which speech is a perfect example (Wright et al., 1997). Yet another account says that dyslexics have a mild impairment to the cerebellum, the region of the brain responsible for automatic processes, co-ordinating perception and action, and motor control and co-ordination (Nicolson et al., 2001). The cerebellum is the little bump at the bottom of the brain, just behind the midbrain where the spinal cord enters the brain (look back at Figure 1.3). Brain imaging suggests that there are processing differences between the cerebellums of normal and dyslexic people (Ramus et al., 2003).

A theory that attempts to bring together the visual and auditory and other deficits is that people with dyslexia have an impairment to the *magnocellular* perceptual pathways in the brain (Stein, 2001, 2003). These pathways, characterised by large cells, respond quickly to contrast, movement, and rapidly varying stimuli; although most clearly understood for visual processing, there seems to be an analogue in the auditory processing system. Furthermore these pathways have particularly string inputs to the cerebellum. So here we have a candidate theory that can bring together many of the phenomena and observations of dyslexia: a genetic abnormality leads to dysfunction of the magnocellular pathways, leading to difficulties in processing rapidly changing visual and auditory processing, as well as abnormal development of the cerebellum leading to difficulties in motor control. While the magnocellular theory provides an impressive integration of a range of data, it's unlikely to be the only explanation of developmental dyslexia because not all people with dyslexia have any obvious visual processing deficit (Lovegrove et al., 1986), and some people with dysfunction of this pathway do not develop dyslexia (Skoyles & Skottun, 2004).

Another explanation at the biological level focuses on the role of the *planum temporale*, a structure that lies at the heart of Wernicke's area, that region of the left hemisphere of the cortex known to play an essential role in processing language. Although the planum temporale is usually significantly larger in the left hemisphere than in the right (up to five times larger, making it the most asymmetric region of the brain), this asymmetry is much less in people with dyslexia (Beaton, 1997). Damage to the planum temporale is associated with difficulties in phonological (sound) processing, and in particular difficulties in processing sounds in real time. Autopsies of four (dead) people with dyslexia found this asymmetry, but also showed abnormalities of the structure consistent with abnormalities of the migration phase of foetal development, when developing neurons move to their final destination in the brain (Galaburda et al., 1985). Again the line of argument is that the reading deficit in developmental dyslexia follows from a primary deficit in processing sounds.

Although Castles and Coltheart argued that there were two distinct subtypes of developmental dyslexia, surface and phonological, most researchers conclude that dyslexics fall on a continuum, with the surface type at one extreme and the phonological at the other (Manis et al., 1996; Wilding, 1990). Those near the surface end have difficulty with irregular words but are not so troubled by non-words and grapheme–phoneme conversion; those nearer the phonological extreme will show the opposite pattern. Those individuals near the middle will have both sorts of difficulty. Children at the surface extreme perform very similarly on a range of tasks to reading-age-matched control children; that is, they "just" seem to have difficulty reading irregular words. It's as though, for some reason, they're learning to read much more slowly than normal – they're delayed readers. Children with signs of phonological dyslexia show other deficits relative to reading-age-matched controls, however: they're impaired at a range of tasks needing phonological skills, including phonological awareness, non-word reading, picking out phonologically distinct words, and reduced short-term memory (e.g. Bradley & Bryant, 1983; Campbell & Butterworth, 1985; Goswami & Bryant, 1990; Metsala et al., 1998).

The idea then is that developmental phonological dyslexia arises from a general phonological deficit, in just the same way as in the one-route triangle model acquired phonological dyslexia arises from a general phonological deficit. Exactly how this system might work is demonstrated in a connectionist model of reading (Harm & Seidenberg, 1999, 2001). These authors showed how the symptoms of developmental phonological dyslexia are generated by damage to the phonological units representing sounds before the model is trained to read. The symptoms of developmental surface dyslexia could be generated in several ways, such as providing less training, making training less effective, and degrading the visual input to the network (resembling a real-life visual impairment). They also showed that it's possible to have a phonological impairment that's severe enough to cause massive disruption to learning to read, but at the same time isn't severe enough to interfere with speech perception or production.

And that, I reckon, is what's wrong with me: I have a mild general phonological deficit. I have difficult in learning new words, manipulating sounds, repeating and remembering non-words, learning foreign languages, needed speech therapy as a child, and all my life have always made many, many speech errors – all characteristics of such a problem. I can get by very nicely, thank you, because of very strong semantic support to words.

Here then we have an account that potentially synthesises all the above. We seem to have two types of biological deficit, one involving some disturbance of visual processing and one involving a disruption of phonological processing, probably arising from some genetic disorder. We have a computational model that shows how a continuum of surface and phonological dyslexia can arise from delayed reading and a general phonological deficit.

The remaining obvious question is how developmental dyslexia should be treated. The first point to make is that just because there's a genetic predisposition doesn't mean that a person will develop full-blown dyslexia. In "at risk" families, scores on measures of phonological skill lie on a continuum; for young children, the higher the score, the greater the likelihood that they will later develop dyslexia

(Pennington & Lefly, 2001; Snowling et al., 2003). What's more, good general language skills, particularly good early vocabulary development, can partly offset the phonological deficit. Nevertheless, the deficit will still be apparent with phonological awareness tasks, and even children classified as normal readers will have some difficulty reading and spelling non-words. So in a family at risk, there might be widespread subtle language difficulties, but other skills can compensate. So one thing that might help would be providing additional training from an early age if children at risk can be identified. Generally training on tasks that introduce and improve phonological awareness from as early as possible is desirable (Bradley & Bryant, 1983; Snowling, 2000). For example, children who were poor at rhyme judgement were trained individually and weekly for two years at tasks such as having to group "hat" with "cat" on the basis of rhyme, but with "hen" on the basis of the initial sound. After four years the experimental group performed significantly better at reading and spelling than the untrained control group. Providing extra training on a range of phonological skills is without doubt the best way to improve the reading ability of young children with developmental dyslexia (particularly those towards the more phonological end of the continuum), but is also the best way to improve the skills of poor readers in general (Hatcher et al., 1994). Training can be advantageous beyond the earliest years: DF, a 10-year-old boy with poor reading ability characterised by surface dyslexia, showed a marked improvement after training on many low-frequency irregular words, while SP, an 11-year-old boy with poor reading characterised by phonological dyslexia, showed improvement after training on phonological awareness skills (Broom & Doctor, 1995a, 1995b).

For children at the surface end of the continuum, training on irregular words, particularly low-frequency words, is a great help. For those whose dyslexia arises because of a visual impairment, improving the child's magnocellular system by training eye fixations has been shown to help in at least some cases (Stein, 2003). Other methods of improving visual clarity and reducing interference might work; there is some anecdotal evidence that orange or yellow paper or overlays or tinted glasses might assist some people, although the experimental evidence is currently a bit scanty (Stein, 2003; Wilkins, 2003; Wilkins & Neary, 1991).

There's no doubt that people with dyslexia are disadvantaged in educational fields requiring literacy – which to some extent is most of them. In the UK it is quite rightly illegal to discriminate against people with dyslexia, and educationalists and employers must make reasonable adjustments. The question naturally arises as to what is a reasonable adjustment.

We do people with dyslexia no favours at all by over-compensating, or by giving them useless or incorrect treatments or adjustments. In some institutions students might be given 15 minutes' extra "reading time" for a three-hour exam. What's the reasoning behind this? It's reasonable for complex exams involving a great deal of reading, but for short exam questions, how will it help at all? For a dyslexic person, the disorder is mainly going to show itself with difficulty in writing and in spelling correctly. How will extra time reading help that? What would help the person most would be help in transcribing, or taking spelling difficulty into account when marking. Similarly instructions given to educationalists are very vague. Stickers on work saying "This person is dyslexic; please take this into account" are common, but how should the marker most fairly take this into account? By ignoring spelling mistakes? More clarity is needed, for the sake of both the dyslexic person, who might not receive the help they need, and the non-dyslexic person, who could end up finding themselves disadvantaged.

How do we understand ambiguous words?

What do the following utterances have in common?

> I'm going to the bank.
> What a lovely pen!
> That's some ball.

Apart from being not terribly interesting, they're all *ambiguous* sentences – they all have more than one meaning. In the first example, we could be off to take out our life savings from the money bank, or for a nice quiet day's fishing on the river bank. In the second, I could be complimenting you on your nice biro, or on your cunningly made area for holding sheep. In the third, I could be praising the little round thing the children are kicking around the park, or the dance extravaganza I'm gazing down at from the balcony. These sentences are ambiguous because the words "bank", "pen", and "ball" (and many others) are ambiguous – they have multiple meanings, or *senses*.

These are words ambiguous both in writing and sound, but some words are ambiguous just when we hear them. These words are called homophones.

> What a lovely night!

When we hear this sentence, we could interpret it to mean the night is very pleasant, or the knight is a darned good-looking chap.

And to complicate things even more, some words can belong to two different syntactic categories:

> Hold on, the plane is going to bank suddenly.

This type of ambiguity, where words have multiple senses, is called lexical ambiguity. In the next chapter I'll introduce another sort of ambiguity, syntactic ambiguity, which occurs when syntactic structures can have more than one interpretation.

Lexical ambiguity is one of the most important sources for humour, particularly most puns, or plays on words. Type "best puns in the world" into your favourite internet search engine and you will find such gems as:

Two silkworms had a race. They ended up in a tie.

This joke gets its humour (such as it is) from the lexical ambiguity of "tie", which can refer either to an identical position in a race or game, or an item of clothing. Or you could look at some clips from the best James Bond puns ("I see you handle your weapon well", which gets its humour from . . . well, you get the idea). You could also try typing "ten worst puns in the world" into Google, and you'll discover that some of the same puns are in both the best ten and worst ten puns of all time. Oh well.

In terms of our model of language processing so far, the same word – or, put more precisely, the same pattern of activation over phonological or orthographic units – is pointing to different patterns of activation across the semantic features, or two different semantic attractors. Yet we rarely make a mistake and end up with the wrong meaning; most of the time we're not even aware that a word is ambiguous. How do we so easily end up with the right meaning?

It's obvious that we use the context around the ambiguous word to latch quickly on to the right meaning. Given:

I'm going to take some cheques to the bank.
The fisherman put his rod down on the river bank.
My pencil's broken – could I borrow your pen?
The farmer rounded up the sheep into the pen.

I doubt that without the preceding preamble you'd even notice the ambiguity. One of the earliest models of how we cope with lexical ambiguity, the *context-guided single-reading lexical access model* (e.g. Schvaneveldt et al., 1976; Simpson, 1981), said that context somehow restricts the access process so that usually only the correct meaning is accessed. The problem with this model is in that word "somehow"; at the time it wasn't understood how context could have such immediate and powerful effects. The context of an utterance is a big thing; it isn't just the other words in the sentence, it's what else you've been talking about in the conversation, what you're looking at, what you've been looking at, all knowledge of the word – context is huge, and potentially any of it could be brought to bear on resolving an instance of lexical ambiguity, while how context works is actually very mysterious.

An alternative early model was the *ordered-access model* (Hogaboam &

Perfetti, 1975). You'll probably have noticed that the different senses of most ambiguous words aren't equally commonly intended. "Pen" has a high-frequency sense (writing instrument) and a low-frequency sense (animal enclosure), as does "bank" (financial institution and river side, although the difference in meaning frequencies isn't as pronounced). There is the complication that frequency is a personal thing: fishermen and financiers will see things differently. Let's talk about the average frequency of sense across people. According to the ordered-access model, when we come across an ambiguous word we check the most frequent sense first against the context to see if it makes sense, and if it does not, then we move on down to the next most frequent sense, and check that.

Early experimenters lacked sufficiently sensitive techniques to make much headway in distinguishing between these models. The breakthrough came with the development of the technique called *cross-modal priming*. In tasks based on this technique participants have to juggle two things at once: they have to listen and watch. In Swinney's (1979) experiment, participants heard little stories such as:

> Rumour had it that, for years, the government building had been plagued with problems. The man was not surprised when he found (several spiders, roaches, and other) bugs1 in the cor2ner of his room.

I'll come back to that 1 and 2 later. The ambiguous word here is of course "bugs". Half the participants heard a version which included the strongly biasing context "several spiders, roaches, and other" which pushes you to one sense of bugs; the other half just heard "found bugs", without any strongly biasing context.

At the same time participants saw words or non-words on a screen in front of them to which they had to make a lexical decision, so they had to press one button if they saw a word, and another if they saw a non-word. Swinney measured the time it took people to make this decision. I'll only talk about what happened when they saw words; in this experiment some non-words are slipped in just to keep participants on their toes so they really do have to read the word and can't keep pressing "yes" all the time. The targets were "ant" (which is a word associated with the biased sense of the word), "spy" (a word associated with the irrelevant sense in the biased context), and "sew" (a neutral word that provides a baseline).

Remember that semantic priming is a very robust effect: it's easier to recognise a word if we've just been exposed to one related in meaning. So if both senses of "bug" are active, people should be faster to respond to both "ant" and "spy" than the baseline, "sew", but if only the biased sense is active, then they should only be faster to respond to "ant", with the irrelevant sense, "spy", being the same as "sew". Swinney found that the pattern of results depended on the timing. Immediately after the ambiguous word "bug" (indicated by the 1 in the example above), both senses were active (both "ant" and "spy" were facilitated), but very soon after, at point 2, after just a few intervening syllables, only the relevant sense, "ant", was facilitated. This result shows that when we come across an ambiguous word, all the senses are activated immediately, but the activation of the irrelevant ones dies away very quickly. A similar experiment measuring how long it takes people to name a word rather than make a lexical decision came to a similar conclusion (Tanenhaus et al., 1979). So we access all the senses first of all, but use the context to decide between them very quickly – within 200 milliseconds.

Chapter 7

Understanding

THE JOYS OF READING Proust include the immaculate prose, the wonderful descriptions of characters that encapsulate almost everything there is about being human, and the very, very long sentences that sometimes seem to start on one page and finish several later. Among the contenders for longest "real" sentence is one 1287 words long, from William Faulkner's novel *Absalom, Absalom!*, according to the *Guinness Book of Records*, although Molly Bloom's soliloquy in James Joyce's *Ulysses* clocks in with one sentence 11,281 words long, and the following 12,931 words long, although I'm not sure I'd count these as real sentences. The point is that contrary to what I might have led you to believe I think so far, we deal with more than one word at a time. We speak mostly in sentences, and we hear and read sentences. But sentences aren't lonely creatures spoken in isolation; they're linked to what's come before and what's coming next. We tell stories, have conversations, read books about something.

The "something" language does isn't random, either. We speak or write with some purpose in mind. In our heads we have a representation of the world, and we use language to convey a part of that representation to other people. I speak to bring about some change in you: to get you to do something, or to inform you of something I don't think you already know. When we speak or write, we have a representation we wish to convey, and your job as listener or reader is to decode that information, integrate it with our existing mental representation of the world, and decide how to act upon it. This process of bringing two mental representations together so they share more than they did before the linguistic interchange is called *alignment* (Pickering & Garrod, 2004). The alignment we achieve doesn't have to be perfect: it just has to be good enough. When I tell you "Felix is on the loose!", I don't have to convey my feelings about dogs, or my knowledge that Felix is good at catching Frisbees, just that Felix is a dog and he's got out of his kennel and something has to be done about it. Similarly as a listener you don't need to analyse every word I say for hidden nuances (although some seem to enjoy doing so) or align your representation of the world perfectly to mine before you do anything; you just have to extract my intention. You might not even need to analyse the sentence perfectly every time if you can get away without doing so. Language understanding, most of the time, has to be just good enough. The cost of this casualness is that we're not always right – sometimes people misunderstand what they're hearing or reading (Ferreira et al., 2002). So when people saw the sentence:

> While Anna dressed the baby played in the crib.

many participants afterwards believed both that the baby played in the crib (correctly) and that Anna had dressed the baby (incorrectly). So in the real world we might not analyse everything perfectly every time, yet clearly we do enough to get by (most of the time).

It's my experience that many students find the study of how we understand sentences to be the most difficult and least interesting part of psycholinguistics. And, I must now shamefully admit, I know what they mean. I think there are three difficulties with the work discussed in this chapter. First, there are many technical terms (e.g. "reduced relative", "relative clause"), and I find it difficult remembering what they all mean. Second, many of the materials used in the experiments in this area strike me as artificial and unnatural – not at all the sort of thing we use in real life. And third, related to this point, I wonder what the more general point of it all is. Obviously we can process reduced relatives (we'll come to what they are later), but why does it matter? Some researchers are very interested in them, but it strikes me as a very specialist topic – almost like train spotting (no offence intended), and not at all the sort of thing a wide-ranging scholar would spend too long on. So writing this chapter is a special quest for me: to minimise the number of technical terms and make them memorable; to discover if we are really troubled by these sorts of sentences in real life; and to discover if this work tells us anything more general about how the mind works.

We call the process of working out the syntactic structure of a sentence *parsing*. When we parse a sentence, we break it down into its constituents – nouns, verbs, adjectives, and so on – and work out how they are related to each other. We can summarise the structure of a sentence such as "the old man jumped quickly into the boat" using a diagram (Figure 7.1).

We call the mechanism responsible for parsing the human sentence processing mechanism – or HSPM for short. The HSPM extracts the meaning of an utterance, and we then have to integrate that meaning into a representation that makes sense with what we already know.

What is grammatical ambiguity?

If language was completely unambiguous things would be much easier, and this chapter would be very short. We'd be able to hear or read a sentence, and

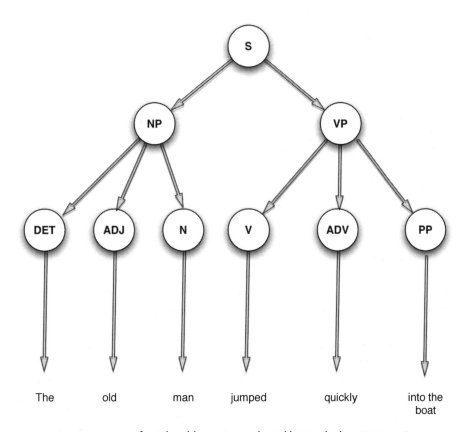

FIGURE 7.1 A parse tree for "The old man jumped quickly into the boat". Note: S = sentence; NP = noun phrase; VP = verb phrase; DET = determiner; ADJ = adjective; N = noun; V = verb; ADV = adverb; PP = prepositional phrase

immediately work out its grammatical structure correctly. We would never have to postpone a decision about what it means or backtrack and reanalyse what we've read.

But life isn't that simple. You're listening to someone speak on the radio: "The". OK so far, not much difficulty understanding what's happening. "The old". No problems yet. "The old man". Easy. "The old man the". What? Has someone made a mistake? "The old man the boats". Uh? Oh, I see. (Take a moment if you still don't.)

Here the sentence is to be understood with "man" as a verb ("man the boats!"), and therefore "old" as a noun, but virtually everyone, when they hear "the old man", at first identifies – *parses* – this structure with "man" as a noun and "old" as an adjective.

I've already talked about lexical ambiguity, and syntactic ambiguity is the other great source of ambiguity and difficulty in understanding language. Some sentences are permanently ambiguous in that we get to the end of them and we can't resolve the ambiguity (by which I mean settle on one unambiguous interpretation) without additional information.

I saw the Pennines flying to Dundee.

Structurally, this sentence is ambiguous. You probably instantly and without any thought settled on the structure corresponding to "When I was flying to Dundee, I saw the Pennines", but it could mean "There I am standing there and all of a sudden I looked up and saw the Pennines flying overhead on their way to Dundee"; well, there are fantasy or science fiction scenarios where it wouldn't be totally impossible. I suppose we could also think of the Pennine family, and we see them peering through their plane window en route to Dundee. Or for something less dramatic:

Visiting relatives can be boring.

Either going to visit them can be boring, or it can be boring when they come to visit us. Both interpretations are nearly always true in my experience.

With these sorts of sentence, we get to the end and that's it. There's no more help, and we just have to work out which is likely to be the correct structure on the basis of the context.

But the worst is yet to come: in addition to permanent ambiguity, we, or our HSPM, have to worry about temporary ambiguity, where we can assign more than one syntactic interpretation to what we've got so far. Later material in the sentence then disambiguates the structure so we are left with just one reading. Now virtually every sentence is ambiguous at some point; if you just hear the first word, "The –", there is an extremely large number of possible continuations and structures that could follow. We could have "the dog" or "the brown dog", "the brown dog chased", "the brown dog was chased", and so on. Let's put aside this trivial sort of temporary ambiguity and stick to parsing where commitment matters.

I saw the man with the binoculars

Let's stop there; that's all you've heard, and what you've heard so far is ambiguous – it's ambiguous between a structure that means "I saw a man, and it was the man who had some binoculars" and one that means "With my binoculars, I saw the man". At some point – and the really big question here is when – we have to choose between these two structures. At some point the temporary ambiguity might be resolved by additional material:

I saw the man with the binoculars that I had just picked up.
I saw the man with the binoculars use them to swat a fly.

In some cases the material might have been preceded by helpful context. In some cases the intended interpretation might remain unclear at the end of the sentence. We have to do the best we can.

At least these sorts of ambiguous sentences don't seem to derail us most of the time. Our HSPM moves along without our noticing; we assign syntactic structures, and usually aren't aware of any ambiguity or conflict. Now try to read the following sentence – and this isn't easy – one word at a time, quickly, without looking ahead. Ready?

The horse raced past the barn fell.

Most people who haven't seen this sentence before get to the end and say "what?" That "fell" doesn't seem to fit there. Your head jerks. Is this even grammatical? You probably had the experience of going back and reanalysing the sentence. What appears to have happened here is that we analyse the structure of the sentence (work out who or what is doing what to what) initially as "There is a horse and it raced past the barn", which is fine until we come to the word "fell". We then have to reanalyse the sentence to come up with a structure that can accommodate "fell". Hence we decide the sentence must mean "There was a horse that was raced past the barn and it fell". Got it? Some people need some time to see the correct structure (that is, one that works without leaving any words over!).

These sorts of temporarily ambiguous sentences, where we have a very strong initial interpretation that turns out to be wrong, are called *garden-path sentences*; we've been led up the garden path. They contain what's called a reduced relative clause. A relative clause is one that modifies a noun. Here the "horse" is the noun, and "raced past the barn" is the relative clause. Often relative clauses are introduced by grammatical words called relativisers, "that" and "which"; if one had been present in this example it would have read:

> The horse that was raced past the barn fell.

And there wouldn't have been a problem because the relativiser would have prevented the structure from being ambiguous. When we omit the relativiser the relative clause becomes a reduced relative, and it's these reduced relatives that cause us trouble. Not all sentences that lead us up the garden path are reduced relatives: "the old man the boats" isn't, but it garden-paths most people.

A note on garden-path sentences: many people find them odd, and some find them ungrammatical. "People never really speak like that!" they say, or "Surely there should be a comma there!", and I have some sympathy with these views. However, we do sometimes speak like that, perhaps more than we think. Just as I broke off from writing this section, I looked, in the gloomy depression- and recession-framed time of writing the first draft, at the financial part of the *Daily Telegraph* only to be met with "Treasury reveals biggest growth forecast cut since records began". I was all right until I got to the word "cut". If we're going to understand how we understand language, we need to understand how we cope with the type of ambiguity found in garden-path sentences; garden-path sentences are a tool to help us study the human sentence parsing mechanism.

With this dash around ambiguity we can identify a number of interrelated issues of potential interest to the psycholinguist. How do we resolve ambiguity? What sorts of information do we use? When we come across ambiguity, do we keep both possible analyses open and only make a choice when we have enough information to make a conclusive decision? Or do we make a best bet as soon as we encounter the ambiguity and, if it turns out to be wrong, go back and reanalyse? And on what basis then do we make the best bet?

How do we deal with temporary ambiguity?

Perhaps the garden-path examples have already given us the answer: after all, when we come across garden-path sentences we have the very strong impression that we are forced to *reanalyse* the sentence. We hear "The horse raced past the barn" and analyse it simply as noun phrase (the horse), a verb (raced), and prepositional phrase (past the barn). We construct the syntactic structure and use that to extract the meaning. But then along comes "fell", nothing fits any more, and so we stop, go back, and reanalyse it correctly this time as a reduced relative.

There are two main theories of how we parse incoming structures. According to the *garden-path model*, we pick the most likely structure on syntactic grounds and carry on with it unless we're forced by subsequent conflicting information to

I saw the Pennines flying to Dundee

reanalyse. According to the *constraint-based model*, we use multiple sources of information to assign a structure. I'll look at these two approaches in more detail, bearing in mind that the key differences emerge when the HSPM comes across syntactically ambiguous material such as a garden-path sentence.

In the garden-path model, we create just one syntactic structure, which means the HSPM has to make a choice – I'll come back to how it chooses among alternatives in a moment. If the choice is correct, we move on. If the first parse turns out to be incompatible with later syntactic, semantic, or pragmatic information, then we have to go back and reanalyse. The garden-path model therefore is a two-stage model, with an initial stage that uses just syntactic information, and a second stage that makes use of any semantic or pragmatic information (Frazier, 1987; Rayner et al., 1983).

In constraint-based models, the parser uses multiple sources of information, called *constraints*, to activate alternative syntactic structures in parallel. Constraints are anything that could influence parsing – syntactic preferences, semantic knowledge about what can do what to what, pragmatic information about the topic of conversation, even the relative frequency of different syntactic structures (Boland et al., 1990; Taraban & McClelland, 1988).

The two main differences between the two models then are, first, whether parsing takes place in one or two stages and, second, whether any kind of information other than syntactic knowledge can affect the initial parse.

The question of how we resolve syntactic ambiguity might seem very narrow, perhaps even tedious, but in fact it addresses one of the most fundamental issues about the design of the mind. Are we made out of little boxes, each doing their own thing, never interfering with each other, forming a strictly regimented regime? This is the East Coast view, and if you read any of Steven Pinker's books, you will get the impression that this is the way things have to be. Or does anything go? Is our mind a laid-back free-for-all society of co-operating individuals always interfering in each others' business? This is the West Coast view, the connectionist one.

How do we decide where to attach phrases?

In the garden-path model, what syntactic information does the parser use to assign the initial structure? It has two biases, *minimal attachment* and *late closure*. These will take a bit of explaining.

According to the principle of minimal attachment, new material should be attached to the syntactic representation we have so far to create the simplest legal structure possible. Of course "simple" needs a formal definition, and more strictly minimal attachment stipulates that incoming material should be attached to the partial syntactic structure using the fewest nodes possible. A *node* is a point in the syntactic structure, and at this point we really do need a diagram and a little knowledge of how we analyse syntactic structures.

According to the principle of late closure, if possible new material should be incorporated into the clause or phrase structure being processed. We also assume the current clause is the main clause of the sentence. If there's any conflict between these two principles, minimal attachment takes precedence. Let's have some fun with parse tree diagrams (Figures 7.2A, 7.2B, and 7.2C).

They're called parse trees because they're supposed to look like upside-down trees, although with branches coming off. They're very useful for showing the structure of a sentence. Here we have the start of a sentence; you hear "The burglars stole –". "The burglars" must be a noun phrase, and "stole" a verb, announcing the start of a noun phrase. So far, so unambiguous. But now suppose you hear "all the statues in the –". How are we to attach this? Let's wait until we hear the

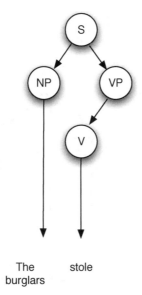

FIGURE 7.2A Parse tree: "The burglars stole"

final word before drawing diagrams, and the final word is either "house" or "night". These two words necessitate different syntactic structures, as can be seen by their associated parse trees.

"In the house" has to be combined directly with "all the statues", so the

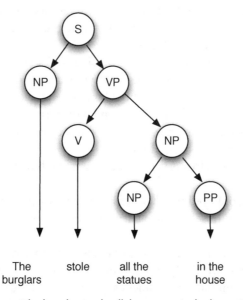

FIGURE 7.2B Parse tree: "The burglars stole all the statues in the house"

195

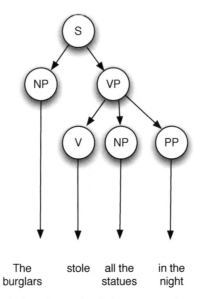

The   stole   all the   in the
burglars   statues   night

FIGURE 7.2C Parse tree: "The burglars stole all the statues in the night"

whole makes "all the statues in the house" a noun phrase. "In the night" has to be combined with the verb, so it is attached as a prepositional phrase to the verb phrase.

Which is the simpler structure – which is the minimal attachment structure? Simply count up the nodes, the circles. The first structure, the noun phrase structure, has seven nodes; the verb phrase structure has six. So according to minimal attachment the second, verb phrase structure is the preferred simpler structure – an important prediction to which I'll return.

A favoured technique for studying parsing looks at people's eye movement while reading text. There are a number of devices available now that enable us to see where people are looking and for how long; one favoured mechanism involves bouncing an infrared beam off the eyeball and monitoring the reflections. Studies of eye movements show that sentences that only make sense when these two principles are violated always seem to cause difficulty.

The first example below is very straightforward, but the second is not.

The criminal confessed that his sins harmed many people.
The criminal confessed his sins harmed many people.

You might find the second sentence to be slightly more difficult to understand. That's because when we deal with the first part of the sentence ("the criminal confessed his sins"), minimal attachment says that we should construct the simplest possible structure, which is for "sins" to be the direct object of "confessed", so "sins" should be the end of the clause; after that it should be a new sentence, or a conjunction such as "and" or "because". The final part of the sentence, "harmed many people" – what we can call the *disambiguating* material, because it resolves any temporary ambiguity – is in conflict with this simple structure, and to resolve this conflict we have to go back and reanalyse (putting the second parsing stage into action, according to the garden-path model). Rayner and Frazier (1987) monitored people's eye movements, and found that this sort of structure did cause temporary difficulty: people looked for a relatively long time in the disambiguating region and looked longer at the second sentence overall than the first. The first sentence above doesn't cause this problem because the word "that" prevents any ambiguity, so people spend a relatively short time looking at the "harmed many people" section.

Other studies show that sentences that violate late closure also cause difficulty. In the second sentence below, the processor tries to attach "a mile and a half" to "jog", because it's treating this material as part of the main clause. But then we get "seems a short distance", which throws a spanner in the works. Frazier and Rayner (1982), again looking at people's eye movements, found that people found the second sentence harder than the first, where the word "this" again prevents any ambiguity.

> Since Alice always jogs a mile and a half this seems a short distance to her.
> Since Alice always jogs a mile and a half seems a short distance to her.

We have data then that are consistent with minimal attachment and late closure, but can semantic knowledge prevent us from being led up the garden path? The results of an experiment by Ferreira and Clifton (1986) suggest not. Consider these two sentences.

> The defendant examined by the lawyer turned out to be unreliable.
> The evidence examined by the lawyer turned out to be unreliable.

The sentence fragment "The noun examined –" is ambiguous; it's consistent with either a nice, simple direct object structure (as in "the defendant examined the evidence") or the more complex reduced relative structure (as in "the defendant examined by the lawyer"). Hold on a moment, I hear you say, surely it depends on what the noun is? I grant you that animate nouns, such as defendants, can be ambiguous in this sort of structure, because they can be both subjects and objects, but what about inanimate nouns, such as "evidence"? As soon as we hear "the evidence examined" we know to expect something like a reduced relative, because evidence can't go round examining things – it's got to be examined *by* something. So while the first of these of two sentences might be difficult, the second should not, because our semantic knowledge of what things can do should prevent the ambiguity. Or at least it should if parsing can make early use of semantic information. But

Ferreira and Clifton found that these two sentences were equally difficult – people were getting garden-pathed by "the evidence examined –" just as much as they were by "the defendant examined –". This result suggests that we make the very first parsing decisions on syntactic grounds alone; the semantic information is quickly used to hasten our way out of the garden path, but it can't prevent us being led up it in the first place.

The analysis of the electrical activity of the brain ("brain waves") supports this two-stage idea. We can attach electrodes to a person's scalp and measure the electrical activity across the brain in response to events – called *event-related potentials* (ERPs). There are two particularly pronounced spikes of interest to our understanding of how we process verbal material. We observe one event called the N400 (so called because it's of negative amplitude and observed 400 milliseconds after the event) after we observe a semantic anomaly – so when you read:

When Alice pressed the switch nothing happened, so she realised she had to change the bulb in the ostrich.

Your brain will show a nice big N400 when you get to "ostrich". Another event, the P600, is of positive amplitude and observed 600 milliseconds after a syntactic anomaly. So when you read:

Alice persuaded to dig it.

your brain will show a glorious P600. Several studies have used these ERPs to map the time course of sentence processing (e.g. Ainsworth-Darnell et al., 1988; Friederici, 2002; Osterhout & Nicol, 1999). For example, Osterhout and Nicol presented participants with sentences containing words that were appropriate, semantically anomalous, syntactically anomalous, or both semantically and syn-tactically anomalous:

The new species of orchid will grow in tropical regions.
The new species of orchid will sing in tropical regions.
The new species of orchid will growing in tropical regions.
The new species of orchid will singing in tropical regions.

The doubly anomalous sentences elicited both an N400 and a P600, with the size of effect being the same as single anomalous sentences. Different parts of the brain seem to respond to syntactic and semantic anomaly, with each being unaffected by the other. Osterhout and Nicol concluded that semantic and syntactic processes are independent.

Other researchers have met these results with more scepticism. It is one thing to say that different parts of the brain store different types of knowledge and deal with different types of processing, and another to say that these processes don't have any influence on each other (Pickering, 1999). While the first claim is relatively uncontroversial, the second is much more so.

How much like a parse tree does this look?

How do multiple constraints operate?

According to constraint-based models, multiple sources of information converge to bias how the HSPM parses sentences. Semantic information can be used from an early stage, and can override pure syntactic biases. Consider the two sentences:

The thieves stole all the paintings in the museum while the guard slept.
The thieves stole all the paintings in the night while the guard slept.

Taraban and McClelland (1988) used a task known as self-paced reading to measure how difficult people found these sentences to understand. In this task people press a key for each new word, and so you can measure how long it takes them to read the whole sentence. The more difficult the sentence is to understand, the reasoning goes, the longer people will take to read it. The first sentence above, with "all the paintings in the museum" forming a noun phrase, is the more complicated syntactic structure according to minimal attachment.

199

An eye-tracking device (photograph Ben Tatler)

Nevertheless, people took longer to read the grammatically simpler second sentence than the more complex first sentence. Taraban and McClelland argued that the meanings of all the words of the first sentence (thieves, paintings, museum) conspire to create a bias for the more complex, non-minimal interpretation. What matters, they argue, aren't syntactic biases, but semantic biases: what cause the parser problems aren't violations of abstract syntactic principles, but violations of semantic expectations. In this type of approach the verb is king: each verb comes with a set of possible roles (called thematic information) about what can do what to what. If you ask a hundred people to complete the sentence "the thieves stole the paintings in the –", they're more likely to complete it with the place the paintings were stolen from (e.g. museum, gallery) than some general setting (in the night, in the day) (Figure 7.3). Taraban and McClelland went on to argue that the earlier studies that showed effects of minimal attachment had in fact done so because the materials had confounded syntactic and semantic biases. When you balance them out, such as here, only semantics matters.

(7 nodes)

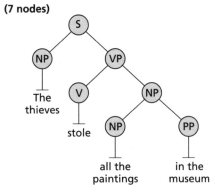

(6 nodes)

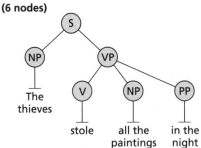

FIGURE 7.3 Noun phrase and verb phrase attachment structures in Taraban and McClelland (1988)

Providing an appropriate semantic context can eliminate the garden-path effect. When we have two similar sentences:

The teachers taught by the Berlitz method passed the test.
The children taught by the Berlitz method passed the test.

The first causes us more difficulty than the second, as measured by the number of people who think it's ungrammatical. We expect children to be taught and teachers to teach, and so the syntactic structure of the second sentence doesn't cause us any difficulty at all (Crain & Steedman, 1985). For the first sentence we have to construct a model where for some reason teachers are being taught something, and it's making sense of this information that's costly. We find the same thing with other materials using different tasks:

The archaeologist examined –
The fossil examined –

Fossils are inanimate and can only be examined, they can't examine. Measures of eye movements show that if semantic constraints are strong enough, people are not garden-pathed by reduced relative constructions such as the following sentence (Trueswell et al., 1994).

The fossil examined by the archaeologist was important.

On the semantic account, there's no such thing as neutral context. Even if no semantic context is provided by the material, we have knowledge and expectations about how the world works, as with teachers teaching in this example. The more assumptions we have to make, the harder the sentence is to understand. This idea is powerful, and casts light on why our old friend, the original garden-path sentence "the horse raced past the barn fell", is difficult.

The horse raced past the barn quickly.
The horse raced past the barn fell.

People find the first sentence much easier to understand than the second. In the first, we only need to think about one horse. The second only really makes sense if there are a number of horses being raced and it was the one that was raced past the barn that fell – otherwise why would the speaker bother mentioning the bit about the barn? So we have to construct a model with more than one horse, which is more effortful than in the first, quick, case.

How specific is the sort of information that can influence parsing? Recent experiments with eye movements suggest we make use of all possible sources of information to help construct the most likely syntactic structure. In the real world, we aren't always limited to hearing or reading a few sentences. What's in front of our eyes is sometimes a rich source of information. Suppose you read:

Put the apple on the towel in the box.

This sentence by itself is ambiguous. It could mean either "there's an apple on a towel, and you should put that in the box" or "there's an apple somewhere else and you should put that on a towel which is in the box". Garden-path theory says that we should always interpret the sentence initially in the second way, with the towel being the destination, because that's the grammatically simpler structure. How we understand this sentence depends on what's in front of our eyes (Tanenhaus et al., 1995). In the one-referent condition of the Tanenhaus et al. experiment, there was an apple on a towel, and another towel in the box. In the two-referent condition, there was one apple on a towel and another on a napkin. In the one-referent condition, participants spent considerable time looking at the incorrect destination, the irrelevant towel, whereas in the two-referent condition they rarely did so. "On the towel" was interpreted as the destination only in the one-referent condition; in the two-referent condition it was interpreted as a modifier of "apple".

Visual information is used to help us decide how to analyse ambiguous material. Furthermore, a similar experiment by Sedivy et al. (1999) showed that people make use of this sort of information very quickly.

Put the apple on the towel – seems easy enough

There is now then a great deal of evidence that people make use of multiple sources of information while constructing a syntactic representation of incoming language. Remember though that an earlier study by Ferreira and Clifton (1986) found that semantic factors can't prevent us from being garden-pathed (with defendants and evidence being examined). How can we explain this apparent contradiction? Trueswell et al. (1994) argued that experiments that failed to find semantic effects on parsing preference did so because the semantic constraints weren't strong enough. Semantic contraints can prevent us being garden-pathed, but only if they're strong enough. It is also interesting to note that the more realistic information there is available (as in the visual world experiment above), the more likely we are to find evidence of interaction.

We have two sources of variation that make a comparison of studies in this area very difficult: we have the strength of the semantic constraint provided by the materials (and this can be difficult to measure independently) and we have different researchers using different experimental techniques (eye movements, ERP, grammaticality judgement, self-paced reading) – and even within a technique such as eye-movement analysis there are different measures to be compared (total reading time, the number of times you look back, the time you spend first looking at something before you move on). So if you don't like somebody else's results, there are plenty of ways out. The debate is far from settled, and this is another area in which the jury is still out (even if many researchers don't think it is). But I can't sit on the wall for ever, and I admit I find the evidence for the constraint-based approach more compelling and powerful.

When we hear or read then, we construct a syntactic representation which we adjust with each incoming word. We do this quickly and mostly effortlessly. The HSPM makes use of every source of information, particularly semantic and pragmatic knowledge, and especially our knowledge of how different verbs behave. If a structure is ambiguous, representations of both structures are kept open, although one is usually more activated than the other. As with the TRACE model of word identification, competition is used to resolve ambiguity (MacDonald et al., 1994). The most activated structure beats the others into submission, which has two implications. The first is that if the less activated structure is very much less activated, but turns out to be the correct one, the HSPM will be momentarily taken aback – which presumably is when we have the strong overt sensation of having been led down the garden path (Tabor & Hutchins, 2004). The second implication is that if competition is high, such as when there are two highly activated competing structures, processing will be difficult, which makes sense and is what we observe.

Where does this leave us with the big issue of modularity? It leaves us near Hollywood on the West Coast. If the multiple-constraints approach is indeed correct, language processing is a free-for-all – or, in Spivey's (2007) terms, it's a *hungry* process, actively seeking possible interpretations, gobbling up as much information as it can as quickly as possible, and looking ahead to see what's left on the linguistic plate.

What do we remember of what we understand?

Think back to the introduction you've just read, and ask yourself what you remember of it. Do you remember every word? Almost certainly not. Do you remember the syntax, the grammatical structure of every sentence? Again, almost certainly not. You might remember the odd word (particularly novel ones like *alignment*), or the odd sentence verbatim, but what you remember – hopefully – is the gist, the general idea.

Several early psycholinguistic experiments confirmed this impression. Sachs (1967) gave participants stories containing sentences such as the following:

He sent a letter about it to Galileo, the great Italian scientist.

She later tested their ability to distinguish this original from three variants of it:

He sent Galileo, the great Italian scientist, a letter about it.
A letter about it was sent to Galileo, the great Italian scientist.
Galileo, the great Italian scientist, sent him a letter about it.

She tested their memory after 0, 80, and 160 intervening syllables – equivalent to about 0, 25, or 50 seconds. She found that unless people were tested immediately they couldn't tell the original from the first two variants, which each change the syntax of the original. In contrast, they were able to distinguish the original from the final version, which changes the meaning of the original, even after some time had elapsed. This result confirms our intuition: people usually dump the details of the wording and syntax as soon as they've extracted the meaning, but retain the meaning for some time.

We don't always dump word order information. Sometimes what we hear is important, or in some way particularly memorable, or just funny. Students remember material from lectures well for a couple of days but in the absence of additional exposure have forgotten most of it after five days (Kintsch & Bates, 1977). A depressing result from this study for educators is that students were no better at remembering the most important points of the lecture than the peripheral material. What students remembered best of all were the announcements and jokes. There's a lesson here.

This conclusion is consistent with the work on eye-witness testimony I discussed earlier.

The conclusion is that processing sentences is just a tool to extract the gist of the meaning. We're not concerned with the details of the words, or the specifics of the syntax, once we've extracted what we think is the intended meaning. It's that intended meaning that's important, and it's that that we try to fit in with our model of the world.

How do we make use of context?

It's not surprising to me that our memory for word order is usually so poor. After all, the goal of language understanding isn't to construct a syntactic representation, but to use that in the short term to extract the meaning of the sentence – to work out how the meanings of words are related, and to connect that meaning with what we already know, and to decide what to do next. It's the bigger picture that matters. How do we paint this bigger picture, and what does the picture look like?

Try reading an advanced text in an area of which you have little or no prior knowledge. It's hard going, isn't it, to say the least? Close the book; how much of it do you remember? Probably very little indeed. The point may be obvious, but we need some context, some background knowledge before we can make sense of what we hear or read. Part of the skill of writing a good textbook is being able to pitch it at a level that provides sufficient context for the novice in the area, without making it boring; part of the skill of being a good student in an area is discovering the gaps in your knowledge and finding that context.

Several classic psycholinguistic experiments show the importance of prior knowledge – and knowing that you know the context. One of the earliest experiments made just this point. Here's a little story:

> The procedure is actually quite simple. First you arrange things into two different groups. Of course, one pile may be sufficient depending on how much there is to do. If you have to go somewhere else due to lack of facilities, that is the next step; otherwise you are pretty well set. It is important not to overdo things. That is, it is better to do fewer things at once than too many. In the short run this might not seem important, but complications can easily arise. A mistake can be expensive as well. At first the whole procedure will seem complicated. Soon, however, it will become just another facet of life. It is difficult to foresee any end to the necessity for this task in the immediate future, but then one can never tell. After the procedure is completed, one arranges the material into different groups again. Then they can be put into their appropriate places. Eventually they will be used once more, and the whole cycle will then have to be repeated. However, that is part of life.

Can you make any sense of it? How much can you remember of it? When presented like this, people recall an average of only 2.8 out of a maximum of 18 ideas in the story (Bransford & Johnson, 1973). Now suppose I'd told you in advance that this story is about washing clothes; your comprehension of and memory for the story would have been much better. In fact people told this context before being given the story to read remembered 5.8 ideas. Interestingly, being given the context *after* hearing the story didn't seem to help much; people recalled only 2.7 ideas, about the same as if they'd had no context.

The context doesn't have to be very much; having a title sometimes is all we need, as was demonstrated in a similar sort of study by Dooling and Lachman (1971), who gave their participants the following story:

> With hocked gems financing him, our hero bravely defied all scornful laughter that tried to prevent his scheme. "Your eyes deceive," he had said. "An egg, not a table, correctly typifies this unexplored planet." Now three sturdy sisters sought proof. Forging along, sometimes through vast calmness, yet more often over turbulent peaks and valleys, days became weeks as doubters spread fearful rumours about the edge. At last, from nowhere, welcome winged creatures appeared signifying monumental success.

You'll probably find this story equally difficult to make any sense of, but with the title "Christopher Columbus's discovery of America", everything falls into place: the three sisters are the ships, the turbulent peaks and valleys the ocean, the edge the supposed edge of the flat earth, welcome winged creatures birds showing land is near. Again, though, the context only helped if presented before the story.

You might say that these are pretty odd stories, designed to be obscure. Context still has striking effects when comprehending more mundane material, as is shown with this story from an experiment by Anderson and Pichert (1978).

> Two boys play hooky from school. They go to the home of one of the boys because his mother is never there on a Thursday. The family is well off. They have a fine old home which is set back from the road and which has attractive grounds. But since it is an old house it has some defects: for example, it has a leaky roof, and a damp and musty cellar. Because the family is wealthy, they have a lot of valuable possessions – such as ten-speed bike, a colour television, and a rare coin collection.

Participants were told in advance that the story was about a house to be considered either from the perspective of a burglar, or from that of a potential house buyer. The perspective supplied influenced what people remembered of the story; so, for example, those reading it from the estate agent perspective would be more likely to recall the leaking roof, and those from the burglar perspective the list of valuable possessions. However, the participants were then given the other perspective – so that if they'd previously been given the burglar perspective they would now be given the estate agent perspective. This shift in perspective aided recall, so that people recalled ideas from the story that they could not previously. This positive effect of shifting perspective might seem to contradict the findings above that you need to know the context before hearing the story, but this difference can be explained in terms of the difficulty and bizarreness of the stories: these very odd stories are too difficult to be rescued by context afterwards. But most of the time, context before and after is a very good thing, and changing your perspective will help you remember more.

How do we go beyond the words?

I have a friend who is a master of not saying what he means, so that you can work out what he really means with quite a bit of knowledge and effort. He is the master of obliqueness: if he means "no", he will say "yes", but in a very roundabout way such that if you know him you can eventually work out that he really means "no". But it takes a lot of work. His words differ from his intentions.

We go beyond the literal meaning of what we read or hear in many ways: we make *inferences* that sometimes go far beyond the meaning of the sentences we come across. Sometimes these are warranted, sometimes not. Sometimes the inferences are made so easily they appear to happen automatically; sometimes we have to really struggle to work out what was intended.

Context can be a curse as well as a blessing, as shown dramatically by an experiment by Sulin and Dooling (1974), who presented this story to their participants:

> Gerald Martin strove to undermine the existing government to satisfy his political ambitions. Many of the people of his country supported his efforts. Current political problems made it relatively easy for Martin to take over. Certain groups remained loyal to the old government and caused Martin trouble. He confronted these groups directly and so silenced them. He became a ruthless, uncontrollable dictator. The ultimate effect of his rule was the downfall of his country.

Half the readers read the story as above, but the other half had "Adolf Hitler" substituted for "Gerald Martin". A little later they were given some sentences and asked if they had read them in the story; some of them really were in the story, but others weren't. Those who had been given the name "Adolf Hitler" were far more likely to think erroneously that they'd actually read "He hated the Jews particularly and so persecuted them" than those given the name "Gerald Martin". So context isn't always a good thing; here (and once again, remember the unreliability of eyewitness testimony, and how we can distort memory with leading questions) context can cause us to remember things we never heard. Our knowledge of the world can provoke errors.

There are three types of inference: logical, bridging, and elaborative. *Logical* inferences are the least interesting: if I tell you "Boris is a bachelor", you can easily infer that Boris doesn't have a wife. We make *bridging* inferences to keep our understanding of the text coherent, to ensure that everything links to everything else. We work, as comprehenders, on the basis that everything makes sense. So if I say,

> Boris had a haircut yesterday. He was happy about it,

who does "he" refer to? Boris, of course. You've made a bridging inference to relate new information to old. I'll deal with how we keep track of pronouns in the next section.

We make *elaborative inferences* when we go beyond the text and use our knowledge of the world to deduce something that isn't in the text. The Gerald Martin example shows how elaborative inferences can sometimes lead us astray. We make inferences to construct a more detailed model depicting what we hear; and given that our memory for what we actually read or hear is quite poor, it should come as no surprise to hear that we are bad at distinguishing the results of elaborative inferences we make from what was actually in the text. This was famously shown in an experiment by Bransford et al. in 1972. They gave people a sentence such as:

Three turtles rested on a floating log and a fish swam beneath them.

After a short delay people were given the following sentence:

Three turtles rested on a floating log and a fish swam beneath it.

They were just as likely to agree that they'd heard the new sentence as the original because if the turtles are on a log then anything that swims beneath the turtles must also swim beneath the log. It's the model of what we hear that we remember, complete with all the inferences we make to construct the model, not the words we hear. If we change just two words in the above sentence, though:

Three turtles were beside a floating log and a fish swam beneath them.

People no longer confuse this sentence with the "beneath it" one because the inference is no longer true.

Obviously the number of potential elaborative inferences that could be made is extremely large. The experimenters could have slipped any plausible information about Hitler into that version of the Gerald Martin story and still confused the participants. There's a considerable amount of evidence that we draw the bridging inferences we need to keep the text making sense automatically, but we only automatically draw elaborative inferences as and when we need to. According to the minimalist hypothesis, we keep the number of elaborative inferences to a minimum, and make them as simple as possible (McKoon & Ratcliff, 1992). The studies we've discussed so far that show that people make inferences have all been rather indirect, looking at people's memory for text, often in the light of confusing distractor items or misleading questions. The longer the delay between presentation and testing, the more errors people make. Now consider these two sentences:

The housewife was learning to be a seamstress and needed practice, so she got out the skirt she was making and threaded the needle.

The director and cameraman were ready to shoot close-ups when suddenly the actress fell from the fourteenth floor.

Participants are given a lexical decision task concurrently with these stories. In this task, if you remember, you have to press one button if you see a word, and another if you see a non-word, and we measure the reaction time to pressing the key. The key target words for these stories are "sew" for the first and "dead" for the second. The word "sew" is strongly semantically associated with the words "seamstress", "threaded", and "needle" in the stories, and consequently its recognition is duly facilitated by the story. What about "dead"? It isn't strongly associated with any of the words in the story, and although it's a very reasonable, indeed likely, elaborative inference, it isn't necessary (and it might not even be true; she might survive, or have her fall broken by something in the way that happens so often in Hollywood). We don't find any facilitation of words like "dead" in these kinds of contexts. Further evidence comes from a study by Singer (1994), who presented participants with sentences like the following:

> The dentist pulled the tooth painlessly. The patient liked the method.
> The tooth was pulled painlessly. The dentist used a new method.
> The tooth was pulled painlessly. The patient liked the new method.

The participants were given a probe sentence to verify and the experimenter measured how long it took the participant to decide if the probe was true or not. The probe was "A dentist pulled a tooth". The first sentence more or less contains the probe, so people are fast to respond YES. In the second sentence people must make the bridging inference that the dentist pulled the tooth to make sense of the material and to maintain a coherent representation of the material. The bridging inference is that the dentist pulled the tooth, and we find that people are just as fast to respond "yes" to the probe with the second sentence as with the first. This result suggests that people make this sort of inference quickly and automatically. However, the third sentence requires an elaborative inference; the dentist isn't mentioned explicitly, so we have to put a bit of work into constructing a model that ties up the tooth, dentist, and patient. So bridging inferences are made automatically when we read text to maintain coherence, and elaborative inferences are made later when necessary.

What can we do with language?

Although I've noted that language serves many functions, from communicating to assisting thought, from play to maintaining social contact, often we speak because we want to have some effect on our listeners (or readers). Speakers have goals, and listeners try to work out what those goals are. Every utterance is a type of *speech act*, with some goal in mind, however trivial (Austin, 1976; Searle, 1969). Searle argued that speech acts fall into five broad categories.

1   *Representatives:* The speaker is asserting what they consider to be a fact (e.g. "Felix is a naughty dog").

2   *Directives:* The speaker is trying to get the listener to do something (e.g. if I ask you "Is Felix a good dog?", I'm trying to get you to give me some information).

3   *Expressives:* The speaker is revealing something about their psychological state (e.g. "I'm very disappointed in Felix").

4   *Declaratives:* The speaker brings about a new state of affairs (e.g. "You're fired!").

5   *Commissives:* The speaker commits themselves to some future action (e.g. "I promise I'll buy Felix a bone tomorrow").

I don't think we should see these as hard and fast categories, as some utterances might straddle two categories ("I'm very disappointed in Felix" conveys something about my psychological state and conveys a belief), but they provide a very useful framework for thinking about the sorts of things language can do. But often there's a mismatch between the literal meaning of what we say and the effects the utterance has, and the philosopher of language J.L. Austin (the initials standing for "John" and the splendid "Langshaw") recognised that each speech act can have three effects, which he called *forces*. If I make an apparently simple request such as:

Can you get me rat poison on the way home from work tonight?

the most obvious effect is that I interpret this utterance as a request that I should purchase some rat poison on my way home from work. Austin called this the *illocutionary force* – what the speaker is trying to get the listener to do. But notice that literally it's not what the utterance says at all; the literal meaning is a question about my ability to get rat poison on my way home from work. Austin called this literal meaning the *locutionary force*. It is possible to imagine scenarios in which the literal meaning of this sort of utterance is the intended one – that is, where the locutionary and illocutionary force match. For example, I might have just broken my leg, having previously offered to get some rat poison on the way home from work. Finally, our utterances can have all sorts of effects: I might annoy you because this is yet another unreasonable demand on your time I've made, or you might think I'm mean and heartless killing all those nice rats, or you might believe I'm going to poison you, or you might just go ahead and get the rat poison. All these effects, some intended, others not, are called the *perlocutionary force* of the utterance.

Utterances like this one, where there's a mismatch between the literal meaning and the intended meaning of the words, are very common. The mismatch, on reflection, is most apparent in this sort of *indirect request* where I'm trying to get you to do something. You might not have noticed it before, but "Can you pass the wine?" is an indirect request – my words don't strictly request you to pass the wine, but instead literally ask if you have the ability to do so. It's a good schoolboy jape to reply "yes" to such requests, and leave it at that. Indirect requests are linked to politeness; the more polite we want to be, the more indirect we become.

> Pass the wine!
> Can you pass the wine?
> Could you please reach over and hand me the wine?
> Could you please think about passing the wine?
> My glass is only half full.
> The wine's lovely.
> Look at the pattern the moonlight creates shining through my empty glass.

Some indirect requests are so common as to have become idioms – frozen sayings that have a well-known meaning of their own. "Can you –" requests are of this type, to the extent that it would be most unusual to have to interpret "Can you pass the wine?" literally as a request about your ability to pass the wine. There comes a point on this list, though, where indirectness is no longer idiomatic, and the listener has to do some real work to draw an elaborative inference about what the speaker's intention is.

We call this sort of conversational inference, where listeners have to compute the intended meaning from the literal meaning, a *conversational implicature*. The way in which we detect a mismatch, and the way in which we seek to resolve the indirectness, was suggested by the linguistic philosopher H.P. Grice (1975). Grice proposed that speakers in a conversation collaborate: adult conversation should be meaningful and purposeful. Only up to a point, surely, you might object, but even just discussing the weather has some conversational goal, and such conversations will still follow the rules. But what are the rules? Grice argued that we follow a *co-operative principle* when speaking, making our contributions such as is required when they are required. To do this, speakers follow four conversational maxims:

1 *Maxim of relevance.* Make your contribution relevant to the aims of the conversation.
2 *Maxim of quantity.* Make your contribution as informative as necessary, but no more so.
3 *Maxim of quality.* Make your contribution true – do not say anything you know to be false.
4 *Maxim of manner.* Be clear; avoid obscurity, ambiguity, and disorder in your speech.

Of these, relevance is probably the most important, and some have argued that the other three maxims are all implied by relevance alone (Sperber & Wilson, 1986, 1987). These maxims are most useful not when the speaker follows them, but when they appear to have violated them. Given the importance of relevance, the following conversation seems very odd:

Bill: What do you think of my new hat?
Ben: What a lovely day it is!

Ben's utterance doesn't seem to follow from what Bill said at all. So odd does this seem that we strive to find some purpose in Ben's utterance – we try to make it relevant. How can we do this? We could make the inference that Ben really doesn't like Bill's new hat, and is trying to avoid the topic. Listeners assume that although on the face of things speakers might appear to be violating one or more of the maxims, deeper down they are not. We reconcile this discrepancy by making an inference – the *conversational implicature*. If you eavesdrop on a few conversations, and are looking for them, conversational implicatures are very common. We have to make one whenever there's a discrepancy between what someone says and the most straightforward reply the other speaker could give.

I don't mean to imply that we spend a great deal of conscious effort in conversation trying to work out what the other person meant, or intended. Sometimes we do; sometimes I've had the experience of realising a couple of hours later, when it's far too late to do anything about it, that the other person was intending something other than they'd said. But on many occasions we draw the inferences necessary to help us make sense of the conversation without even noticing that we're doing so.

How do we link new information with old?

Relevance means that what we say or hear is in some way linked to what has come before. Language wouldn't be of much use if every sentence was spoken in isolation, without any connection to the past. There are two different tasks for speakers and listeners. The speaker has to relate the new material that they wish to convey to the old so as to ease the work of the listener, and the listener has to integrate the new information with the old.

Here's a little story.

Felix chased a cat. The cat found a small hole and he ran into it. The dog had to give up the chase. He sat outside the hole for a while looking disappointed. After five minutes he went off to chase some rabbits. It was sad to watch.

Not a terribly exciting story, perhaps, but an interesting one from a psycholinguistic point of view. Notice how with multi-sentence stories we get a picture of events unfolding in time. Think about that first "he"; what does it refer to? I think most people won't hesitate to say "the cat". But now look at the second "he", and say what that refers to; this time it's Felix, the dog. In fact it's interesting that we know that Felix is a dog, because it isn't explicitly stated anywhere. Working out what refers to what in a story entails problems of establishing the *reference*. What we seem to be doing when we read a story such as this is that we construct some sort of model, and then we create entities in that model to represent the actors and objects in our story, and then we try to keep track of who's what. We call the thing first mentioned the *antecedent* (Felix) and subsequent different expressions referring to the antecedent (he, the dog) *anaphors*.

One way in which we keep track of reference is that we try to keep the number of entities in our mental model of the story to a minimum. Once we've introduced dear old Felix, we don't then postulate that "the dog" refers to something new. The word "the" is a cue; we wouldn't normally use "the" here to introduce a new dog; whereas "a dog" would imply something new in the story, "the dog" implies something has already been introduced.

Most troublesome are all those pronouns, "he" and "it". The first "he" refers to the cat, but the second "he", soon after, to Felix the dog. How do we decide what pronouns refer to? It turns out that we use a number of strategies based on cues from the sentence.

Sometimes it's very straightforward; there is only the referent, as below.

Felix was very happy; he caught the pesky rabbit.

We prefer to match the anaphors to antecedents in the same relative position, a strategy called *parallel function* (Sheldon, 1974).

Bill sold Ben his car because he no longer needed it.
Bill sold Ben his car because he needed it.

The first sentence is easy to understand because "he", the subject of the second clause, refers to Bill, the subject of the first clause. People find the second more difficult because the subject of the second clause does not refer to the subject of the first. And when we have a sentence such as:

Bill hated Ben so he kicked him.

The meaning and relative position of the antecedents and pronouns conspire to make reference assignment straightforward. *Gender* is another straightforward cue. Given:

Alice told Bill to get lost because he had annoyed her

it's trivial to work out to whom "he" and "her" refer. We access information about gender very quickly: eye-movement studies show that if people look at cartoons with male and female characters, they can use the gender of the pronoun to look at the correct picture within 200 milliseconds; if gender isn't a cue (as is the case if all the characters in the picture are male or female), people take much longer to work out to whom the pronoun is referring (Arnold et al., 2000).

The meaning of the sentence is another cue. In the following two examples you are likely to assign different antecedents to the pronouns because the meanings of the verbs imply things: it's the person who hates who is most likely to kick, and the person who is offended who is most likely to react.

> Bill hated Ben, so he kicked him.
> Bill offended Ben, so he sent him to Coventry.

Pronouns are processed more quickly the more recently the antecedent has been explicitly mentioned. Psycholinguists talk about items being in focus; we can think of these referents as being the most active in our representation of the text because of their recency and importance. We can only really use pronouns when an item is in focus. If we have the sentence:

> Bill was driving to Birmingham.

it's perfectly acceptable to follow it with "He became tired", because he refers to Bill, who is in explicit focus; but to follow it with "It broke down" would sound distinctly odd, because the antecedent of "it" is presumably Bill's car, which isn't in explicit focus. The less in focus an antecedent is, the more difficult it is to retrieve it (Sanford & Garrod, 1981). If I suddenly spring on you:

> He ran back to his kennel and drank some water

it's going to take you some time to work out that we're back to talking about dear old Felix again.

We clearly have several strategies for computing the antecedents of anaphors. How do we choose the best one? We seem to use them in parallel. Badecker and Straub (2002) discuss a parallel constraint model, similar to the interactive activation models of word recognition and the constraint-satisfaction models of parsing, where all possible cues contribute in parallel to the activation of possible antecedents in the mental model of the discourse. If all the cues converge, anaphoric resolution is fast and straightforward; if they conflict, resolution is slower, and might even come to need conscious, attentional processing.

The second, related way in which we have to mingle old and new information is based on the idea of focus. We can think of the focus of the text or discourse as moving along as we come to new material and events happen. Here is my entry for the next Booker Prize:

> Felix slept until late most mornings. He'd get up, chase a few chipmunks, and drink some water. Then he'd wander around the cabbage patch and drink some more water. One day a cat came into the garden. Felix went wild. He chased the cat round and round until it went into a hole. He sat patiently outside. Eventually he worked out it was too small for him and then he gave up. He had some more water from his bucket and went back to sleep. When we got home the cabbage patch was ruined. The bucket was empty and the cat was still down the hole. It took some time before it ventured out.

Notice how the focus of the story moves along, and how effortlessly we assign referents to pronouns. If we jumble the sentences up, the overall meaning of the story is preserved, but the flow of the focus is disrupted, and assigning antecedents to anaphors is now very difficult.

> He had some more water from his bucket and went back to sleep. It took some time before it ventured out. Eventually he worked out that it was too small for him and then he gave up. Felix went wild. He sat patiently outside. Felix slept until late most mornings. When we got home the cabbage patch was ruined. He'd get up, chase a few chipmunks, and drink some water. The bucket was empty and the cat was still down the hole. Then he'd wander around the cabbage patch and drink some more water. One day a cat came into the garden. He chased the cat round and round until it went into a hole.

Speakers and writers don't speak and write like this. Although it might seem obvious that we are most likely to present events in the order in which they happen, speakers go further than that: they try to make the listener's job as straightforward as possible. There's a contract between speaker and listener to present new information so that it can be readily assimilated into what is already known, a contract that's been called the *given–new contract* (Haviland & Clark, 1974). We find it harder to understand new material that violates the given–new contract, and find it easier to understand a new sentence where the link between the new material and the old is explicit rather than when it has to be inferred.

How do we construct a model of what we hear?

Here's a simple little story. Once again, I mean it really is simple, so don't get too excited.

The lawn runs up to the flower bed. The rose bush is in front of the dahlias, with the fence behind. On the right of the rose bush, as you look towards the fence, are some violets. On the left of the rose bush are some daisies. Behind the violets is a big sunflower. Bill comes along and waters the sunflower. He accidentally steps back and treads on . . .

I did tell you it wasn't terribly exciting! But now ask yourself, what does Bill trample to death? The violets of course. How do you know?

Reflect on this for a moment. I formed some kind of picture, an image of the story. You might not have done exactly the same, but you probably constructed a model of some sort to represent what was depicted in the story. This sort of model goes by several different names: a *situational model*, a *mental model*, sometimes just a model. Let's go for brevity and stick with what I've been calling it so far, the mental model (e.g. Johnson-Laird, 1983).

The mental model, then, is our representation of what we're reading, or what we're talking about. It consists of all the activated word meanings involved tied together in some way to show the relation between them. The most active meanings will be present in our limited short-term memory. Exactly how the model is constructed, and how the meanings are tied together, is shown by Walter Kintsch's *construction–integration model* (Kintsch, 1988). The most important part of the model is a propositional network that ties together all the elements of the text. A *proposition* is the smallest unit of meaning that can be put into a propositional form – a verb operating on a noun. Propositions would be "Felix sleeps", "cat runs" "is in hole", "Felix chases", and so on. All these simple propositions can be connected together into a network that represents the complete meaning of the text. When you've read and understood material, all you're left with is a propositional network; most of the surface details have been dispensed with.

We construct the propositionally network incrementally. As new material comes in, we integrate it with the propositional network. We keep some propositions active in our working memory; these are the most recent, and what we consider to be the most important. Given its limited capacity, we can only keep a few propositions active in working memory at any time; it's these that we find easier to find the antecedents for when we come across an anaphor. As we construct the propositional network, we might come across some contradictions, but these are resolved by a process of spreading activation and competition as I've discussed before. New portions of the network are continually being integrated with the existing structure to expand the size of the propositional network. As it grows, we can search the network, and use it to deduce answers to questions such as "What did Bill trample on?"

The model can account for several key findings in the comprehension literature. The more complex the material, in terms of the number of propositions, the longer it takes to read, because the longer the model takes to construct. We remember the most salient propositions better because they tend to be held in working memory for longer because they're the most useful propositions in constructing the network. We confuse inferences with the original material because we dump the source of the information as soon as we've constructed a stable network; all that matters is how propositions are connected, not how they became connected. The construction–integration model also predicts the ease with which we can read different sorts of material: text that makes it easy to construct a network, and that is constructed so that key propositions are likely to remain active in focus in working memory, should be the easiest to read. Material that keeps on bringing up different material that isn't in working memory, but that instead has to be inferred or brought from the network into working memory (by a process called a *reinstatement search*), is more difficult (Kintsch & Vipond, 1979). Individual differences in working memory span affect reading skill; clearly, the larger the span, the easier the person is going to find reading to be (Daneman & Carpenter, 1980). One lesson for writers here is that you can make your material easy to read by trying to minimise the number of times the reader has to dip into their propositional network by keeping important material in focus, by making referents as obvious as possible, and by constructing the flow of the text so that the focus assists the reader by keeping the most important propositions active.

Where does humour in language come from?

Brain damage can affect our ability to understand language in many different ways. I'm going to defer discussion of how it affects our ability to parse sentences until the next chapter. Brain damage can affect comprehension in a number of ways. I've already shown how understanding print can be disrupted by developmental and acquired dyslexia, and unsurprisingly there are types of brain damage that lead to difficulty in understanding spoken words. One of the most striking deficits in understanding language is known as *pure word deafness*. Patients with pure word deafness can read, write, and speak quite normally, but have great difficulty in understanding speech. They have extremely poor auditory comprehension and cannot repeat words back. On the other hand their hearing is normal, and they can identify musical instruments and other non-speech sounds (Saffran et al., 1976). The problem with pure word deafness patients must lie in constructing a pre-lexical code for speech.

A very rare variant is called *word meaning deafness*, in which the symptoms are similar to pure word deafness except the patient can also repeat words. The first case study was of a patient living in Edinburgh in the 1890s (Bramwell, 1897/1984); a more recent case was reported by Kohn and Friedman in 1986. Word meaning deafness shows that there must be a route that enables us to gain access to the sounds of words, and be able to repeat them back, but that bypasses meaning.

In the next chapter I'll talk about the consequences of damage to Wernicke's area of the brain, but patients with this sort of damage show difficulty in understanding speech and following conversations as well as pronounced difficulties in production. They also have difficulty in maintaining the coherence of discourse (Christiansen, 1995). And damage to the frontal lobes of the brain will lead to difficulty in controlling language, running conversations, and inhibiting appropriate material.

In this section though, I want to focus on the consequences of damage to the right hemisphere of the brain, which leads to an impairment to the ability to follow connected discourse without an impairment to recognising words or parsing sentences (Caplan, 1992). In particular, this sort of damage leads to a difficulty in understanding humour. Much as I wish I could write one, this section isn't an instruction manual on how to be funny. There are many different types and sources of humour: slapstick, puns, surreal, intellectual, incongruous, and the coarse and vulgar. It's unlikely that a single mechanism underlies all of these. But let's tell a joke.

> The quack was selling a potion which he claimed would make men live to a great age. He claimed he himself was hale and hearty and over 300 years old. "Is he really as old as that?" asked a listener of the youthful assistant. "I can't say", said the assistant, –

Now which of the following punchlines would be most likely to make them roll around the aisles?

1   "I've only worked with him a hundred years."
2   "I don't know how old he is."
3   "There are over three hundred days in a year."

The first, of course; the second is a coherent but non-humorous continuation, and the third just incoherent. Patients with right-hemisphere damage aren't very good at picking the funny continuation (Brownell et al., 1983); indeed, they often choose the incoherent ending. People with right-hemisphere damage find it particularly difficult to see implied meaning (something that is of course essential for understanding humour), make decisions about appropriateness, and integrate information (Myers & Mackisack, 1990). None of this is to say that patients with left-hemisphere damage might not have some difficulty in appreciating humour; after all, if you can't understand what's being said, you're unlikely to find it very funny, although you might be able to have a good laugh at the person saying it.

The right hemisphere isn't just important for understanding humour in language. It seems to play a more general role in helping us with the pragmatics of language – helping us understand how language is used and what we do with language. Damage to the right hemisphere interferes with our ability to use non-verbal cues, to follow the rules of conversation, and to go beyond the words (see Kolb & Whishaw, 2003, for a review). People with right-hemisphere damage have difficulty in understanding metaphor and figurative language (time is a river, the raindrops exploded on the window) – I think the relation with humour is obvious.

Chapter 8

Speaking

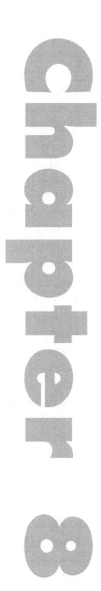

I DRIFTED INTO PSYCHOLINGUISTICS. They say that people become interested in psychology because they want to understand what's wrong with themselves, and that's true in my case. All my life I've messed up what I've meant to say. I'm perfectly articulate on paper but sometimes feel pretty dreadful when speaking. I slur my speech and often say the opposite of what I mean (which makes my lectures fun). I now think this all happens because of the general phonological deficit I have that I described earlier.

The obvious problem with making a lot of mistakes is that it makes the job of the listener very difficult. There's less room for error in producing language than in understanding it, and talking is hard work. When you're listening or reading, you can afford to take it easy now and then. If you hear "mutter cat mutter chase mutter mutter dog" you can interpret this as meaning "The cat chases the dog" and you'd be right most of the time. Speakers don't have this room. They have to say "A cat chases the dog" and always pay attention to those little details the listeners don't always have to bother with. (Although some say that when I speak it often sounds like "mutter mutter dog".)

In other words, when you're reading and listening, you can "be statistical" a lot of the time: you can live with inaccuracy, incomplete inputs, and making a guess at what you're hearing or reading. As long as you understand the content to an appropriate extent you've done all you need to. But when you're speaking, there's little room for error. People don't go round saying the odd word and hoping the listener will fill in the gaps.

There are, however, still elements of unpredictability in speech production. When you start speaking you don't always know what you're going to end up saying. Next time you have a conversation with someone, spend some effort on trying to work out what you're doing while talking. How far do you plan ahead when you're speaking? I find it's quite variable, and depends on the context. In a very formal situation – such as when I'm introducing a speaker, or making an important announcement to a class – I might prepare every word before I start speaking. (I then might have difficulty remembering what I'd planned to say, and might still mix up my carefully prepared words.) In an informal conversation over coffee, I might start speaking with no conscious idea of how I'm going to end up. And after a few drinks . . . Most of the time it's in between: I have some idea about what I'm going to say, I know how I'm going to start, but I don't always know the details of the wording at the end of what I want to say.

Can we learn from our mistakes?

I've already mentioned how many mistakes I make while I'm talking. Over the years I've jotted down the slips of the tongue I've made; it's a fun way of doing research. Sitting in a wine bar talking and writing down the occasional speech error beats hours programming a computer to run a lexical decision experiment.

Of course I'm not unique in making errors while talking (although I think I make more than most). Speech is full of mistakes. We slur our speech. We get words wrong. We mix sounds up. We mix sentences up. We say the opposite of what we intend. Sometimes there are long pauses before we get the words out. We call these mistakes speech errors, and they don't just pass the time nicely in the bar, they tell us a great deal about speech production. Of particular interest are slips of the tongue, when we mix up sounds, words, or sentences. I estimate I make six or seven a day, on average. In the last few days I've said "Is this the special Swish one?" (instead of "Swiss one"), and "look, concrete blocks" (instead of granite blocks).

Here's one of the most famous speech errors ever made.

A maniac for weekends

The target – what the speaker intended to say – was "a weekend for maniacs" (Fromkin, 1971). What's going on here? The words "weekend" and "maniacs" have been exchanged – but not quite. The plural ending of "maniacs" has been left in touch, in place. The word "maniac" has been ripped from it, and put where "weekend" should be. "Weekend" meanwhile picks up the plural ending. But let's look a bit closer at this; think about how we pronounce the plural ending in "maniacs" and "weekends"; they're actually different, with an "s" sound in the former and a "z" sound in the latter. And here although the speaker intended to say "maniacs" with an "s" sound, it actually came out as "weekends" with a "z" sound; the plural ending stayed in place, but changed its form to suit the word to which it is in the end attached.

There is a fairly obvious explanation for this error, and the explanation reveals the basics of how we plan speech. It makes sense to think of speaking as involving two different processes: retrieving the words and constructing a frame into which we then insert the words. What happens with this sort of exchange error is simply that we put the words into the wrong slots in the frame. I'll explain what this frame looks like in the next section, but it's apparent that the plural ending is part of the frame. That is, we don't immediately retrieve a word in its plural form; instead we retrieve a word, and then insert it into a slot that's marked for plural. It must be like this because the words and their plural endings can become so easily divorced, as in this example and many, many others. But the plural ending can't be spelled out in fine phonetic detail at first, because otherwise the plural ending wouldn't accommodate its sound to the sound of the word that ends up in the slot. It must therefore start out in some abstract form, like just "plural". The words are inserted into the attached slot, and only then is the sound of the plural ending spelled out in detail. That's a lot to learn from just one speech error; I and others have collected many thousands, and have used regularities in these collections of errors, or *corpora*, to map out how we produce speech.

We make a large number of different types of slips of the tongue, and it's convenient to have a framework with which we can classify them. We can do this readily by considering for each error what unit of speech is involved, and what mechanism of error has generated the slip. Units include individual sounds (phonemes, and in fact features of phonemes, such as whether a sound is voiced or not, or where the vocal apparatus is constricted in producing it), syllables, words, and phrases; mechanisms include deletion, addition, substitution, exchange, anticipation, and perseveration. A few examples from my own corpus of naturally occurring slips of the tongue should make this clear:

- I still *v*eel very full. (Target: I still feel very full. The "v" of very has been anticipated at the start of "feel" – these sorts of errors are called *anticipations*.)
- I'm suspicious of people who wear base*p*all hats on TV. (Target: I'm suspicious of people who wear baseball hats on TV. The "p" of people (and possibly suspicious) has *perseverated*, or lingered too long, substituting for the "b" in "baseball – these sorts of errors are called *perseverations*.)

223

- I can't disgree with it. (Target: I can't disagree with it. A sound has been deleted in "disagree".)
- I want to yook *l*ung. (Target: I want to look young. Two sounds have been exchanged. This error is an example of a spoonerism, discussed below.)
- Use my *towel* as a *back*. (Target: Use my back as a towel. Two words have been exchanged.)
- There's already a *raw*. (Target: There's already a rule, or There's already a law. The two words "rule" and "law" have blended together.)
- The *hedgerow* is looking good. (Target: The rockery is looking good. The word "rockery" has been substituted by another word, "hedgerow", related in meaning.)
- All sorts of *papers*. (Target: All sorts of potatoes. The word "potatoes" has been substituted by another, "papers", this time related in sound.)
- My tummy swolled up again. (Target: My tummy swelled up again and My tummy has swollen up again. Two different phrases have blended together.)

These examples illustrate the variety of slips of the tongue we observe in spontaneous speech, and the range of mechanisms that give rise to them. The classification might strike you as quite mundane. Most of the errors are low-level sound errors; about 10% of errors are word substitutions, where we say a different word to that intended. Of course, providing a classification based on mechanisms such as exchanges and substitutions doesn't provide an explanation of why these slips happen, just how. To explain why we need to dig deeper, and think about the relative activation level of features, sounds, words, and phrases.

Of course, the speech error everyone (who's not a psycholinguist) really wants to know about is the Freudian slip. These errors, according to Freud (1901/1975), happen when the repressed unconscious or suppressed conscious bubbles to the surface. Freud saw Freudian slips everywhere, not just in speech: in forgetting, in bungled actions (or action slips, as we now call them), in writing, in not being able to remember names, in forgetting things from childhood, even in apparently chance actions and encounters. Some of Freud's descriptions are quite lengthy, sometimes covering several pages in explanations that strike me as very contrived. Here are a few simple, shorter examples.

A gentleman was expressing his condolences to a young lady who husband had recently died. He intended to say: "You will find consolation in devoting [*widmen* in German] yourself to your children". Instead of *widmen* he said *widwen* – a non-word. Whereas I would describe this as a phonological perseveration error, with the /w/ of the initial syllable perseverating and substituting for /m/, Freud accounted for it in terms of a suppressed thought of the gentleman: "a young and pretty widow [*Witwe*] will soon enjoy fresh sexual pleasures". Note that even if the error was in part caused by an intrusion of *Witwe*, there's no reason to assume a sexual motivation for it; the speaker might have been thinking of saying "I am sorry that you've become a widow". Who knows, without interviewing the speaker? (Freud's Example 23, from Chapter V, Slips of the tongue)

A lady was asked what regiment her son was with. She replied: "With the 42nd Murderers", instead of Mortars [*Morder* instead of *Morser*]. This error is explicable as a simple sound error. (Freud's Example 26)

A professor said: "In the case of the female genitals, in spite of many temptations [*Versuchungen*] – I beg your pardon, experiments [*Versuche*] . . ." This admittedly embarrassing error is probably simply a substitution of one word for a phonologically similar one, as in my "papers potatoes" example above. (Freud's Example 37)

A doctor said to a lady suspected of having Graves' disease: "You are about a goitre taller than your sister" instead of "head taller" [*Kropf* instead of *Kopf*]. This is another phonological error, although it might reflect an intruding thought. (Freud's Example 20)

I'm not saying that Freudian slips, as Freud conceptualised them, never occur in speech, but they're very rare. I can't think of a single example in my corpus of several thousand slips that is explained most simply in terms of a repressed sexual thought. Some errors do undoubtedly occur because of the intrusion of thoughts: the final example above might be of that type. Most people have experienced thinking something and then inadvertently saying it instead of what you'd meant to say. Here is a harmless example from my collection: "We'll be having lunch in 12 hours", instead of "in three hours"; I'd just been thinking "We'll have lunch at twelve thirty" and then worked out how long away that was. Notice here how a number has substituted for another number, and in the Graves' disease example how the two words sound similar; this observation suggests that a single error can have several causes, that a substitution is more likely to occur if the target is similar to the intrusion in some way: an important point to which I'll return.

Sometimes we'll probably never know for sure what the speaker was thinking and therefore how the error happened. As I was writing this book, the current British Prime Minister, Gordon Brown, said in Question Time at the House of Commons "we not only saved the world" instead of "saved the banks". Given the way in which the credit crisis had seen a resurgence in Mr Brown's fortunes, and the credit being given to him by other world leaders, we can only speculate about what was going on in his mind.

Less famous than the Freudian slip, but nevertheless familiar to many, is the *spoonerism*, when the initial sound of two words exchange, although more loosely it's used for any exchange of two sounds. Here are some of my examples:

- "A bit of mawn lowing", instead of "a bit of lawn mowing".
- "I've dropped stripping sweat", instead of "I've stopped dripping sweat".
- "They decided it by a toin coss" instead of "they decided it by a coin toss".

Spoonerisms are named after the Reverend William Archibald Spooner (1844–1930), the Warden of New College, Oxford, who was particularly prone to making such errors, including such gems as:

- You have hissed all my mystery lectures.
- You have tasted the whole worm.
- The Lord is a shoving leopard.
- Three cheers for the queer old dean!

Care to guess for a moment what the intended utterances were? They were "missed all my history lectures", "wasted the whole term", "loving shepherd", and "dear old queen". There is some doubt as to the authenticity of some of the errors attributed to the Reverend Spooner; some might be apocryphal, some made by others, some deliberate plays or jokes on words. Spooner himself apparently claimed that the only spoonerism he ever genuinely uttered was "kinkering kongs their titles take". However, given that speech errors are relatively common and are universal, it would be surprising if he hadn't made many more; one of the difficulties of collecting speech errors is that people don't always notice when they make them. If he did indeed make an inordinate number, we should suspect some pathology at work; I, in common with a recent US President, also make an above average number. I attribute this blunder abundance to my general phonological deficit.

What is the Garrett model of speech production?

We've seen from the "maniac for weekends" example that speech production can be thought of as retrieving words and sticking them into a marked frame. The distinction between planning the syntax and retrieving the words is the basis of one of the earliest models of speech production, the Fromkin-Garrett model, arising independently from the work of the American linguist Vicky Fromkin and the American psycholinguist Merrill Garrett (Fromkin, 1971; Garrett, 1975, 1976, 1980).

In addition to the placing of words in the wrong slots, there are two other important observations about speech error data that provide important constraints on our model of speech production. First, Garrett observed that when words swap with each other, or one word substitutes for another, the two words are always of the same type. We divide words into content words and function words: content words do the semantic work of the language, and comprise nouns, verbs, adjectives, and adverbs. There's a very large number of content words, and we occasionally make new ones up (from television to geek). Function words are the ones that do all the grammatical work of the language, including determiners (the, some, a), prepositions (to, at, in), conjunctions (and, because, so), relativisers (that, which), question words (where, how), and pronouns (she, he, it, her, him). Function words are generally very common in the language, but there's just a small number of them, and we don't add new ones; they change very slowly (we don't after all have too many thees and thous these days). Content words only ever exchange for other content words. I've collected many thousands of speech errors over many years, and I can't think of a single exception to this law – and it's unusual for there not to be exceptions in psychology. What can explain it? Content words and function words are clearly very different types of beast, a conclusion supported by brain imaging studies that show they tend to be processed in different parts of the brain (Pulvermüller, 1999). We process them in different ways when we speak.

The second observation is that errors involving sounds and errors involving whole words are subject to different kinds of constraint. Sound errors, including anticipations, exchanges, and perseverations, are constrained by distance, not by word type, while word errors are constrained by grammatical category, not distance. Here are some examples:

- And ty the time (instead of "and by the time").
- Toin coss (instead of "coin toss").
- Make a dimmer (instead of "make a dinner").
- I got it wrong trying to get it right (instead of "I got it right trying to get it wrong"; yes, really).
- It cost seven thousand miles to take about ninety miles (instead of "it cost seven thousand pounds to take about ninety miles")

The first three errors, involving sounds, illustrate that the source of the error and the place where the intrusion happens tend to be close together. Typically, sound errors involve adjacent words, or words with just one intervening word; almost inevitably the two words involved are in the same clause. On the other hand, they don't show any constraint of word type, with parts of function word and content word ("by" and "time" in the first error), and nouns and verbs being mixed regardless. The word errors, though, tend to involve words interacting over longer distances, and content words always interact with content words, and nouns tend to interact with nouns, verbs with verbs, adjective with adjectives, and so on. The conclusion is that sound errors and word errors happen at different times.

In the Fromkin-Garrett model, speech production takes place on a number of levels. We start with the *message level*, where we formulate an intention to convey a particular message, such as an intention to communicate the idea that Bill chased the cat in the past. The format of representation of this stage is a bit vague in these models; it is important to note though that the details of individual words are not specified at the message level – at least in the Fromkin-Garrett model. It's pretty vague; the message level is often the forgotten level of speech production. I can speculate a bit though, in terms of the concepts I've introduced so far. Clearly the intention must refer to particular objects and concepts. It makes sense to think that we're starting with the same sort of representation as we end up with in comprehension, so a propositional network must play some role. But our semantic networks are "messy": first, things are massively interconnected, and we are situated in the world, so our representation is connected to words and percepts; and second the networks are leaky, so when we think about concepts, we know we get activation of related concepts both horizontally (think of a lion and you might think a little bit of a tiger) and vertically (down to words and up to perceptual information). We can think of the message level as our semantic network, but with several attractors active simultaneously, the pattern of activation shifting in time, sometimes lighting up associated inputs and outputs. But I repeat, this is all speculative, and goes far beyond what was in the original model, which was rather like a "thought" bubble in a cartoon.

We then use the intention to construct a *functional-level* representation. At the functional level concepts are selected and the relation between them specified, but the representation isn't spelt out in syntactic detail. So the functional level would be something like:

- *Actor*: Bill
- *Action*: chase
- *Object*: cat, known
- *Time*: past

We next linearise this representation into one where order matters – that is, we spell out the syntactic frame of the sentence, to form a *positional-level* representation:

Noun 1 Action + Past Determiner-known Noun 2

We can then insert the phonological forms of the appropriate content words into the slots and retrieve the phonological forms of the function words to form the sound-level representation. Finally, the *sound-level representation* is translated into a format that can drive the articulatory apparatus (Figure 8.1).

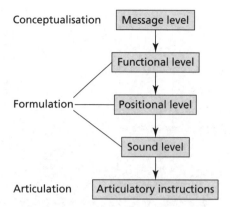

FIGURE 8.1 Garrett's model of speech production, showing how the stages correspond to the processes of conceptualisation, formulation, and articulation. Based on Garrett (1975, 1976)

Errors involving words happen when we assign specific concepts to the functional level. Distance doesn't matter because the functional level isn't yet spelt out in syntactic detail; it is for the type of role, so it's similar roles that tend to get confused. Sound errors happen at the sound level, where distance matters because we can retain only a limited amount of material in the phonological buffer we've prepared for output.

Note that although we have several distinct levels of processing, there is no necessity that we have to finish one level of processing before we move on to the next. We don't construct the functional-level representation, turn it wholesale into a positional and then into a sound-level representation of the sentence, before moving on to the next sentence. It's thought, by looking at things such as the distance over which sounds interact in errors, that we construct the sound level a phrase at a time. We might well be thinking of the next message-level representation while we're still constructing the sound-level representation of part of the previous one.

How do we retrieve words?

Getting the content words when speaking is for me the most fascinating aspect of language. We go from some internal representation of the meaning of a word to the sounds; if we take recognition in reverse, we start with the semantic attractor and move to the constituent sounds of the word. We call this process *lexicalisation*. First, we have to specify the correct attractor, or meaning, or concept; we have to specify that's it's DOG we want to say, not PUPPY or CAT or POODLE. Second, we have to retrieve the sounds that make up the word. It's apparent therefore that lexicalisation is a two-stage process: specifying the meaning followed by specifying the sounds.

Fat cat – or he was until we put him on a diet

As soon as we appreciate this insight, it should be apparent why we get two types of word substitution error. In the examples I gave earlier, there were some where the target and intrusion were related in meaning, and others where they were related in sound. Here are a few more examples:

- glass → cup
- red → white
- words → letters
- conform → confirm
- bed → bread
- risking → resting

The distinction between semantically based and phonologically based word substitutions was first discussed in detail by Fay and Cutler (1977). Fay and Cutler called the phonological errors *malapropisms*, after Mrs Malaprop, a character in Sheridan's 1775 play *The Rivals*, in turn named after malapropos (inopportune, inadvertent), who got in trouble by trying to use big impressive words she didn't quite get right:

I have laid Sir Anthony's preposition before her.
I laid my positive conjunctions on her, never to think of the fellow again.

Malapropisms have been used to comic effect in literature, theatre, and television ever since, my favourites including "What are you incinerating?" (instead of "insinuating", from *Steptoe and Son*, and "We heard the ocean is infatuated with sharks", instead of "infested", from *Laurel and Hardy*). Malapropisms are errors of ignorance (or perhaps over-ambition) rather than knowing the target and retrieving the wrong word, so I'll just call these two types of error semantic word substitutions and phonological word substitutions. Semantic substitutions happen when we're selecting the meaning of the word; phonological substitutions happen when we try to use this meaning to select the sound of the word. If you think about running the Hinton and Shallice model in reverse, you should get the idea.

I've been a bit fast and loose so far with this description of lexicalisation as a two-stage process. Most recent theories of speech production invoke the concept of a *lemma* as an intermediate stage between meaning and sounds (Levelt, 1989, 2001). We don't go straight from a semantic representation to the sounds, but instead go through an intermediate level where we've identified a specific word and accessed its semantic and syntactic properties, but this is prior to detailing the sounds of the words. Everyone agrees that something comes between semantic features and phonemes; the debate among researchers is exactly what, and what information is associated with it. Now, you say, why is production different from recognition? Why didn't I talk about lemmas there? Implicitly I did; a lemma in word recognition is the lexical entry for every word – or if you want to follow the extreme connectionist viewpoint, and not talk about lexical entries, you still need the hidden units. Something has to mediate meaning and sounds.

We can get further insight into how we produce words from studies of brain imaging of people naming pictures (Indefrey & Levelt, 2000, 2004). Very broadly speaking, production involves activation spreading from the back of the brain to the front. When people first see a picture and have to name it, we of course first see activation associated with visual processing and object recognition. Activation then spreads from the occipital regions of the brain where this happens to the temporal lobe in the left hemisphere, particularly the region around the pronounced bump called the temporal gyrus. This region seems to be associated with semantic processing. Activation then spreads to Wernicke's region, where the meaning is associated with the broad phonology of the word; and finally Broca's region becomes activated as we prepare the syllables, phonemes, and prosody of the word. Visual and conceptual processing takes on average about 175 milliseconds; finding the best word takes place between 150 and 225 milliseconds; accessing the phonology occurs between 250 and 330 milliseconds; and preparing the details of the pronunciation of the word starts around 450 milliseconds after seeing the picture to be named.

Experimental evidence from picture naming supports this general model. A useful technique in studying speech production is called *picture–word interference*; you give a person a picture to name, and at the same time you give them an auditory presentation of a word to which they have to make a lexical decision. The important thing about this technique is that we can vary exactly when the participants hear the word relative to seeing the picture. There is a complication that whereas with word recognition items related in meaning speed up or facilitate recognition, in production items related in meaning can interfere with others, making naming slower – so you're slower to name a picture of a giraffe if the word "lion" is superimposed on the picture. Let's not worry about that too much for now, but just consider when things related in meaning and things related in sound have their effects. Early on after seeing a picture, we get an effect of meaning, so that the target word (the one people hear and to which they have to make a response) has to be related in meaning to the picture; later it has to be related in sound to have any effect (Levelt et al., 1991). All of this, remember, takes place in less than half a second after seeing a picture.

I showed in the chapter on word recognition that there's a considerable amount of evidence that recognition is an interactive process – that the different modules of understanding language are a bit leaky, so that context can affect aspects of word recognition or which syntactic structure we prefer. What about producing words? Before we can consider the evidence we really need to think about what this notion of interactivity means a little more deeply. There are really two separate notions involved when we talk about interactivity, *feedback* and *cascading processing*. Feedback is the easier of these two ideas to explain: it's simply that later levels of processing can feed back and affect earlier. When you get into debt and pay increasing amounts of interest, having less money to spend and having to borrow more and more, then having to pay ever increasing amounts of interest so that you then have to borrow yet more – that's feedback in action. Fortunately feedback in language processing isn't quite as gloomy. We've seen it in several connectionist models so far: for example in the Tippett and Farah model of naming in dementia making object naming more robust, the TRACE model of spoken word recognition, and the Hinton and Shallice model of semantics and deep dyslexic reading, where feedback connections from the clean-up units to the semantic features allow semantic attractors to develop.

Cascading processing is like one of those indoor waterfalls where water falls into one receptacle until it fills up, and then water falls out of that one into another beneath, and so on. If we've got a system comprising several connected levels of processing (as virtually all cognitive psychology models posit), with activation flowing between levels, there are two ways in which we can move from one level to another. We could deal with each level one by one, so that we wait until we have decided on just one winner at that level; or we could allow activation to trickle forward – *cascade*, as we call it – so that later levels of processing can start work while earlier ones are themselves still working.

I'll make this issue of cascading versus discrete processing concrete with a simplified example from lexicalisation. Suppose we see a picture of a big cat – in fact it's a tiger. (It doesn't matter if we want to start by thinking of an idea rather than looking at a picture. In both cases we process the picture and identify the appropriate concept (tiger).) We then start finding the semantically and syntactically specified item, the lemma, that corresponds to this concept. The concept of course activates the associated TIGER lemma, but activation will spread to items that overlap with it to some extent semantically – say all the other big cats

The models diverge in what happens next. The discrete model is very straightforward. Although early on a number of semantically related lemmas are active along with the target:

    Concept: TIGER
    Lemmas: TIGER Jaguar Leopard Cheetah Puma Panther

processing continues until one and only one lemma is left standing:

    Concept: TIGER
    Lemma: TIGER

Then, and only then, the lemmas start activating their corresponding sounds and to a lesser extent, by spreading activation, words that overlap with the selected lemma in sound:

    Lemma: TIGER
    Sounds: TIGER Trigger Table

The process is repeated until one sound-form is left, and we say "tiger".

The cascading model is more complex. The semantic representations activate their corresponding lemmas, but all these lemmas immediately start sending activation down to the sound level; they don't have to wait for just one lemma to be chosen. So at some point we might have them all active at the same time:

    Concept: TIGER
    Lemmas: TIGER Jaguar   Leopard
    Sounds: TIGER Trigger   Table Jaguar Jagged Leopard
               Leaping Leper

The critical difference is that the cascaded model predicts that the sounds of words like "leper" and "leaping" might get activated, to a small extent, because leopard is still active at the lemma level. The cascade model is much more promiscuous about what gets simultaneously activated.

Many models have both cascading activation and feedback – TRACE is a model of this type. Activation flows continuously from the feature level to the letter level, where several candidate letters can be active simultaneously; we don't need to recognise just one letter with absolute certainty before we start activating the words. All the activated letters start activating the words to which they're connected. At the same time, activation can spread back down from the word level to the letter level and hence back to the feature level. It's an ever-shifting, highly dynamic pattern of activation spreading through vast, interconnected networks; but the neural networks of the brain are several orders of magnitude larger.

Evidence for feedback in lexicalisation comes yet again from a detailed analysis of slips of the tongue. There are two well-known types of bias that make some slip outcomes more likely than others, called familiarity bias and similarity bias. The *familiarity bias* is that outcomes of errors that are more familiar are more likely than those that are less familiar. A familiarity bias is demonstrated most clearly with sound errors, such as:

- A negative feedback leep ensues (instead of "feedback loop" – perseveration of the "ee" sound from "feedback").
- I want to yook lung (instead of "look young", spoonerism with initial consonants exchanged)
- Washed up the peasant pooh (instead of "pheasant pooh", anticipation of "p")

Here we have three sound errors that result in real words – leap, lung, and peasant. Of course, by chance some sound errors will result in words, but it's mathematically straightforward to compute the chance rate at which this should happen, and the number of lexical outcomes we observe in sound errors far exceeds this rate (Dell & Reich, 1981; Stemberger, 1985). What's more, we can induce speech errors experimentally, by getting people to read pairs of words presented very quickly (e.g. BARN DOOR); in an experimental setting we can manipulate the words so we know exactly what the chance of lexical outcomes should be. Once again, sound errors result in words far more than we would expect by chance (Baars et al., 1975). We also observe this lexical bias in languages other than English, such as Spanish (Hartsuiker et al., 2006).

Given that we know that sound errors happen relatively late in the speech production process, after we've accessed the representation of the words, how can whether or not an error outcome is a word affect the chance of it happening? What's steering these late-stage sound errors to word outcomes? There are two plausible explanations, and speech production probably involves a bit of both. As we speak we monitor (sometimes, at least!) what we say. We occasionally detect errors in our speech – we know this because people sometimes stop and correct their errors, or halfway through an exchange error they stop so that they don't produce the second part of the exchange. It's very likely that we sometimes detect upcoming errors before we say them out aloud. Although, as we know, phenomenology can be misleading, we certainly occasionally have this impression. It's also likely that the more egregious the upcoming error is, the more likely we are to spot and censor it. Error outcomes that are words are more likely to slip past our internal censor. The second explanation is feedback: words can feed activation down to the sound level to provide a support that just isn't available for non-word outcomes. You can think of it as a kind of resonance, or as words being attractors, or words providing a glue that sticks certain sound combinations available – they all amount to the same thing. Connectionist modelling of lexicalisation, using an interactive activation architecture similar to TRACE, shows that these mechanisms really can give rise to different types of error in the right proportions (Dell, 1986, 1988; Harley, 1993).

The *similarity bias* is the finding that errors are more likely to occur the more similar the target and intrusion sound. The most straightforward example is with word substitutions. I noted above that we find semantic and phonological word substitutions; we also observe many *mixed* errors, where there is a similarity in both sound and meaning between the target and substitution, such as:

- No meat by the front door (instead of "mint by the front door")
- Catalogue (instead of "calendar")
- Colon (instead of "comma").

Once again we would expect some mixed errors by chance, but we find many more than we should do unless something was happening (Dell & Reich, 1981, Harley, 1984; Stemberger, 1985). In an interactive system, mixed errors are straightforward to account for by feedback: possible intrusions can receive activation from both overlap in meaning and overlap in sound in a way that pure semantic and pure phonological errors cannot. Once again, connectionist simulations of production show that these interactive models can explain the proportions of errors found.

The issue of whether or not processing in lexicalisation is discrete or cascading is more controversial than the issue of feedback, and for many the jury is still out. There's a large amount of literature on what is called *mediated priming* – as we saw above, in a cascading system a word such as "couch" should prime "sofa" by meaning, and if activation is cascading through the system this should then be able to prime "soda" through sound. Mediated priming can only easily be explained by cascading activation. Many experiments have found mediated priming in picture naming (e.g. Cutting & Ferreira, 1999; Peterson & Savoy, 1998), while others have not (Levelt et al., 1991). The technique is very sensitive to the details of the materials used and the strength of the relations between the primes and the targets; however, the fact that we find mediated priming in at least some conditions is difficult to explain in discrete models.

The predominance of the evidence then suggests that lexicalisation takes place in two stages, that activation cascades between stages, and that later levels feed back to influence earlier ones (Figures 8.2, 8.3).

Name this object. (The right answer is TRACTOR; see me if you had difficulty)

Why are words sometimes on the tip of our tongue?

Just before I started to write this section, I did something daft. I went to a car park I've been to a hundred times before, and got to the exit with the card, put it in the slot, to discover I'd forgotten to pay in the car park. How daft. A phrase came to mind for someone forgetful and distracted as me – a something professor. Quite a long phrase. It became annoying.

And then a few minutes later it came to me – absentminded. "Absentminded" was a word that was on the "tip of my tongue", and we call these states when we know the word, but just can't retrieve it, *tip-of-the-tongue* (TOT) states. Although TOTs must have been experienced since humans started to speak, and Freud gave some wonderful examples in the *Psychopathology of Everyday Life*, they were first studied methodically by Brown and McNeill in 1966. They gave students definitions of low-frequency words. Here are a few such definitions.

- A navigational instrument used in measuring angular distances, especially the altitude of the sun, moon, and stars at sea.
- An incarnation, a descent into human form, or the temporary manifestation of a continuing entity, these days used of computer games.
- The branch of theology that's concerned with the study of the end of the world.

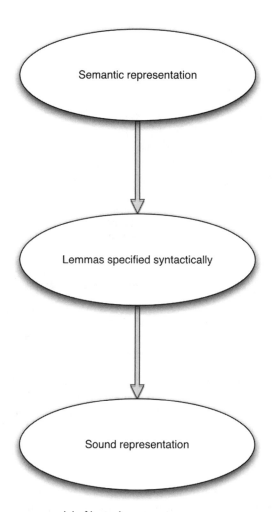

FIGURE 8.2 The two-stage model of lexical access

They're not meant to be easy! Stop and think for a moment if you don't the know the answers. The answers are "sextant", "avatar", and "eschatology". With this sort of task, people report that the answer is on the tip of their tongues over 10% of the time. This rate might seem quite high, but there's nothing like feeling you're being tested to pile on the stress; just look at contestants in quiz shows who obviously know the answer but can't retrieve it, and particularly those who forget the answer between pressing the buzzer and coming to speak. Quiz shows are fertile lands for TOT-hunters.

TOTs are accompanied by a strong feeling of knowing. Obviously when the TOT is resolved – either by the person remembering spontaneously (and this can take some time; I've experienced TOTs persisting, on and off of course, for a

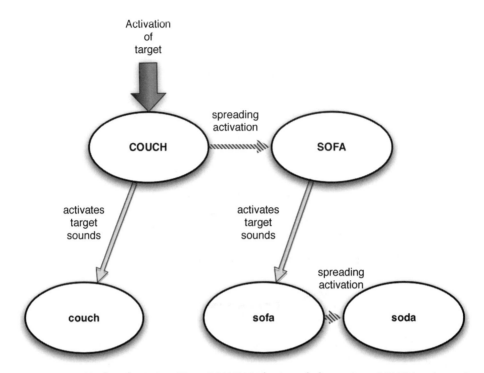

FIGURE 8.3 Mediated priming. Here COUCH is the intended meaning. COUCH activates its semantic neighbour, SOFA, a word related in meaning to COUCH. "Sofa" then activates a similar sounding word, SODA. Although the activation has to travel through a number of intervening links to get the sounds of "soda", in a cascading model, just like the mail, some should get through

couple of weeks) or being told the answer – the word has to be the right one. They're also often not an all-or-nothing experience; sometimes people can retrieve partial information about the word: they might know how many syllables it's got, or its stress pattern (DA-de-de for "avatar"), or be able to remember some sounds from the word, typically the initial sound. Quite often other words, called inter-lopers, come spontaneously to mind – typically phonological neighbours of the target, such as "secant", "sextet", or "sexton", and occasionally semantic neighbours, such as "astrolabe". The number of TOTs we experience increases with age, and can be considered a hallmark of cognitive ageing (James & Burke, 2000).

Clearly TOTs fit in very well with the two-stage model of lexicalisation; we've completed the first stage, that of selecting the meaning of the word, but can't complete the second, retrieving the sounds. There are two explanations of why we can't complete this second stage. In the first, the *blocking hypothesis*, these inter-lopers play a critical role; according to this model, they aren't just the casual by-product of failed memory, but actively get in the way of our remembering the correct word (Jones & Langford, 1987). It's as though our view of the person at the centre of the scrum is obscured by all these other, stronger players holding them down. One might object that not all TOTs generate interlopers, but we don't have to be aware of the competitors for them to be troublesome.

The second explanation is called the *partial activation* hypothesis. Most of the time we get TOTs with rare words, or in stressful conditions, or as we age, suggesting that it's just more difficult to retrieve the target because it's only weakly represented. Not enough activation is getting down to it from higher levels. There's a considerable amount of evidence favouring the partial activation hypothesis over the blocking hypothesis. First, presenting words related in sound to the targets in a TOT task actually reduces the probability that the person is going to be in a TOT state, not increasing it as blocking would predict (James & Burke, 2000). Second, bilingual speakers are more prone to making TOTs, presumably because as they must speak each of the languages less in total than a monolingual speaker, the connections between meanings and sounds are slightly weaker because they don't get strengthened by practice as much (Gollan & Acenas, 2004). Finally, the blocking hypothesis predicts that words with many phonological neighbours – words that sound like the target – should be more prone to TOTs, because there are words to block the target. But they're not; in fact they're less prone. It's those odd-sounding words that have few neighbours that are more likely to suffer TOTs (Harley & Bown, 1998). To give a simple example, "ball" and "growth" are roughly as common as each other, but whereas there are few words that sound like "growth", there are many that sound like "ball" ("call", "fall", "bell", to name just a few). All other things being equal, we get more TOTs on words like "ball" than on words like "growth". Rather than getting in the way, neighbouring words provide support, and words that like this support are more difficult to retrieve. We suffer from TOTs, then, when for whatever reason insufficient activation is obtained from meaning to sound (Burke et al., 1991).

As well as being fascinating in their own right, TOTs make a useful tool for exploring speech production. Although English does not mark gender (whether a noun is masculine, feminine, or neuter), many languages do, including Italian. There is some evidence that Italian speakers when in a TOT can retrieve the gender of the word they're stuck on (Vigliocco et al., 1997); as gender is a syntactic property of words, this finding means that people can retrieve syntactic properties of words independently of the phonology. (Of course people can tell whether or not the word they search for is a noun or a verb, say, but the syntactic context and planning process supplies this knowledge too straightforwardly for it to be interesting.) This result supports the idea of a semantically and syntactically specified lemma accessed prior to any retrieval of sounds, although the exact interpretation is controversial because what we find depends on the details of how researchers run these sorts of experiments (Caramazza, 1997).

How do we plan syntax?

We have to get the syntax right when we speak, and we have to do it right. We don't have the leisure we have in writing when, as I've just done, I've stood up halfway through a sentence, wandered around, admired the melting snow, and wondered what on earth I'm going to say next.

Although the size of the planning unit in production might be variable, the evidence from word exchange errors suggests that we typically sketch out the content and meaning in clause-size chunks, but the fact that sound errors typically happen over much shorter distances suggests that we only retrieve and plan the detailed sound of what we're going to say a few words at a time. Picture–word interference studies confirm that we only get effects of sound similarity for a word or two (Meyer, 1996); and perhaps more surprisingly, we don't always retrieve the verb before we start speaking, even though as we've seen the verb plays an essential role in determining the syntax of the sentence. Again using the picture–word interference paradigm, we only get semantic interference between a verb and the auditory decision word if the verb is close to the beginning of the sentence (Schriefers et al., 1998). Another useful technique in studying the production of syntax is to get people to describe simple pictures, and measure how long it takes them to start speaking. We find that people take longer to start producing single-clause sentences beginning with a complex noun phrase containing two lemmas, such as:

The dog and the kite move above the house

than for similar sentences that start just with a simple noun phrase containing one lemma, such as:

The dog moves above the kite and the house.

So although we might not plan much of the sentence, we do seem to retrieve at least the lemmas of the first phase, and we might start initiating the process of retrieving later ones, even if we don't get much further (Smith & Wheeldon, 1999). We say that speech production is *incremental* in as much as we make much of it up as we go along, rather than planning everything we're going to say in detail before we start speaking.

Although we may not always know for sure what the verb is going to be when we start speaking, choosing the verb is one of the most important aspects of planning a sentence. The verb tells you what sort of things can go in your sentence: if you choose an intransitive verb (one that doesn't take an object), you have to construct a very different sort of syntactic frame from when you choose a transitive verb (one that must take an object), and if you choose a verb that takes both a direct and an indirect object, you are allowed yet another type of construction. If you choose the passive form of a verb, you are committed to yet another type of structure, as these examples show:

Felix sleeps.
Felix chases the cat.
Felix gave the cat a good fright.
The cat was chased by Felix.

A number of factors interact to determine how we begin our sentence, and the work of the American psycholinguist Kay Bock has cast a great deal of light on this area (e.g. Bock, 1982, 1987). More accessible items, those that are easier to retrieve, tend to be placed earlier in the sentence, presumably simply because they by definition are the first to come to mind (Bock & Warren, 1985). Accessible items include high-frequency ones, more concrete words, and of course those things that we've been talking about most recently. Placing recently mentioned items early also has the advantage of bridging between old material and new, and helps us fulfil the given–new category I discussed in the last chapter: we typically provide "given" information before "new' (Bock & Irwin, 1980). As I've repeatedly said, we don't speak sentences in isolation, and we don't (usually) go out of our way to make the listener's job more difficult than it need be. If we're using a transitive verb, and one noun is animate and the other inanimate, we tend to make the animate noun the subject of the sentence. We wouldn't place the inanimate object first, and necessitate a passive construction, unless there was some good reason, such as if we want to emphasise that object, or distinguish it from another.

Felix knocked over his bowl.
It was the bowl (not the bucket) that Felix knocked over.

Imitation is the sincerest form of flattery, they say, and we imitate more than we think. Do you find sometimes that when you speak, you're starting to imitate another person? Have you ever noticed that you're starting to sound like the person you're speaking to? We tend to use the same words, the same turns of phrase, and even syntactic structures that the other speaker has just used (Schenkein, 1980).

This point is made most forcibly with the syntactic priming paradigm, where we can influence the syntactic structures a speaker chooses by exposing them to sentences with a particular structure (Bock, 1986). A common method of demonstrating syntactic priming is to get people to read sentences aloud, and then describe a simple picture. Although they are completely free to describe the picture as they wish, they tend to use the same syntactic structure as in the sentence they read aloud. Suppose we have a picture of Bill handing the weedkiller to Ben. Most people will use one of two syntactic structures to describe this heartening horticultural scene, either what's called a prepositional-object structure:

> Bill handed the weedkiller to Ben

or a double-object structure:

> Bill handed Ben the weedkiller.

We can influence which they choose by priming them appropriately, so that prior to describing the picture they repeat one of:

> The robot sold a dodo to Carl.
> The robot sold Carl a dodo.

If people hear a prepositional-object structure, they're more likely to then use that in spontaneous speech, but if they hear a double-object structure, they're more likely to use that. It does seem to be the underlying syntactic structure that's primed; researchers have eliminated the possibility that obtaining the effect depends on reusing particular words, or the tense of the verb, or its number, or its aspect (Pickering & Branigan, 1998). So the following two sentences are equally effective at biasing people to the prepositional-object structure:

> Bill bakes a cake for Ben.
> Bill took a cake to Ben.

The verb is different, the tense is different, and the prepositions are different, but both prime the same structure. And as it's clearly the underlying syntactic structure that persists, as you might expect the following two sentences do not bias us to prepositional-object structures equally well:

> Bill brought a book to Ben.
> Bill brought a book to study.

Here the words are very similar, containing the same verbs and preposition "to", but whereas the first is a true prepositional-object structure, the second is a noun-phrase structure. In spite of the great similarity between the two sentences the second is totally ineffective for biasing people towards prepositional-object structures (Bock & Loebell, 1990). So we don't need to have the same verb or grammatical words to get priming, and word order alone doesn't do it: what seems to be persisting is a representation of the underlying relations between things.

This kind of syntactic persistence can last for a surprisingly long time. It's been observed with at least 10 intervening sentences between the prime and the biased sentence (Bock & Griffin, 2000). It's also been shown experimentally for structures people have heard other people produce, and shown in the recall of sentences read on a computer screen as well as in spontaneous speech (Branigan et al., 2000; Potter & Lombardi, 1998). Clearly syntactic persistence is a robust effect, and probably arises for at least three reasons. First, it smoothes and co-ordinates communication – it helps the process of alignment between speaker and listener I mentioned in the last two chapters. It's easier to understand and compare two sentences if they have similar forms. Second, priming is a striking effect of human cognition; virtually anything that can be primed is primed. Why should syntax be exempt? Third, we re-use syntax because we're a little bit lazy. We're good at finding shortcuts, and again, why should syntax be exempt?

Another problem facing speakers in production is ensuring that the different parts of the sentence *agree* with each other. We face agreement issues with matching possessives and pronouns to the right gender:

Bill gave all *his* money to Alice; she kissed *him* but kept all *hers*.

But agreement is a particular issue with regard to the *number* of things involved.

Bill was weeding in his garden.
Bill and Ben were weeding in their garden.
The man does his work.
The women do their work.

We occasionally get agreement wrong in spontaneous speech. Here is an example from my corpus:

What was her name? (Instead of "his name").

However, agreement errors aren't at all common in spontaneous speech, at least in my corpus. Here's another example, this time from Bock and Eberhard (1993):

Membership in these unions were voluntary.

So although it's a tricky task co-ordinating the different parts of the sentence, we seem to manage it quite well. When we do make an error, we have a particular tendency to make the verb agree with a noun that's closer than the subject of the sentence with which it should be agreeing – so here we get "were" instead of "was" because the verb is agreeing with the plural "unions" rather than the singular "membership". We call this sort of slip an attraction error, because the verb gets attracted to the number of a close noun. Although not that common in spontaneous speech, in an elegant and important series of experiments Bock and her colleagues managed to induce a suitably high rate of attraction errors in speech using a sentence completion task (Bock & Cutting, 1992; Bock & Eberhard, 1993; Bock &

Miller, 1991). Participants in the experiment are presented with a sentence fragment and have to complete the sentence in any way they wish. A high rate of errors in this task gives us enough data to be able to explore the process of agreement. So participants might be given the following fragments to complete:

The player on the court –
The player on the courts –
The player on the course –

Let's suppose the person chooses to continue it with "was very good"; if they make an agreement error, it would be "were very good". The first fragment is straightforward and does not produce agreement errors. The second generates many agreement errors because although the word controlling the verb ("player") is singular, the nearest noun, "courts", is plural, so we get attraction errors. The final fragment is the most interesting one; although the noun "course" is of course singular, it ends with an "s" sound, so if the sound of the plural ending matters it could conceivably trick our production system into thinking that it's a plural – we can call such words pseudoplurals. In fact pseudoplurals do not generate attraction agreement errors. On the other hand, irregular plurals that don't have an "s" on the end, such as "men" and "mice", generate just as many errors as do regular plurals ("boys" and "dogs"). So once again it's not the sound of the word that matters, but the plural in some more underlying, abstract form.

The degree of attraction isn't determined by the superficial distance between the verb and the disruptive local noun but the underlying syntactic structure, as was demonstrated in an elegant experiment by Vigliocco and Nicol (1998). They used a variant of the sentence completion task where participants were given a sentence fragment and a word they had to use in their continuation, such as:

The helicopter for the flights + safe.

A correct continuation would be to introduce a verb and make it agree with the subject of the sentence, "helicopter", as in the following typical continuation:

The helicopter for the flights was safe.

But because we have a disruptive local plural noun, "flights", as you would now expect, people made many agreement errors such as:

The helicopter for the flights were safe.

Participants then had to generate questions from the starting materials, such as:

Is the helicopter for the flights safe?

Note that in the question form the verb ("is") has been moved some way from the potentially disruptive noun ("flights") – in fact the local noun is now the singular subject of the sentence, "helicopter". So if all that matters is the superficial proximity of words, we shouldn't get any agreement errors such as:

Are the helicopter for the flights safe?

But we do; in fact we observe just as many as with the original materials. So it's not the superficial word order that matters, but the underlying, more abstract syntactic representation that focuses on relationships between words. It's proximity in the underlying syntactic representation, not the superficial order of words, that matters and that leads to number agreement errors. (I now note that in writing the first draft of that sentence I made a number agreement error, writing "words, that matters and that lead to", making "lead" agree with "words" rather than "the underlying syntactic representation. Perhaps agreement errors are after all around us all the time.)

We need two complementary processes to ensure that agreement runs smoothly (Bock et al., 2004; Eberhard et al., 2005). First, we need a process that Bock et al. call *marking* to take account of the number of things we're talking about: is it one man, or two or more? We then mark the verb as singular or plural depending on that number. We then need to take into account any peculiarities of what we're talking about. Suppose we're talking about things like scissors, tongs, glasses, or trousers – more specifically, one pair of scissors, tongs, glasses, or trousers. "Scissors", "tongs", "glasses", and "trousers" are odd words; even though we might be, and indeed usually are, talking about one pair of trousers at the message level, we treat "trousers" as a plural, and therefore have to mark the verb as plural. We always say "the trousers are too long", and should never say "the trousers is too long". Talking of trousers, "pants" behaves in the same way; we say "here are your pants", not "here is your pant". Just to complicate things more, the plural of these words stays the same, so we can say:

Here is your pair of pants.
Here are your pants.
Here are your two pairs of pants.
I have just glued your pants together, and here are two pairs of pants.

Such words are called pluralia tantum (single: plurale tantum), and yes, they are confusing. With these words we need to override the syntactic process of marking with a process that takes account of the form, the *morphology* as we call it, of the subject, a process that Bock et al. call *morphing*. Both stages can go wrong; the

245

plurale tantum can give rise to attraction errors, as below, or we can fail to morph appropriately:

The time to find the scissors are now.

Interestingly, pronouns are more prone to this sort of attraction error than nouns, so we find more errors of the sort:

The key to the cabinets disappeared. They were never found again.

This difference confirms what we might already have expected – pronouns and nouns are treated in different ways when we plan syntax.

The final difficulty with agreement arises from mass nouns, which are singular nouns naming undifferentiated masses of things – sand, dust, water, furniture, and so on. Mass nouns can be easily distinguished from count nouns, such as grain, molecule, chair, in several ways: for example, we can precede count nouns directly with numerals, but we have to modify mass nouns (we have "a hundred grains", but not "a hundred sands"; instead we would have to say something like "a hundred grains of sand"; we have to say "we have too much water", but can say "we have too many molecules"). Although mass nouns refer to collections of things (sand is lots of grains of sand, water is lots of molecules of water), we have to use the singular form of the verb: "the sand is hot" is right, and "the sand are hot" is wrong. It's more straightforward with mass nouns referring to undifferentiated masses of things like sand, water, and metal, but trickier when we get to mass nouns like furniture and cutlery that refer to more easily countable individual things. We have to ensure we get the agreement right. Trickier still are nouns that take plural or singular forms of verbs depending on the specific sense in which we use the word, such as "government" and "committee", i.e. if we are talking about the thing as a whole or the members of the group. We should say:

The committee have now taken their seats

although there is a case for "the committee has now taken". Yet we should prefer:

The committee has come to a decision.

But few would lose any sleep over which way round "have" and "has" should be here. Perhaps this distinction is dying away; I find it difficult to get too enthused about this one any longer. In as much as we do care, these sorts of agreement decisions are often not automatic, and may require considerable reflection on what sense is being used, by which time the listener might well have given up and gone to talk to someone else, particularly at a party.

How do we control conversations?

There are of course some people who appear to relish interrupting and butting in, but most of the time conversations run pretty smoothly with only one person talking and, perhaps more impressively, without long gaps between speakers. How do we manage to avoid all speaking at the same time? How do we know when the other person is at last ready to shut up and let me speak?

Conversations have a structure: Bill says something, Ben says something, Bill says something else, and so on. We say that speakers take *turns*. Turns vary in their length and the amount of information they convey. While someone is having their turn, the other person need not remain totally unresponsive; they nod in agreement, they look at the other person, they pull faces, they make sounds like "yeah" and "oh no", in general maintaining contact and expressing sympathy (or not) with the speaker, a process we call *back-channel communication* (Yngve, 1970).

It might seem self-evident that we take it in turns to speak, but it's less evident how we co-ordinate the turn-taking so well: it's estimated that while less than 5% of conversation consists of speaking overlapping, the average gap between turns is just a few tenths of a second (Ervin-Tripp, 1979). Turn-taking is fairly straightforward when we use adjacency pairs that formalise the first speaker and second speaker interacting in a stylised way, with greetings ("hello!" "hello!"), question and answer ("how are you?" "very poorly thank you"), and offer–acceptance pairs ("I'll wash your pants for you" "thanks"), but otherwise listeners have to rely on a range of semantic, syntactic, and prosodic cues to work out when the other person is likely to have finished (Sacks et al., 1974). Pauses are quite good indicators of *transitional relevant places* where a change of speaker might arise, but given that the gap between speakers' turns is on average so short, either we're very quick at spotting them or we make use of other cues too (or probably both). Pauses are in any case easily overridden: a speaker who says "then he said he was going to murder me, and then –" is unlikely to be yielding the floor, however long the pause, dramatic or otherwise. We can use several non-linguistic means to indicate that we wish either to yield the floor or to carry on talking: the pitch of our voice tails off, the intensity falls, we look at the other person (while we tend to look away when we wish to carry on speaking), we make gestures, and we try and fill our pauses with ums and ers and other little words ("right", "OK", "yeah"). If speakers fail to emit the right cues, they tend to get interrupted more than they should; it's been argued that Lady Thatcher, the ex-Prime Minister, was interrupted so often by interviewers because she unconsciously displayed these turn-yielding cues at inappropriate points (Beattie et al., 1982). And we all know people who refuse to emit turn-yielding cues in their seemingly interminable monologues.

247

How does brain damage affect language?

I've noted several times that damage to parts of the adult brain, particularly the left cortex, as a result of a stroke, disease, or trauma, can lead to *aphasia*, an impairment of spoken language. These impairments naturally differ depending on which specific parts of the brain are damaged, and are most apparent in production, where, in a manner of speaking, the person can get away with less.

It should already be apparent that the two regions of the left hemisphere called Broca's and Wernicke's areas are particularly important for language (see Figure 1.3 again). The French physician Paul Broca (1824–1880) first discovered the importance of the region that now has his name. Before the advent of modern brain scanning and imaging technologies, the only way to work out which parts of the brain had been damaged was after death, with an autopsy. Broca carried out a series of autopsies that suggested that this region, towards the back of the left frontal lobe, played a particularly important part in speech. All patients who had difficulty in producing fluent speech seemed to have damage in that region. His most famous case study was that in 1861 of a person whose real name was Leborgne but who was nicknamed "Tan" because of his inability to produce sounds other than this and "a few obscenities". "Tan" turned out in the autopsy to have a large lesion, caused by advanced syphilis, in what we now call Broca's region.

A little later, the Prussian physician Carl Wernicke (1848–1905) investigated a different sort of speech difficulty. He noted that not all patients with language difficulties suffered from damage to Broca's area, and that damage to a region of the left temporal lobe results in problems in understanding language. Wernicke went on to describe a model of language processing in the brain that, along with the work of the American neurologist Norman Geschwind, gave rise to the Wernicke-Geschwind model and that is still accepted as a reasonable account today, even if it doesn't account for the complexities and subtleties of language processing. The basic idea is that language production involves the flow of activation from structures towards the rear of the left hemisphere through Wernicke's area, to Broca's area, and then to the control of the articulatory apparatus (Geschwind, 1972).

Damage localised to Broca's area leads to slow, hesistant, laborious speech, with obvious articulation difficulties. Because of these features this type of problem is called *non-fluent* aphasia. Here's an example:

> Ah . . . Monday . . . ah Dad and Paul . . . and Dad . . . hospital. Two . . . ah . . . doctors . . . and ah . . . thirty minutes . . . and yes . . . ah . . . hospital. And er Wednesday . . . nine o'clock. And er Thursday, ten o'clock . . . doctors. Two doctors . . . and ah . . . teeth.
>
> (Goodglass, 1976, p. 238)

Contrast this with the speech of someone with damage to Wernicke's area:

Well, this is . . . mother is away here working her work out o' here to get her better, but when she's looking, the two boys in the other part. One their small tile into her time here. She's working another time because she's getting, too . . ."

(Goodglass & Geschwind, 1976, p. 410)

In contrast with the speech of someone with damage to Broca's area, the speech of a person with damage to Wernicke's area is usually fast and fluent, so this type of aphasia is often called *fluent aphasia*.

What's going on here? It's tempting to contrast the fluent but rather meaningless speech resulting from damage to Wernicke's area with the non-fluent but meaningful speech resulting from damage to Broca's area and conclude that Wernicke's region controls meaning and Broca's syntax, and in a sense that would be along the right lines, but too simplistic. We need to look at each in more detail.

Non-fluent aphasia is characterised by difficulties with articulation and difficulties in producing syntax. A reasonable generalisation here is that Broca's area is responsible for sequencing and controlling order, both of the movements necessary to produce words and the words necessary to form sentences. It's the lack of syntax that's most striking in non-fluent aphasia; all we seem to be seeing is isolated content words – and mostly nouns at that. If we can remember that far back, it's reminiscent of Bickerton's proto-language. The content words are appropriate, and we can deduce the sense of what the person intends from them, but they are not produced in any kind of sentence structure. This type of speech, where syntax is missing or greatly impoverished, is called *agrammatism*. Agrammatism has three characteristics: there's a sentence construction deficit, so that the speech is made up of isolated words rather than fitting into sentences; content words, particularly nouns, are much better preserved than function words; and the other grammatical elements of language, the inflections that modify words, such as turning nouns into plurals and modifying the tense of verbs, are also absent. And although it was thought for some time that the comprehension of non-fluent aphasics was left intact, it's been discovered that their ability to understand complex syntax when semantic cues are removed is impaired (Caramazza & Berndt, 1978). Suppose I say to you:

The dog is being chased by the cat

and show you a picture of a dog chasing a cat; you should have no difficulty in spotting that the sentence doesn't match the picture. Non-fluent aphasics find this task very difficult, presumably because the semantic cues about how things normally behave don't help here. Instead, they're forced to rely on syntactic processing, and they're not very good at syntactic processing. Further experiments have shown that people with agrammatism haven't lost syntactic knowledge, but they do have difficulty in using it to work out who is doing what to what (Schwartz et al., 1987).

We have then a cluster of symptoms in agrammatism that all relate to difficulty producing and understanding syntax. Whether or not these symptoms cohere, or whether we can sometimes find some without others – particularly whether we always observe production and comprehension deficits together – has in the past been a matter of intense debate (Badecker & Caramazza, 1985; Caplan, 1986; Miceli et al., 1983), but clearly Broca's region plays a central role in planning syntax. We can also identify that syntactic planning involves the separable components of constructing the sentence frame and retrieving grammatical elements (function words and word endings).

Fluent aphasia is characterised by fluent speech, but it's often difficult to discern what the speaker means. The comprehension of fluent aphasics is always obviously poor or very poor. In contrast, the syntax of these speakers is relatively well preserved: the speakers speak in syntactically well-formed sentences, with plenty of function words, and the word endings, as far as one can tell, are often appropriate. Wernicke's aphasics often fail to recognise that their speech is aberrant, and may even become annoyed with others for failing to understand them (Marshall et al., 1998). What seems to have gone wrong in fluent aphasia is that the ability to produce syntax is preserved, but the ability to access the meanings of words and select the correct lemmas is impaired. Fluent aphasics tend to make many word substitutions (called *paraphasias* in aphasia research), broadly similar in nature to those made by people without brain damage, but they make many, many more of them. Some also make up words, creating *neologisms*, which may or may not be obvious distortions of real words. Here are some examples of all of these:

- Scroll → letters (semantic paraphasia)
- Pencil → pepper (phonological or "formal" paraphasia)
- Thermometer → typewriter (unrelated paraphasia)
- Octopus → Opupkus (derived neologism)
- ? → Kwailai (unrelated neologisms)

Speech replete with neologisms is often called jargon aphasia. Here is an example of the connected speech of a severe jargon aphasic describing a picture of a boy and a girl taking some cookies from behind their mother's back (from Buckingham, 1981, p. 54) – I've taken some liberties in simplifying the transcription:

You mean like this boy? I mean noy, and this, uh, neoy. This is a kaynit, kahken. I don't say it, I'm not getting anything from it. I'm getting, I'm getting dime from it, but I'm getting from it. These were ekspresez, ahgrashenz, and with the type of mahkanic is standing like this . . . and then the . . . I don't know what she goin other than. And this is deli this one is the one and this one and this one and . . . I don't know.

We might not usually notice it, but we often hesitate very slightly before less common words; indeed, the tip-of-the-tongue state can be seen as a big – sometimes very big – hesitation before uncommon words. Jargon aphasics do the same thing, and they're more likely to hesitate before a paraphasia or neologism (Butterworth, 1979). What's more, neologisms are more common when the presumed word the person is trying to say is low in frequency (Ellis et al., 1983). If we look at the use of hand gestures made by neologistic speakers, they're normal – up to a point.

When we speak, we make two sorts of gestures: batonic, for emphasis, thumping your clenched fist down on the table, and iconic, which are loosely related to the meaning of the word you're saying. We might be talking about going round in circles, while gesturing the shape of a circle. KC, a patient with jargon aphasia, largely gestured normally, but when he came to gesture before a neologism, the gestures would be incomplete, starting normally but then fading away (Butterworth et al., 1981). The conclusion from all this is that patients such as KC seem to know the meaning of at least some of the words with which they're having difficulty, but, because the words are low in frequency, are having difficulty retrieving the lemma or the sounds. Sometimes there's sufficient activation of the phonemes for the word to be recognisable, but on other occasions there is not, so unrelated neologisms reflect almost random activation of the phoneme level.

A third type of difficulty aphasic speakers face is in retrieving names, a problem called *anomia*. Virtually all types of aphasia are accompanied by some degree of anomia, although often it is so common as to be the defining characteristic. Given that I've argued above for a two-stage model of lexicalisation, it should come as no surprise that we observe two types of anomia. In some patients the ability to access lemmas seems to be impaired. Howard and Orchard-Lisle (1984) describe the case of JCU, who had great difficulty naming objects. She also made a lot of semantic errors in both production and comprehension. Her naming performance could be greatly improved if she was given the first sound of the word, suggesting that the sounds were intact and still there; so, shown a picture of a tiger, the cue "t" would help elicit the right response. She was also easily led astray by a misleading cue; if she was shown the same picture of a tiger and given the cue "l" she would say "lion". Although her recognition of objects was excellent, and she scored highly on most tests of semantic ability, she found it difficult to distinguish items in a semantic matching task where the items were very similar – where she had to match a picture of an onion to a peapod when the distractor was an apple. The likely explanation of JCU's problem was that she was confusing semantically similar items because her semantic representations were weakened by her brain damage, leading to the activation of several competing lemmas. Phonological cues helped to resolve this competition, either for better or for worse.

Contrast this type of semantic–lexical anomia with the case of EST (Kay & Ellis, 1987). EST was another anomic patient, but he performed well on the semantic tasks JCU was bad at; he wasn't at all prone to the effects of semantic distraction, and he could provide detailed information about the word he couldn't retrieve. He found it difficult to retrieve much phonological information at all. He performed much worse with low-frequency names, and phonological cueing was of little assistance; neither could he be misled into producing a semantic competitor with an incorrect sound. Clearly EST's problems are very different from those of JCU. He seems able to access the lemma, but his problems seem to lie in getting to the sounds of the word. Given a two-stage model, this pattern is exactly what we expect: some patients have difficulty accessing the right lemma, and others accessing the sounds given that they've accessed the lemma. Other patients might find both difficult, of course!

The viability of explaining lexical access difficulties in aphasia is supported by computational modelling. Dell et al. (1997) simulated naming errors using an interactive two-stage model (the model is called the DSMSG model after the authors). Activation flows in cascade fashion from the semantic feature level to the lemma level, and then to the phoneme level, with feedback from a level to the one above. This basic architecture should now be very familiar. Dell et al. simulated brain damage by reducing the strengths of the connections between levels (the weights on the connections), or by decreasing the decay rate of the activated units. Once a unit is activated, it has to return to its resting level – we can't have units remaining highly activated for ever. Usually this decay is quite rapid. Dell et al. found that reducing the connection strengths had the effect of producing a large increase in the number of non-word errors, and a small increase in the number of semantic and phonological word substitutions, while increasing the rate of decay increased the number of semantic and phonological errors, although with very large decay rates the number of non-word errors increases too. Hence it's possible to map out a surface depending on the amount of damage caused by reduced connection weights and increased decay. Dell et al. then measured the exact proportion of semantic, phonological, and non-word (jargon) substitution errors produced by 21 fluent aphasic patients, and showed that they all lay somewhere on this surface. In the original model the connection weights were reduced globally in the model, but we can get an even better fit to the data if we reduce the semantic-to-lemma and lemma-to-phoneme connection weights separately (Foygel & Dell, 2000). In particular, the revised model can account for patients who make exclusively semantic errors and others who make exclusively phonological errors, and can also account for performance on repeating words as well as naming pictures (Dell et al., 2007; Schwartz et al. 2006). The model also accounts for the patterns of speech of two brothers with a progressive aphasia caused by a degenerative brain disease (Croot et al., 1999); one brother's speech is modelled very well by reduced connection strengths between units, while the other's is modelled very well by an abnormally high rate of decay of activation.

Although speech production is obviously a very different task from understanding language, we can explain both normal and brain-damaged behaviour using the same general principles: interactive networks through which activation can spread.

Chapter 9

End

I^{N THIS CHAPTER} I'm going to tidy up a few loose ends and talk about a few other points of interest. If there is a theme to this chapter, it's individual differences. We vary in just about every other way imaginable, so it would be amazing if we didn't vary in our language skills. Indeed, I've already discussed several ways in which we do. Some people are better readers than others; we all know some people who are depressingly fluent and articulate, while some of us mumble our way through lives. Some people stutter, some very badly. We've seen that children even start their language journeys differently; there's variation in the age at which we start to speak; and we've even seen that there's some systematic variation in the first words children start to produce. We've seen that we carry on acquiring language and developing our language skills in late childhood and beyond; I think I only became a more than competent writer five years ago, and it took a lot of hard work – and perhaps even then I'm fooling myself. No sooner do we get good at something, than we start to lose it, as ageing and the cumulative effects of toxins take their toll. We've also seen how some are unluckier than others, being involved in accidents that cause a brain injury, or have one or more strokes, or suffer from a neurodegenerative illness. I hope I've shown how psycholinguists have learned a great deal from these different sorts of brain damage.

In this chapter I want to begin by looking at two particular sorts of difference, gender and age.

My favourite tipple, but also Enemy of the Neuron

Are there sex differences in language?

Sex differences are often controversial. It's perhaps naive to be surprised by the amount of controversy they can generate. But why should it be surprising if there are some sex differences in the brain and behaviour, given there are such pronounced and manifest differences in other ways? Of course, we must always be careful about drawing a conclusion about the cause of sex differences; some if not all of the difference could be explicable in terms of cultural differences – boys and girls are brought up in different ways, with different expectations and experiences.

With these caveats in mind, there are nevertheless differences that appear to be robust and have their origin in differences in brain structure and the effects of sex hormones. It's widely believed that women are "better" at language than men, and there is some basis for this belief. On average, girls develop verbal skills faster than boys, while boys have a slight edge in some aspects of mathematical and spatial development (Kimura, 1999; Kolb & Whishaw, 2003). Women tend to perform better on linguistic tasks, some memory tasks, mathematical calculation, and fine motor movements, while men tend to perform better on mathematical reasoning, motor tasks involving directing something towards a target, and spatial tasks, particularly those involving some degree of mental rotation.

Sex differences in language have been known and speculated about for a long time, largely because they are among the most obvious of the cognitive differences. Girls tend to start talking before boys, by an average of about one month, and have higher verbal fluency, larger vocabularies, and better verbal memory. They're better readers and spellers, and the incidence of developmental dyslexia and other disorders such as stuttering is considerably lower in females than in males. In general the speech of girls is more clearly enunciated than the speech of boys. Females produce, on average, longer sentences than males, and make fewer errors. There's some evidence for greater cerebral asymmetry in the male brain, with women having more interhemispheric connections, with parts of the corpus callosum – the tract of nerve fibres that connects the two hemispheres of the brain – being significantly large in women (Baron-Cohen, 2003; Kolb & Whishaw, 2003). These findings are supported by autopsy studies and brain imaging, and also by the effects of brain damage: damage to one hemisphere has more pronounced effects on language (for damage to the left hemisphere) and motor and spatial skills (for damage to the right) for women. Somehow the lower degree of lateralisation might lead to a slight processing advantage, probably because females are better able to use both hemispheres, at least partly, and here two is better than one. Some of the developmental differences might also reflect the faster maturation of girls – and this difference in maturation rate might in turn be linked to the greater degree of lateralisation in boys, because the more slowly a person matures, the greater the time available for the development of a more pronounced cerebral asymmetry (Kolb & Whishaw, 2003). It should be said that not everyone agrees with these conclusions. In a meta-analysis – an analysis of many analyses – of brain imaging of lateralisation effects on language tasks, Sommer et al. (2004) found no significant difference in lateralisation on language tasks between women and men, and concluded that it is unlikely that differences in lateralisation in language play a large role in cognitive sex differences.

Some of the differences, particularly in later life, are likely to have a cultural origin – or at least a very roundabout biological origin, depending on your view of the biological contribution to cultural differences. It will perhaps come as no surprise to learn that men are significantly more likely to interrupt the other speaker than are women, and men are even more likely to interrupt a woman than another man (Anderson & Leaper, 1998).

Sex differences in verbal ability have one important consequence for the psycholinguist: we have to be careful to control for, or at least take account of, gender in our experiments. Running an experiment where one group is all male and the other all female is asking for trouble.

How does ageing affect language?

Sadly joints and bones aren't the only things that deteriorate as we age. Although the cognitive consequences of ageing are normally relatively slight, at least early on, eventually old age starts to get us – and it's possible that we might start to show a decline in some cognitive tasks in our 40s (Rhodes, 2004). It's useful to distinguish between normal ageing and pathological ageing; in pathological ageing cognition and performance are affected by neurodegenerative illnesses such as Alzheimer's disease or Parkinson's disease. As we get older, the probability of an individual having accrued damage from an accident or stroke increases.

There are two broad approaches to how cognitive abilities change with age: one approach maintains that ageing has a general effect so that there is a decline across all abilities, as a result of either decreasing cognitive resources or a general slowing in our speed of processing, while the other approach says that the decline of more specific processes, such as our ability to inhibit responses, is responsible for the cognitive changes seen (Banich, 2004). Whichever ultimately turns out to be correct, some brain regions, and some aspects of behaviour, do seem more sensitive to ageing's effects. With normal ageing, declarative memory (memory of facts) fails faster than procedural memory (memory of how to do things). Declarative memory typically starts to decline slightly from the age of approximately 60, although it should be noted that there are very large variations between people (Hedden & Gabrieli, 2004).

Language is *relatively* spared by ageing. As we might expect from the above, those aspects of language that depend on declarative memory retrieval are more sensitive than those that depend on procedural memory. So syntax is generally well preserved until the end, while word retrieval suffers more. Even so, semantic and autobiographical memory are better preserved than episodic memory and working memory. Given this broad pattern, and the less forgiving nature of production, age-related changes are more apparent in speech production than in understanding. We see more forgetting of names, slower reaction times, more errors, more hesitations, and more TOT states. The evidence suggests that the difficulty comes from accessing the sounds of words; we see a parallel difficulty with increasing age in spelling (James & Burke, 2000). Proper names – particularly those not used recently – tend to be particularly prone to loss and to causing a TOT state. When in a TOT, older people produce less partial information and fewer interlopers than younger adults. The sounds of words are particularly prone to loss because they're "at the end of the line"; semantic representations are rich with many semantic features contributing to the meaning of each word, offering a high degree of protection to word meanings; phonological representation, particularly for low-frequency words with few neighbours, does not have this protection.

Frontal regions of the brain – those responsible for planning, executive processing, and inhibition – seem to be particularly prone to the effects of ageing (Banich, 2004). Given this finding, those aspects of language dependent on executive processes, such as the control of conversation, the ability to inhibit excessive responding, and our ability to use metaknowledge – our ability to reflect upon and manipulate our knowledge, in this case our knowledge of language – will be prone to gradual disruption.

Although generally language is better preserved than other cognitive abilities, there is an exception. *Primary progressive aphasia* is a type of dementia that characteristically begins with the prominent progressive loss of language abilities. The disease is related to Alzheimer's disease, but the degeneration begins in the fronto-temporal regions of the brain that we know are particularly important for language. As with language impairments caused by brain trauma, there are both fluent and non-fluent types. The fluent type is associated with the loss of semantic knowledge, knowledge about word meanings, and, as its first symptom, a disorder called *semantic dementia*. Semantic dementia is an exception to my statement above that generally semantic knowledge is among the last things to go in ageing. Although fortunately quite rare, in recent years semantic dementia has been much studied by psychologists, because of the window it provides on how the brain stores and structures semantic information (Hodges et al., 1992; Warrington, 1975).

We have a lot to look forward to! The elderly have some advantages: they have greater experience and expertise, and have larger vocabularies. The good news is that we can help ourselves by taking care of ourselves, enjoying a good diet, and taking physical and mental exercise. There comes a point though when the damage from within and without is too much, and beyond that point the rest is silence.

What were those issues again?

You should now have an opinion on whether my friend is right. Is psycholinguistics boring? Is there something special about language? The answer to the first question is of course no, and the second, yes and no, as most answers are.

My initial paradox was if on the one hand language processes are specific to language, then why should we find them to be particularly interesting? But on the other, if they reflect general processing then why should we focus just on language? I hope I've convinced you that while language is special, it's not so special that we can't learn many important things from it. There are two good reasons for devoting a great deal of effort to understanding the psychology of language. First, language is just so important to our lives and our cognition. I've shown that language and thought are inextricably intertwined; there is no way that we could understand thought without understanding language. Second, in as much as language does make use of general-purpose cognitive processes – statistical learning, the construction of elaborate representations – it does so in a way that is more complex and pervasive than any other aspect of cognition. Language is a window to the mind. Steven Pinker (2007), in the final chapter of *The Stuff of Thought*, presents a fascinating list of things that the structure of language tells us about how humans construct a representation of the world based on time, space, and causality: for example, we differentiate things, states, places, and goals; things are differentiated into human and non-human, animate and inanimate, solid and aggregate, and how they are laid out in space.

The differences between researchers sometimes seem less than they first appear. Does language make use of knowledge specific to language? The East Coasters say yes, and against them we could level the charge that it's all very specific and therefore uninteresting. But the mechanisms that use that knowledge are still surely not specific to language. The West Coasters say no, language arises as a result of the way in which the mind processes material with the sorts of statistical regularities (and irregularities) that language has; against them we could levy the charge that they should broaden their horizons a bit and look at something more general, but oh, how impressive language is. And by examining the way in which general-purpose cognitive processes cope with the materials of language, we learn a great deal about those processes, perhaps things that couldn't be learned any other way.

Let's return briefly to the important issues I raised in the first chapter. Without duplicating this book, it's possible to comment generally on them.

First, is our language behaviour governed by the use of rules or by multiple constraints and statistical regularities? When we hear a complex sentence, do we try to work out its structure according to the rules of grammar, or make use of our experience to tell us what the structure of that sort of sentence has usually been in the past? One of the recurring themes of this book is that language processing has an important statistical component centred around constraint satisfaction and integrating multiple sources of information. Of course not all processing can be probabilistic: we start off with some idea of what we're going to say (normally!); children receive a great deal of help in segmenting speech into sounds; and we must place great store on the input in comprehension.

A great deal is made of the distinction between rule-governed language and exceptions, as though this is a fundamental dichotomy. However, the dichotomy isn't as clear-cut as it might first seem. First, there is some order in some of the irregularity. The past tense of "drink" ("drank"), while irregular (we don't say "drinked"), resembles the past tense of "sink" and "shrink". A second, related point is that it's possible to express all the contingencies of language on a continuum from simple (the majority of items that are without exception rule-governed), through those that are a little irregular, to those that need to be expressed with more complex contingencies (e.g. "You pronounce -ave as in save and gave except after an h"). That is, although the mappings in language are not totally regular, they're certainly not totally random either, but somewhere in between; we can say language is *quasi-regular* (Seidenberg, 2005).

Can we do without rules completely? Although parsing and production might have probabilistic aspects, it's difficult to see how we could dump rules altogether from syntax. And although, as I've said many times before, introspection can be misleading, we certainly sometimes feel like we're following a rule.

Second, where does knowledge come from? Is it innate and in our genes, or is it learned? The question of how much knowledge a baby is born with has been a central one in the history of philosophy. The question is one of degree: how much specific knowledge about language are we born with? Is some knowledge about language encoded in our genes, or do we just pick it up using general-purpose cognitive mechanisms? Everyone agrees something has to be innate; the only question is how much. Much progress has been made in the past decade, largely as a result of computational modelling, showing how we can acquire language and explain aspects of it that were previously thought to necessitate domain-specific innate knowledge using general-purpose learning algorithms (by general-purpose I mean used throughout cognition, not just by language). Once again this programme is an empirical one: how much can we explain (by modelling) without invoking special knowledge? Of course, just because we can model something without special knowledge doesn't mean that we don't in fact use it, but it's parsimonious to assume that if general knowledge is sufficient for learning to occur, that's the way we do it. Parsimony is an important principle in science (although it isn't always apparent which is the more economical option).

Third, is processing modular or interactive? I've shown that there's a great deal of evidence for interaction: for cascading processing and for feedback. It's a free-for-all, but it's not a game without any rules. The brain has structure – it's divided into interacting parts responsible for particular aspects of behaviour. The environment has structure and imposes constraints on us. The mind has structure, but it's a leaky structure; there are processing modules in language, but they're leaky ones. Our knowledge of meaning or of the world can affect at any early stage which word we think we're hearing or which sentence structure we're preferring.

Is there a "grand model" of language processing in the brain?

I've presented a general account of language processing – it would be far too grand to call it a model – where we can identify a number of language modules: visual word recognition, spoken word recognition, the human sentence processing mechanism, the system that produces syntax, and the lexicalisation process. Each of these modules consists of a number of linked levels of processing. I've also shown the importance of the idea of activation spreading through a network of massively

261

interconnected features. The general mechanisms involved – levels of simple units massively interconnected by weighted connections along which activation can spread – are surely general to all psychology, not just language; it's a way of describing the mind that's highly effective. How do these modules fit together?

The triangle model of reading is one approach to a limited domain, but it's possible to go much further. Figure 9.1 gives a model of language processing from

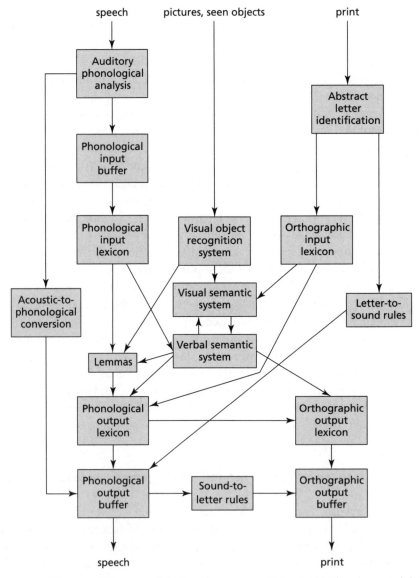

FIGURE 9.1 The overall structure of the language system. It is possible that the speech lemma system is unnecessary, or that other links to lemmas need to be introduced

Harley (2008). This model is in turn based on a model used for neuropsychological testing of language disorders (Ellis & Young, 1988; Kay, Lesser, & Coltheart, 1992). It's based on the sort of neuropsychological dissocations we find (and don't find). There's no need to go through it in detail, and many would take issue with the necessity for some of the boxes (the triangle modellers would dispense with the dual-route aspect), but it shows the sort of model we can construct. It shows how we can take different inputs (speech and print) and use them to access meaning and construct a representation of discourse, or convert them to speech (through repetition or reading aloud) or print (through writing to dictation or copying). It also shows the architecture of how we might generate speech and writing afresh from our internal goals and representation.

You might think it ironic that I conclude with what seems to the most extreme "boxology" model yet, particularly after sounding off against the approach in the first chapter, but this is meant to do nothing more than show what sort of general account of language we can develop, and how the components of language might be related to one another. Just to consider one process in slightly more depth, let's take single-word repetition. If I say a non-word, SPRIT, you can (I hope) repeat it aloud; from this we can conclude that it is not essential to access the lexicon in order to be able to repeat a string of sounds. This idea is supported by the condition known as word meaning deafness, where some patients with brain damage can repeat words back, but can not understand those words. To take another example: some patients have difficulty in producing speech but are much more fluent at writing, suggesting the phonological and orthographic output systems part company somewhere along the line (Bub & Kertesz, 1982). You could have a few hours of fun by taking the model and predicting what types of neuropsychological disorders you might find if particular connections were destroyed.

The next stage is to relate our model to the brain. The Wernicke-Geschwind model was the first attempt to relate language to the brain, and more recent models have gone much further. Ullman (2004) details a model of the interaction of language and memory and how they relate to brain structures, distinguishing between a declarative memory for facts – the lexicon, where knowledge about words is stored – in the left temporal lobe of the brain, and a procedural memory for grammar to act on words, based on a distinct neural circuit making use of parts of the frontal lobes, the basal ganglia, and the cerebellum. Essentially this is a distinction between words and syntax, or between facts and rules that operate on those facts. While the details of the model are beyond the scope of this book, the key point is that we are now at the point where we can begin to integrate how the brain and mind work to give complete models of whole facets of human behaviour.

What's the future?

Einstein reputedly once said, "It's very difficult to predict ... the future." I've written several books and papers in which I've either tried to guess or been made to think about the shape of things to come, and every time I've been largely wrong. So I don't think there's much to be gained by speculating what psycholinguistics will be like in five or ten years – science moves too quickly. But it does need enthusiastic, motivated, clever researchers to tackle some of the most fundamental problems about what it means to be human. Why not join them?

Next

WHAT SHOULD YOU READ NEXT? Where better to start than my text *The Psychology of Language* (third edition, published by Psychology Press in 2008)? It goes into the topics in this book, as well as several others, in greater detail. There is now a great deal of information freely available on the internet. Wikipedia has many good articles about the topics in this book, with links and suggestions for further reading. You are always cautioned that Wikipedia might not be entirely reliable, but I've yet to find any egregious errors in things I know about. Sometimes, however, analysis might be biased or selective. So be careful.

Steven Pinker's (1994, 1999, 2007) three books on language are good, readable places to start to get an idea of the East Coast view of language – that language is a special faculty that is based on rules, and depends on language-specific innate knowledge.

There are two recent large, comprehensive, but expensive handbooks of psycholinguistics that between them cover the complete area in detail and contain many thousands of further references (Gaskell, 2007; Traxler & Gernsbacher, 2006).

The following are suggestions for further reading, chapter by chapter.

1 Language

Crystal's (1997) *Cambridge Encyclopedia of Language* is an excellent place to find out more about linguistics – the study of language and languages. It's particularly clear on the sounds and rules of languages.

Price (1984) is an excellent account of the history of the languages of Britain. Most of my account of the history of Welsh comes from this book, although

Wikipedia also has an excellent section on the Welsh language and the history of the Welsh language. I used the Shakespeare insult generator from http://petelevin.com/shakespeare.htm. Bryson (1990) is very good on the history of English.

Steven Pinker has written an excellent series of books (*The Language Instinct, Words and Rules*, and *The Blank Slate*), all from the viewpoint that language is a special faculty, that it is a rule-based system, and that it relies on innate knowledge.

Christiansen and Kirby's (2003) collection of papers *Language Evolution* is the best book I know of on the subject. You might find it hard going, but by the end of it you'll know nearly everything there is to know on the subject. A critique of the fossil evidence that Neanderthals could speak is provided by DeGusta, Gilbert, and Turner (1999). Renfrew (2007) is a fascinating description of early man, the flowering of culture in the Palaeolithic, with discussion of what language might have done.

See Harley (2004) for a discussion – and the sources – of the different metaphors for the mind. Really we should distinguish between metaphors of the mind itself, and metaphors suggesting what we can and cannot learn about the mind by looking at damage to the brain, but the range is interesting and amusing to note.

2 Animals

Wikipedia has a good section on ants in general, and ant communication and pheromones in particular. People are fascinated by the sounds produced by whales and dolphins, but I've been unable to locate a good introductory reference. The Wikipedia entry again is good if short, but does include samples of sounds.

The debate between Kako (1999a, 1999b) and Pepperberg (1999) raises questions about the grammatical abilities of animals that have been taught some language, including Alex. It's worth reading to gain some idea of what some people would need to see to accept that these animals are truly using language – and some of the reasons why these criteria might be too strong. *Alex & Me* (Pepperberg, 2008) is a more popular account of Pepperberg's work with Alex.

Chimpanzees mourn their dead – they might also be susceptible to romantic love, and it has even been suggested that they can appreciate a beautiful sunset. For more on these ideas see the work of the animal researcher Jane Goodall. Her website www.janegoodall.org is a good place to start.

There's an enormous literature on cross-fostering chimpanzees and attempts to teach them language. An excellent description of the Kelloggs' work with Gua is provided by Benjamin and Bruce (1982). The life of Nim Chimpsky is sympathetically described by Hess in her 2008 book *Nim Chimpsky: The Chimp who Would be Human*. A popular account of Kanzi can be found in Sue Savage-Rumbaugh's and Roger Lewin's (1994) book of that name.

3 Children

Kuhl (2004) provides a short overview of research on all areas of early language acquisition, emphasising the multiple constraints that help a child to learn without too much prior knowledge. Altmann's (1997) book on psycho-linguistics has a good section on language in the womb, and is generally a good read for the beginner. Fernald and Marchman (2006) provide an excellent detailed review of language in infancy, covering both comprehension and production. For more detail, Clark (2009) is a recent and very well received text. Bloom's (2000) *How Children Learn the Meaning of Words* is a readable book all about that topic.

There are a number of excellent pages in Wikipedia about pidgins and creoles, with many fascinating examples. Bickerton's (2008) is a good general book on creoles. I discovered the Creole song at: www.mamalisa.com/blog/looking-for-a-french-creole-song-from-trinidad. It has been performed by a group called La Compagnie Creole. There has been much debate about how we process irregular verbs and how children acquire the past tense; see also Pinker and Ullman (2002) and Plunkett and Marchman (1991, 1993). See Fernald and Marchman again for a brief review of the current status of the nativist–empiricist debate.

The idea that you need negative information to be able to learn powerful grammars – specifically, those with infinite recursion – is called Gold's Theorem (Gold, 1967). Pinker (1994) gives an excellent description of linguistic universals and parameter setting. Elman et al.'s (1996) book *Rethinking Innateness* is now a classic reference on alternatives to nativism, arguing that we need to look at exactly what children say, and pay attention to the language to which children are exposed. The idea that "less is more" has not been accepted by everyone. Rohde and Plaut (1999) argued that while less might be more for the constrained worlds of these computer simulations, with more realistic stimuli less is definitely less. For more on the importance of recursion, and whether recursion alone makes us special, see Fitch and Hauser (2004), Jackendoff and Pinker (2005), and Pinker and Jackendoff (2005)

There is some debate about whether or not the brain suddenly becomes less flexible around the age of 16, or whether the decline is a more gradual one. Birdsong and Molis (2001) repeated Johnson and Newport's experiment with native Spanish speakers learning English, and found no sudden discontinuity. Elman et al. (1996) argued that Johnson and Newport's (1989) original data were fitted just as well by a curved line as one showing a discontinuity.

For stories on the "original language", the original reference is Fromkin et al. (1974), but several websites go into further detail. Shattuck's (1994) account of the Wild Boy of Aveyron, *The Forbidden Experiment*, is an excellent and easy read. Some controversy surrounds feral children. Many of the accounts are second- and third-hand, and some may be hoaxes; Serge Aroles in his 2007 book *L'Enigme des Enfants-Loup* ("The enigma of wolf children") is particularly damning, arguing that not a single case of abandoned children surviving for long periods in the wild, or being reared by animals, stands up to scrutiny. The animals apparently capable of raising children include wolves (several times), bears, gazelles, monkeys, chimpanzees, dogs, cattle, and sheep; having some familiarity with sheep, I find this final claim particularly incredible. There is an excellent website devoted to feral children at www.feralchildren.com, and Wikipedia provides an exhaustive review of all known cases. There is also the film *The Apple* (Makhmalbaf, 1998) about the story of the rehabilitation of the Iranian twins Zahra and Massoumeh Naderi, who were kept in isolation by their father until they were about 12 years old. For a more recent and accessible account of Genie, see Rymer (1993). For another recent general and popular account of feral children, see Newton (2002).

Dorothy Bishop's (1997) book *Uncommon Understanding* is an excellent text on specific language impairments and developmental disorders of language. The chapter on neural plasticity in language in Huttenlocher (2002) is a good review of the area.

For a recent review of research on bilingualism, see Bialystock (2001a) and Genesee and Nicoladis (2006). Wikipedia has a good page on language education. There are several other methods not mentioned in the main text. One of the most famous is the proprioceptive, or feedback, method, which tries to engage all the senses and involve as much movement and activity as possible. You speak as loudly as possible. A well-received text on second language learning and teaching is that of Cook (2008).

4 Thought

For two very different overviews of cognitive development, I recommend the books by Flavell et al. (2002) and Goswami (2008). The former has a more Piagetian bias, the latter a more neuroscience one. I note that there are other case studies showing a low correlation between verbal abilities and non-verbal IQ; a review is provided by Rondal (1998), with emphasis on exceptional language abilities of some people with Down syndrome. There is some dispute about the strength of the conclusions that can be drawn from such case studies (e.g. Levy, 1996), but it's difficult to see how they show anything other than the limitations of the cognition hypothesis. Some think that the case for preserved or even superior language abilities in children with Williams syndrome has been overstated (e.g. Brock, 2007). The collection edited by Piattelli-Palmarini (1980) summarises the classic debate between Piaget and Chomsky on nativism and language held at the Abbaye de Royaumont near Paris in 1975.

Hoff-Ginsberg (1997) has a good section on dialogue, monologues, Piaget, and Vygotsky. Goswami (2008) presents a very good account of Vygotsky's work. There are several introductory books on Chomsky (who is by far the most highly cited social scientist in the world). The most approachable, particularly if you enjoy the cartoon approach, is *Introducing Chomsky* (Maher & Groves, 2004). I like the rather more staid and detailed *Chomsky* in the Fontana Modern Masters series (Lyons, 1991).

I recommend Orwell's (1949) novel *Nineteen Eighty-Four* to anyone who hasn't read it. The appendix on the details of Newspeak is one appendix you shouldn't skip. Pinker (1994) has a very good section on the Sapir-Whorf hypothesis, with some interesting snippets of information on how it came about. One of the best more advanced recent collections of work on Sapir-Whorf is Gumperz and Levinson (1996). Pinker discusses the circularity of Whorf's arguments from translations; the circularity was first pointed out by Lenneberg (1953) and Brown (1958). It does on occasion seem that we have it in for Whorf. He gets a very bad press. As he said, he had more than one hypothesis. He died tragically young and carried out most of his research as an unpaid amateur; he nevertheless made some exceptional contributions to linguistics, particularly in deciphering the Mayan hieroglyphs (Pullum, 1991).

Pinker (2007) writes very sensibly on the Sapir-Whorf hypothesis. The debate about the number of Inuit words for snow was formerly about the number of Eskimo words for snow; but as the Inuit of Canada (where Boas carried out his work) consider the word "Eskimo" offensive, I've avoided it. The Pullum article is reprinted with a new introduction in his 1991 *The Great Eskimo Vocabulary Hoax*, a collection of entertaining essays particularly good at debunking common linguistic misconceptions, although some of the articles are more linguistically technical. The uncertainty about the number of words for snow depends on your definition of "word" and how lax you want to be about counting something as referring to snow; although Pullum gives just two on one page, on another he accepts the number could be as high as a dozen. There is at least one online English–Inuit dictionary available that looks very respectable; when I typed in "snow" I got over 30 words, but many of these look like compounds. But as Pullum rightly says, so what? I can't resist mentioning his delightful phrase "these lexically profligate hyperborean nomads".

What about those euphemisms? "Adult movie" means pornography, "economical with the truth" means "lying" (or, at least, failing to correct mistaken impressions), "tired and emotional" means drunk, and "I need to wash my hands" means I want to go to the lavatory (which, I suppose, is itself just another euphemism; few *just* want to go and look at the toilet). "Tired and emotional" originated in the British magazine *Private Eye* in a spoof on a Labour politician. "Economical with the truth" was first used by the British Cabinet Secretary Sir Robert Armstrong in the Spycatcher trial of 1986, although in turn it is an adaptation of a quote from Edmund Burke. The US military are legendary for their euphemisms, having given us also "pacification" (bombing to utter destruction), "enhanced coercive interrogation technique" (torture), "sleep management" (sleep deprivation), and "rendition" (kidnap). For anyone interested in how those in power abuse language to make themselves and their actions more presentable and opaque, I recommend Poole's (2007) *Unspeak*.

The recent flurry of research on language and numerical cognition is reviewed by Gelman and Butterworth (2005). They conclude that cultural and lifestyle differences account for differences manipulating number; as they point out, it would be surprising if there were no effects of language on cognition, but it's another thing altogether to maintain that it's the causal underpinning of our abilities. As for Captain Cook's ships . . . in the same section that I write about the dangers of checking sources and stories getting distorted, I'm ashamed and embarrassed to say that I have no idea where I heard this story, or even if I'm repeating it correctly: Hambling (2007) gives an overview.

The colour naming research has spawned considerable controversy. Rosch's experimental procedure was challenged by Lucy and Shweder (1979), who argued that Rosch's focal colours were perceptually more discriminable – further away in colour space – than the non-focal colours, but this conclusion was in turn challenged by Kay and Kempton (1984). There is a good page on the Navajo language in Wikipedia.

"English has basic colour terms corresponding to all the focal colours." It does now, but "orange", derived from the Spanish name for the fruit, naranja, is a relatively recent addition, being first recorded in late mediaeval times, around the time of Henry VIII. Before that English used a construction corresponding to "yellow-red", "geoluhread". Wikipedia has good entries on colours.

Bloom's work on counter-factuals in Chinese has, perhaps unsurprisingly, been the subject of some debate. In particular Au (1983, 1983) and Liu (1985) claimed that Bloom's Chinese sentences just weren't very good translations from the original English, which is that the Chinese group seemed to perform worse, a point in turn denied by Bloom (1984). Not understanding a word of Chinese, it would be prudent if I avoided making too strong a statement, but it's my impression that there are nevertheless some differences in the ease with which people can understand counter-factual statements depending on the ease with which their language can express them.

For a well-known feminist angle on sexist language, see Spender (1980).

5 Meaning

The two chapters I've just mentioned on concepts and categories – by Eysenck and Keane (2005) and Reisberg (2007) – are both relevant here. Recent excellent overviews of this area are provided by Vigliocco and Vinson (2007) and Moss et al. (2007).

The man with the Chinese dictionary is of course just a reference to the philosopher John Searle's Chinese Room argument, which he uses to show that a computer, or artificial intelligence system, can never really be said to understand anything (see Searle, 1980). The article generated more debate than virtually any other in psychology, but the version I've presented seems incontrovertible (at least to me; see the original article for some of the comments and Searle's reply).

Hesperus and Phosphorus are discussed by Frege and Kripke (see, for example, Kripke, 1980). The later Greeks realised the two were the same, but thought, reasonably enough, that they were still different manifestations of the same thing. The Babylonians apparently knew all the time that they were the same thing. Johnson-Laird (1983) gives a very good and clear discussion of these matters.

There's a very large literature in linguistics and anthropology on the semantics of kinship terms; I suggest you just Google the topic for further information. The linguistic approach to decomposing all languages into a small number of features is describing it in a natural semantic metalanguage; they talk about semantic primes or atoms, but it's the same thing as features. For a full list of the semantic primitives see the Wikipedia page on natural semantic metalanguage, or one of Wierzbicka's books (e.g. 1996). Pinker (2007) discusses the structure of verbs, and also talks about the sorts of semantic elements that seem to be fundamental to the language of thought. On the subject of the definition of "game", Wikipedia has a fascinating entry; it is worth examining some of the features of "game" on that page. The most famous attempts to distinguish experimentally between decompositional and non-decompositional semantics were those of Fodor et al. (1975, 1980). However, it's very difficult to design experiments with all the necessary experimental controls. The main exponent of the unitary semantics idea, where each word corresponds to a single concept that is not decomposed, is the East Coast philosopher and linguist Jerry Fodor (e.g. 1981). Pinker (2007) discusses this approach, and the difficulties with it, amusingly and in detail. Because some concepts have to be innate, if every word has its own underlying concept, Fodor seems committed to the conclusion that we have tens of thousands of concepts that must be innate. One difficulty I have with this sort of idea is in seeing how genes code these innate concepts; after all, genes describe how proteins should be synthesised, and don't store knowledge like little seeds that blossom after birth. But perhaps it's just ignorance or a failure of imagination on my part.

"We know from various sources about the reading performance of the right hemisphere of the brain." There has been much research on this topic, including studies of competent adult readers who have lost all their left hemisphere (Patterson et al., 1989), and particularly the reading performance of material presented to the left side of the visual field in split-brain patients. These patients have had the tract of nerve fibre that connects the left and right hemispheres of the brain, the corpus callosum, severed as a treatment to prevent the spread of severe epilepsy. Because of the way in which the eyes are wired to the brain, the left side of the visual field in each eye goes to the right visual cortex, and the right side of the visual field goes to the left cortex. Hence these patients provide an opportunity to present material to just one hemisphere. Reading performance by the right hemisphere is, as you would cxpcct, very poor indeed; they are generally unable to read aloud at all, but can sometimes match pictures to printed words, although they do make semantic errors in this task. It should be noted, though, that this research generated considerable controversy (for just a flavour, see Gazzaniga, 1983; Zaidel, 1983; Zaidel & Peters, 1981).

The standard reference for connectionist models of semantics is the book *Semantic Cognition* by Rogers and McClelland (2004). A paper that pursues the same line as the Hinton and Shallice original, but explaining the phenomena in more detail, particularly the effect of imageability, is Plaut and Shallice (1993). The idea that concrete words have richer semantic representations originated from Greg Jones (1985). To demonstrate the imageability effect the model needs to incorporate the reading aloud process itself, so the design is much more complex. Nevertheless, the same general principles apply. An example of work showing the sensitivity of people with dementia to the quality of the picture they have to name is Kirshner et al. (1984).

The general approach of using computational models to simulate reading and memory has been greatly advanced by Harm and Seidenberg (2004). They model the normal process of reading print for meaning (rather than just sound, which is what many models focus upon).

Semantic category-specific disorders have generated a great deal of controversy; see Capitani et al. (2003) for a review. Originally the controversy was about whether the disorder even existed, with critics arguing that the results were spurious, arising from a failure to control properly for frequency and the complexity of the pictures used (e.g. Funnell & Sheridan, 1992; Stewart et al., 1992). However, we still find the same pattern of impairment when materials are suitably controlled. The fact that we observe a double dissociation – some patients are bad with living things and good with non-living, while others show the reverse pattern – is difficult to explain away. The dissociations of living things and other categories are discussed in detail by Caramazza and Shelton (1998). With regard to decomposing the sensory features into a finer grained representation, Warrington and McCarthy (1987) proposed that we depend on shape more to recognise animals, and colour to recognise foodstuffs; while this idea sounds plausible, there isn't any independent evidence for it. I've talked elsewhere about the nature of functional information (Harley & Grant, 2004). There's plenty of evidence that very young infants can already distinguish between living and non-living things (Quinn & Eimas, 1996).

Eysenck and Keane (2005) describe both conceptual web approaches and situated cognition (Chapter 9). For examples of good popular writing on the interconnectedness of everything, and the wider implications of the idea, I recommend Barabasi (2002) and Buchanan (2002). For another introductory account of latent semantic analysis (LSA), see Landauer et al. (1998).

One of the themes of this book is that language has two purposes, to communicate and as a means of expediting and controlling thought, but from an early age these purposes become inextricably intertwined. This of course was Vygotsky's view, and similar to the views espoused by Terence Deacon (1997) in his account of the evolution of language and symbolic processing. For more on the use of language as communication, see Herb Clark's excellent (1996) book *Using Language*.

Latent semantic analysis is one of a number of very similar approaches. It goes by several other names: the conceptual web approach, the hyperspace analogue to language (HAL), and high-dimensional memory (HDM). Barsalou (1999) and Glenberg and Robertson (2000) criticise the approach; see Burgess (2000), though, for a reply. The essence of the critique is that LSA approaches do not provide a way of grounding the system in perception or action. The idea of meaning through co-occurrence is an old one; we've already talked about certain words like "bread" and "butter" being associated. The idea of association as a basis of meaning dates back to Aristotle; the problem with association is that knowing two words are associated doesn't tell us anything about the way in which they share meaning. The relationships between "happy" and "blissful", "dog" and "tail", and "good" and "bad" are all very different, even though the words of each pair are very highly associated.

The dog is Felix, who owns my friend and colleague Nadine Martin. He's a German short-haired pointer, or so I'm assured. My reader Bill pointed out to me that this name is confusing because it's a cat's name, not a dog. I thought about changing it, but decided to sacrifice clarity for truth. Felix is a dog.

Most texts of cognitive psychology have a chapter on concepts and categories; I particularly like those in Eysenck and Keane (2005) and Reisberg (2007). The idea that some members of categories are better exemplars of the category than others is important, and gives rise to the model in which categories are represented by an abstract, idealised exemplar called the prototype (Rosch, 1978). Eysenck and Keane cover the ideas of situated cognition in more depth.

6 Words

The factors that influence word processing are discussed in much more detail in my text (Harley, 2008). For frequency, see Whaley (1978); for different aspects of frequency, particularly how it should be measured, see Gernsbacher (1984); for age-of-acquisition, see Morrison and Ellis (1995, 2000) and Bonin et al. (2004); for neighbourhood effects, see Andrews (1989); and for form-based priming, see Forster and Davis (1984) and Scarborough et al. (1977). The classic recent reference for semantic priming is Meyer and Schvaneveldt (1971), although it was first demonstrated by Cattell in 1888.

See McQueen (2007) for a short summary of the main issues in modern research on speech recognition. The phoneme restoration effect has generated a considerable amount of controversy. People can report the missing phoneme, and say they "heard" it, but what does that mean? Does the restoration really occur at the perceptual level, or does it occur later? People are notoriously poor at self-report of this kind of thing. See Fodor (1983) and Samuel (1996) for discussion. At the time of writing, typing "phoneme restoration demonstration" and "McGurk effect demonstration" into your favourite search engine should generate several online examples, including on YouTube.

The best recent compendium for everything to do with visual word recognition and reading is *The Science of Reading*, edited by Margaret Snowling and Charles Hulme (2005). In addition, there are several relevant chapters in both the Gaskell (2007) and Traxler and Gernsbacher (2006) handbooks.

I've simplified the cohort and particularly the TRACE models. The cohort model needs a mechanism to recover from errors; if you mishear, or if there's an error on the first sound of a word, there's no apparent way of the system ever recovering. Marslen-Wilson addressed this flaw in a later version of the model by dropping the all-or-none aspect; candidates aren't completely eliminated from the cohort in the face of disconfirmatory evidence, but their activation levels are greatly reduced. My description of TRACE doesn't address the issue of time, the fact that the /t/ sounds at the start and end of words like TAINT are different. The model deals with time by cutting it into discrete slices.

The extent to which context, top-down information, feedback – call it what you like – influences speech recognition is a contentious issue. The article by Norris et al. (2000) argues that it has no effect at all. It's a particularly useful source because the article is followed by peer commentators offering different points of view. Norris et al. propose an alternative computational called MERGE (SHORT-LIST in its earlier form) where there's no feedback between the lexical and prelexical units. Critics argue that the model is too narrow and does include an implicit form of feedback. The experimental data on the topic are complex and prone to dispute.

Eysenck and Keane (2005) give a more detailed introductory description of the dual-route cascaded model. Both the DRC and triangle model have generated enormous discussion, and there is a very large literature of critique and counter-critique; see Harley (2008) and Eysenck and Keane (2005) for summaries and further references. For two biased accounts see Coltheart (2005) and Plaut (2005), and for another overview of connectionist models of reading, see Seidenberg (2005). The topic of whether or not phonological dyslexia is necessarily accompanied by a general phonological deficit, as the triangle model necessarily predicts, is one full of controversy (see for example Coltheart, 1996; Farah et al., 1996; Vliet et al., 2004). For more on the triangle model and surface dyslexia, see Woollams et al. (2007). For more on brain imaging of reading, see Chen et al. (2002), who used fMRI brain imaging to examine Chinese readers making lexical decision tasks. Chinese has the familiar logographic "picture-like" script, which relies wholly on direct lexical access and cannot use any letter–sound conversion process, and also a letter-based script called "Pinyin" which is based just on assembled phonology.

These two very different scripts provide a unique tool for examining reading. As might be expected, both scripts activate many of the same areas of the brain, but some regions showed greater amounts of activation for one or the other script.

Again, while these results are consistent with the dual-route mode, they don't show that this model is right and the triangle model wrong; the results support the idea that there is a division of labour in reading, but it is much less clear what that division of labour is.

There are several books on literacy and learning to read. A good recent popular account with which to start is Wolf (2007). Goswami (2008) contains a good, if more advanced, chapter. See Byrne (2005) for a recent description of theories of reading development. For a reply to Castles and Coltheart's critique of phonological awareness as a prerequisite of reading skills, see Hulme et al. (2005). Seymour (2005) and Ziegler and Goswami (2005) provide good recent reviews of phonological awareness, learning to read, and differences between language. See the final two chapters in Snowling and Hulme (2005) for more on teaching reading. For an overview of developmental dyslexia, see Vellutino and Fletcher (2005). Wikipedia has a good web page on dyslexia, covering some of the recent controversies in the press. For more that contributes to this discussion, see Vellutino et al. (2004). For references to dyslexia as a middle class disease, just type "dyslexia middle class disease" into Google for a torrent of references – I generated 49,000 hits to wade through. There are probably many more now. Have fun. See Nicolson and Fawcett (2007) for a more recent take on the cerebellar hypothesis, and Beaton (2004) for a general review of developmental dyslexia, with emphasis on the underlying neurological disorder(s). There are many, many references talking about the types of phonological impairments shown by children at the phonological dyslexia pole of the continuum. I've given just a representative and historic few in the text; see Harley (2008, p. 251) for a more comprehensive list.

For a full discussion of early models and experiments on lexical ambiguity, including the phoneme-monitoring task (where you have to press a button when you hear a particular sound; early experiments showed that we're slower to detect the target when it comes immediately after an ambiguous word, even when the word is in a strongly biasing context), see Harley (2008, p. 200). For a short review of the more recent work on ambiguity, see Sereno et al. (2003).

7 Understanding

There were several papers about the same time that introduced constraint-based models. In addition to those listed, see Tanenhaus et al. (1989) and MacDonald et al. (1994). The volume edited by Henderson and Ferreira (2004) is an excellent source of material on the relation between language, the visual world, and eye movements, in the context of both language processing and production. There are connectionist models of parsing making use of competition and attractor networks;

examples include McRae et al. (1998), Tabor and Tanenhaus (1999), and Tabor et al. (1997).

There's much more to parsing than has been covered in this brief discussion of the main theoretical issues. My text (Harley, 2008) covers several other topics, including cross-linguistic differences in parsing, other models of parsing (of which Van Gompel et al.'s, 2001, *unrestricted race* model is among the most interesting and important), how we deal with syntactic category ambiguity (e.g. "Trains" can be either a noun or a verb), gaps and fillers, and the neuropsychology of parsing comprehension. For a review and summary of the current issues in parsing, see Pickering and Van Gompel (2006), Tanenhaus (2007), and Van Gompel and Pickering (2007).

I've simplified and embellished Kintsch's construction–integration model, making the description consistent with the terminology I've used elsewhere.

Caplan (1992) has an excellent section on right-hemisphere brain damage, humour, and disorders of discourse processing. For a recent paper on metaphor and the right hemisphere, see Schmidt et al. (2007).

8 Speaking

A good collection of papers on all aspects of speech production can be found in Wheeldon (2000). There are sections on speech production in both the Gaskell (2007) and Traxler and Gernsbacher (2006) handbooks.

For the fruits of my labours in collecting speech errors, see Harley (1984, 1990). For a fun account of speech errors, read Erard's (2007) *Um*. Wikipedia has a good entry on the Reverend Spooner and examines the authenticity of the spooner-isms attributed to him. See Reason and Mycielska (1982) for a psychological perspective on Freudian slips.

Phonological word substitutions are much less common in my corpus than semantic ones, and they are often less convincing – as is apparent from this sample. Often they have alternative explanations in terms of mechanisms such as sound deletions. I think they do happen, but they are rare. The best example I can think of is from Fromkin (1971), where a speaker said "Liszt's Hungarian restaurant" instead of "Liszt's Hungarian rhapsody". Wikipedia has an extensive list of mala-propisms in literature and on screen.

I've simplified the discussion of lemmas and the evidence for the two-stage model; see my text (Harley, 2008) for a fuller discussion of the issues involved. For an integration of the brain imaging and experimental work on semantic interfer-ence and the timing of lexicalisation, see Maess et al. (2002). The status of lemmas is a bit more controversial than I've presented it; everyone agrees that lexicalisation is a two-stage process, but there is less agreement on how the stages work in detail and the nature of the representations involved (Rapp & Goldrick, 2000, 2004). There's evidence similar to the ability to retrieve gender in TOTs from Italian speakers with brain damage; they can't retrieve the sounds of the words, but they can access information about gender (Badecker et al., 1995). On the other hand, a model where lemmas are syntactically and semantically specified predicts that if people in TOTs can retrieve partial sound information they should always be able to retrieve the gender of the word, as we must go through lemmas to get to sound. However, the data suggest that gender and sound information are independent, so this is yet another case where for some the jury is still out (Caramazza & Miozzo, 1997, 1998; Miozzo & Caramazza, 1997; Roelofs et al., 1998).

According to Wikipedia on pluralia tantum – and here I will have to take its word for it – *inålvor* ("intestines") is such a word too. Intestines and bowels are close to being pluralia tantum in English too, but I do hear people talking about "the bowel" and, more interestingly, "my intestine".

There are many websites giving advice about plural forms of nouns like company, collective, and committee: www.askoxford.com is good, and I particularly enjoyed www.alt-usage-english.org, which thoughtfully points out that if you say "the government is killing people", you mean something like it's ordered its army to go in and shoot people, or blockade the country and starve people to death, but if you say "the government are killing people", you mean the individual members are wading in there with their machetes and machine guns doing the job themselves. Definitely not a distinction for automatic processing.

Wikipedia has excellent biographies of Broca and Wernicke. For a more recent model of language processing and the brain, but one that still isn't a million miles away from the Wernicke-Geschwind model, see Ullman (2004). I have given just a couple of key references in the debate on the status of agrammatism; there are many others, some of which delve into questions about the best way to study brain damage and cognition (are experiments with groups of patients valid, or should we restrict ourselves to single-case studies?; for a selection, try Bates et al., 1991; Caramazza, 1991; Goodglass & Menn, 1985; McCloskey & Caramazza, 1988; Schwartz, 1987). Some of these exchanges are the most vituperative I know of in the literature. The examples of paraphasias and neologisms come from Ellis (1985), Martin and Saffran (1992), and Martin et al. (1994).

Dell et al.'s (1997) model has not gone without criticism. (As they say, if no one criticises you, the model probably isn't good enough.) The debate centres on how brain damage should be simulated in a connectionist model, and how good a fit between the model and real-life data has to be before we're happy. I refer the dedicated to Dell et al. (2000), Foygel and Dell (2000), Ruml and Caramazza (2000), and Ruml et al. (2000).

Where, you might wonder, is the East Coast–West Coast debate in all this? The Dell et al. approach is the West Coast model. There is an alternative, the WEAVER model and its variants, of Pim Levelt and Ardi Roelofs and colleagues of Nijmegen in the Netherlands (Levelt et al., 1999; Roelofs, 1992, 1997). But although the models differ in whether there is cascading processing and feedback, and how the meanings of words are represented, they agree on the basics: lexicalisation takes place in two stages and involves the spread of activation through a network.

9 End

Steven Pinker's (2002) *The Blank Slate* is an excellent overview of genetic influences on behaviour, nature versus nurture, language, and sex differences. For an overview of sex differences in behaviour, including language, I recommend Baron-Cohen's (2003) *The Essential Difference* and Susan Pinker's (2008) *The Sexual Paradox* (yes, they are related). Kolb and Whishaw (2003) have an excellent description of sex differences in behaviour, including the biology (Chapter 12 in the fifth edition).

Banich (2004) gives a good short review of the neuropsychology of ageing, although all good texts of biological psychology should have a section. See Burke and Shafto (2004) for a review of ageing and language production.

Ullman (2007) reviews the literature on the biocognition of language. In addition to Ullman's (2001, 2004) procedural/declarative model, other grand models of language–brain integration include the neurocognitive model of auditory sentence comprehension (Friederici, 2002) and the memory, unification, and control framework (Hagoort, 2005); see Bornkessel-Schlesewsky and Friederici (2007) for a review.

Glossary

Acoustics   The study of the physical properties of sounds.

Acquired disorder   A disorder caused by brain damage is acquired if it affects an ability that was previously intact (contrasted with *developmental disorder*).

Activation   Can be thought of as the amount of energy possessed by something. The more highly activated something is, the more likely it is to be output.

AD   Alzheimer's disease or dementia: often there is some uncertainty about the diagnosis, so this is really short-hand for "probable Alzheimer's disease" or "dementia of the Alzheimer's type".

Adjective   A describing word (e.g. "red").

Adverb   A word that modifies a verb (e.g. "quickly").

Affix   A *bound morpheme* that cannot exist on its own, but must be attached to a *stem* (e.g. re-, -ing). It can come before the main word, when it is a *prefix*, or after, when it is a *suffix*.

Agent   The *thematic role* describing the entity that instigates an action.

Agrammatism   Literally, "without grammar"; a type of *aphasia* distinguished by an impairment of syntactic processing (e.g. difficulties in sentence formation, inflection formation, and parsing).

Anaphor   A linguistic expression for which the *referent* can only be determined by taking another linguistic expression into account, namely the anaphor's *antecedent* (e.g. "Vlad was happy; *he* loved the vampire" – here *he* is the anaphor and *Vlad* is the antecedent).

Anomia   Difficulty in naming objects.

Antecedent   The linguistic expression that must be taken into account in order to determine the *referent* of an *anaphor* ("*Vlad* was happy; he loved the vampire" – here *he* is the anaphor and *Vlad* the antecedent). Often the antecedent is the thing for which a pronoun is being substituted.

Aphasia   A disorder of language, including a defect or loss of *expressive* (production) or *receptive* (comprehension) aspects of written or spoken language as a result of brain damage.

Argument structure   The pattern of thematic roles that a particular verb takes (e.g. *Agent* GIVES the *Theme* to the *Goal*).

Articulatory apparatus   The parts of the body responsible for making the physical sounds of speech (e.g. tongue, lips, larynx).

ASL   American Sign Language (sometimes called AMESLAN).

Assimilation   The influence of one sound on the articulation of another, so that the two sounds become slightly more alike.

Attachment   Concerns how phrases are connected together to form syntactic structures. In "The vampire saw the ghost with the binoculars" the *prepositional phrase* ("with the binoculars") can be attached to either the first noun phrase ("the vampire") or the second ("the ghost").

Attachment preference   A preference for how an *attachment* should be formed.

Attentional processing   Processing that is non-obligatory, generally uses working memory space, is prone to dual-task interference, is relatively slow, and may be accessible to consciousness. (The opposite is *automatic* processing.)

Attractor   A point in the connectionist attractor network to which states are attracted.

Automatic processing   Processing that is unconscious, fast, obligatory, facilitatory, does not involve working memory space, and is generally not susceptible to dual-task interference. (The opposite is *attentional* processing.)

Auxiliary verb   A linking verb used with other verbs (e.g. in "You *must have* done that", "must" and "have" are auxiliaries).

Babbling   An early stage of language, starting at the age of about five or six months, where the child repetitively combines consonants and vowels into syllable-like sequences (e.g. "babababababa").

Back-propagation   An algorithm for learning input–output pairs in connectionist networks. It works by alternately reducing the error between the actual output and the desired output of the network.

Basic level   The level of representation in a hierarchy that is the default level (e.g. "dog" rather than "terrier" or "animal").

Bilingual   Speaking two languages.

Bilingualism   The ability to speak two languages. There are three types depending on when *L2* (the second language) is learned relative to *L1*: simultaneous (L1 and L2 learned about the same time), early sequential (L1 learned first but L2 learned relatively early, in childhood), and late (in adolescence onwards).

Body   The same as a *rime*: the final vowel and terminal consonants.

Bootstrapping   The way in which children can increase their knowledge when they have some, such as inferring syntax when they have semantics.

Bottom-up   Processing that is purely data-driven.

Bound morpheme   A *morpheme* that cannot exist on its own (e.g. un, ent).

Broca's aphasia   A type of *aphasia* that follows from damage to Broca's region of the brain, characterised by: many dysfluencies; slow, laborious speech; difficulties in articulation; *agrammatism*.

Buffer   A store for temporary storage, usually of a sequence of items (e.g. *phonemes*) that either have just been input or are about to be output.

Cascade model   A type of processing where information can flow from one level of processing to the next before the first has finished processing; contrast with *discrete stage model*.

Categorical perception   Perceiving things that lie along a continuum as belonging to one distinct category or another.

CDS   Child-directed speech. The speech of carers to young children that is modified to make it easier to understand (sometimes called *motherese*).

Class   The grammatical class of a word is the major grammatical category to which a word belongs, e.g. noun, adjective, verb, adverb, determiner, preposition, pronoun.

Clause   A group of related words containing a *subject* and a *verb*.

Closed-class item   Same as *grammatical element*.

Co-articulation   The way in which the articulatory apparatus takes account of the surrounding sounds when a sound is articulated; as a result, a sound conveys information about its neighbours.

Competence   Our knowledge of our language, as distinct from our linguistic *performance*.

Complement   What describes the *subject* after a *copulative verb* (e.g. "the most important thing is *that you're alive*"); *subordinate clauses* can also complement adjectives ("I am sure *that you made a mistake*").

Complementiser   A category of words (e.g. "that") used to introduce a *subordinate clause*.

Conjunction   A part of speech that connects words within a sentence (e.g. "and," "because").

Connectionism   An approach to cognition that involves computer simulations with many simple processing units, and where knowledge comes from learning statistical regularities rather than explicitly presented rules.

Consonant   A sound produced with some constriction of the airstream, unlike a *vowel*.

Constituent   A linguistic unit that is part of a larger linguistic unit.

Content word   One of the enormous number of words that convey most of the meaning of a sentence: nouns, verbs, adjectives, adverbs. Content words are the same as *open-class words*. Contrasted with *function word*.

Controlled processing   Processing requiring central resources, the same as *attentional processing*: the opposite of *automatic processing*.

Conversation maxim   A rule that helps us to make sense of conversation.

Copulative verb   A linking verb that links the subject of a sentence with its predicate; in English it's usually some form of the verb "to be". The construction can express identity, membership of a class, or attribution of a property.

Corpus   Body or collection of something, such as a collection of slips of the tongue or samples of words.

Counterfactual   A statement that runs counter to the actual state of affairs (e.g. "if the moon were made out of cheese then there'd be a lot of happy mice").

Creole   A *pidgin* that has become the language of a community through an evolutionary process known as "creolisation".

Cross-linguistic   Involving a comparison across languages.

Deep dyslexia   Disorder of reading characterised by semantic reading errors.

Deep dysphasia   Disorder of repetition characterised by *semantic* repetition errors.

Derivation   A word that is grammatically derived from another, changing the meaning and often the grammatical category (e.g. "entertainment" from "entertain").

Derivational morphology   The study of derivational inflections.

Determiner   A grammatical word that determines the number of a noun (e.g. "the", "a", "an", "some").

Developmental disorder   A disorder where the normal development or acquisition of a process (e.g. reading) is affected.

Diphthong   A type of vowel that combines two vowel sounds (e.g. in "boy", "cow", and "my").

Discourse   Linguistic units composed of several sentences.

Discrete stage model   Processing model where information can only be passed to the next stage when the current one has completed its processing (contrast with *cascade model*).

Dissociation   A process is dissociable from other processes if brain damage can disrupt it while leaving the others intact.

Distributional information   Information about what tends to co-occur with what; for example, the knowledge that the letter "q" is almost always followed by the letter "u", or that the word "the" is always followed by a noun, are instances of distributional information.

Double dissociation   A pattern of dissociations whereby one patient can do one task but not another, whereas another patient shows the reverse pattern.

Dysgraphia   Disorder of writing.

Dyslexia   Disorder of reading.

EEG   Electroencephalography: a means of measuring electrical potentials in the brain by placing electrodes across the scalp.

Episodic memory   Knowledge of specific episodes (e.g. what I had for breakfast this morning, or what happened in the library yesterday).

ERP   Event-related potential: electrical activity in the brain after a particular event. An ERP is a complex electrical waveform related in time to a specific event, measured by *EEG*.

Expressive   To do with production.

Facilitation   Making processing faster, usually as a result of priming. It is the opposite of *inhibition*.

Figurative speech   Speech that contains non-literal material, such as *metaphors* and similes (e.g. "he ran like a leopard").

Formal paraphasia   Substitution in speech of a word that sounds like another word (e.g. "caterpillar" for "catapult"). Sometimes called a form-related *paraphasia*.

Function word   One of the limited numbers of words that do the grammatical work of the language (e.g. *determiners, prepositions, conjunctions* – such as "the", "a", "to", "in", "and", "because"). Contrasted with *content word*.

Garden-path sentence   A type of sentence where the syntactic structure leads you to expect a different conclusion from that which it actually has (e.g. "The horse raced past the barn fell").

Gating   A task that involves revealing progressively more of the sound of a word.

Gender   Some languages (e.g. French and Italian) distinguish different cases depending on their gender – male, female, or neuter.

Generative grammar   A finite set of rules that will produce or generate all the sentences of a language (but no non-sentences).

Glottal stop   A sound produced by closing and opening the glottis (the opening between the vocal folds); an example is the sound that replaces the /t/ sound in the middle of "bottle" in some dialects of English (e.g. in parts of London).

Goal   The *thematic role* of where the theme is going to.

Grammar   The set of syntactic rules of a language.

Grammatical elements   Collective name for *function words* and *inflections*.

Grapheme   A unit of written language that corresponds to a *phoneme* (e.g. "steak" contains four graphemes: s t ea k).

Hemidecortication   Complete removal of the cortex of one side of the brain.

Hidden unit   A unit from the hidden layer of a connectionist network that enables the network to learn complex input–output pairs by the *back-propagation* algorithm. The hidden layer forms a layer between the input and output layers.

Homograph   Different words that are spelled the same; they may or may not be pronounced differently, e.g. "lead" (as in what you use to take a dog for a walk) and "lead" (as in the metal).

Homonym   A word with two meanings (e.g. "bank").

Homophone   Two words that sound the same.

Idiom   An expression particular to a language, whose meaning cannot be derived from its parts (e.g. "kick the bucket").

Imageability   A semantic variable concerning how easy it is to form a mental image of a word: "rose" is more imageable than "truth".

Implicature   An inference that we make in conversations to maintain the sense and relevance of the conversation.

Inference   The derivation of additional knowledge from facts already known; this might involve going beyond the text to maintain coherence or to elaborate on what was actually presented.

Infinitive   A verb preceded by "to" that can act like a noun: "*To eat* is my goal".

Inflection   A grammatical change to a verb (changing its tense, e.g. -ed) or noun (changing its number, e.g. -s or "mice").

Inflectional morphology   The study of *inflections*.

Inhibition   This word has two uses. In terms of processing it means slowing processing down. In this sense priming may lead to inhibition. Inhibition is the opposite of *facilitation*. In comprehension it is closely related to the idea of *suppression*. In terms of networks it refers to how some connections decrease the amount of activation of the target unit.

Inner speech   The voice we hear in our head; speech that is not overtly articulated.

Intransitive verb   A verb that does not take an object (e.g. "The man laughs").

L1   The language learned first by bilingual people.

L2   The language learned second by bilingual people.

LAD   Language acquisition device: Chomsky argued that children hear an impoverished language input and therefore need the assistance of an innate language acquisition device in order to acquire language.

Lemma   A level of representation of a word between its *semantic* and phonological representations; it is syntactically specified, but does not yet contain sound-level information; it is the intermediate stage of two-stage models of *lexicalisation*.

Lexeme   The phonological word-form, in a format where sounds are represented.

Lexical   To do with words.

Lexical access   Accessing a word's entry in the *lexicon*.

Lexicalisation   In speech production, going from *semantics* to sound.

Lexicon   Our mental dictionary.

LSA   Latent *semantic* analysis – a means of acquiring knowledge from the co-occurrence of information.

Main clause   A part of a sentence that can stand alone.

Malapropism A type of speech error where a similar-sounding word is substituted for the target (e.g. saying "restaurant" instead of "rhapsody").

Manner of articulation The way in which the airstream is constricted in speaking (e.g. stop).

Maturation The sequential unfolding of characteristics, usually governed by instructions in the genetic code.

Mediated priming (Facilitatory) priming through a *semantic* intermediary (e.g. "lion" to "tiger" to "stripes").

Meta-analysis A statistical technique for summarising and comparing a number of independent studies.

Metaphor A figure of speech that works by association, comparison, or resemblance (e.g. "He's a tiger in a fight", "The leaves swam around the lake").

Millisecond 1/1000th (one thousandth) of a second – response times are typically given in milliseconds. Abbreviated to ms.

Minimal pair A pair of words that differ in meaning when only one sound is changed (e.g. "pear" and "bear").

Modifier A part of speech that is dependent on another, which it modifies or qualifies in some way (e.g. adjectives modify nouns).

Modularity The idea that the mind is built up from discrete modules; its resurgence is associated with the American philosopher Jerry Fodor, who said that modules cannot tinker around with the insides of other modules. A further step is to say that the modules of the mind correspond to identifiable neural structures in the brain.

Monosyllabic A word having just one *syllable*.

Morpheme The smallest unit of meaning (e.g. "dogs" contains two, dog + plural s).

Morphology The study of how words are built up from *morphemes*.

Nativism The idea that knowledge is innate.

Natural kind A category of naturally occurring things (e.g. animals, trees).

Neologism A "made-up word" that is not in the dictionary. Neologisms are usually common in the speech of people with jargon *aphasia*.

Non-word A string of letters that does not form a word. Although most of the time non-words mentioned in psycholinguistics refer to pronounceable non-words (*pseudowords*, e.g. "blunk"), not all non-words need be pronounceable (e.g. "lbnkb").

Noun The syntactic category of words that can act as names and can all be *subjects* or *objects* of a *clause*; all things are nouns.

Noun phrase A grammatical *phrase* based on a *noun* (e.g. "the red house"), abbreviated to NP.

Number The number of a verb is whether one or more subjects are doing the action (e.g. "the ghost was" but "the ghosts were").

Object The person, thing, or idea that is acted on by the *verb*. In the sentence

"The cat chased the dog", "cat" is the *subject*, "chased" the *verb*, and "dog" is the object. Objects can be either direct or indirect – in the sentence "She gave the dog to the man," "dog" is the direct object and "the man" is the indirect object.

Offline An experimental task that does not tap processing as it actually happens (e.g. memory tasks).

Online An experimental task that does tap processing as it actually happens (e.g. measuring reading time).

Onset The beginning of something. It has two meanings. The onset of a stimulus is when it is first presented. The onset of a printed word is its initial consonant cluster (e.g. "sp" in "speak").

Open-class word Same as *content word*.

Orthographic To do with the written form.

Orthotactic To do with constraints on the legal combinations of *graphemes* (e.g. STDEAK is not orthotactically legal).

Ostensive You can define an object ostensively by pointing to it.

Over-extension When a child uses a word to refer to things in a way that is based on particular attributes of the word, so that many things can be named using that word (e.g. using "moon" to refer to all round things, or "stick" to all long things, such as an umbrella).

Paralexia A reading word substitution error.

Parameter A component of Chomsky's theory that governs aspects of language and is set in childhood by exposure to a particular language.

Paraphasia A spoken word substitution.

Parsing Analysing the grammatical structure of a sentence.

Participle A type of verbal phrase where a *verb* is turned into an *adjective* by adding -ed or -ing to the verb: "We live in an *exciting* age".

Patient The *thematic role* of a person or thing acted on by the *agent*.

Performance Our actual language ability, limited by our cognitive capacity, distinct from our *competence*.

Phoneme A sound of the language; changing a phoneme changes the meaning of a word.

Phonetics The acoustic detail of speech sounds and how they are articulated.

Phonological awareness Awareness of sounds, measured by tasks such as naming the common sound in words (e.g. "bat" and "ball"), and deleting a sound from a word (e.g. "take the second sound of bland"); thought to be important for reading development but probably other aspects of language too.

Phonological dyslexia A type of *dyslexia* where people can read words quite well but are poor at reading *non-words*.

Phonology The study of sounds and how they relate to languages; phonology describes the sound categories each language uses to divide up the space of possible sounds.

Phonotactic   Sequential constraints that operate on adjacent phonetic segments.

Phrase   A group of words forming a grammatical unit beneath the level of a *clause* (e.g. "up a tree"). A phrase does not contain both a *subject* and a *predicate*. In general, if you can replace a sequence of words in a sentence with a single word without changing the overall structure of the sentence, then that sequence of words is a phrase.

Pidgin   A type of language, with reduced structure and form, without any native speakers of its own, which is created by the contact of two peoples who do not speak each other's native languages.

Place of articulation   Where the airstream in the articulatory apparatus is constricted.

Polysemous words   Words that have more than one meaning.

Pragmatics   The aspects of meaning that do not affect the literal truth of what is being said; these concern things such as choice from words with the same meaning, implications in conversation, and maintaining coherence in conversation.

Predicate   The part of the *clause* that gives information about the subject (e.g. in "The ghost is laughing", "The ghost" is the *subject* and "is laughing" is the predicate).

Prefix   An *affix* that comes before the *stem* (e.g. *dis*-interested). Contrast with *suffix*.

Preposition   A grammatical word expressing a relation (e.g. "to", "with", "from").

Prepositional phrase   A phrase beginning with a *preposition* (e.g. "with the telescope," "up the chimney").

Priming   Affecting a response to a target by presenting a related item prior to it; priming can have either facilitatory or inhibitory effects.

Pronoun   A grammatical class of words that can stand for *nouns* or *noun phrases* (e.g. "she", "he", "it").

Proposition   The smallest unit of knowledge that can stand alone: it has a truth value; that is, a proposition can be either true or false.

Prosody   To do with duration, pitch, and loudness.

Prototype   An abstraction that is the best example of a category.

Pseudohomophone   A *non-word* that sounds like a word when pronounced (e.g. "nite").

Pseudoword   A string of letters that forms a pronounceable *non-word* (e.g. "smeak").

Psycholinguistics   The psychology of language

Receptive   To do with comprehension.

Recurrent network   A type of connectionist network that is designed to learn sequences. It does this by means of an additional layer of units, called context units, that stores information about past states of the network.

Recursion   Something that defines something in terms of itself, or a rule that calls itself, such as a syntactic structure that can repeat building the structure using the same rule.

Reduced relative   A relative *clause* that has been reduced by removing the relative *pronoun* and "was" ("The horse raced past the barn fell").

Reference   What things refer to.

Referent   The thing in the world (or model) to which a word refers. In the sentence, "The vampire cooked his eggs and then he made some tea", "The vampire" and "he" have the same referent.

Relative clause   A *clause* normally introduced by a relative *pronoun* that modifies the main *noun* ("The horse that was raced past the barn fell" – here the relative clause is "that was raced past the barn").

Repetition priming   (Facilitatory) priming by repeating a stimulus.

Rime   The end part of a word that produces the rhyme (e.g. the rime constituent in "rant" is "ant", or "eak" in "speak"): more formally, it is the VC or VCC (vowel–consonant or vowel–consonant–consonant) part of a word.

Saccade   A fast movement of the eye, for example to change the fixation point when reading.

Schema   A means for organizing knowledge.

Script   A script for procedural information (e.g. going to the doctor's).

Segmentation   Splitting speech up into constituent *phonemes*.

Semantic   To do with meaning.

Semantic feature   A unit that represents part of the meaning of a word.

Semantic memory   A memory system for the long-term storage of facts (e.g. a robin is a bird; Paris is the capital of France).

Semantic priming   Priming, usually facilitatory, obtained by the prior presentation of a stimulus related in meaning (e.g. "doctor"–"nurse").

Semantics   The study of meaning.

Sentence   A group of words that expresses a complete thought, indicated in writing by the capitalisation of the first letter, and ending with a period (full stop). Sentences contain a *subject* and a *predicate* (apart from a very few exceptions, notably one-word sentences such as "Stop!").

Sequential bilingualism   *L2* acquired after *L1* – this can be either early in childhood or later.

Short-term memory   Limited memory for recent events (abbreviated to STM).

Simultaneous bilingualism   *L1* and *L2* acquired simultaneously.

SLI   Specific language impairment – a developmental disorder affecting just language.

SOA   Short for stimulus–onset asynchrony – the time between the onset (beginning) of the presentation of one stimulus and the onset of another. The time between the offset (end) of the presentation of the first stimulus and the onset of the second is known as stimulus offset–onset asynchrony.

Source   The *thematic role* of where the *theme* is moving from.

Span   The number of items (e.g. digits) that a person can keep in *short-term memory*.

Speech act   An utterance defined in terms of the intentions of the speaker and the effect that it has on the listener.

Spoonerism   A type of speech error where the initial sounds of two words get swapped (named after the Reverend William A. Spooner, who is reported as saying things such as "You have tasted the whole worm" instead of "You have wasted the whole term").

Stem   The root *morpheme* to which *bound morphemes* can be added.

Stroke   The sudden appearance of symptoms following an interruption to the blood flow in the brain.

Subject   The word or phrase that the sentence is about: the *clause* about which something is predicated (stated). The subject of the *verb*: who or what is doing something. More formally it is the grammatical category of the *noun phrase* that is immediately beneath the sentence node in the phrase structure tree; the thing about which something is stated.

Sublexical   Correspondences in spelling and sound beneath the level of the whole word.

Subordinate clause   A clause that cannot stand alone, usually flagged by "who", "that", "which"; in "The vampire who was running for president kicked the bucket", "The vampire kicked the bucket" is the main clause, and "who was running for president" is the subordinate clause.

Sucking-habituation paradigm   A method for examining whether or not very young infants can discriminate between two stimuli. The child sucks on a special piece of apparatus; as the child habituates to the stimulus, their sucking rate drops, but if a new stimulus is presented, the sucking rate increases again, but only if the child can detect that the stimulus is different from the first.

Suffix   An *affix* that comes after the *stem* (e.g. laugh*ing*). Contrast with *prefix*.

Suppression   In comprehension, suppression is closely related to *inhibition*. Suppression is the attenuation of *activation*, while *inhibition* is the blocking of activation. Material must be activated before it can be suppressed.

Surface dyslexia   A type of *dyslexia* where the person has difficulty with exception words.

Syllable   A rhythmic unit of speech (e.g. po-lo contains two syllables); it can be analysed in terms of *onset* and *rime* (or rhyme), with the rime further being analysable into nucleus and coda. Hence in "speaks", "sp" is the onset, "ea" the nucleus, and "ks" the coda; together "eaks" forms the rime.

Syndrome   A medical term for a cluster of symptoms that cohere as a result of a single underlying cause.

Syntactic roles   Set of roles derived from word order information, including the grammatical *subject* and *object*.

Syntax The rules of word order of a language.

Telegraphic speech A type of speech used by young children, marked by syntactic simplification, particularly in the omission of *function words*.

Tense The tense of a *verb* is whether it is in the past, present, or future (e.g. "she gave", "she gives", and "she will give").

Thematic role The set of *semantic* roles in a sentence that conveys information about who is doing what to whom, as distinct from the *syntactic roles* of *subject* and *object*. Examples include *agent* and *theme*.

Theme The thing that is being acted on or being moved.

Tip-of-the-tongue (TOT) When you know that you know a word, but you cannot immediately retrieve it (although you might know its first sound, or how many syllables it has).

Top-down Processing that involves knowledge coming from higher levels (such as predicting a word from the context).

Transcortical aphasia A type of language disturbance following brain damage characterised by relatively good repetition but poor performance in other aspects of language.

Transformation A grammatical rule for transforming one syntactic structure into another (e.g. turning an active sentence into a passive one).

Transformational grammar A system of *grammar* based on *transformations*, introduced by Chomsky.

Transitive verb A *verb* that takes an *object* (e.g. "The cat hit the dog").

Unaspirated A sound that is produced without an audible breath (e.g. the /p/ in "spin").

Unilingual Speaking one language.

Unit The simplest element, usually of a network.

Universal grammar The core of the grammar that is universal to all languages, and which specifies and restricts the form that individual languages can take.

Unvoiced A sound that is produced without vibration of the vocal cords, such as /p/ and /t/ – the same as voiceless and without voice.

Verb A syntactic class of words expressing actions, events, and states, and which have *tenses*.

Verb argument structure The set of possible themes associated with a *verb* (e.g. a person gives something to someone – or *agent–theme–goal*).

Voice onset time The time between the release of the constriction of the airstream when we produce a consonant, and when the vocal cords start to vibrate. Abbreviated to VOT.

Voicing Consonants produced with vibration of the vocal cords.

Vowel A speech sound produced with very little constriction of the airstream, unlike a *consonant*.

Wernicke's aphasia A type of *aphasia* resulting from damage to Wernicke's area of the brain, characterised by poor comprehension and fluent, often meaning-less speech with clear word-finding difficulties.

Word The smallest unit of *grammar* that can stand alone.

Word class Syntactic category.

Working memory In the USA, often used as a general term for *short-term memory*. According to the British psychologist Alan Baddeley, working memory has a particular structure comprising a central executive, a short-term visuo-spatial store, and a phonological loop (although the model continues to develop).

References

Adams, M.J. (1990). *Beginning to read: Thinking and learning about print.* Cambridge, MA: MIT Press.

Ainsworth-Darnell, K., Shulman, H.G., & Boland, J.E. (1998). Dissociating brain responses to syntactic and semantic anomalies: Evidence from event-related potentials. *Journal of Memory and Language, 38,* 112–130.

Aksu-Koc, A.A., & Slobin, D. (1985). The acquisition of Turkish. In D. Slobin (Ed.), *The crosslinguistic study of language acquisition* (Vol. 1, *The data,* pp. 839–880). Hillsdale, NJ: Lawrence Erlbaum Associates, Inc.

Altmann, G.T.M. (1997). *The ascent of Babel.* Oxford, UK: Oxford University Press.

Anderson, K.J., & Leaper, C. (1998). Metaanalyses of gender effects on conversational interruption: Who, what, when, where, and how. *Sex Roles, 39,* 225–252.

Anderson, R.C., & Pichert, J.W. (1978). Recall of previously unrecallable information following a shift in perspective. *Journal of Verbal Learning and Verbal Behavior, 12,* 1–12.

Andrews, S. (1989). Frequency and neighborhood effects on lexical access: Activation or search? *Journal of Experimental Psychology: Learning, Memory, and Cognition, 15,* 802–814.

Arensburg, B., Tillier, A.M., Vandermeersch, B., Duday, H., Schepartz L.A., & Rak, Y. (1989). A Middle Palaeolithic human hyoid bone. *Nature, 338,* 758–760.

Arnold, J.E., Eisenband, J.G., Brown-Schmidt, S., & Trueswell,

J.C. (2000). The rapid use of gender information: Evidence of the time course of pronoun resolution from eyetracking. *Cognition, 76,* B13–B36.

Aroles, S. (2007). *L'enigme des enfants-loup.* Paris: Publibook.

Au, T.K. (1983). Chinese and English counterfactuals: The Sapir-Whorf hypothesis revisited. *Cognition, 15,* 155–187.

Au, T.K. (1984). Counterfactuals: In reply to Alfred Bloom. *Cognition, 17,* 289–302.

Austin, J.L. (1976). *How to do things with words* (2nd ed.). Oxford, UK: Oxford University Press. [First edition published 1962.]

Baars, B.J., Motley, M.T., & MacKay, D.G. (1975). Output editing for lexical status from artificially elicited slips of the tongue. *Journal of Verbal Learning and Verbal Behavior, 14,* 382–391.

Badecker, W., & Caramazza, A. (1985). On considerations of method and theory governing the use of clinical categories in neurolinguistics and cognitive neuropsychology: The case against agrammatism. *Cognition, 20,* 97–125.

Badecker, W., Miozzo, M., & Zanuttini, R. (1995). The two-stage model of lexical retrieval: Evidence from a case of anomia with selective preservation of gender. *Cognition, 57,* 193–216.

Badecker, W., & Straub, K. (2002). The processing role of structural constraints on the intepretation of pronouns and anaphors. *Journal of Experimental Psychology: Learning, Memory, and Cognition, 28,* 748–769.

Baker, C. (2006). *Foundations of bilingual education and bilingualism* (4th ed.). Clevedon, UK: Multilingual Matters.

Balota, D.A. (1990). The role of meaning in word recognition. In D.A. Balota, G.B. Flores d'Arcais, & K. Rayner (Eds.), *Comprehension processes in reading* (pp. 9–32). Hillsdale, NJ: Lawrence Erlbaum Associates, Inc.

Banich, M.T. (2004). *Cognitive neuroscience and neuropsychology* (2nd ed.). Boston: Houghton Mifflin.

Barabasi, A. (2002). *Linked: How everything is connected to everything else and what it means for business, science, and everyday life.* New York: Plume Books.

Bargh, J.A., Chen, M., & Burrows, L. (1996). Automaticity of social behavior: Direct effects of trait construct and stereotype activation on action. *Journal of Personality and Social Psychology, 71,* 230–244.

Baron, J., & Strawson, C. (1976). Use of orthographic and word-specific knowledge in reading words aloud. *Journal of Experimental Psychology: Human Perception and Performance, 2,* 386–393.

Baron-Cohen, S. (2003). *The essential difference.* Harmondsworth, UK: Penguin.

Barsalou, L. (1999). Perceptual control systems. *Behavioral and Brain Sciences, 22,* 577–660.

Barsalou, L. (2003). Situated simulation in the human conceptual system. *Language and Cognitive Processes, 18,* 513–562.

Barsalou, L. (2008). Grounded cognition. *Annual Review of Psychology, 59,* 617–645.

Bartlett, F.C. (1932). *Remembering: A study in experimental and social psychology.* Cambridge, UK: Cambridge University Press.

Batchelder, E.O. (2002). Bootstrapping the lexicon: A computational model of infant speech segmentation. *Cognition, 83,* 167–206.

Bates, E., Marchman, V., Thal, D., Fenson, L., Dale, P.S., Reznick, J.S., et al. (1994). Developmental and stylistic variation in the composition of early vocabulary. *Journal of Child Language*, 21, 85–123.

Bates, E., McDonald, J., MacWhinney, B., & Applebaum, M. (1991). A maximum likelihood procedure for the analysis of group and individual data in aphasia research. *Brain and Language*, 40, 231–265.

Beaton, A.A. (1997). The relation of planum temporale asymmetry and morphology of the corpus callosum to handedness, gender, and dyslexia: A review of the evidence. *Brain and Language*, 60, 252–322.

Beaton, A.A. (2004). *Dyslexia, reading and the brain: A sourcebook of psychological and biological research*. Hove, UK: Psychology Press.

Beattie, J., Cutler, A., & Pearson, M. (1982). Why is Mrs Thatcher interrupted so often? *Nature*, 300, 744–747.

Behrend, D.A., Rosengren, K.S., & Perlmutter, M. (1992). The relation between private speech and parental interactive style. In R.M. Diaz & L.E. Berk (Eds.), *Private speech: From social interaction to self-regulation* (pp. 85–100). Hillsdale, NJ: Lawrence Erlbaum Associates, Inc.

Bellugi, U., Lichtenberger, L., Mills, D., Galaburda, A., & Korenberg, J.R. (1999). Bridging cognition, the brain and molecular genetics: Evidence from Williams syndrome. *Trends in Neurosciences*, 22, 197–207.

Benjamin, L.T., & Bruce, D. (1982). From bottle-fed chimp to bottlenose dolphin: A contemporary appraisal of Winthrop Kellogg. *Psychological Record*, 32, 461–482.

Berlin, B., & Kay, P. (1969). Basic color terms: Their universality and evolution. Berkeley, CA: University of California Press.

Bernstein, B. (1961). Social structure, language, and learning. *Educational Research*, 3, 163–176.

Betts, C. (1976). *Culture in crisis: The future of the Welsh language*. Wales: Ffynnon Press.

Bialystock, E. (2001a). *Bilingualism in development: Language, literacy and cognition*. Cambridge, UK: Cambridge University Press.

Bialystock, E. (2001b). Metalinguistic aspects of bilingual processing. *Annual Review of Applied Linguistics*, 21, 169–181.

Bialystock, E., Craik, F.I.M., Klein, R., & Viswanathan, M. (2004). Bilingualism, aging, and cognitive control: Evidence from the Simon task. *Psychology and Aging*, 19, 290–303.

Bickerton, D. (1984). The language bioprogram hypothesis. *Behavioral and Brain Sciences*, 7, 173–221.

Bickerton, D. (1990). *Language and species*. Chicago: Chicago University Press.

Bickerton, D. (2008). *Bastard tongues*. New York: Hill & Wang.

Birdsong, D., & Molis, M. (2001). On the evidence for maturational constraints in second-language acquisition. *Journal of Memory and Language*, 44, 235–249.

Bishop, D. (1983). Linguistic impairment after left hemidecortication for infantile hemiplegia? A reappraisal. *Quarterly Journal of Experimental Psychology*, 35A, 199–207.

Bishop, D.V.M. (1997). *Uncommon understanding: Development and disorders of language comprehension in children*. Hove, UK: Psychology Press.

Bloom, A.H. (1981). *The linguistic shaping of thought: A study in the impact of thinking in China and the West*. Hillsdale, NJ: Lawrence Erlbaum Associates, Inc.

Bloom, A.H. (1984). Caution – the words you use may affect what you say: A response to Au. *Cognition*, 17, 275–287.

Bloom, L. (1970). *Language development: Form and function in emerging grammars*. Cambridge, MA: MIT Press.

Bloom, P. (2000). *How children learn the meaning of words*. Cambridge, MA: Bradford Books.

Boas, F. (1911). Introduction to the handbook of North American Indians (Vol. 1). *Bureau of American Ethology Bulletin*, 40 (Part 1).

Bock, J.K. (1982). Toward a cognitive psychology of syntax: Information processing contributions to sentence formulation. *Psychological Review*, 89, 1–47.

Bock, J.K. (1986). Syntactic persistence in language production. *Cognitive Psychology*, 18, 355–387.

Bock, J.K. (1987). An effect of accessibility of word forms on sentence structure. *Journal of Memory and Language*, 26, 119–137.

Bock, J.K., & Cutting, J.C. (1992). Regulating mental energy: Performance units in language production. *Journal of Memory and Language*, 31, 99–127.

Bock, J.K., & Eberhard, K.M. (1993). Meaning, sound and syntax in English number agreement. *Language and Cognitive Processes*, 8, 57–99.

Bock, J.K., Eberhard, K.M., & Cutting, J.C. (2004). Producing number agreement: How pronouns equal verbs. *Journal of Memory and Language*, 51, 251–278.

Bock, J.K., & Griffin, Z.M. (2000). The persistence of structural priming: Transient activation or implicit learning. *Journal of Experimental Psychology: General*, 129, 177–192.

Bock, J.K., & Irwin, D.E. (1980). Syntactic effects of information availability in sentence production. *Journal of Verbal Learning and Verbal Behavior*, 19, 467–484.

Bock, J.K., & Loebell, H. (1990). Framing sentences. *Cognition*, 35, 1–39.

Bock, J.K., & Miller, C.A. (1991). Broken agreement. *Cognition*, 23, 45–93.

Bock, J.K., & Warren, R.K. (1985). Conceptual accessibility and syntactic structure in sentence formulation. *Cognition*, 21, 47–67.

Boland, J.E., Tanenhaus, M.K., & Garnsey, S.M. (1990). Evidence for the immediate use of verb control information in sentence processing. *Journal of Memory and Language*, 29, 413–432.

Bonin, P., Barry, C., Méot, A., & Chalard, M. (2004). The influence of age of acquisition in word reading and other tasks: A never ending story? *Journal of Memory and Language*, 50, 456–476.

Bornkessel-Schlesewsky, I.D., & Friederici, A.D. (2007). Neuroimaging studies of sentence and discourse comprehension. In M.G. Gaskell (Ed.), *The Oxford handbook of psycholinguistics* (pp. 407–424). Oxford, UK: Oxford University Press.

Bornstein, S. (1985). On the development of colour naming in young children: Data and theory. *Brain and Language*, 26, 72–93.

Boroditsky, L. (2001). Does language shape thought?: Mandarin and English speakers' conception of time. *Cognitive Psychology*, 43, 1–22.

Bowerman, M. (1990). Mapping thematic roles onto syntactic functions: Are children helped by innate linking rules? *Linguistics*, 28, 1253–1289.

Bradley, L., & Bryant, P. (1983). Categorizing sounds and learning to read – A causal connection. *Nature*, 301, 419–421.

Braine, M.D.S. (1976). Children's first word combinations. *Monographs of the Society for Research in Child Development*, 41 (Serial No. 164).

Bramwell, B. (1897). Illustrative cases of aphasia. *Lancet*, 1, 1256–1259. [Reprinted in *Cognitive Neuropsychology* (1984), 1, 249–258.]

Branigan, H.P., Pickering, M.J., & Cleland, A.A. (2000). Syntactic co-ordination in dialogue. *Cognition*, 75, B13–B25.

Bransford, J.D., Barclay, J.R., & Franks, J.J. (1972). Sentence memory: A constructive versus interpretive approach. *Cognitive Psychology*, 3, 193–209.

Bransford, J.D., & Johnson, M.K. (1973). Consideration of some problems of comprehension. In W.G. Chase (Ed.), *Visual information processing* (pp. 383–438). New York: Academic Press.

Brock, J. (2007). Language abilities in Williams syndrome: A critical review. *Development and Psychopathology*, 19, 97–127.

Broom, Y.M., & Doctor, E.A. (1995a). Developmental phonological dyslexia: A case study of the efficacy of a remediation programme. *Cognitive Neuropsychology*, 12, 725–766.

Broom, Y.M., & Doctor, E.A. (1995b). Developmental surface dyslexia: A case study of the efficacy of a remediation programme. *Cognitive Neuropsychology*, 12, 69–110.

Brown, R. (1958). *Words and things*. New York: Free Press.

Brown, R. (1973). *A first language: The early stages*. London: George Allen & Unwin.

Brown, R., & Hanlon, C. (1970). Derivational complexity and order of acquisition in child speech. In J.R. Hayes (Ed.), *Cognition and the development of language* (pp. 11–53). New York: Wiley.

Brown, R., & Lenneberg, E.H. (1954). A study in language and cognition. *Journal of Abnormal and Social Psychology*, 49, 454–462.

Brown, R., & McNeill, D. (1966). The "tip of the tongue" phenomenon. *Journal of Verbal Learning and Verbal Behavior*, 5, 325–337.

Brownell, H.H., Michel, D., Powelson, J.A., & Gardner, H. (1983). Surprise but not coherence: Sensitivity to verbal humor in right hemisphere patients. *Brain and Language*, 18, 20–27.

Bruner, J. S. (1983). *Child's talk: Learning to use language*. New York: W.W. Norton.

Bryant, P. (1998). Sensitivity to onset and rhyme does predict young children's reading: A comment on Muter, Hulme, Snowling, and Taylor (1997). *Journal of Experimental Child Psychology*, 71, 29–37.

Bryson, B. (1990). *Mother tongue*. London: Penguin Books.

Bub, D., Cancelliere, A., & Kertesz, A. (1985). Whole-word and analytic translation of spelling to sound in a non-semantic reader. In K.E. Patterson, J.C. Marshall, & M. Coltheart (Eds.), *Surface dyslexia: Neuropsychological and cognitive studies of phonological reading* (pp. 15–34). Hove, UK: Lawrence Erlbaum Associates Ltd.

Bub, D., & Kertesz, A. (1982). Evidence for logographic processing in a patient with preserved written over oral single word naming. *Brain*, 105, 697–717.

Buchanan, M. (2002). *Nexus: Small worlds and the groundbreaking science of networks*. New York: W.W. Norton.

Buckingham, H.W. (1981). Where do neologisms come from? In J.W. Brown (Ed.), *Jargon-aphasia* (pp. 39–62). New York: Academic Press.

Burgess, C. (2000). Theory and operational definitions in computational memory models: A response to Glenberg and Robertson. *Journal of Memory and Langauge*, 43, 402–408.

Burgess, C., & Lund, K. (1997). Representing abstract words and emotional connotation in high-dimensional memory space. In *Proceedings of the Cognitive Science Society* (pp. 61–66). Hillsdale, NJ: Lawrence Erlbaum Associates, Inc.

Burke, D., MacKay, D.G., Worthley, J.S., & Wade, E. (1991). On the tip of the tongue: What causes word finding failures in young and older adults? *Journal of Memory and Language*, 30, 237–246.

Burke, D.M., & Shafto, M. (2004). Aging and language production. *Current Directions in Psychological Science*, 13, 21–25.

Butterworth, B. (1979). Hesitation and the production of neologisms in jargon aphasia. *Brain and Language*, 8, 133–161.

Butterworth, B., Reeve, R., Reynolds, F., & Lloyd, D. (2008). Numerical thought with and without words: Evidence from indigenous Australian children. *Proceedings of the National Academy of Sciences of the United States of America*, 105, 13179–13184.

Butterworth, B., Swallow, J., & Grimston, M. (1981). Gestures and lexical processes in jargonaphasia. In J. Brown (Ed.), *Jargonaphasia* (pp. 113–124). New York: Academic Press.

Byrne, B. (2005). Theories of learning to read. In M.J. Snowling & C. Hulme (Eds.), *The science of reading: A handbook* (pp. 104–119). Oxford, UK: Blackwell.

Campbell, R., & Butterworth, B. (1985). Phonological dyslexia and dysgraphia in a highly literate subject: A developmental case with associated deficits of phonemic processing and awareness. *Quarterly Journal of Experimental Psychology Section A*, 37, 435–475.

Cantalupo, C., & Hopkins, W.D. (2001). Asymmetric Broca's area in great apes. *Nature*, 414, 505.

Capitani, E., Laiacona, M., Mahon, B., & Caramazza, A. (2003). What are the facts of semantic category-specific deficits? A critical review of the clinical evidence. *Cognitive Neuropsychology*, 20, 213–261.

Caplan, D. (1986). In defense of agrammatism. *Cognition*, 24, 263–276.

Caplan, D. (1992). *Language: Structure, processing, and disorders*. Cambridge, MA: MIT Press.

Caramazza, A. (1991). Data, statistics, and theory: A comment on Bates, McDonald, MacWhinney, and Applebaum's "A maximum likelihood procedure for the analysis of group and individual data in aphasia research". *Brain and Language*, 41, 43–51.

Caramazza, A. (1997). How many levels of processing are there in lexical access? *Cognitive Neuropsychology*, 14, 177–208.

Caramazza, A., & Berndt, R.S. (1978). Semantic and syntactic processes in aphasia: A review of the literature. *Psychological Bulletin*, 85, 898–918.

Caramazza, A., & Miozzo, M. (1997). The relation between syntactic and phonological knowledge in lexical access: Evidence from the "tip-of-the-tongue" phenomenon. *Cognition*, 64, 309–343.

Caramazza, A., & Miozzo, M. (1998). More is not always better: A response to Roelofs, Meyer, and Levelt. *Cognition*, 69, 231–241.

Caramazza, A., & Shelton, J.R. (1998). Domain-specific knowledge systems in the brain: The animate–inanimate distinction. *Journal of Cognitive Neuroscience*, 10, 1–34.

Carey, S., & Bartlett, E. (1978). Acquiring a single new word. *Proceedings of the Stanford Child Language Conference*, 15, 17–29.

Carmichael, L., Hogan, H.P., & Walter, A.A. (1932). An experimental study of the effect of language on the reproduction of visually presented forms. *Journal of Experimental Psychology*, 15, 73–86.

Carroll, J.B., & Casagrande, J.B. (1958). The function of language classifications in behavior. In E.E. Maccoby, T.M. Newcomb, & E.L. Hartley (Eds.), *Readings in social psychology* (3rd ed., pp. 18–31). New York: Holt, Rinehart & Winston.

Casey, B.J., Thomas, K.M., & McCandliss, B. (2001). Applications of magnetic resonance imaging to the study of development. In C.A. Nelson & M. Luciano (Eds.), *Handbook of developmental cognitive neuroscience* (pp. 137–147). Cambridge, MA: MIT Press.

Castles, A., & Coltheart, M. (1993). Varieties of developmental dyslexia. *Cognition*, 47, 149–180.

Castles, A., & Coltheart, M. (2004). Is there a causal link from phonological awareness to success in learning to read? *Cognition*, 91, 77–111.

Cattell, J.M. (1947). On the time required for recognizing and naming letters and words, pictures and colors. In *James McKeen Cattell, Man of science* (Vol. 1, pp. 13–25). Lancaster, PA: Science Press. [Originally published 1888.]

Cheeta (2008). *Me Cheeta: The autobiography*. New York: Fourth Estate.

Chen, Y., Fu, S., Iversen, S.D., Smith, S.M., & Matthews, P.M. (2002). Testing for dual brain processing routes in reading: A direct contrast of Chinese character and Pinyin reading using fMRI. *Journal of Cognitive Neuroscience*, 14, 1088–1098.

Chomsky, N. (1959). Review of B.F. Skinner, *Verbal Behavior*. *Language*, 35, 26–57.

Chomsky, N. (1965). *Aspects of the theory of syntax*. Cambridge, MA: MIT Press.

Chomsky, N. (1975). *Reflections on language*. New York: Pantheon.

Chomsky, N. (1980). *Rules and representations*. Oxford: Blackwell.

Christiansen, J. A. (1995). Coherence violations and propositional usage in the narratives of fluent aphasics. *Brain and Language*, 51, 291–317.

Christiansen, M.H., & Kirby, S. (2003). *Language evolution*. Oxford, UK: Oxford University Press.

Clark, E.V. (1973). What's in a word? On the child's acquisition of semantics in his first language. In T.E. Moore (Ed.), *Cognitive development and the acquisition of language* (pp. 65–110). New York: Academic Press.

Clark, E.V. (2009). *First language acquisition* (2nd ed.). Cambridge, UK: Cambridge University Press.

Clark, H.H. (1996). *Using language*. Cambridge, UK: Cambridge University Press.

Clark, H.H., & Clark, E.V. (1977). *Psychology and language: An introduction to psycholinguistics*. New York: Harcourt Brace Jovanovich.

Collins, A.M., & Loftus, E.F. (1975). A spreading-activation theory of semantic processing. *Psychological Review*, 82, 407–428.

Collins, A.M., & Quillian, M.R. (1969). Retrieval time from semantic memory. *Journal of Verbal Learning and Verbal Behavior*, 8, 240–247.

Coltheart, M. (1980). Deep dyslexia: A right hemisphere hypothesis. In M. Coltheart, K.E. Patterson, & J.C. Marshall (Eds.), *Deep dyslexia* (pp. 326–380). London: Routledge & Kegan Paul. [2nd ed., 1987.]

Coltheart, M. (1985). Cognitive neuropsychology and the study of reading. In M.I. Posner & O.S.M. Marin (Eds.), *Attention and performance XI* (pp. 3–37). Hillsdale, NJ: Lawrence Erlbaum Associates, Inc.

Coltheart, M. (1996). Phonological dyslexia: Past and future issues. *Cognitive Neuropsychology*, 13, 749–762.

Coltheart, M. (2004) Are there lexicons? *Quarterly Journal of Experimental Psychology*, 57A, 1153–1171.

Coltheart, M. (2005). Modeling reading: The dual-route approach. In M.J. Snowling & C. Hulme (Eds.), *The science of reading: A handbook* (pp. 6–23). Oxford, UK: Blackwell.

Coltheart, M., Rastle, K., Perry, C., Langdon, R., & Ziegler, J. (2001). DRC: A dual route cascaded model of visual word recognition and reading aloud. *Psychological Review*, 108, 204–256.

Conrad, C. (1972). Cognitive economy in semantic memory. *Journal of Experimental Psychology*, 92, 149–154.

Cook, V. (2008). *Second language learning and language teaching* (4th ed.). London: Hodder Arnold.

Corballis, M. (2004). On the origins of modernity: Was autonomous speech the critical factor? *Psychological Review*, 111, 543–552.

Crain, S., & Steedman, M.J. (1985). On not being led up the garden path: The use of context by the psychological parser. In D. Dowty, L. Karttunen, & A. Zwicky (Eds.), *Natural language parsing* (pp. 320–358). Cambridge, UK: Cambridge University Press.

Croot, K., Patterson, K.E., & Hodges, J.R. (1999). Familial progressive aphasia: Insights into the nature and deterioration of single word processing. *Cognitive Neuropsychology*, 16, 705–747.

Cross, T.G. (1978). Mother's speech and its association with rate of linguistic development in young children. In N. Waterson & C. E. Snow (Eds.), *The development of communication* (pp. 199–216). Chichester, UK: Wiley.

Crystal, D. (1986). Prosodic development. In P. Fletcher & M. Garman (Eds.), *Language acquisition* (2nd ed., pp. 174–197). Cambridge, UK: Cambridge University Press.

Crystal, D. (1997) *Cambridge encyclopaedia of language*. Cambridge, UK: Cambridge University Press.

Curtiss, S. (1977). Genie: A psycholinguistic study of a modern-day "wild child". London: Academic Press.

Cutting, J.C., & Ferreira, V. (1999). Semantic and phonological information flow in the production lexicon. *Journal of Experimental Psychology: Learning, Memory, and Cognition*, 25, 318–344.

Daneman, M., & Carpenter, P.A. (1980). Individual differences in working memory and reading. *Journal of Verbal Learning and Verbal Behavior*, 19, 450–466.

Davidoff, J. (2001). Language and perceptual categorisation. *Trends in Cognitive Sciences*, 5, 382–387.

Davidoff, J., Davies, I., & Roberson, D. (1999). Colour categories in a stone-age tribe. *Nature*, 398, 203–204.

Davis, K. (1947). Final note on a case of extreme social isolation. *American Journal of Sociology*, 52, 432–437.

Deacon, T. (1997). *The symbolic species*. Harmondsworth, UK: Penguin Books.

De Boysson-Bardies, B., Sagart, L., & Durand, C. (1984). Discernible differences in the babbling of infants according to target language. *Journal of Child Language*, 11, 1–15.

DeCasper, A.J., Lecanuet, J.P., Maugais, R., Granier-Deferre, C., & Busnel, M.C. (1994). Fetal reactions to recurrent maternal speech. *Infant Behavior and Development*, 17, 159–164.

DeGusta, D., Gilbert, W.H., & Turner, S.P. (1999). Hypoglossal canal size and hominid speech. *Proceedings of the National Academy of Sciences of the United States of America*, 96, 1800–1804.

Dehaene, S. (2000). *The number sense: How the mind creates mathematics*. Oxford, UK: Oxford University Press.

Dell, G.S. (1986). A spreading-activation theory of retrieval in sentence production. *Psychological Review*, 93, 283–321.

Dell, G.S. (1988). The retrieval of phonological forms in production: Tests of predictions from a connectionist model. *Journal of Memory and Language*, 27, 124–142.

Dell, G.S., Martin, N., & Schwartz, M.F. (2007). A case-series test of the interactive two-step model of lexical access: Predicting word repetition from picture naming. *Journal of Memory and Language*, 56, 490–520.

Dell, G.S., & Reich, P.A. (1981). Stages in sentence production: An analysis of speech error data. *Journal of Verbal Learning and Verbal Behavior*, 20, 611–629.

Dell, G.S., Schwartz, M.F., Martin, N., Saffran, E.M., & Gagnon, D.A. (1997). Lexical access in aphasic and nonaphasic speakers. *Psychological Review*, 104, 801–838.

Dell, G.S., Schwartz, M.F., Martin, N., Saffran, E.M., & Gagnon, D.A. (2000). The role of computational models in the cognitive neuropsychology of language: A reply to Ruml and Caramazza. *Psychological Review*, 107, 635–645.

De Villiers, P.A., & De Villiers, J.G. (1979). *Early language*. London: Fontana/Open Books.

Dooling, D.J., & Lachman, R. (1971). Effects of comprehension on retention of prose. *Journal of Experimental Psychology*, 88, 216–222.

Duncker, K. (1945). On problem-solving. *Psychological Monographs*, 58 (5, Whole No. 270).

Dunlea, A. (1989). *Vision and the emergence of meaning: Blind and sighted children's early language*. Cambridge, UK: Cambridge University Press.

Eberhard, K.M., Cutting, J.C., & Bock, J. (2005). Making syntax of sense: Number agreement in sentence production. *Psychological Review*, 112, 531–559.

Ehri, L.C. (1992). Reconceptualizing the development of sight word reading and its relationship to recoding. In P. Gough, L. Ehri, & R. Treiman (Eds.), *Reading acquisition* (pp. 107–143). Hillsdale, NJ: Lawrence Erlbaum Associates, Inc.

Ehri, L.C. (1997). Learning to read and learning to spell are one and the same, almost. In C.A. Perfetti, L. Rieben, & M. Fayol (Eds.), *Learning to spell: Research, theory, and practice across languages* (pp. 237–269). Mahwah, NJ: Lawrence Erlbaum Associates, Inc.

Ehri, L.C., Nunes, S.R., Stahl, S.A., & Willows, D.M. (2001). Systematic phonics instruction helps students learn to read: Evidence from the National Reading Panel's meta-analysis. *Review of Educational Research*, 71, 393–447.

Eimas, P.D., & Corbit, L. (1973). Selective adaptation of linguistic feature detectors. *Cognitive Psychology*, 4, 99–109.

Eimas, P.D., Miller, J.L., & Jusczyk, P.W. (1987). On infant speech perception and the acquisition of language. In S. Harnad (Ed.), *Categorical perception* (pp. 161–195). New York: Cambridge University Press.

Elliott, J., & Place, M. (2004). *Children in difficulty: A guide to understanding and helping.* London: Routledge.

Ellis, A.W. (1985). The production of spoken words: A cognitive neuropsychological perspective. In A.W. Ellis (Ed.), *Progress in the psychology of language* (Vol. 2, pp. 107–145). Hove, UK: Lawrence Erlbaum Associates Ltd.

Ellis, A.W., & Young, A.W. (1988). *Human cognitive neuropsychology.* Hove, UK: Lawrence Erlbaum Associates Ltd. [Augmented edition with readings, 1996.]

Ellis, N.C., & Hennelly, R.A. (1980). A bilingual word-length effect: Implications for intelligence testing and the relative ease of mental calculations in Welsh and English. *British Journal of Psychology*, 71, 43–52.

Ellis, A.W., Miller, D., & Sin, G. (1983). Wernicke's aphasia and normal language processing: A case study in cognitive neuropsychology. *Cognition*, 15, 111–144.

Elman, J.L. (2005). Connectionist models of cognitive development: Where next? *Trends in Cognitive Sciences*, 9, 111–117.

Elman, J.L., Bates, E.A., Johnson, M.H., Karmiloff-Smith, A., Parisi, D., & Plunkett, K. (1996). *Rethinking innateness: A connectionist perspective on development.* Cambridge, MA: Bradford Books.

Elowson, A.M., Snowdon, C.T., & Lazaro-Perea, C. (1998). Infant "babbling" in a nonhuman primate: Complex vocal sequences with repeated call types. *Behaviour*, 135, 643–664.

Entus, A.K. (1977). Hemispheric asymmetry in processing of dichotically presented speech sounds. In S.J. Segalowitz & F.A. Gruber (Eds.), *Language development and neurological theory* (pp. 63–73). New York: Academic Press.

Erard, M. (2007). *Um: Slips, stumbles, and verbal blunders and what they mean.* New York: Anchor Books.

Ervin-Tripp, S. (1979). Children's verbal turntaking. In E. Ochs & B.B. Schieffelin (Eds.), *Developmental pragmatics* (pp. 391–414). New York: Academic Press.

Eysenck, M.W., & Keane, M.T. (2005) *Cognitive psychology: A student's handbook.* Hove, UK: Psychology Press.

Farah, M.J., & McClelland, J.L. (1991). A computational model of semantic memory impairment: Modality-specificity and emergent category-specificity. *Journal of Experimental Psychology: General*, 120, 339–357.

Farah, M.J., Stowe, R.M., & Levinson, K.L. (1996). Phonological dyslexia: Loss of a reading-specific component of the cognitive architecture? *Cognitive Neuropsychology*, 13, 849–868.

Fay, D., & Cutler, A. (1977). Malapropisms and the structure of the mental lexicon. *Linguistic Inquiry*, 8, 505–520.

Fernald, A. (1991). Prosody and focus in speech to infants and adults. *Annals of Child Development*, 8, 43–80.

Fernald, A., & Marchman, V.A. (2006). Language learning in infancy. In M.J. Traxler & M.A. Gernsbacher (Eds.), *Handbook of psycholinguistics* (2nd ed., pp. 1026–1071). Amsterdam: Elsevier.

Ferreira, F., & Clifton, C. (1986). The independence of syntactic processing. *Journal of Memory and Language*, 25, 348–368.

Ferreira, F., Ferraro, V., & Bailey, K.G.D. (2002). Good-enough representations in language comprehension. *Current Directions in Psychological Science*, 11, 11–15.

Fiebach, C.J., Friederici, A.D., Muller, K., & von Cramon, D.Y. (2002). fMRI evidence for dual routes to the mental lexicon in visual word recognition. *Journal of Cognitive Neuroscience*, 14, 11–23.

Fisher, S.E., & Marcus, G.F. (2006). The eloquent age: Genes, brains, and the evolution of language. *Nature Reviews Genetics*, 7, 9–20.

Fisher, S.E., Marlow, A.J., Lamb, J., Maestrini, E., Williams, D.F., Richardson, A.J., et al. (1999). A quantitative-trait locus on chromosome 6p influences different aspects of developmental dyslexia. *American Journal of Human Genetics*, 64, 146–156.

Fitch, W.T., & Hauser, M.D. (2004). Computational constraints on syntactic processing in a nonhuman primate. *Science*, 303, 377–380.

Fitch, W.T., Hauser, M.D., & Chomsky, N. (2005). The evolution of the language faculty: Clarifications and implications. *Cognition*, 97, 179–210.

Flavell, J.H., Miller, P.H., & Miller, S.A. (2002). *Cognitive development* (4th ed.). Upper Saddle River, NJ: Prentice Hall.

Fodor, J.A. (1981). *Representations*. Cambridge, MA: MIT Press.

Fodor, J.A. (1983). *The modularity of mind*. Cambridge, MA: Bradford Books.

Fodor, J.A., Bever, T.G., & Garrett, M.S. (1974). *The psychology of language*. New York: McGraw-Hill.

Fodor, J.A., Garrett, M.F., Walker, E.C.T., & Parkes, C.H. (1980). Against definitions. *Cognition*, 8, 263–367.

Fodor, J.D., Fodor, J.A., & Garrett, M.F. (1975). The psychological unreality of semantic representations. *Linguistic Inquiry*, 6, 515–531.

Forster, K.I., & Davis, C. (1984). Repetition priming and frequency attenuation in lexical access. *Journal of Experimental Psychology: Learning, Memory, and Cognition*, 10, 680–698.

Fouts, R.S., Fouts, D.H., & Van Cantford, T.E. (1989). The infant Loulis learns signs from cross-fostered chimpanzees. In R.A. Gardner, B.T. Gardner, & T.E. Van Cantford (Eds.), *Teaching sign language to chimpanzees* (pp. 280–292). Albany, NY: SUNY Press.

Foygel, D., & Dell, G.S. (2000). Models of impaired lexical access in speech production. *Journal of Memory and Language*, 43, 182–216.

Frankell, A.S. (1998). Sound production. In B. Wursig & J.G.M. Thewissen (Eds.), *Encyclopedia of marine mammals* (pp. 1126–1137). New York: Academic Press.

Frazier, L. (1987). Sentence processing: A tutorial review. In M. Coltheart (Ed.), *Attention and performance XII: The psychology of reading* (pp. 559–586). Hove, UK: Lawrence Erlbaum Associates Ltd.

Frazier, L., & Rayner, K. (1982). Making and correcting errors during sentence comprehension: Eye movements in the analysis of structurally ambiguous sentences. *Cognitive Psychology*, 14, 178–210.

Freud, S. (1975). *The psychopathology of everyday life* (Trans. A. Tyson). Harmondsworth, UK: Penguin. [Originally published 1901.]

Friederici, A. D. (2002). Towards a neural basis of auditory sentence processing. *Trends in Cognitive Sciences*, 6, 78–84.

Fromkin, V. A. (1971). The non-anomalous nature of anomalous utterances. *Language*, 51, 696–719. [Reprinted in V.A. Fromkin (Ed.) (1973), *Speech errors as linguistic evidence* (pp. 215–242). The Hague: Mouton.]

Fromkin, V., Krashen, S., Curtiss, S., Rigler, D., & Rigler, M. (1974). The development of language in Genie: A case of language acquisition beyond the "critical period". *Brain and Language*, 1, 81–107.

Frost, R. (1998). Toward a strong phonological theory of visual word recognition: True issues and false trails. *Psychological Bulletin*, 123, 71–99.

Funnell, E. (1983). Phonological processes in reading: New evidence from acquired dyslexia. *British Journal of Psychology*, 74, 159–180.

Funnell, E., & Sheridan, J. (1992). Categories of knowledge? Unfamiliar aspects of living and non-living things. *Cognitive Neuropsychology*, 9, 135–153.

Galaburda, A.M., Sherman, G.F., Rosen, G.D., Aboitiz, F., & Geschwind, N. (1985). Developmental dyslexia: Four consecutive patients with cortical anomalies. *Annals of Neurology*, 18, 222–233.

Gardner, R.A., & Gardner, B.T. (1969). Teaching sign language to a chimpanzee. *Science*, 165, 664–672.

Gardner, R.A., & Gardner, B.T. (1975). Evidence for sentence constituents in the early utterances of a child chimpanzee. *Journal of Experimental Psychology: General*, 104, 244–267.

Garrett, M.F. (1975). The analysis of sentence production. In G. Bower (Ed.), *The psychology of learning and motivation* (Vol. 9, pp. 133–177). New York: Academic Press.

Garrett, M.F. (1976). Syntactic processes in sentence production. In R.J. Wales & E.C.T. Walker (Eds.), *New approaches to language mechanisms* (pp. 231–255). Amsterdam: North Holland.

Garrett, M.F. (1980). Levels of processing in sentence production. In B. Butterworth (Ed.), *Language production: Vol. 1. Speech and talk* (pp. 177–220). London: Academic Press.

Garrod, S. C., & Sanford, A. J. (1977). Interpreting anaphoric relations: The integration of semantic information while reading. *Journal of Verbal Learning and Verbal Behavior*, 16, 77–90.

Gaskell, M.G. (Ed.). (2007). *The Oxford handbook of psycholinguistics*. Oxford, UK: Oxford University Press.

Gaskell, M.G., & Marslen-Wilson, W.D. (2002). Representation and competition in the perception of spoken words. *Cognitive Psychology*, 45, 220–266.

Gathercole, V.C. (1985). "He has too much hard questions": The acquisition of the linguistic mass-count distinction in much and many. *Journal of Child Language*, 12, 395–415.

Gazzaniga, M. (1983). Right hemisphere language following brain bisection: A 20-year perspective. *American Psychologist*, 38, 525–537.

Gelman, R., & Butterworth, B. (2005). Number and language: How are they related? *Trends in Cognitive Sciences*, 9, 6–10.

Genesee, F., & Nicoladis, E. (2006). Bilingual first language acquisition. In E. Hoff & M. Schatz (Eds.), *Handbook of language development* (pp. 324–342). Oxford: Blackwell.

Gernsbacher, M.A. (1984). Resolving 20 years of inconsistent interactions between lexical familiarity and orthography, concreteness, and polysemy. *Journal of Experimental Psychology: General*, 113, 256–281.

Geschwind, N. (1972). Language and the brain. *Scientific American*, 226, 76–83.

Gilbert, A.L., Regier, T., Kay, P., & Ivry, R.B. (2006). Whorf hypothesis is supported in the right visual field but not the left. *Proceedings of the National Academy of Sciences of the United States of America*, 103, 489–494.

Gleason, H.A. (1961). *An introduction to descriptive linguistics*. New York: Holt, Rinehart & Winston.

Gleitman, L.R. (1990). The structural sources of word meaning. *Language Acquisition*, 1, 3–55.

Glenberg, A. (2007). Language and action: Creating sensible combinations of ideas. In M.G. Gaskell (Ed.), *The Oxford handbook of psycholinguistics* (pp. 362–370). Oxford, UK: Oxford University Press.

Glenberg, A.M., & Robertson, D.A. (2000). Symbol grounding and meaning: A comparison of highdimensional and embodied theories of meaning. *Journal of Memory and Language*, 43, 379–401.

Glucksberg, S., & Weisberg, R.W. (1966). Verbal behavior and problem solving: Some effects of labeling in a functional fixedness problem. *Journal of Experimental Psychology*, 71, 659–664.

Glushko, R. J. (1979). The organization and activation of orthographic knowledge in reading aloud. *Journal of Experimental Psychology: Human Perception and Performance*, 5, 674–691.

Gold, E.M. (1967). Language identification in the limit. *Information and Control*, 16, 447–474.

Goldin-Meadow, S., So, W.C., Ozyurek, A., & Mylander, C. (2008). The natural order of events: How speakers of different languages represent events nonverbally. *Proceedings of the National Academy of Sciences*, 105, 9163–9168.

Goldinger, S.D., Luce, P.A., & Pisoni, D.B. (1989). Priming lexical neighbours of spoken words: Effects of competition and inhibition. *Journal of Memory and Language*, 28, 501–518.

Golinkoff, R.M., Mervis, C.B., & Hirsh-Pasek, K. (1994). Early object labels: The case for lexical principles. *Journal of Child Language*, 21, 125–155.

Gollan, T.H., & Acenas, L.R. (2004). What is a TOT? Cognate and translation effects on tip-of-the-tongue states in Spanish–English and Tagalog–English bilinguals. *Journal of Experimental Psychology: Learning, Memory, and Cognition*, 30, 246–269.

Gombert, J.E. (1992). *Metalinguistic development* (Trans. T. Pownall). London: Harvester Wheatsheaf. [Originally published 1990.]

Goodglass, H. (1976). Agrammatism. In H. Whitaker & H.A. Whitaker (Eds.), *Studies in neurolinguistics* (Vol. 1, pp. 237–260). New York: Academic Press.

Goodglass, H., & Geschwind, N. (1976). Language disorders (aphasia). In E.C. Carterette & M.P. Friedman (Eds.), *Handbook of perception: Vol. VII. Language and speech* (pp. 389–428). New York: Academic Press.

Goodglass, H., & Menn, L. (1985). Is agrammatism a unitary phenomenon? In M.-L. Kean (Ed.), *Agrammatism* (pp. 1–26). New York: Academic Press.

Gopnik, M. (1997). Language deficits and genetic factors. *Trends in Cognitive Sciences*, 1, 5–9.

Gopnik, M., & Goad, H. (1997). What underlies inflection errors in SLI? *Journal of Neurolinguistics*, 10, 109–237.

Gopnik, M., & Meltzoff, A.N. (1986). Relations between semantic and cognitive development in the one-word stage: The specificity hypothesis. *Child Development*, 57, 1040–1053.

Gordon, P. (1985). Evaluating the semantic categories hypothesis: The case of the count/mass distinction. *Cognition*, 20, 209–242.

Gordon, P. (2004). Numerical cognition without words: Evidence from Amazonia. *Science*, 306, 496–499.

Goswami, U. (1986). Children's use of analogy in learning to read: A developmental study. *Journal of Experimental Child Psychology*, 42, 73–83.

Goswami, U. (1993). Towards an interactive analogy model of reading development: Decoding vowel graphemes in beginning reading. *Journal of Experimental Child Psychology*, 56, 443–475.

Goswami, U. (2008). *Cognitive development: The learning brain*. Hove, UK: Psychology Press.

Goswami, U., & Bryant, P. (1990). *Phonological skills and learning to read*. Hove, UK: Psychology Press.

Greenberg, J.H. (1963). Some universals of grammar with particular reference to the order of meaningful elements. In J.H. Greenberg (Ed.), *Universals of language* (pp. 58–90). Cambridge, MA: MIT Press.

Grice, H.P. (1975). Logic and conversation. In P. Cole & J. Morgan (Eds.), *Syntax and semantics: Vol. 3. Speech acts* (pp. 41–58). New York: Academic Press.

Grosjean, F. (1980). Spoken word recognition processes and the gating paradigm. *Perception and Psychophysics*, 28, 267–283.

Gumperz, J., & Levinson, S. (1996). *Rethinking linguistic relativity*. Cambridge, UK: Cambridge University Press.

Hagoort, P. (2005). On Broca, brain, and binding: A new framework. *Trends in Cognitive Science*, 9, 416–423.

Hambling, D. (2007). I see no ships. *Fortean Times*, February. Available online at: www.forteantimes.com/strangedays/science/20/questioning_perceptual_blindness.html

Harley, B., & Wang, W. (1997). The critical period hypothesis: Where are we now? In

A.M.B. de Groot & J.F. Kroll (Eds.), *Tutorials in bilingualism: Psycholinguistic perspectives* (pp. 19–51). Mahwah, NJ: Lawrence Erlbaum Associates, Inc.

Harley, T.A. (1984). A critique of top-down independent levels models of speech production: Evidence from non-plan-internal speech production. *Cognitive Science*, 8, 191–219.

Harley, T.A. (1990). Environmental contamination of normal speech. *Applied Psycholinguistics*, 11, 45–72.

Harley, T.A. (1993). Phonological activation of semantic competitors during lexical access in speech production. *Language and Cognitive Processes*, 8, 291–309.

Harley, T.A. (2004). Does cognitive neuropsychology have a future? *Cognitive Neuropsychology*, 21, 3–16.

Harley, T.A. (2008). *The psychology of language* (3rd ed.). Hove, UK: Psychology Press.

Harley, T.A., & Bown, H.E. (1998). What causes a tip-of-the-tongue state? Evidence for lexical neighbourhood effects in speech production. *British Journal of Psychology*, 89, 151–174.

Harley, T.A., & Grant, F. (2004). The role of functional and perceptual attributes: Evidence from picture naming in dementia. *Brain and Language*, 91, 223–234.

Harm, M.W., & Seidenberg, M.S. (1999). Phonology, reading acquisition, and dyslexia: Insights from connectionist models. *Psychological Review*, 106, 491–528.

Harm, M.W., & Seidenberg, M.S. (2001). Are there orthographic impairments in phonological dyslexia? *Cognitive Neuropsychology*, 18, 71–92.

Harm, M.W., & Seidenberg, M.S. (2004). Computing the meanings of words in reading: Cooperative division of labor between visual and phonological processes. *Psychological Review*, 111, 662–720.

Harste, J., Burke, C., & Woodward, V. (1982). Children's language and world: Initial encounters with print. In J. Langer & M. Smith-Burke (Eds.), *Bridging the gap: Reader meets author* (pp. 105–131). Newark, DE: International Reading Association.

Hart, J., Berndt, R.S., & Caramazza, A. (1985). Category-specific naming deficit following cerebral infarction. *Nature*, 316, 439–440.

Hartsuiker, R.J., Anton-Méndez, I., Roelstraete, B., & Costa, A. (2006). Spoonish Spanerisms: A lexical bias effect in Spanish. *Journal of Experimental Psychology: Learning, Memory, and Cognition*, 32, 949–953.

Hatcher, P.J., Hulme, C., & Ellis, A.W. (1994). Ameliorating early reading failure by integrating the teaching of reading and phonological skills: The phonological linkage hypothesis. *Child Development*, 65, 41–57.

Hauk, O., Johnsrude, I., & Pulvermuller, F. (2004). Somatotopic representation of action words in human motor and premotor cortex. *Neuron*, 41, 301–307.

Haviland, S.E., & Clark, H.H. (1974). What's new? Acquiring new information as a process of comprehension. *Journal of Verbal Learning and Verbal Behavior*, 13, 515–521.

Hayes, C. (1951). *The ape in our house*. New York: Harper.

Hayes, K.J., & Nissen, C.H. (1971). Higher mental functions of a home-raised chimpanzee. In A.M. Schrier & F. Stollnitz (Eds.), *Behaviour of nonhuman primates* (Vol. 4, pp. 60–115). New York: Academic Press.

Hedden, T., & Gabrieli, J.D.E. (2004). Insights into the ageing mind: A view from cognitive neuroscience. *Nature Reviews Neuroscience*, 5, 87–97.

Heider, E.R. (1972). Universals in colour naming and memory. *Journal of Experimental Psychology*, 93, 10–20.

Henderson, J.M., & Ferreira, F. (Eds.) (2004). *The interface of language, vision, and action: Eye movements and the visual world*. Hove, UK: Psychology Press.

Henderson, L. (1982). *Orthography and word recognition in reading*. London: Academic Press.

Hernandez, A.E., Fernandez, E.M., & Aznar-Besé, N. (2007). Bilingual sentence processing. In G. Gaskell (Ed.), *The Oxford handbook of psycholinguistics* (pp. 371–384). Oxford, UK: Oxford University Press.

Hess, E. (2008). *Nim Chimpsky: The chimp who would be human*. New York: Bantam Press.

Hindley, P. (2005). Development of deaf and blind children. *Psychiatry*, 4, 45–48.

Hinton, G.E., & Shallice, T. (1991). Lesioning an attractor network: Investigations of acquired dyslexia. *Psychological Review*, 98, 74–95.

Hodges, J.R., Patterson, K.E., Oxbury, S., & Funnell, E. (1992). Semantic dementia: Progressive fluent aphasia with temporal lobe atrophy. *Brain*, 115, 1783–1806.

Hoff, E. (2003). The specificity of environmental influence: Socioeconomic status affects early vocabulary development via maternal speech. *Child Development*, 74, 1368–1378.

Hoff-Ginsberg, E. (1997). *Language development*. Pacific Grove, CA: Brooks/Cole.

Hoffman, C., Lau, I., & Johnson, D.R. (1986). The linguistic relativity of person cognition. *Journal of Personality and Social Psychology*, 51, 1097–1105.

Hogaboam, T.W., & Perfetti, C.A. (1975). Lexical ambiguity and sentence comprehension: The common sense effect. *Journal of Verbal Learning and Verbal Behavior*, 14, 265–275.

Howard, D., & Orchard-Lisle, V. (1984). On the origin of semantic errors in naming: Evidence from the case of a global aphasic. *Cognitive Neuropsychology*, 1, 163–190.

Hulme, C., Snowling, M., Caravolas, M., & Carroll, J. (2005). Phonological skills are (probably) one cause of success in learning to read. *Scientific Studies of Reading*, 9, 351–366.

Hunt, E., & Agnoli, F. (1991). The Whorfian hypothesis: A cognitive psychology perspective. *Psychological Review*, 98, 377–389.

Huttenlocher, P.R. (2002). *Neural plasticity: The effects of environment on the development of the cerebral cortex*. Cambridge, MA: Harvard University Press.

Indefrey, P., & Levelt, W.J.M. (2000). The neural correlates of language production. In M. Gazzaniga (Ed.), *The new cognitive neurosciences* (2nd ed., pp. 845–865). Cambridge, MA: MIT Press.

Indefrey, P., & Levelt, W.J.M. (2004). The spatial and temporal signatures of word production components. *Cognition*, 92, 101–144.

Jackendoff, R., & Pinker, S. (2005). The nature of the language faculty and its implications for evolution of language (Reply to Fitch, Hauser, and Chomsky). *Cognition*, 97, 211–225.

Jackson, D.E., & Ratnieks, F.L.W. (2006). Communication in ants. *Current Biology*, 16, R570–R574.

Jacobsen, E. (1932). The electrophysiology of mental activities. *American Journal of Psychology*, 44, 677–694.

Jakobson, R. (1968). *Child language: Aphasia and phonological universals*. The Hague: Mouton.

James, L.E., & Burke, D.M. (2000). Phonological priming effects on word retrieval and tip-of-the-tongue experiences in young and older adults. *Journal of Experimental Psychology: Learning, Memory, and Cognition*, 26, 1378–1391.

Jared, D., & Seidenberg, M.S. (1991). Does word identification proceed from spelling to sound to meaning? *Journal of Experimental Psychology: General*, 120, 358–394.

Joanisse, M.F., & Seidenberg, M.S. (1998). Specific language impairment: A deficit in grammar or processing? *Trends in Cognitive Sciences*, 2, 240–247.

Joanisse, M.F., & Seidenberg, M.S. (2003). Phonology and syntax in specific language impairment: Evidence from a connectionist model. *Brain and Language*, 86, 40–56.

Johnson, J.S., & Newport, E.L. (1989). Critical period effects in second language learning: The influence of maturational state on the acquisition of English as a second language. *Cognitive Psychology*, 21, 60–99.

Johnson-Laird, P.N. (1983). *Mental models*. Cambridge, UK: Cambridge University Press.

Johnston, R., & Watson, J.E. (2007). *Teaching synthetic phonics*. Exeter, UK: Learning Matters.

Jolicoeur, P., Gluck, M.A., & Kosslyn, S.M. (1984). Pictures and names: Making the connection. *Cognitive Psychology*, 16, 243–275.

Jones, G.V. (1985). Deep dyslexia, imageability, and ease of predication. *Brain and Language*, 24, 1–19.

Jones, G.V., & Langford, S. (1987). Phonological blocking in the tip of the tongue state. *Cognition*, 26, 115–122.

Jones, S.R., & Fernyhough, C. (2007). Thought as action: Inner speech, self-monitoring, and auditory verbal hallucinations. *Consciousness and Cognition*, 16, 391–399.

Just, M.A., & Carpenter, P.A. (1987). *The psychology of reading and language comprehension*. Newton, MA: Allyn & Bacon.

Kako, E. (1999a). Elements of syntax in the systems of three language-trained animals. *Animal Learning and Behavior*, 27, 1–14.

Kako, E. (1999b). Response to Pepperberg; Herman and Uyeyama; and Shanker, Savage-Rumbaugh, and Taylor. *Animal Learning and Behavior*, 27, 26–27.

Kaminski, J., Call, J., & Fischer, J. (2004). Word learning in a domestic dog: Evidence for "fast mapping. *Science*, 304, 1682–1683.

Katz, J.J., & Fodor, J.A. (1963). The structure of a semantic theory. *Language*, 39, 170–210.

Kay, J., & Ellis, A. W. (1987). A cognitive neuropsychological case study of anomia: Implications for psychological models of word retrieval. *Brain*, 110, 613–629.

Kay, J., & Marcel, A.J. (1981). One process, not two in reading aloud: Lexical analogies do the work of nonlexical rules. *Quarterly Journal of Experimental Psychology*, 33A, 397–414.

Kay, J., Lesser, R., & Coltheart, M. (1992). *Psycholinguistic assessments of language processing in aphasia (PALPA): An introduction*. Hove, UK: Lawrence Erlbaum Associates Ltd.

Kay, P., & Kempton, W. (1984). What is the Sapir-Whorf hypothesis? *American Anthropologist*, 86, 65–79.

Kegl, J., Senghas, A., & Coppola, M. (1999). Creations through contact: Sign language emergence and sign language change in Nicaragua. In M. DeGraff (Ed.), *Comparative grammatical change: The intersection of language acquisition, Creole gensis, and diachronic syntax* (pp. 179–237). Cambridge, MA: MIT Press.

Kellogg, W.N., & Kellogg, L.A. (1933). *The ape and the child*. New York: McGraw-Hill.

Kennedy, A., & Pynte, J. (2005). Parafoveal-on-foveal effects in normal reading. *Vision Research*, 45, 153–168.

Kersten, A.W., & Earles, J.L. (2001). Less really is more for adults learning a miniature artificial language. *Journal of Memory and Language*, 44, 250–273.

Kimura, D. (1999). *Sex and cognition*. Cambridge, MA: MIT Press.

Kintsch, W. (1988). The use of knowledge in discourse processing: A construction–integration model. *Psychological Review*, 95, 163–182.

Kintsch, W., & Bates, E. (1977). Recognition memory for statements from a classroom lecture. *Journal of Experimental Psychology: Human Learning and Memory*, 3, 187–197.

Kintsch, W., & Vipond, D. (1979). Reading comprehension and readability in educational practice and psychological theory. In L.G. Nilsson (Ed.), *Perspectives in memory research* (pp. 329–366). Hillsdale, NJ: Lawrence Erlbaum Associates, Inc.

Kirshner, H.S., Webb, W.G., & Kelly, M.P. (1984). The naming order of dementia. *Neuropsychologia*, 22, 23–30.

Kohn, S.E., & Friedman, R.B. (1986). Word-meaning deafness: A phonological–semantic dissociation. *Cognitive Neuropsychology*, 3, 291–308.

Kolb, B., & Whishaw, I.Q. (2003). *Fundamentals of human neuropsychology* (5th ed.). New York: W.H. Freeman & Co.

Kovacs, A.M., & Mehler, J. (2009). Cognitive gains in 7-month-old bilingual infants. *Proceedings of the National Academy of Sciences of the United States of America*, 106, 6556–6560.

Krashen, S.D. (1982). *Principles and practices in second language acquisition*. Oxford, UK: Pergamon.

Krashen, S. (2003). *Explorations in language acquisition and use: The Taipei lectures*, Portsmouth, NH: Heinemann.

Krause, J., Lalueza-Fox, C., Orlando, L., Enard, W., Green, R.E., Burbaro, H.A., et al. (2007). The derived FOXP2 variant of modern humans was shared with Neandertals. *Current Biology*, 17, 1908–1912.

Kripke, S. (1980). *Naming and necessity*. Cambridge, MA: Harvard University Press.

Krutzen, M., Mann, J., Heithaus, M.R., Connor, R.C., Bejder, L., & Sherwin, W.B. (2005). Cultural transmission of tool use in bottlenose dolphins. *Proceedings of the National Academy of Sciences of the United States of America*, 102, 8939–8943.

Kuczaj, S.A. (1977). The acquisition of regular and irregular past tense forms. *Journal of Verbal Learning and Verbal Behavior*, 16, 589–600.

Kuhl, P.C. (2000). A new view of language acquisition. *Proceedings of the National Academy of Sciences of the United States of America*, 97, 11850–11857.

Kuhl, P.C. (2004). Early language acquisition: Cracking the speech code. *Nature Reviews Neuroscience*, 5, 831–843.

Kuhl, P.K., & Miller, J.D. (1975). Speech perception by the chinchilla: Voiced–voiceless distinction in alveolar plosive consonants. *Science*, 190, 69–72.

Labov, W. (1972). *Language in the inner city: Studies in Black English Vernacular*. Philadelphia: University of Pennsylvania Press.

Lai, C.S.L., Fisher, S.E., Hurst, J.A., Vargha-Khadem, F., & Monaco, A.P. (2001). A forkhead-domain gene is mutated in a severe speech and language disorder. *Nature*, 413, 519–523.

Lambert, W.E., Tucker, G.R., & d'Anglejan, A. (1973). Cognitive and attitudinal consequences of bilingual schooling. *Journal of Educational Psychology*, 85, 141–159.

Landau, B., & Gleitman, L.R. (1985). *Language and experience: Evidence from the blind child*. Cambridge, MA: Harvard University Press.

Landauer, T.K., & Dumais, S.T. (1997). A solution to Plato's problem: The latent semantic analysis theory of acquisition, induction, and representation of knowledge. *Psychological Review*, 104, 211–240.

Landauer, T.K., Foltz, P.W., & Laham, D. (1998). An introduction to latent semantic analysis. *Discourse Processes*, 25, 259–284.

Lantz, D., & Stefflre, V. (1964). Language and cognition revisited. *Journal of Abnormal Psychology*, 69, 472–481.

Lee, A.C.H., Graham, K.S., Simons, J.S., Hodges, J., & Patterson, K.E. (2002). Regional brain activations differ for semantic features but not categories. *NeuroReport*, 13, 1497–1501.

Lenneberg, E.H. (1953). Cognition and ethnolinguistics. *Language*, 29, 463–471.

Lenneberg, E.H. (1967). *The biological foundations of language*. New York: Wiley.

Lennie, P. (1984). Recent developments in the physiology of color vision. *Trends in Neurosciences*, 7, 243–248.

Leopold, W.F. (1939–1949). *Speech development of a bilingual child: A linguist's record* (5 vols.). Evanston, IL: Northwestern University Press.

Levelt, W.J.M. (1989). *Speaking: From intention to articulation*. Cambridge, MA: MIT Press.

Levelt, W.J.M. (2001). Spoken word production: A theory of lexical access. *Proceedings of the National Academy of Sciences of the United States of America*, 98, 13464–13471.

Levelt, W.J.M., Roelofs, A., & Meyer, A.S. (1999). A theory of lexical access in speech production. *Behavioral and Brain Sciences*, 22, 1–75.

Levelt, W.J.M., Schriefers, H., Vorberg, D., Meyer, A.S., Pechmann, T., & Havinga, J. (1991). The time course of lexical access in speech production: A study of picture naming. *Psychological Review*, 98, 122–142.

Levy, Y. (1996). Modularity of language reconsidered. *Brain and Language*, 55, 240–263.

Levy, Y., & Schlesinger, I.M. (1988). The child's early categories: Approaches to language acquisition theory. In Y. Levy, I.M. Schlesinger, & M.D.S. Braine (Eds.), *Categories and processes in language acquisition* (pp. 261–276). Hillsdale, NJ: Lawrence Erlbaum Associates, Inc.

Lewis, V. (1987). *Development and handicap*. Oxford, UK: Blackwell.

Liberman, A.M., Harris, K.S., Hoffman, H.S., & Griffith, B.C. (1957). The discrimination of speech sounds within and across phoneme boundaries. *Journal of Experimental Psychology*, 53, 358–368.

Liberman, I.Y., Shankweiler, D., Fischer, F.W., & Carter, B. (1974). Explicit syllable and phoneme segmentation in the young child. *Journal of Experimental Child Psychology*, 18, 201–212.

Lieberman, P., & Crelin, E.S. (1971). On the speech of Neanderthal man. *Linguistic Inquiry*, 2, 203–222.

Lieven, E.V.M. (1994). Crosslinguistic and crosscultural aspects of language addressed to children. In C. Gallaway & B.J. Richards (Eds.), *Input and interaction in language acquisition* (pp. 56–73). Cambridge, UK: Cambridge University Press.

Liu, L.G. (1985). Reasoning counter-factually in Chinese: Are there any obstacles? *Cognition*, 21, 239–270.

Locke, J.L. (1983). *Phonological acquisition and change.* New York: Academic Press.

Loftus, E.F., & Palmer, J.C. (1974). Reconstruction of automobile destruction: An example of the interaction between language and memory. *Journal of Verbal Learning and Verbal Behavior*, 13, 585–589.

Lovegrove, W., Martin, F., & Slaghuis, W. (1986). A theoretical and experimental case for a visual deficit in specific reading disability. *Cognitive Neuropsychology*, 3, 225–267.

Lucy, J.A., & Shweder, R.A. (1979). Whorf and his critics: Linguistic and nonlinguistic influences on colour memory. *American Anthropologist*, 81, 581–615.

Lund, K., Burgess, C., & Atchley, R.A. (1995). Semantic and associative priming in high-dimensional semantic space. *Proceedings of the Seventeenth Annual Conference of the Cognitive Science Society*, 660–665.

Lyons, J. (1991). *Chomsky* (3rd ed.). London: Fontana.

MacDonald, M.C., Pearlmutter, N.J., & Seidenberg, M.S. (1994). The lexical nature of syntactic ambiguity resolution. *Psychological Review*, 101, 676–703.

Maess, B., Friederici, A.D., Damian, M., Meyer, A.S., & Levelt, W.J.M. (2002). Semantic category interference in overt picture naming: Sharpening current density localization by PCA. *Journal of Cognitive Neuroscience*, 14, 455–462.

Maher, J., & Groves, J. (2004). *Introducing Chomsky.* Cambridge, UK: Icon Books.

Manis, F.R., Seidenberg, M.S., Doi, L.M., McBride-Chang, C., & Petersen, A. (1996). On the bases of two subtypes of developmental dyslexia. *Cognition*, 58, 157–195.

Markman, E.M. (1979). Realizing that you don't understand: Elementary school children's awareness of inconsistencies. *Child Development*, 50, 643–655.

Markman, E.M. (1990). Constraints children place on word meanings. *Cognitive Science*, 14, 57–77.

Marshall, J.C., & Newcombe, F. (1966). Syntactic and semantic errors in paralexia. *Neuropsychologia*, 4, 169–176.

Marshall, J.C., & Newcombe, F. (1973). Patterns of paralexia: A psycholinguistic approach. *Journal of Psycholinguistic Research*, 2, 175–199.

Marshall, J., Robson, J., Pring, T., & Chiat, S. (1998). Why does monitoring fail in jargon aphasia? Comprehension, judgement, and therapy evidence. *Brain and Language*, 63, 79–107.

Marslen-Wilson, W.D. (1990). Activation, competition, and frequency in lexical access.

In G.T.M. Altmann (Ed.), *Cognitive models of speech processing* (pp. 148–172). Cambridge, MA: MIT Press.

Marslen-Wilson, W.D., & Welsh, A. (1978). Processing interactions and lexical access during word recognition in continuous speech. *Cognitive Psychology*, 10, 29–63.

Martin, N., Dell, G.S., Saffran, E.M., & Schwartz, M.F. (1994). Origins of paraphasia in deep dysphasia: Testing the consequences of a decay impairment to an interactive spreading activation mode of lexical retrieval. *Brain and Language*, 47, 609–660.

Martin, N., & Saffran, E. M. (1992). A computational account of deep dysphasia: Evidence from a single case study. *Brain and Language*, 43, 240–274.

Masataka, N. (1996). Perception of motherese in a signed language by 6-month-old deaf infants. *Developmental Psychology*, 32, 874–879.

McClelland, J.L., & Elman, J.L. (1986). The TRACE model of speech perception. *Cognitive Psychology*, 18, 1–86.

McCloskey, M., & Caramazza, A. (1988). Theory and methodology in cognitive neuropsychology: A response to our critics. *Cognitive Neuropsychology*, 5, 583–623.

McGurk, H., & MacDonald, J. (1976). Hearing lips and seeing voices. *Nature*, 264, 746–748.

McKoon, G., & Ratcliff, R. (1992). Inference during reading. *Psychological Review*, 99, 440–466.

McQueen, J.M. (2007). Eight questions about spoken word recognition. In M.G. Gaskell (Ed.), *The Oxford handbook of psycholinguistics* (pp. 38–53). Oxford, UK: Oxford University Press.

McRae, K., Spivey-Knowlton, M.J., & Tanenhaus, M.K. (1998). Modeling the influence of thematic fit (and other constraints) in on-line sentence comprehension. *Journal of Memory and Language*, 38, 283–312.

Mechelli, A., Crinion, J.T., Noppeney, U., O'Doherty, J., Ashburner, J., Frackowiak, R.S., et al. (2004). Structural plasticity in the bilingual brain. *Nature*, 431, 757.

Mehler, J., Jusczyk, P.W., Lambertz, G., Halsted, N., Bertoncini, J., & Amiel-Tison, C. (1988). A precursor of language acquisition in young infants. *Cognition*, 29, 143–178.

Metsala, J.L., Stanovich, K.E., & Brown, G.D.A. (1998). Regularity effects and the phonological deficit model of reading disabilities: A metaanalytic review. *Journal of Educational Psychology*, 90, 279–293.

Meyer, A.S. (1996). Lexical access in phrase and sentence production: Results from picture–word interference experiments. *Journal of Memory and Language*, 35, 477–496.

Meyer, D.E., & Schvaneveldt, R.W. (1971). Facilitation in recognizing pairs of words: Evidence of a dependence between retrieval operations. *Journal of Experimental Psychology*, 90, 227–235.

Miceli, G., Mazzucci, A., Menn, L., & Goodglass, H. (1983). Contrasting cases of Italian agrammatic aphasia without comprehension disorder. *Brain and Language*, 19, 65–97.

Miller, K.F., & Stigler, J. (1987). Counting in Chinese: Cultural variations in a basic cognitive skill. *Cognitive Development*, 2, 279–305.

Mintz, T.H. (2003). Frequent frames as a cue for grammatical categories in child directed speech. *Cognition*, 90, 91–117.

Miozzo, M., & Caramazza, A. (1997). Retrieval of lexical-syntactic features in tip-of-the-tongue states. *Journal of Experimental Psychology: Learning, Memory, and Cognition*, 23, 1410–1423.

Miyake, A., Emerson, M.J., Padilla, F., & Ahn, J. (2004). Inner speech as a retrieval aid for task goals: The effects of cue type and articulatory suppression in the random task cuing paradigm. *Acta Psychologica*, 115, 123–142.

Molfese, D.L. (1977). Infant cerebral asymmetry. In S.J. Segalowitz & F.A. Gruber (Eds.), *Language development and neurological theory* (pp. 21–35). New York: Academic Press.

Morais, J., Bertelson, P., Cary, L., & Alegria, J. (1986). Literacy training and speech segmentation. *Cognition*, 24, 45–64.

Morrison, C.M., & Ellis, A.W. (1995). Roles of word frequency and age of acquisition in word naming and lexical decision. *Journal of Experimental Psychology: Learning, Memory, and Cognition*, 21, 116–133.

Morrison, C.M., & Ellis, A.W. (2000). Real age of acquisition effects in word naming. *British Journal of Psychology*, 91, 167–180.

Morton, J., & Patterson, K.E. (1980). A new attempt at an interpretation, or, an attempt at a new interpretation. In M. Coltheart, K. E. Patterson, & J. C. Marshall (Eds.), *Deep dyslexia* (pp. 91–118). London: Routledge & Kegan Paul. [2nd ed., 1987.]

Moss, H.E., Tyler, L.K., & Taylor, K.I. (2007). Conceptual structure. In M.G. Gaskell (Ed.), *The Oxford handbook of psycholinguistics* (pp. 217–234). Oxford, UK: Oxford University Press.

Mowrer, O.H. (1960). *Learning theory and symbolic processes*. New York: Wiley.

Muter, V., Hulme, C., Snowling, M., & Taylor, S. (1998). Segmentation, not rhyming, predicts early progress in learning to read. *Journal of Experimental Child Psychology*, 71, 3–27.

Myers, P., & Mackisack, E.L. (1990). Right hemisphere syndrome. In L.L. LaPointe (Ed.), *Aphasia and related neurogenic language disorders* (pp. 177–195). New York: Thieme.

Nagy, E. (2006). From imitation to conversation: The first dialogues with human neonates. *Infant and Child Development*, 14, 223–232.

Nelson, K. (1973). Structure and strategy in learning to talk. *Monographs of the Society for Research in Child Development*, 38 (Serial No. 149).

Nelson, K. (1987). What's in a name? *Journal of Experimental Psychology: General*, 116, 293–296.

Newport, E.L. (1990). Maturational constraints on language learning. *Cognitive Science*, 14, 11–28.

Newton, M. (2002). *Savage girls and wild boys*. London: Faber & Faber.

Nicolson, R.I., & Fawcett, A.J. (2007). Procedural learning difficulties: Reuniting the developmental disorders? *Trends in Neurosciences*, 30, 135–141.

Nicolson, R.I., Fawcett, A.J., & Dean, P. (2001). Developmental dyslexia: The cerebellar deficit hypothesis. *Trends in Neurosciences*, 24, 508–511.

Norris, D., McQueen, J.M., & Cutler, A. (2000). Merging information in speech recognition: Feedback is never necessary. *Behavioral and Brain Sciences*, 23, 299–370.

Oller, D.K., & Eilers, R.E. (1988). The role of audition in infant babbling. *Child Development, 59*, 441–449.

Oppenheim, G., & Dell, G.S. (2008). Inner speech slips exhibit lexical bias, but not the phonemic similarity effect. *Cognition, 106*, 528–537.

Orwell, G. (1949). *Nineteen eighty-four*. Harmondsworth, UK: Penguin.

Osgood, C.E., & Sebeok, T.A. (Eds.) (1954). *Psycholinguistics: A survey of theory and research problems*. Bloomington, IN: Indiana University Press.

Osterhout, L., & Nicol, J. (1999). On the distinctiveness, independence, and time course of the brain responses to syntactic and semantic anomalies. *Language and Cognitive Processes, 14*, 283–317.

Pansky, A., & Koriat, A. (2004). The basic-level convergence effect in memory distortions. *Psychological Science, 15*, 52–59.

Patterson, K., Graham, N., & Hodges, J.R. (1994). The impact of semantic memory loss on phonological representations. *Journal of Cognitive Neuroscience, 6*, 57–69.

Patterson, K.E., & Morton, J. (1985). From orthography to phonology: An attempt at an old interpretation. In K.E. Patterson, J.C. Marshall, & M. Coltheart (Eds.), *Surface dyslexia: Neuropsychological and cognitive studies of phonological reading* (pp. 335–359). Hove, UK: Lawrence Erlbaum Associates Ltd.

Patterson, K., Vargha-Khadem, F., & Polkey, C. E. (1989). Reading with one hemisphere. *Brain, 112*, 39–63.

Pennington, B.F., & Lefly, D.L. (2001). Early reading development in children at family risk for dyslexia. *Child Development, 72*, 816–833.

Pepperberg, I. (1999). Rethinking syntax: A commentary on E. Kako's "Elements of syntax in the systems of three language-trained animals". *Animal Learning and Behavior, 27*, 15–17.

Pepperberg, I. (2002). *The Alex studies: Cognitive and communicative abilities of grey parrots*. Cambridge, MA: Harvard University Press.

Pepperberg, I. (2008). *Alex & me*. New York: Collins.

Pérez-Pereira, M., & Conti-Ramsden, G. (1999). *Language development and social interaction in blind children*. Hove, UK: Psychology Press.

Peterson, R.R., & Savoy, P. (1998). Lexical selection and phonological encoding during language production: Evidence for cascaded processing. *Journal of Experimental Psychology: Learning, Memory, and Cognition, 24*, 539–557.

Petitto, L.A., & Marentette, P.F. (1991). Babbling in the manual mode: Evidence for the ontogeny of language. *Science, 251*, 1483–1496.

Piaget, J. (1926). *The language and thought of the child*. London: Routledge & Kegan Paul.

Piattelli-Palmarini, M. (Ed.) (1980). *Language and learning: The debate between Jean Piaget and Noam Chomsky*. London: Routledge & Kegan Paul.

Pica, P., Lerner, C., Izard, V., & Dehaene, S. (2004). Exact and approximate arithmetic in an Amazonian indigene group. *Science, 306*, 499–503.

Pickering, M.J. (1999). Sentence comprehension. In S. Garrod & M.J. Pickering (Eds.), *Language processing* (pp. 123–153). Hove, UK: Psychology Press.

Pickering, M.J., & Branigan, H.P. (1998). The representation of verbs: Evidence from syntactic priming in language production. *Journal of Memory and Language, 39*, 633–651.

Pickering, M.J., & Garrod, S. (2004). Toward a mechanistic psychology of dialogue. *Behavioral and Brain Sciences*, 27, 169–226.

Pickering, M.J., & Van Gompel, R.P.G. (2006). Syntactic parsing. In M.J. Traxler & M.A. Gernsbacher (Eds.), *Handbook of psycholinguistics* (2nd ed., pp. 455–503). Oxford, UK: Oxford University Press.

Pine, J.M. (1994). Environmental correlates of variation in lexical style: Interactional style and the structure of the input. *Applied Psycholinguistics*, 15, 355–370.

Pinker, Steven (1984). *Language learnability and language development*. Cambridge, MA: MIT Press.

Pinker, Steven (1994). *The language instinct*. Harmondsworth, UK: Penguin.

Pinker, Steven (1999). *Words and rules*. London: Weidenfeld & Nicolson.

Pinker, Steven (2001). Talk of genetics and vice versa. *Nature*, 413, 465–466.

Pinker, Steven (2002). *The blank slate*. Harmondsworth, UK: Penguin.

Pinker, Steven (2007). *The stuff of thought*. Harmondsworth, UK: Penguin.

Pinker, Steven, & Jackendoff, R. (2005). The faculty of language: What's special about it? *Cognition*, 95, 201–236.

Pinker, Steven, & Prince, A. (1988). On language and connectionism: Analysis of a parallel distributed processing model of language acquisition. *Cognition*, 28, 59–108.

Pinker, Steven, & Ullman, M.T. (2002). The past and future of the past tense. *Trends in Cognitive Science*, 6, 456–463, and Reply, 472–474.

Pinker, Susan (2008). *The sexual paradox*. London: Atlantic.

Plaut, D.C. (2005). Connectionist approaches to reading. In M.J. Snowling & C. Hulme (Eds.), *The science of reading: A handbook* (pp. 24–38). Oxford, UK: Blackwell.

Plaut, D.C., McClelland, J.L., Seidenberg, M.S., & Patterson, K.E. (1996). Understanding normal and impaired word reading: Computational principles in quasi-regular domains. *Psychological Review*, 103, 56–115.

Plaut, D.C., & Shallice, T. (1993). Deep dyslexia: A case study of connectionist neuropsychology. *Cognitive Neuropsychology*, 10, 377–500.

Plunkett, K., & Marchman, V. (1991). U-shaped learning and frequency effects in a multilayered perceptron: Implications for child language acquisition. *Cognition*, 38, 43–102.

Plunkett, K., & Marchman, V. (1993). From rote learning to system building: Acquiring verb morphology in children and connectionist nets. *Cognition*, 48, 21–69.

Poole, S. (2007). *Unspeak*. London: Abacus.

Potter, M.C., & Lombardi, L. (1998). Syntactic priming in immediate recall of sentences. *Journal of Memory and Language*, 38, 265–282.

Premack, D. (1971). Language in chimpanzee? *Science*, 172, 808–822.

Premack, D. (1976). *Intelligence in ape and man*. Hillsdale, NJ: Lawrence Erlbaum Associates, Inc.

Premack, D., & Premack, A. (1983). *The mind of an ape*. New York: Norton.

Price, G. (1984). *The languages of Britain*. London: Arnold.

Pruetz, J.D., & Bertolani, P. (2007). Savanna chimpanzees, *Pan troglodytes verus*, hunt with tools. *Current Biology*, 17, 412–417.

Pullum, G.K. (1989). The great Eskimo vocabulary hoax. *Natural Language and Linguistic Theory*, 7, 275–281.

Pullum, G.K. (1991). *The great Eskimo vocabulary hoax and other irreverent essays on the study of language*. Chicago: University of Chicago Press.

Pullum, G.K., & Scholz, B.C. (2002). Empirical assessment of stimulus poverty evidence. *Linguistic Review*, 19, 9–50.

Pulvermüller, F. (1999). Words in the brain's language. *Behavioral and Brain Sciences*, 22, 253–336.

Pulvermüller, F., Shtyrov, Y., & Illmoniemi, R.J. (2003). Spatio-temporal patterns of neural language processing: An MEG study using minimum-norm current estimates. *NeuroImage*, 20, 1020–1025.

Quay, L.C., & Blaney, R.L. (1992). Verbal communication, nonverbal communication, and private speech in lower and middle socioeconomic status preschool children. *Journal of Genetic Psychology*, 153, 129–138.

Quinn, P.C., & Eimas, P.D. (1996). Perceptual organization and categorization in young infants. In C. Rovee-Collier & L.P. Lipsitt (Eds.), *Advances in infancy research* (Vol. 10, pp. 2–36). Norwood, NJ: Ablex.

Ramus, F., Rosen, S., Dakin, S.C., Day, B.L., Castellote, J.M., White, S., et al. (2003). Theories of developmental dyslexia: Insights from a multiple case study of dyslexic adults. *Brain*, 126, 841–865.

Rapp, B., & Goldrick, M. (2000). Discreteness and interactivity in spoken word production. *Psychological Review*, 107, 460–499.

Rapp, B., & Goldrick, M. (2004). Feedback by any other name is still interactivity: A reply to Roelofs (2004). *Psychological Review*, 111, 573–578.

Rayner, K., Carlson, M., & Frazier, L. (1983). The interaction of syntax and semantics during sentence processing: Eye movements in the analysis of semantically biased sentences. *Journal of Verbal Learning and Verbal Behavior*, 22, 358–374.

Rayner, K., & Frazier, L. (1987). Parsing temporarily ambiguous complements. *Quarterly Journal of Experimental Psychology*, 39A, 657–673.

Rayner, K., & Pollatsek, A. (1989). *The psychology of reading*. Englewood Cliffs, NJ: Prentice Hall.

Read, C., Zhang, Y., Nie, H., & Ding, B. (1986). The ability to manipulate speech sounds depends on knowing alphabetic writing. *Cognition*, 24, 31–44.

Reason, J.T., & Mycielska, K. (1982). *Absent-minded? The psychology of mental lapses and everyday errors*. Englewood Cliffs, NJ: Prentice Hall.

Reisberg, D. (2007). *Cognition: Exploring the science of the mind* (3rd Media ed.). New York: Norton.

Renfrew, C. (2007). *Prehistory*. London: Phoenix.

Rhodes, M.G. (2004). Age-related differences in performance on the Wisconsin card-sorting test: A meta-analytic review. *Psychology of Aging*, 19, 482–494.

Rips, L.J., Shoben, E.J., & Smith, E.E. (1973). Semantic distance and the verification of semantic relations. *Journal of Verbal Learning and Verbal Behavior*, 12, 1–20.

Roberson, D., Davies, I., & Davidoff, J. (2000). Color categories are not universal: Replications and new evidence from a stone-age culture. *Journal of Experimental Psychology: General*, 129, 369–398.

Rodriguez-Fornells, A., Rotte, M., Heinze, H.J., Nosselt, T., & Munte, T. (2002). Brain potential and functional MRI evidence for how to handle two languages with one brain. *Nature*, 415, 1026–1029.

Roelofs, A. (1992). A spreading-activation theory of lemma retrieval in speaking. *Cognition*, 42, 107–142.

Roelofs, A. (1997). The WEAVER model of word-form encoding in speech production. *Cognition*, 64, 249–284.

Roelofs, A., Meyer, A.S., & Levelt, W.J.M. (1998). A case for the lemma/lexeme distinction in models of speaking: Comment on Caramazza and Miozzo (1997). *Cognition*, 69, 219–230.

Rogers T.T., & McClelland, J.L. (2004). *Semantic cognition*. Cambridge, MA: Bradford Books.

Rohde, D.L.T., & Plaut, D.C. (1999). Language acquisition in the absence of explicit negative evidence: How important is starting small? *Cognition*, 72, 67–109.

Rondal, J.A. (1998). Cases of exceptional language in mental retardation and Down syndrome: Explanatory perspectives. *Down Syndrome Research and Practice*, 5, 1–15.

Rosch, E. (1973). Natural categories. *Cognitive Psychology*, 4, 328–350.

Rosch, E. (1978). Principles of categorization. In E. Rosch & B. Lloyd (Eds.), *Cognition and categorization* (pp. 27–48). Hillsdale, NJ: Lawrence Erlbaum Associates, Inc.

Rosch, E., Mervis, C.B., Gray, W., Johnson, D., & Boyes-Braem, P. (1976). Basic objects in natural categories. *Cognitive Psychology*, 8, 382–439.

Rowe, M.L. (2008). Child-directed speech: Relation to socioeconomic status, knowledge of child development and child vocabulary skill. *Journal of Child Language*, 35, 185–205.

Rumelhart, D.E., & McClelland, J.L. (1986). On learning the past tense of English verbs. In D.E. Rumelhart, J.L. McClelland, & the PDP Research Group, *Parallel distributed processing: Vol. 2. Psychological and biological models* (pp. 216–271). Cambridge, MA: MIT Press.

Ruml, W., & Caramazza, A. (2000). An evaluation of a computational model of lexical access: Comment on Dell et al. (1997). *Psychological Review*, 107, 609–634.

Ruml, W., Caramazza, A., Shelton, J.R., & Chialant, D. (2000). Testing assumptions in computational theories of aphasia. *Journal of Memory and Language*, 43, 217–248.

Rymer, R. (1993). *Genie*. London: Joseph.

Sachs, J.S. (1967). Recognition memory for syntactic and semantic aspects of connected discourse. *Perception and Psychophysics*, 2, 437–442.

Sachs, J., Bard, B., & Johnson, M.L. (1981). Language with restricted input: Case studies of two hearing children of deaf parents. *Applied Psycholinguistics*, 2, 33–54.

Sacks, H., Schegloff, E.A., & Jefferson, G. (1974). A simplest systematics for the organization of turn-taking in conversation. *Language*, 50, 696–735.

Saffran, E.M., Marin, O.S.M., & Yeni-Komshian, G.H. (1976). An analysis of speech perception in word deafness. *Brain and Language*, 3, 209–228.

Saffran, J.R., Aslin, R.N., & Newport, E.L. (1996). Statistical learning by 8-month-old infants. *Science*, 274, 1926–1928.

Samuel, A.G. (1996). Does lexical information influence the perceptual restoration of phonemes? *Journal of Experimental Psychology: General*, 125, 28–51.

Sanford, A.J., & Garrod, S.C. (1981). *Understanding written language*. Chichester, UK: Wiley.

Santa, J.L., & Ranken, H.B. (1972). Effects of verbal coding on recognition memory. *Journal of Experimental Psychology*, 93, 268–278.

Savage-Rumbaugh, E.S. (1987). Communication, symbolic communication, and language: A reply to Seidenberg and Petitto. *Journal of Experimental Psychology: General*, 116, 288–292.

Savage-Rumbaugh, E.S., & Lewin, R. (1994). *Kanzi: The ape at the brink of the human mind*. New York: Wiley.

Savage-Rumbaugh, E.S., McDonald, K., Sevcik, R.A., Hopkins, W.D., & Rupert, E. (1986). Spontaneous symbol acquisition and communicative use by pygmy chimpanzees (*Pan paniscus*). *Journal of Experimental Psychology: General*, 115, 211–235.

Savage-Rumbaugh, E.S., Murphy, J., Sevcik, R.A., Brakke, K.E., Williams, S.L., & Rumbaugh, D.M. (1993). Language comprehension in ape and child. *Monographs of the Society for Research in Child Development*, 58 (Whole Nos. 3–4).

Scarborough, D.L., Cortese, C., & Scarborough, H.S. (1977). Frequency and repetition effects in lexical memory. *Journal of Experimental Psychology: Human Perception and Performance*, 3, 1–17.

Schaeffer, H.R. (1975). Social development in infancy. In R. Lewin (Ed.), *Child alive* (pp. 32–39). London: Temple Smith.

Schenkein, J. (1980). A taxonomy for repeating action sequences in natural conversation. In B. Butterworth (Ed.), *Language production: Vol. 1. Speech and talk* (pp. 21–48). London: Academic Press.

Schmidt, G.L., DeBuse, C.J., & Seger C.A. (2007). Right hemisphere metaphor processing? Characterizing the lateralization of semantic processes. *Brain and Language*, 100, 127–141.

Schriefers, H., Teruel, E., & Meinshausen, R.M. (1998). Producing simple sentences: Results from picture–word interference experiments. *Journal of Memory and Language*, 39, 609–632.

Schumacher, J., Hoffmann, P., Schmal, C., Schulte-Korne, G., & Nothen, M.M. (2007). Genetics of dyslexia: The evolving landscape. *Journal of Medical Genetics*, 44, 289–297.

Schvaneveldt, R.W., Meyer, D.E., & Becker, C.A. (1976). Lexical ambiguity, semantic context, and visual word recognition. *Journal of Experimental Psychology: Human Perception and Performance*, 2, 243–256.

Schwartz, M.F. (1987). Patterns of speech production deficit within and across aphasia syndromes: Application of a psycholinguistic model. In M. Coltheart, G. Sartori, & R. Job (Eds.), *The cognitive neuropsychology of language* (pp. 163–199). Hove, UK: Lawrence Erlbaum Associates Ltd.

Schwartz, M.F., Dell, G.S., Martin, N., Gahl, S., & Sobel, P. (2006). A case-series test of the interactive two-step model of lexical access: Evidence from picture naming. *Journal of Memory and Language*, 54, 228–264.

Schwartz, M.F., Linebarger, M., Saffran, E., & Pate, D. (1987). Syntactic transparency and sentence interpretation in aphasia. *Language and Cognitive Processes*, 2, 85–113.

Schwartz, M.F., Marin, O.S.M., & Saffran, E.M. (1979). Dissociations of language function in dementia: A case study. *Brain and Language*, 7, 277–306.

Searle, J. (1969). *Speech acts*. Cambridge, UK: Cambridge University Press.

Searle, J. (1980). Minds, brains, and programs. *Behavioral and Brain Sciences*, 3, 417–457.

Sedivy, J.C., Tanenhaus, M. K., Chambers, C.G., & Carlson, G.N. (1999). Achieving incremental semantic interpretation through contextual representation. *Cognition*, 71, 109–147.

Seidenberg, M.S. (2005). Connectionist models of word reading. *Current Directions in Psychological Science*, 14, 238–242.

Seidenberg, M.S., & McClelland, J.L. (1989). A distributed developmental model of word recognition. *Psychological Review*, 96, 523–568.

Seidenberg, M.S, & Petitto, L.A. (1979). Signing behaviour in apes: A critical review. *Cognition*, 7, 177–215.

Seidenberg, M.S., & Petitto, L.A. (1987). Communication, symbolic communication, and language: Comment on Savage-Rumbaugh, Macdonald, Sevcik, Hopkis, and Rubert (1986). *Journal of Experimental Psychology: General*, 116, 279–287.

Semenza, C., & Zettin, M. (1988). Generating proper names: A case of selective inability. *Cognitive Neuropsychology*, 5, 711–721.

Senghas, A., Kita, S., & Ozyurek, A. (2004). Children creating core properties of language: Evidence from an emerging sign language in Nicaragua. *Science*, 305, 1779–1782.

Sereno, S.C., Brewer, C.C., & O'Donnell, P.J. (2003). Context effects in word recognition: Evidence for early interactive processing. *Psychological Science*, 14, 328–333.

Seymour, P.H.K. (2005). Early reading development in European orthographies. In M.J. Snowling & C. Hulme (Eds.), *The science of reading: A handbook* (pp. 296–315). Oxford, UK: Blackwell.

Seymour, P.H.K., & Elder, L. (1986). Beginning reading without phonology. *Cognitive Neuropsychology*, 3, 1–36.

Seymour, P.H.K., & Evans, H.M. (1994). Levels of phonological awareness and learning to read. *Reading and Writing*, 6, 221–250.

Shallice, T., & Warrington, E.K. (1975). Word recognition in a phonemic dyslexic patient. *Quarterly Journal of Experimental Psychology*, 27, 187–199.

Shattuck, R. (1994). *The forbidden experiment*. New York: Kodansha International.

Sheldon, A. (1974). The role of parallel function in the acquisition of relative clauses in English. *Journal of Verbal Learning and Verbal Behavior*, 13, 272–281.

Siegel, J.A., & Siegel, W. (1977). Categorical perception of tonal intervals: Musicians can't tell sharp from flat. *Perception and Psychophysics*, 21, 399–407.

Simpson, G.B. (1981). Meaning dominance and semantic context in the processing of lexical ambiguity. *Journal of Verbal Learning and Verbal Behavior*, 20, 120–136.

Sinclair-deZwart, H. (1973). Language acquisition and cognitive development. In T.E. Moore (Ed.), *Cognitive development and the acquisition of language* (pp. 9–26). New York: Academic Press.

Singer, M. (1994). Discourse inference processes. In M.A. Gernsbacher (Ed.), *Handbook of psycholinguistics* (pp. 479–516). San Diego, CA: Academic Press.

Skoyles, J., & Skottun, B.C. (2004). On the prevalence of magnocellular deficits in the visual system of non-dyslexic individuals. *Brain and Language*, 88, 79–82.

Smith, M., & Wheeldon, L. (1999). High level processing scope in spoken sentence production. *Cognition*, 73, 205–246.

Smith, N.V. (1973). *The acquisition of phonology: A case study*. Cambridge, UK: Cambridge University Press.

Smith, N., & Tsimpli, I.M. (1995). *The mind of a savant: Language learning and modularity*. Oxford, UK: Blackwell.

Smith, S.M., Brown, H.O., Thomas, J.E.P., & Goodman, L.S. (1947). The lack of cerebral effects of d-tubocurarine. *Anesthesiology*, 8, 1–14.

Snow, C.E. (1977). The development of conversation between mothers and babies. *Journal of Child Language*, 4, 1–22.

Snow, C.E. (1994). Beginning from baby talk: Twenty years of research on input and inter- action. In C. Gallaway & B.J. Richards (Eds.), *Input and interaction in language acquisition* (pp. 3–12). Cambridge, UK: Cambridge University Press.

Snow, C.E., & Hoefnagel-Hohle, M. (1978). The critical period for language acquisition: Evidence from second language learning. *Child Development*, 49, 1114–1128.

Snow, C.E., & Juel, C. (2005). Teaching children to read: What do we know about how to do it? In M.J. Snowling & C. Hulme (Eds.), *The science of reading: A handbook* (pp. 501–520). Oxford, UK: Blackwell.

Snowling, M.J. (2000). *Dyslexia* (2nd ed.). Oxford, UK: Blackwell.

Snowling, M., Gallagher, A., & Frith, U. (2003). Family risk of dyslexia is continuous: Individual differences in the precursors of reading skill. *Child Development*, 74, 358–373.

Snowling, M.J., & Hulme, C. (Eds.) (2005). *The science of reading: A handbook*. Oxford, UK: Blackwell.

Sokolov, J.L., & Snow, C.E. (1994). The changing role of negative evidence in theories of language development. In C. Gallaway & B.J. Richards (Eds.), *Input and interaction in language acquisition* (pp. 38–55). Cambridge, UK: Cambridge University Press.

Sommer, I.E.C., Aleman, A., Bouma, A., & Kahn, R.S. (2004). Do women really have more bilateral language representation than men? A meta-analysis of functional imaging studies. *Brain*, 127, 1845–1852.

Spender, D. (1980). *Man made language*. London: Routledge & Kegan Paul.

Sperber, D., & Wilson, D. (1986). *Relevance: Communication and cognition*. Oxford: Blackwell.

Sperber, D., & Wilson, D. (1987). Précis of *Relevance: Communication and cognition*. *Behavioral and Brain Sciences*, 10, 697–754.

Spivey, M. (2007). *The continuity of mind*. Oxford, UK: Oxford University Press.

Stein, J. (2001). The magnocellular theory of developmental dyslexia. *Dyslexia*, 7, 12–36.

Stein, J. (2003). Visual motion sensitivity and reading. *Neuropsychologia*, 41, 1785–1793.

Stemberger, J.P. (1985). An interactive activation model of language production. In A.W. Ellis (Ed.), *Progress in the psychology of language* (Vol. 1, pp. 143–186). Hove, UK: Lawrence Erlbaum Associates Ltd.

Stern, K., & McClintock, M.K. (1998). Regulation of ovulation by human pheromones. *Nature*, 392, 177–179.

Stewart, F., Parkin, A.J., & Hunkin, N.M. (1992). Naming impairments following recovery from herpes simplex encephalitis: Category-specific? *Quarterly Journal of Experimental Psychology*, 44A, 261–284.

Stroop, J.R. (1935). Studies of interference in serial verbal reactions. *Journal of Experimental Psychology*, 18, 643–622.

Struhsaker, T.T. (1967). Behavior of vervet monkeys and other Cercopithecines. *Science*, 156, 1197–1203.

Sulin, R.A., & Dooling, D.J. (1974). Intrusion of a thematic idea in retention of prose. *Journal of Experimental Psychology*, 103, 255–262.

Sundberg, M.L. (1996). Toward granting linguistic competence to apes. *Journal of the Experimental Analysis of Behavior*, 65, 477–492.

Swinney, D.A. (1979). Lexical access during sentence comprehension: (Re)consideration of context effects. *Journal of Verbal Learning and Verbal Behavior*, 18, 545–569.

Sykes, J.L. (1940). A study of the spontaneous vocalizations of young deaf children. *Psychological Monograph*, 52, 104–123.

Tabor, W., & Hutchins, S. (2004). Evidence for self-organised sentence processing: Digging-in effects. *Journal of Experimental Psychology: Learning, Memory and Cognition*, 30, 431–450.

Tabor, W., Juliano, C., & Tanenhaus, M.K. (1997). Parsing in a dynamical system: An attractor-based account of the interaction of lexical and structural constraints in sentence processing. *Language and Cognitive Processes*, 12, 211–271.

Tabor, W., & Tanenhaus, M.K. (1999). Dynamical models of sentence processing. *Cognitive Science*, 23, 491–515.

Tanenhaus, M.K. (2007). Spoken language comprehension: Insights from eye movements. In M.G. Gaskell (Ed.), *The Oxford handbook of psycholinguistics* (pp. 309–326). Oxford, UK: Oxford University Press.

Tanenhaus, M.K., Carlson, G.N., & Trueswell, J.C. (1989). The role of thematic structure in interpretation and parsing. *Language and Cognitive Processes*, 4, 211–234.

Tanenhaus, M.K., Leiman, J.M., & Seidenberg, M.S. (1979). Evidence for multiple stages in the processing of ambiguous words in syntactic contexts. *Journal of Verbal Learning and Verbal Behavior*, 18, 427–440.

Tanenhaus, M.K., Spivey-Knowlton, M.J., Eberhard, K.M., & Sedivy, J.C. (1995). Integration of visual and linguistic information in spoken language comprehension. *Science*, 268, 1632–1634.

Taraban, R., & McClelland, J.L. (1988). Constituent attachment and thematic role assignment in sentence processing: Influences of content-based expectations. *Journal of Memory and Language*, 27, 597–632.

Terrace, H.S., Petitto, L.A., Sanders, R.J., & Bever, T. (1979). Can an ape create a sentence? *Science*, 206, 891–902.

Tettamanti, M., Buccino, G., Saccuman, M.C., Gallese, V., Danna, M., Scifo, P. et al. (2005). Listening to action-related sentences activates fronto-parietal motor circuits. *Journal of Cognitive Neuroscience*, 17, 273–281.

Thomas, E.L., & Robinson, H.A. (1972). Improving reading in every class: A sourcebook for teachers. Boston: Allyn & Bacon.

Thomas, M.S.C. (2003). Limits on plasticity. *Journal of Cognition and Development*, 4, 95–121.

Tippett, L.J., & Farah, M.J. (1994). A computational model of naming in Alzheimer's disease: Unitary or multiple impairments? *Neuropsychology*, 8, 1–11.

Tomasello, M. (1992). The social bases of language acquisition. *Social Development*, 1, 67–87.

Traxler, M.J., & Gernsbacher, M.A. (Eds.). (2006). *Handbook of psycholinguistics* (2nd ed.). Amsterdam: Elsevier.

Trueswell, J.C., Tanenhaus, M.K., & Garnsey, S.M. (1994). Semantic influences on parsing: Use of thematic role information in syntactic disambiguation. *Journal of Memory and Language*, 33, 285–318.

Ullman, M.T. (2001). A neurocognitive perspective on language: The declarative/procedural model. *Nature Reviews Neuroscience*, 2, 717–726.

Ullman, M.T. (2004). Contributions of memory circuits to language: The declarative/ procedural model. *Cognition*, 92, 231–270.

Ullman, M.T. (2007). The biocognition of the mental lexicon. In M.G. Gaskell (Ed.), *The Oxford handbook of psycholinguistics* (pp. 267–286). Oxford, UK: Oxford University Press.

Valian, V. (1986). Syntactic categories in the speech of young children. *Developmental Psychology*, 22, 562–579.

Van Gompel, R.P.G., & Pickering, M.J. (2007). Syntactic parsing. In M.G. Gaskell (Ed.), *The Oxford handbook of psycholinguistics* (pp. 289–307). Oxford, UK: Oxford University Press.

Van Gompel, R.P.G., Pickering, M.J., & Traxler, M.J. (2001). Reanalysis in sentence processing: Evidence against constraint-based and two-stage models. *Journal of Memory and Language*, 45, 225–258.

Van Orden, G.C., Johnston, J.C., & Hale, B.L. (1988). Word identification in reading proceeds from spelling to sound to meaning. *Journal of Experimental Psychology: Learning, Memory, and Cognition*, 14, 371–386.

Van Orden, G.C., Pennington, B.F., & Stone, G.O. (1990). Word identification in reading and the promise of subsymbolic psycholinguistics. *Psychological Review*, 97, 488–522.

Vargha-Khadem, F., Watkins, K., Alcock, K., Fletcher, P., & Passingham, R. (1995). Praxic and nonverbal cognitive deficits in a large family with a genetically transmitted speech and language disorder. *Proceedings of the National Academy of Sciences of the United States of America*, 92, 930–933.

Vellutino, F.R., & Fletcher, J.M. (2005). Developmental dyslexia. In M.J. Snowling & C. Hulme (Eds.), *The science of reading: A handbook* (pp. 362–378). Oxford, UK: Blackwell.

Vellutino. F.R., Fletcher, J.M., Snowling, M.J., & Scanlon, D.M. (2004). Specific reading disability (dyslexia): What have we learned in the past four decades? *Journal of Child Psychology and Psychiatry*, 45, 2–40.

Vigliocco, G., Antonini, T., & Garrett, M.F. (1997). Grammatical gender is on the tip of Italian tongues. *Psychological Science*, 8, 314–317.

Vigliocco, G., & Nicol, J. (1998). Separating hierarchical relations and word order in language production: Is proximity concord syntactic or linear? *Cognition*, 68, B13–B29.

Vigliocco, G., & Vinson, D.P. (2007). Semantic representation. In M.G. Gaskell (Ed.), *The Oxford handbook of psycholinguistics* (pp. 195–215). Oxford, UK: Oxford University Press.

Vigliocco, G., Vinson, D.P., Lewis, W., & Garrett, M.F. (2004). Representing the meanings of object and action words: The featural and unitary semantic space hypothesis. *Cognitive Psychology*, 48, 422–488.

Vliet, E.C., Miozzo, M., & Stern, Y. (2004). Phonological dyslexia without phonological impairment. *Cognitive Neuropsychology*, 21, 820–839.

Von Frisch, K. (1974). Decoding the language of bees. *Science*, 185, 663–668.

Vygotsky, L. (1934). *Thought and language* (Trans. E. Hanfman & G. Vakar, 1962). Cambridge, MA: MIT Press.

Warren, R.M. (1970). Perceptual restoration of missing speech sounds. *Science*, 167, 392–393.

Warren, R.M., & Warren, R.P. (1970). Auditory illusions and confusions. *Scientific American*, 223, 30–36.

Warrington, E.K. (1975). The selective impairment of semantic memory. *Quarterly Journal of Experimental Psychology*, 27, 635–657.

Warrington, E.K., & McCarthy, R. (1987). Categories of knowledge: Further fractionation and an attempted integration. *Brain*, 110, 1273–1296.

Warrington, E.K., & Shallice, T. (1984). Category-specific semantic impairments. *Brain*, 107, 829–854.

Watanabe, S., Sakamoto, J., & Wakita, M. (1995). Pigeon's discrimination of paintings by Monet and Picasso. *Journal of the Experimental Analysis of Behavior*, 63, 165–174.

Watson, J.B. (1913). Psychology as the behaviorist views it. *Psychological Review*, 20, 158–177.

Waxman, S. R. (1999). Specifying the scope of 13-month-olds' expectations for novel words. *Cognition*, 70, B35–B50.

Weir, R.H. (1962). *Language in the crib*. The Hague: Mouton.

Werker, J.F., & Tees, R.C. (1984). Crosslanguage speech development: Evidence for perceptual reorganization during the first year of life. *Infant Behavior and Development*, 7, 49–63.

Whaley, C.P. (1978). Word–nonword classification time. *Journal of Verbal Learning and Verbal Behavior*, 17, 143–154.

Wheeldon, L. (Ed.). (2000). *Aspects of language production*. Hove, UK: Psychology Press.

Whitehouse, A.J.O., Mayberry, M.T., & Durkin, K. (2006). Inner speech impairments in autism. *Journal of Child Psychology and Psychiatry*, 47, 857–865.

Whorf, B.L. (1956). *Language, thought, and reality*. Cambridge, MA: MIT Press.

Wierzbicka, A. (1996). *Semantics: Primes and universals*. Oxford, UK: Oxford University Press.

Wierzbicka, A. (2004). Conceptual primes in human languages and their analogues in animal communication and cognition. *Language Sciences*, 26, 413–441.

Wilding, J. (1990). Developmental dyslexics do not fit in boxes: Evidence from the case studies. *European Journal of Cognitive Psychology*, 2, 97–131.

Wilkins, A.J. (1971). Conjoint frequency, category size, and categorization time. *Journal of Verbal Learning and Verbal Behavior*, 10, 382–385.

Wilkins, A. (2003). *Reading through colour: How coloured filters can reduce reading difficulty*. London: Wiley.

Wilkins, A.J., & Neary, G. (1991). Some visual, optometric and perceptual effects of coloured glasses. *Ophthalmic and Physiological Optics*, 11, 163–171.

Wilks, Y. (1976). Parsing English II. In E. Charniak & Y. Wilks (Eds.), *Computational semantics* (pp. 155–184). Amsterdam: North Holland.

Wittgenstein, L. (1953). *Philosophical investigations* (Trans. G.E.M. Ancombe). Oxford, UK: Blackwell.

Wolf, M. (2007). *Proust and the the squid: The story and science of the reading brain.* Cambridge, UK: Icon Books.

Woollams, A.M., Lambon Ralph, M.A., Plaut, D.C., & Patterson, K. (2007). SD-squared: On the association between semantic dementia and surface dyslexia. *Psychological Review*, 114, 316–339.

Wright, B., Lombardino, L.J., King, W.M., Puranik, C.S., Leonard, C.M., & Merzenich, M.M. (1997). Deficits in auditory temporal and spectral resolution in language-impaired children. *Nature*, 387, 176–178.

Xu, F. (2002). The role of language in acquiring object kind concepts in infancy. *Cognition*, 85, 223–250.

Yamada, J.E. (1990). *Laura: A case for the modularity of language.* Cambridge, MA: MIT Press.

Yngve, V. (1970). On getting a word in edgewise. *Papers from the Sixth Regional Meeting of the Chicago Linguistic Society* (Vol. 6, pp. 567–577). Chicago: Chicago Linguistic Society.

Zaidel, E. (1983). A response to Gazzaniga: Language in the right hemisphere, convergent perspectives. *American Psychologist*, 38, 542–546.

Zaidel, E., & Peters, A.M. (1981). Phonological encoding and ideographic reading by the disconnected right hemisphere. *Brain and Language*, 14, 205–234.

Ziegler, J.C., & Goswami, U. (2005). Reading acquisition, developmental dyslexia, and skilled reading across languages: A psycholinguistic grain size theory. *Psychological Bulletin*, 131, 3–29.

Author index

Aboitiz, F. 179
Acenas, L. R. 239
Adams, M. J. 174
Agnoli, F. 104
Ahn, J. 91
Ainsworth-Darnell, K. 198
Aksu-Koc, A. A. 63
Alcock, K. 75
Alegria, J. 172
Aleman, A. 257
Altmann, G. T. M. 51, 267
Anderson, K. J. 257
Anderson, R. C. 207
Andrews, S. 273
Antonini, T. 239
Anton-Méndez, I. 234
Applebaum, M. 277
Arensberg, B. 15
Arnold, J. E. 215
Aroles, S. 267
Ashburner, J. 51, 52, 85
Aslin, R. N. 55
Atchley, R. A. 142
Au, T. K. 270
Austin, J. L. 210, 211
Aznar-Besé, N. 84

Baars, B. J. 234
Badecker, W. 215, 250, 277
Bailey, K. G. D. 188

Baker, C. 86
Balota, D. A. 147
Banich, M. T. 258, 259, 278
Barabasi, A. 272
Barclay, J. R. 209
Bard, B. 81
Bargh, J. A. 109
Baron, J. 159, 177
Baron-Cohen, S. 257
Barry, C. 245, 273
Barsalou, L. 143, 273
Bartlett, E. 58, 101
Batchelder, E. O. 55
Bates, E. 56
Bates, E. A. 267, 277
Beaton, A. A. 179, 275
Beattie, J. 247
Becker, C. A. 183
Behrend, D. A. 96
Bejder, L. 35
Bellugi, U. 94
Benjamin, L. T. 266
Berlin, B. 106, 107
Berndt, R. S. 138, 249
Bernstein, B. 113
Bertelson, P. 172
Bertolani, P. 39
Betts, C. 9
Bever, T. G. 42, 43
Bialystock, E. 85, 268

Mackisack, E. L. 219
MacWhinney, B. 277
Maess, B. 276
Maestrini, E. 178
Maher, J. 269
Mahon, B. 272
Manis, F. R. 179
Mann, J. 35
Marantette, P. F. 53
Marcel, A. J. 162, 163
Marchman, V. A. 55, 56, 267
Marcus, G. F. 16
Marin, O. S. M. 163, 218
Markman, E. M. 58, 66
Marlow, A. J. 178
Marshall, J. C. 129, 160, 250
Marslen-Wilson, W. D. 150, 151, 274
Martin, F. 178, 179
Martin, N. 252, 273, 277
Masataka, N. 61
Matthews, P. M. 274
Maugais, R. 51
Mayberry, M. T. 91
Mayer, C. 18
Mazzucci, A. 250
McBride-Chang, C. 179
McCandliss, B. 178
McCarthy, R. 15, 138, 139, 272
McClelland, J. L. 71, 139, 151, 164, 165, 194, 199, 200, 201, 272
McClintock, M. K. 32
McCloskey, M. 277
McDonald, J. 277
McGurk, H. 150, 274
McKoon, G. 209
McNeill, D. 236
McQueen, J. M. 273, 274
McRae, K. 276
Mechelli, A. 85
Mehler, J. 51, 52, 85
Meinshausen, R. M. 240
Meltzoff, A. N. 93
Menn, L. 250, 277
Méot, A. 273
Meringer, R. 18
Mervis, C. B. 58, 121
Merzenich, M. M. 178
Metsala, J. L. 180
Meyer, A. S. 232, 235, 240, 276, 277
Meyer, D. E. 183, 273
Miceli, G. 250
Michel, D. 219
Miller, C. A. 244

Miller, D. 251
Miller, J. D. 149
Miller, J. L. 149
Miller, K. F. 104
Miller, P. H. 92, 93, 268
Miller, S. A. 92, 93, 268
Mills, D. 94
Mintz, T. H. 65
Miozzo, M. 274, 277
Miyake, A. 91
Molfese, D. L. 83
Molis, M. 267
Monaco, A. P. 75
Morais, J. 172
Morrison, C. M. 273
Morton, J. 130
Moss, H. E. 270
Motley, M. T. 234
Mowrer, O. H. 53
Muller, K. 161
Munte, T. 85
Murphy, J. 45
Muter, V. 173
MvDonald, K. 44
Mycielska, K. 276
Myers, P. 219
Mylander, C. 112

Nagy, E. 69
Neary, G. 181
Nelson, K. 45, 56
Newcombe, F. 129, 160
Newport, E. L. 55, 74, 77, 78, 267
Newton, M. 268
Nicol, J. 198, 244
Nicoladis, E. 84, 85, 268
Nicolson, R. I. 179, 275
Nie, D. 172
Nissen, C. H. 39
Noppeney, U. 51, 52, 85
Norris, D. 274
Nosselt, T. 85
Nothen, M. M. 178
Nunes, S. R. 174

O'Doherty, J. 51, 52, 85
O'Donnell, P. J. 275
Oller, D. K. 53
Oppenheim, G. 91
Orchard-Lisle, V. 251
Orlando, L. 15
Orwell, G. 99, 269
Osgood, C. E. 17
Osterhout, L. 198

333

Subject index